14X09

11 X 02

FROM RESISTANCE
TO REVOLUTION

FROM RESISTANCE
TO REVOLUTION

*Colonial Radicals
and the Development of American
Opposition to Britain, 1765–1776*

by *PAULINE MAIER*

ALFRED A. KNOPF

New York 1974

THIS IS A BORZOI BOOK
PUBLISHED BY ALFRED A. KNOPF, INC.

Copyright © 1972 by Pauline Maier

Library of Congress Cataloging in Publication Data

Maier, Pauline, 1938–   . From resistance to revolution.

Includes bibliographical references.

1. U. S.—History—Revolution—Causes. I. Title.
E210.M27   973.3   74–154904
ISBN 0–394–46190–8

Manufactured in the United States of America

PUBLISHED MAY, 18, 1972
REPRINTED ONCE
THIRD PRINTING, OCTOBER 1974

For my parents

The Revolution of the United States was the result of a mature and reflecting preference for freedom, not of a vague or ill-defined craving for independence. It contracted no alliance with the turbulent passions of anarchy, but its course was marked, on the contrary, by a love of order and law.

—Alexis de Tocqueville,
Democracy in America

CONTENTS

———————◦∞◦———————

PREFACE

—————·◦∞◦·—————

WHEN THE AMERICAN REVOLUTIONARIES first came to
interest me nearly nine years ago, prevailing historical interpretation suggested they were not worth serious study. Prop-
aganda was the key concept: revolutionary writings revealed
only how a handful of agitators, dedicated to independence
for their own psychic or material satisfactions, manipulated
the mass of colonists. By now it seems surprising that this view
remained convincing for so long.

No leader, not even the most outspoken American partisan,
was anti-British when the long evolution of events that culminated in revolution first began. Affection for Britain, her
constitutional monarchs and government, pervaded the private
correspondence as well as public pronouncements of the Sons
of Liberty,* who organized against Britain's Stamp Act of
1765. Separation was to be shunned; independence was men-

* The term "Sons of Liberty" in the capitalized version refers here
to the resistance organizations formed throughout the American continent during the Stamp Act crisis and those organizations that formed
or were reconstituted later under that name. The term was also used
generically for all those who were fervent in liberty's cause, as is explained in Chapter 4. The uncapitalized version, "sons of liberty," will
refer here, then, to all who supported the American cause actively,
whether or not they can be linked with an organization. American
partisans accepted the designation proudly, for it summarized their
self-image well. In the hands of Loyalists or royal officials, however,
the term could refer indiscriminately to anyone who perpetrated any
disorderly or illegal act.

tioned only as a gloomy possibility which, hopefully, timely
action could preclude.

Development and change have become, then, an important
historical problem: When and why did the colonists reshape
their views of the Mother Country and her once revered constitution? The discussion of American actions can now also
be reopened. What type of response to British "oppression"
did colonial leaders advocate? How did the Americans' changing assessments of their political situation within the British
governing system affect their tactics? Response was deliber-
ately related to political disillusionment. As the Americans
moved in definable stages away from their loyalty of 1765,
so they abandoned step by step the tactic of resistance that opposed only discrete aspects of London's rule for revolution and
a rejection of all British authority.

To understand the emergent revolutionary movement, this
study concentrates upon men in the vanguard of opposition to
Britain, whom I have chosen to call "radicals." The term has
pitfalls. The word itself is an anachronism, since it was first
applied to political groups only in the nineteenth century. (Observers in the 1760's and 1770's sometimes used the word
"violent" much as we use "radical," without necessarily im-
plying the commission of acts of violence in the modern sense,
which has itself encouraged historical confusion.) "Radical"
is, nonetheless, a legitimate and in fact technically exact word
for describing men who most thoroughly criticized British
governing practices, seeking always a return to what they
considered traditional principles of British rule.

I do not use the word as the old "Progressive" historians
did, to denote a stable group of persons who emerged in the
1760's or earlier and continued on into the 1780's, constantly
struggling for greater political democracy. No such group
existed. The movement against Britain was largely decentral-
ized. Anything resembling central direction emerged only
rarely before the first Continental Congress in 1774. Still,
there was considerable consultation between local leaders who
sought each other out from the Stamp Act crisis on, and it is
this largely informal intercolonial cadre and the men of like
sentiments whom I designate as "radical." They constituted
the nucleus of opposition to Britain. Through them one can

follow a series of increasingly damaging assessments of Britain as well as the progressive elaboration of resistance tactics and organization, which began with the Sons of Liberty of 1765–6, then was continued within the nonimportation movement of 1768–70, the Tea Act resistance, and the associations and committees that flowered after 1773. These men took widely different positions on the political issues that arose once independence was decided upon.

Naturally enough, there was a turnover in radical personnel as the nature of American opposition changed between 1765 and 1776. John Dickinson of Pennsylvania offers a notable example: he more than any other individual articulated the radical position in the 1760's, but found activism increasingly uncomfortable in the 1770's. Meanwhile, others joined the radical groups or became leaders. A significant group of men, however, emerged as strong American partisans during the Stamp Act crisis and remained in the forefront of opposition to Britain on into the war: Christopher Gadsden in Charleston; Cornelius Harnett in North Carolina; Richard Henry Lee in Virginia; John Lamb and Isaac Sears in New York; Samuel Adams in Boston, or the peripatetic Thomas Young, who opposed the Stamp Act as a Son of Liberty in Albany, then migrated to Boston, thence from 1774 to Newport, and finally Philadelphia, finding a home always within the local radical group.

It is the personal letters and public statements of such men and their colleagues, along with the newspapers they published and supported, that provide the basis for the interpretations offered here—although accounts of events by less committed colonists and by British officials have also been consulted. To a large extent, above all in Part III, this book is therefore a study of political perception. By modern standards the radicals' interpretations of events often appear partial, skewed, inaccurate: the colonists never understood, for example, how the self-serving aid of those Irish parliamentary oligarchs known as "undertakers" made the Americans' friends, the Irish "patriots," seem so powerful within Ireland in the late 1760's, or how many strands of political interests the English petition movement contained. As a result they overestimated the strength of their supporters abroad. In other cases the Americans perceived political processes correctly, but judged them by standards far different from those of modern historians or influential Englishmen of their own era. The emoluments that built a majority for the Crown in the English Parliament they saw only as corruption. The toleration the Crown extended to Catholics at home, in Grenada, and the West Indies they perceived only as a replay of Stuart efforts to re-entrench despotism. But accuracy of perception or interpretation according to the modern viewpoint or even that of Georgian England is irrelevant for understanding the escalation of colonial opposition. American decisions were necessarily based upon the information filtered back to the colonies and interpreted from a provincial view.

Point of view raises the issue of the mentality colonists brought to shaping evidence, that is, the issue of ideology. Here I am particularly indebted to Bernard Bailyn, from whom I received my introduction to the American Revolution, and who supervised the doctoral dissertation upon which this book is based. I share with him, above all, a conviction that the set of ideas brought together in the "Real Whig" tradition of seventeenth- and eighteenth-century England are of central importance in explaining the American Revolution; that, in fact, the revolutionary movement takes on consistency and form only against the background of English revolutionary tradition. Not that every colonist spent his evenings reading Francis Hutcheson's *System of Moral Philosophy* or the other works summarized here in Chapter 2. Some did; others at least encountered important arguments from political philosophers in their local newspapers. In any case, the formal works of Whig revolutionary theory furnish in systematic compass the tenets expressed in more fragmented fashion by lettered as well as unlettered colonists and, indeed, by many Londoners as well.

To acknowledge the importance of ideology in the evolution of the American revolutionary movement is not, however, to claim that ideology explains why men became revolutionaries. Motivation remains the most elusive of historical problems, and efforts to attribute it to any one cause, or to identify conceptual structures as causes in themselves, seem to me inadequate. "Real Whig" ideas provided a program for inter-

preting civil society and political life. Given the events of the
decade before 1776, they helped create a logical thrust toward
revolution and independence. But Whig ideology alone did not
separate revolutionaries from Loyalists; indeed, Loyalist writers often shared many of the assumptions of a Gadsden or the
Adamses. Other factors—economic or political interest, family
ties, religious affiliation, temperament and psychology—were
crucial to the political destinations of individual colonists. For
those who wish to pursue the choice for or against revolution
among particular individuals or groups, the fruitful question
must be not merely whether political ambitions or economic
interests caused loyalty or disloyalty, but how these or other
relevant considerations encouraged, permitted, or retarded adherence to a revolutionary argument that was in its own terms
rational and compelling. Insofar as motivation can be understood, I suspect that the path is through comparative biography. That is, through a different book than this, which
bypasses differences of personality, interest, and origin to emphasize the political conclusions and strategy individuals
shared in a common trajectory toward revolution and independence.

I have emphasized here the radicals' concern for order not
because it fits current uneasiness about protest, but because
it is historically significant. Colonial leaders, like many mod-
ern-day "revolutionaries," quickly learned that unrestrained
popular violence was counter-productive. They organized resistance in part to contain disorder. Building associations to
discipline opposition, they gradually made popular self-rule,
founded upon carefully designed "social compacts," a reality.
Out of the struggle with Britain emerged not merely separation, but the beginnings of American republican government.

Sections of the book draw upon two articles, "Popular Uprisings and Civil Authority in Eighteenth-Century America"
and "John Wilkes and American Disillusionment with Britain," which appeared in *The William and Mary Quarterly*
(January 1970 and July 1963) and are used with the permission of its editor.

Several friends and associates have read the manuscript in
whole or part and offered many useful suggestions: John
Murrin, Richard D. Brown, Thomas N. Brown, Richard

Bushman, Mary Beth Norton, Oscar Handlin, and Bernard
Bailyn. Charles S. Maier has had reason to regret his suggestion that I write a graduate course paper on John Wilkes,
which became the genesis of this book. For years now he has
read and edited my manuscript, bringing to it insights from
his own reading in European history and the social sciences.
Another important debt incurred in the preparation of this
book is to Professor Arthur Smithies, Alice Methfessel, and
the staff and members of Kirkland House of Harvard University, who for several years made available to me a place to
think and write within an atmosphere peculiarly suited for the
work of learning. I would also like to thank Marjorie Durand,
who made intelligent corrections while typing the manuscript;
Briana Murphy, who helped check the footnotes; my editor,
Jane Garrett; the staffs of the Massachusetts, Rhode Island,
New-York, and Pennsylvania Historical Societies, the Houghton, Beinecke, and New York Public Libraries, and the Massachusetts Archives within the United States, as well as the
Public Record Office, British Museum, William Salt, and
Sheffield Central Libraries in England for their consistent
helpfulness in making accessible relevant manuscript mate-
rials, and Lord Dartmouth for making the Dartmouth Papers
available. All of the libraries and archives whose manuscripts
are cited have kindly granted permission for quotation herein.
Research was financed in part by grants from the American
Association of University Women, the George B. and Rosa
Schoen and Samuel E. and Lily B. Green Fund, Harvard
University, and the University of Massachusetts. Finally, I
want to thank my family, and my colleagues and students at
the University of Massachusetts, Boston, for the encouragement, help, and stimulation they offered in the years during
which this book was completed.

                                                    Pauline Maier

Cambridge, Massachusetts
July 1971

Abbreviations

(*Used in the Footnotes*)

———◦◦———

BM	British Museum; London
BM Add. Mss.	British Museum Additional Manuscripts; London
Boston Gaz.	*Boston Gazette;* Boston, Massachusetts
Conn. Gaz.	*Connecticut Gazette;* New Haven
CSM *Pubs.* (*Trans.*)	*Publications of the Colonial Society of Massachusetts* (*Transactions* . . .); Boston
HLRO	House of Lords Record Office; London
HUL	Houghton Library, Harvard University; Cambridge, Massachusetts
MA	Massachusetts Archives; State House, Boston
Mass. Spy	*Massachusetts Spy;* Boston and Worcester
MdHS	Maryland Historical Society; Baltimore
MHS	Massachusetts Historical Society; Boston
MHS *Colls.*	*Collections of the Massachusetts Historical Society;* Boston
MHS *Procs.*	*Proceedings of the Massachusetts Historical Society;* Boston
N.C. Col. Recs.	*The Colonial Records of North Carolina,* ed. William L. Saunders (Raleigh, 1886–90)

New London Gaz.	*New London Gazette;* New London, Connecticut
N.J. Col. Docs.	*Documents Relating to the Colonial History of the State of New Jersey; Archives of the State of New Jersey,* ed. William A. Whitehead *et al.* (Newark, Trenton, Paterson, 1880–1949)
N.Y. Col. Docs.	*Documents Relative to the Colonial History of the State of New York,* ed. E. B. O'Callaghan (Albany, 1853–87)
N.Y. Gaz.	*New York Gazette;* New York
N.Y. Jour.	*New York Journal;* New York
NYHS	New-York Historical Society; New York
NYHS *Colls.*	*Collections of the New-York Historical Society;* New York
NYPL	New York Public Library, Manuscripts Division, Astor, Lenox and Tilden Foundations; New York
Pa. Gaz.	*Pennsylvania Gazette;* Philadelphia
Pa. Jour.	*Pennsylvania Journal;* Philadelphia
PRO	Public Record Office; London, England

The files cited are:

Adm.	Admiralty
CO	Colonial Office
PC	Privy Council
SP	State Papers
Treas.	Treasury
TS	Treasury Solicitor

Prov. Gaz.	*Providence Gazette;* Providence, Rhode Island
R.I. Col. Recs.	*Records of the Colony of Rhode Island and Providence Plantations* (Providence, 1856–65)
Reps. R. C. C. B.	*Reports of the Record Commissioners of the City of Boston* (Boston, Mass.)
RIHS	Rhode Island Historical Society; Providence
S.C. Gaz.	*South Carolina Gazette;* Charleston
UVa	University of Virginia Library; Charlottesville
Va. Gaz.	*Virginia Gazette;* Williamsburg
W. M. Q.	*The William and Mary Quarterly,* Third Series

PART ONE

TRADITIONS

CHAPTER ONE

———————————— ❦ ————————————

POPULAR UPRISINGS
AND CIVIL AUTHORITY

EIGHTEENTH-CENTURY AMERICANS accepted the existence of popular uprisings with remarkable ease. Riots and tumults, it was said, happened "in all governments at all times." To seek a world completely free of them was vain; it was to pursue "a blessing denied to this life, and reserved to complete the felicity of the next."[1] Not that extra-legal uprisings were encouraged. They were not. But in certain circumstances, it was understood, the people would rise up almost as a natural force, much as night follows day, and this phenomenon often contributed to the public welfare. The colonists' attitude depended in large part upon a tradition of popular uprisings that also shaped the forms of popular force during the revolutionary era. The existence of such a tradition meant, moreover, that the people, or, as their opponents said, the mob, entered the struggle with Britain as an established social force, not as an agency newly invented to serve the ends of radical leadership.

1. John Adams in Charles F. Adams, ed., *The Works of John Adams* (Boston, 1850–6), IV, 77, 80 (quoting Algernon Sidney). An extended version of this chapter with more comprehensive bibliographical references appeared as Pauline Maier, "Popular Uprisings and Civil Authority in Eighteenth-Century America," *W. M. Q.*, XXVII (1970), 3–35.

[I]

Not all American eighteenth-century popular uprisings were the same, of course. Some involved no more than disorderly vandalism; some were in effect traditional brawls, like the celebrations of Pope's Day in New England every November 5; and some involved resistance to lawful authority on the part of a minority interest group. But there was yet another strain of uprisings so persistent that it became characteristic of prominent colonial incidents. Repeatedly, insurgents defended the urgent interests of their communities when lawful authorities failed to act. This had been true of the famous late-seventeenth-century Virginia tobacco uprisings: only after their provincial assembly was prevented from meeting, and thus from curtailing production so as to avert economic crisis, did insurgents begin tearing up tobacco plants. In Maryland's Prince George County, tobacco "rioting" was similarly carried on by men in "despair of any relief from the legislature." Massive rural uprisings in New Jersey and the Carolinas during the mid-eighteenth century also intervened to punish outlaws, secure land titles, or prevent the abuses of public officials only after efforts to work through established procedures failed, and the colonists became convinced that justice and security had to be imposed by the people directly. In proprietary North Carolina, the "resort to force and violence was . . . a common occurrence, almost the habit of the country"; and even after 1731, when the colony came under Crown rule, "scarce a decade passed that did not see the people in arms to redress official grievances."[2] The Boston mob intervened repeatedly to keep foodstuffs in the colony during times of dearth (1710, 1713, 1729) and to destroy bawdy houses (1734, 1737, 1771); in the mid-1770's, uprisings in Marblehead, Massachusetts, and Norfolk, Virginia, acted to protect their communities from a threat of smallpox

2. Richard L. Morton, *Colonial Virginia* (Chapel Hill, 1960), I, 303–4; Charles A. Barker, *The Background of the Revolution in Maryland* (New Haven, 1940), 91; "A State of Facts Concerning the Riots and Insurrections in New Jersey . . . ," *N.J. Col. Docs.*, VII, 207–26; Richard M. Brown, *The South Carolina Regulators* (Cambridge, Mass., 1963); *N.C. Col. Recs.*, VIII, vii–x.

after official actions proved inadequate. And in New London, Connecticut, insurgents prevented a radical religious sect, the Rogerenes, from disturbing normal Sunday services, "a practice they . . . [had] followed more or less for many years past; and which all the laws made in that government, and executed in the most judicious manner could not put a stop to."[3]

These incidents indicate a readiness among many Americans to act outside the bounds of law, but they cannot simply be described as anti-authoritarian. Often—as in the Boston whorehouse riot of 1734 or the Norfork smallpox incident—local magistrates openly countenanced or participated in the crowd's activities. Contemporary political structure can to a large extent explain this confluence of popular force and magisterial inclination. Certainly within New England communities, where the town meeting ruled, and to some extent in New York, where aldermen and councilmen were annually elected, local magistrates were closely linked to the communities they served; and even in Philadelphia, with its lethargic closed corporation, or Charleston, which lacked regular town government, authority was normally exerted by provincials who had an immediate sense of local sentiment. Provincial assemblies also acted to keep public policy in accord with local demands. Of course, this identity of local magistrates with the popular will was imperfect, and occasional uprisings did turn against domestic colonial institutions—in Pennsylvania in 1764, for example, when the "Paxton Boys" complained that their assembly had failed to protect them adequately against the Indians. But uprisings over local issues proved *extra-institutional* in character more often than they were anti-institutional: they served the community where no law existed, or intervened beyond what magistrates thought they could do officially to cope with a local problem.

3. Carl Bridenbaugh, *Cities in the Wilderness* (New York, 1964), 196, 383, 388, 389; Anne Rowe Cunningham, ed., *Letters and Diary of John Rowe* (Boston, 1903), 218. Smallpox incidents: John Adams as "Novanglus" in Adams, *Works of John Adams*, IV, 76–7; Salem news of January 25 and February 1 in *Prov. Gaz.*, February 5 and 12, 1774; and "Friend to the Borough and county of Norfolk" in *Va. Gaz.* (Purdie and Dixon), *Postscript* September 8, 1768. Rogerenes: *Conn. Gaz.*, April 5, 1766.

The case was different when imperial rule was involved. There legal authority emanated from a capital an ocean away, where the colonists had no integral voice in the formation of policy, and governmental decisions were based largely upon the reports of "King's men" who sought above all to promote the King's interests. When London's legal authority and local interest conflicted, efforts to implement the edicts of royal officials were often answered by uprisings, and it was not unusual in these cases for local magistrates to participate or openly sympathize with the insurgents. Attempts to enforce the White Pine Acts of 1722 and 1729, for example, met widespread forceful resistance, sometimes to the extent that royal officials were forced to abandon the task.[4] Two other imperial efforts similarly provoked local uprisings in the colonies long before 1765 and continued to do so in long-established ways during the revolutionary period: impressment and customs enforcement.

As early as 1743, the colonists' violent opposition to impressment was said to indicate a "Contempt of Government." Captains had been "mobbed," the admiralty complained, "others imprisoned, and afterwards held to exorbitant Bail, and are now under Prosecutions." Colonial governors, despite their offers, furnished captains with little real aid either to procure seamen or "even protect them from the Rage and Insults of the People." Two days of severe rioting answered Commodore Charles Knowles's efforts to sweep Boston Harbor for able-bodied men in November 1747. Again in 1764, when Rear Admiral Lord Colville sent out orders to procure men in principal harbors between Casco Bay and Cape Henlopen, uprisings met the ships at every turn. When the *St. John* sent out a boat to seize a recently impressed deserter from a Newport wharf, a crowd protected him, captured the boat's officer, and hurled stones at the crew; later, fifty Newporters joined the colony's gunner at Fort George in opening fire on the King's ship itself. Under threat to her master, the *Chaleur* was forced to release four fishermen seized off Long Island; and when that ship's captain went ashore at New York, his

4. Bernhard Knollenberg, *Origin of the American Revolution, 1759–1766* (New York, 1965), 126, 129; Robert G. Albion, *Forests and Sea Power* (Cambridge, Mass., 1926), 262–3, 265.

boat was seized and burned in the Fields. In the spring of
1765, after the *Maidstone* capped a six-month siege of Newport Harbor by seizing "all the Men" out of a brigantine from
Africa, a band of about five hundred men similarly seized a
ship's officer and burned one of her boats on the Common.
Impressment also met mass resistance at Norfolk in 1767 and
was a major cause of the famous *Liberty* riot at Boston in
1768.[5]

Like the impressment uprisings, which in most instances
sought to protect or rescue men from the "press," the customs
incidents tried to impede the customs service in enforcing
British laws. Tactics varied; and although incidents occurred
long before 1764—in 1719, for example, Caleb Heathcote
reported a "riotous and tumultuous" rescue of seized claret
by Newporters—their frequency increased after the Sugar
Act was passed and customs enforcement efforts were
tightened. The 1764 rescue of the *Rhoda* in Rhode Island
preceded a theft in Dighton, Massachusetts, of the cargo
from a newly seized vessel, the *Polly*, by a mob of some forty
men with blackened faces. In 1766 again a customs official's
home in Falmouth (Portland), Maine, was stoned while "Persons unknown and disguised" stole sugar and rum that had
been impounded that morning. Attacks upon customs officials
enjoyed a long history, but the punishment of informers was
particularly favored: in 1770, Massachusetts's Lieutenant
Governor Thomas Hutchinson noted that many persons would

---

5. Admiralty to Gov. George Thomas, September 26, 1743, in
Samuel Hazard *et al.*, eds., *Pennsylvania Archives* (Philadelphia,
1852–1949), I, 639. Knowles: Charles H. Lincoln, ed., *The Correspondence of William Shirley . . . 1731–1760* (New York, 1912), I,
406–19, and Thomas Hutchinson, *History of the Province of Massachusetts Bay*, ed. Lawrence S. Mayo (Cambridge, Mass., 1936), II,
330–3. *St. John* and *Maidstone*: R.I. Col. Recs., VI, 427–30; "O.G."
in *Newport Mercury* (R.I.), June 10, 1765; David Lovejoy, *Rhode
Island Politics and the American Revolution, 1760–1776* (Providence,
1958), 36–9. *Chaleur:* Knollenberg, *Origin*, 180. George G. Wolkins,
"The Seizure of John Hancock's Sloop 'Liberty,'" MHS *Procs.*, LV
(1921–3), 239–84. Also Jesse Lemisch, "Jack Tar in the Street:
Merchant Seamen in the Politics of Revolutionary America," *W.M.Q.*,
XXV (1968), 391–3, and Neil R. Stout, "Manning the Royal Navy in
North America, 1763–1775," *American Neptune*, XXIII (1963),
179–81.

join in such an affair "who would scruple joining in acts of violence against any other persons." Even the South Carolina attorney general publicly attacked an informer in 1701 while crying out "this is the Informer, this is he that will ruin the country." Similar assaults on customs functionaries occurred decades later, in New Haven in 1766 and 1769, and New London in 1769, for example, and were then often distinguished by their brutality. In 1771, Providence tidesman Jesse Saville was seized, stripped, bound hand and foot, tarred and feathered, had dirt thrown in his face, then was beaten and "almost strangled." Even more thorough assaults upon two other Rhode Island tidesmen occurred in July 1770 and upon Collector Charles Dudley in April 1771. Customs vessels, too, came under direct attack: the *St. John* was shelled at Newport in 1764 where the customs ship *Liberty* was sunk in 1769—both episodes that served as prelude to the destruction of the *Gaspée* outside Providence in 1772.[6]

Such incidents were not confined to New England. Philadelphia witnessed some of the most savage attacks, and even the surveyor of Sassafras and Bohemia in Maryland—an office long a sinecure, since no ships entered or cleared in Sassafras or Bohemia—met with violence when he tried to execute his

6. Heathcote letter, Newport, September, 7, 1719, *R.I. Col. Recs.*, IV, 259–60; Lovejoy, *Rhode Island Politics*, 35–9. *Polly*: Edmund S. and Helen M. Morgan, *The Stamp Act Crisis* (rev. edn., New York, 1963), 59, 64–7, and *Prov. Gaz.*, April 27, 1765. Falmouth: collector and comptroller of Falmouth, August 19, 1766, PRO, Treas. 1/453, 182, and Appendix I of Josiah Quincy, Jr., *Reports of Cases Argued and Adjudged in the Superior Court . . . of Massachusetts Bay, between 1761 and 1772* (Boston, 1865), 446–7. Hutchinson to the Earl of Hillsborough (secretary of state for America), Boston, October 31, 1770, in MA, XXVI, 400. Cecil Headlam, ed., *Calendar of State Papers, Colonial Series, America and the West Indies, 1701* (London, 1910), 651. New Haven: Arnold's account in Malcolm Decker, *Benedict Arnold* (Tarrytown, N.Y., 1932), 27–9; Lawrence H. Gipson, *Jared Ingersoll* (New Haven, 1920), 277–8. New London: documents of July 1969 in PRO, Treas. 1/471. Saville: *N.Y. Jour.*, July 6, 1769, and Saville to collector and comptroller of customs at Newport, May 18, 1769, PRO, Treas. 1/471. Later Rhode Island incidents: Dudley and John Nicoll to Gov. [Joseph Wanton, Jr.], August 1, 1770, PRO, Treas. 1/471; Dudley to commissioners of customs at Boston, Newport, April 11, 1771, PRO, Treas. 1/482; and documents on the destruction of the *Liberty* in PRO, Treas. 1/471.

office in March 1775. After seizing two wagons of goods being carried overland from Maryland toward Duck Creek, Delaware, the officer was overpowered by a "licentious mob" that kept shouting "Liberty and Duck Creek forever!" as it went through the hours-long ritual of tarring and feathering him and threatening his life. And at Norfolk, Virginia, in the spring of 1766 an accused customs informer was tarred and feathered, pelted with stones and rotten eggs, and finally thrown in the sea, where he nearly drowned. Even Georgia saw customs violence before independence, and one of the rare deaths resulting from a colonial riot occurred there in 1775.[7]

Although the White Pine, impressment, and customs uprisings were distinctive in that they uniformly opposed British authority, they had much in common with many more exclusively local incidents. The community's immediate welfare was at stake, not the satisfaction of any anti-British prejudices. The White Pine Acts reserved to the Crown all white pine trees, whatever their fitness for the navy, and prevented colonists from using them for lumber even where white pine constituted the principal forest growth. As a result, the acts "operated so much against the convenience and even necessities of the inhabitants," Surveyor John Wentworth explained, that "it became almost a general interest of the country" to frustrate their execution. Impressment offered a still more urgent threat: the affected port, as Massachusetts's Governor William Shirley explained in 1747, was drained of mariners both by the impressment itself and by the

---

7. Philadelphia: William Sheppard to commissioners of customs, April 21, 1769, and John Swift to commissioners of customs, October 13, 1769, both in PRO, Treas. 1/471; Swift to customs commissioners, November 15, 1770, and related documents in PRO, Treas. 1/476. Maryland: documents in PRO, Treas. 1/513. Virginia: William Smith to Jeremiah Morgan, April 3, 1766, PRO, CO 5/1331, f. 80. W. W. Abbot, *The Royal Governors of Georgia, 1754–1775* (Chapel Hill, 1959), 174–5.

These customs uprisings should be distinguished from the organized opposition to Britain that emerged in 1765. There was no radical program of customs obstruction *per se.* Customs incidents were above all local in character and, at least before the Townshend Revenue Act, devoid of explicit ideological justifications.

flight of navigation to safer provinces, driving the wages for any remaining seamen upward. When the press was of long duration, moreover, or when it took place during a normally busy season, it could mean serious shortages of food or firewood for winter, and a general attrition of the commercial life that sustained all strata of society in trading towns. Commerce seemed even more directly attacked by British trade regulations, particularly by the proliferation of customs procedures in the mid-1760's that appeared to be in no American's interest, and by the Sugar Act, which seemed to threaten the foreign West Indian trade that sustained the economies of colonies like Rhode Island. As a result, even when only a limited contingent of sailors participated in a customs incident, officials could suspect—as did the deputy collector at Philadelphia in 1770—that the mass of citizens "in their Hearts" approved of it.[8]

Opposition to impressment and customs enforcement in itself was not, moreover, the only cause of the so-called impressment or customs "riots." The complete narratives of these incidents indicate again not only that the crowd acted to support local interests, but that it sometimes enforced the will of local magistrates by extra-legal means. Although British officials blamed the *St. John* incident upon that ship's customs and impressment activities, colonists insisted that the confrontation began when some sailors stole a few pigs and chickens from a local miller and the ship's crew refused to surrender the thieves to Newport officials. Two members of the Rhode Island Council then ordered the gunner of Fort George to detain the schooner until the accused seamen were delivered to the sheriff, and "many People went over to the Fort to assist the Gunner in the Discharge of his Duty." Only after this uprising did the ship's officers surrender the accused men.[9] Similarly, the 1747 Knowles impressment riot

8. Wentworth quoted in Knollenberg, *Origin*, 124–5; Shirley to Duke of Newcastle, December 31, 1747, in Lincoln, *Shirley Correspondence*, I, 420–3; John Swift to customs commissioners, November 15, 1770, PRO, Treas. 1/476.

9. Gov. Samuel Ward's report to the Treasury lords, October 23, 1765, Ward Mss., RIHS, Box I, f. 58; deposition of Daniel Vaughn (the gunner at Fort George), July 8, 1764, Chalmers Papers, Rhode

in Boston and the 1765 *Maidstone* impressment riot in Newport broke out after governors' requests for the release of impressed seamen had gone unanswered, and only after the
outbreak of violence were the governors' requests honored.
The crowd that first assembled on the night the *Liberty* was
destroyed in Newport also began by demanding the allegedly
drunken sailors who that afternoon had abused and shot at
a colonial captain, Joseph Packwood, so that they could be
bound over to local magistrates for prosecution.[10]

In circumstances such as these, uprisings occurred only
after the normal channels of redress had proven inadequate.
The main thrust of the colonists' resistance to the White
Pine Acts had always been made in their courts and legislatures. Violence broke out for the most part only in local
situations where no alternative was available. Even the burning of the *Gaspée* in June 1772—which was inspired by the
immediate needs of Rhode Islanders, not by revolutionary
goals—was a last resort. Three months before the incident,
a group of prominent Providence citizens complained about
the ship's wanton severity with all vessels along the coast and
the colony's governor pressed their case with the fleet's admiral. The admiral, however, supported the *Gaspée*'s commander, Lieutenant William Dudingston; and thereafter, the
Providence Gazette claimed, Dudingston became "more
haughty, insolent and intolerable," "personally ill treating
every master and merchant of the vessels he boarded, stealing
sheep, hogs, poultry, &c. from farmers round the bay, and
cutting down their fruit and other trees for firewood." Redress
from London was possible but time-consuming, and in the
meantime the colony was approaching what its governor called
"the deepest calamity" as supplies of food and fuel were cur-

---

Island, f. 41, NYPL. British accounts: Lt. Thomas Hill's account in
James Munro, ed., *Acts of the Privy Council of England, Colonial
Series* (London, 1912), VI, 374–6, and the report of John Robinson
and John Nicoll to customs commissioners, August 30, 1765, PRO,
PC 1/51, Bundle I (53a).

10. On Knowles and *Maidstone* incidents, seen *n.* 5 above. Documents on the *Liberty* affair in PRO, Treas. 1/471, especially deposition
of Capt. William Reid, July 21, 1769, and that of John Carr, the
second mate, who indicates that the crowd soon forgot its scheme of
delivering crew members to the magistrates.

tailed and prices, especially in Newport, rose steeply. It was significant that John Brown finally led those Providence men who seized the moment in June when the *Gaspée* ran aground near Warwick, for it was he who had spearheaded the effort in March 1772 to win redress through the normal channels of government.[11]

Although popular uprisings were, then, an integral part of eighteenth-century American life, they were not distinctive to America. Colonial uprisings shared many characteristics with those in Britain. The word "mob" connoted for Englishmen the lowest rank of society, the "*mobile vulgus*," an effective fourth estate beyond the King, Lords, and Commons; but the studies of George Rudé have indicated that British insurgents were not uniformly drawn from any one social group.[12] In America, too, largely because uprisings grew out of concerns shared by most segments of the community, the "rioters" were not necessarily confined to the seamen, servants, Negroes, and boys generally described as the staple components of the colonial mob. A member of the prominent Gillman family who was a mill owner and a militia officer organized the uprising against the King's surveyor of the woods at Exeter, New Hampshire, in 1754. "All the principal Gentlemen in Town" were supposedly present when a customs informer was tarred and feathered at Norfolk in 1766; Captain Jeremiah Morgan complained about the virtually universal participation of Norfolkers in an impressment incident of 1767; and persons of standing also participated in the town's smallpox uprising of 1774. Merchant Benedict Arnold admitted leading a New Haven mob against an informer in 1766; New London merchants Joseph Packwood and Nathaniel Shaw commanded the crowd that first accosted Captain William Reid the night the *Liberty* was destroyed at Newport in 1769, just as John Brown, a leading Providence

---

11. Joseph J. Malone, *Pine Trees and Politics* (Seattle, 1964), 8–9 and *passim*. Adm. Montagu to Gov. Wanton, April 8, 1772; Wanton to Hillsborough, June 16, 1772, and Ephraim Bowen's narrative in *R.I. Col. Recs.*, VII, 60, 62–73, 90–2, 174–5. *Prov. Gaz.*, January 9, 1773.

12. George Rudé, *The Crowd in History: A Study of Popular Disturbances in France and England, 1730–1848* (New York, 1968), 204–5.

merchant, led the *Gaspée*'s attackers. Charles Dudley reported in April 1771 that the men who beat him in Newport "did not come from the . . . lowest class of Men," but were "stiled Merchants and the Masters of their Vessels." Similarly in Maryland, Customsman Robert Moreton claimed that "most of [his attackers] were the principal Merchants in Baltimore and Fells Point." And again in 1775, Robert Stratford Byrne claimed that many of his Maryland and Pennsylvania assailants were "from Appearance . . . Men of Property."[13]

Eighteenth-century crowds in England and also France were, Rudé has concluded, remarkably single-minded and discriminating.[14] In America, too, targets were characteristically related to grievances: the Norfolk rioters isolated inoculated persons where they would be least dangerous; customs rioters attacked only customs officials and informers. The Boston mob was so domesticated that it refused to riot on Saturday and Sunday nights, which were considered holy by New Englanders.[15] Equally striking was the tendency of crowds in England and America to avoid bloodshed. Up into the nineteenth century, G. Kitson Clark has reminded us, English society lacked the civility and refinements of the modern age—this was the age of the cockfight, when mothers brought their children to witness the hangings at Tyburn. Yet no deaths were inflicted by the Wilkes, Anti-Irish, or "No Popery" mobs, and only single fatalities resulted from other upheavals such as the Porteous riots of 1736. Insurgents did not abstain from damaging or destroying their victims' property, but "it was authority rather than the crowd that was conspicuous for its violence to life and limb." All 285 casualties of London's Gordon Riots of 1780, for example, were

13. Malone, *Pine Trees and Politics*, 112; Morgan quoted in Lemisch, "Jack Tar," 391; William Smith to Morgan, April 3, 1766, PRO, CO 5/1331, f. 80. Decker, *Benedict Arnold*, 27–9; deposition of Capt. William Reid on the *Liberty* affair, July 21, 1769, PRO, Treas. 1/471; Ephraim Bowen's narrative on the *Gaspée* affair, *R.I. Col. Recs.*, VII, 68–73; Dudley to customs commissioners, April 11, 1771, PRO, Treas. 1/482; Robert Moreton to commissioners of customs, May 28, 1773, Gilmor Papers, MdHS, III, 98. Byrne deposition in PRO, Treas. 1/513.

14. Rudé, *Crowd in History*, 60, 253–4.

15. Joseph Harrison's testimony in MHS *Procs.*, LV (1921–3), 254.

rioters.[16] Total casualty figures for American uprisings were then naturally still lower than for those in the Mother Country, since a regular army was less at the ready for use against colonial mobs.

Even the causes of incidents were remarkably alike on both sides of the Atlantic. The uprisings over grain exportations during times of dearth, the attacks on brothels, press gangs, royal forest officials, and customsmen, all had their counterparts in seventeenth- and eighteenth-century England. Even the Americans' hatred of the customs establishment mirrored the Englishman's traditional loathing of excisemen. Like the customsmen in the colonies, they seemed to descend into localities armed with extraordinary prerogative powers. Often, too, English excisemen were "thugs and brutes who beat up their victims without compunction or stole or wrecked their property" and against whose extravagances little redress was possible through the law.[17]

Charges of an identical character were made in the colonies against customsmen and, particularly after 1763, when naval officers were given commissions in the customs service, the Royal Navy as well. The incidents related by "A PUMKIN" in a 1773 *New London Gazette* were characteristic of this often-mentioned victimization of colonists, regardless of social rank, by the "King's men" in the colonies. A few days earlier, the "PUMKIN" claimed, a royal vessel had seized a brig going to Boston with molasses, and before releasing it His Majesty's servants had stolen "two Duffil Great-Coats, two pair Duffil Trowsers, one Frock, two pair Oznabrigs Trowsers, and three Pillow cases, which they stript off the poor Seamen's Pillows." On entering the harbor they hailed a poor oysterman with a boat "not worth 10 1.," abused him and then took five bushels of his oysters. The next day, they halted a two-mast boat from New Haven, manned by two boys and carrying a barrel of currant wine, a gift from a New Haven gentleman to a friend in New London. "After repeated

---

16. G. Kitson Clark, *The Making of Victorian England* (London, 1962), 58–62; Rudé, *Crowd in History*, 255–7.

17. Max Beloff, *Public Order and Popular Disturbances, 1660–1714* (London, 1938), *passim*; Albion, *Forests and Sea Power*, 263; J. H. Plumb, *England in the Eighteenth Century* (Baltimore, 1961 [orig. pub., Oxford, 1950]), 66.

Execrations, in their usual Form," the letter reported, "they tap'd the Wine, drew out about Half and then dissmiss'd the Boat." Two days later, they accosted a sixty-year-old man named Vail entering the harbor in a sloop from Long Island. When, on orders, Vail—"a gentleman of pretty interest upon Long Island"—failed to lower his anchor fast enough, the royal ship shot at him and ordered him onto the cruiser, where the captain reviled him "in the most abusive Way, and as he had no Oysters or Currant Wine and did not produce any Money," had him beaten.[18]

Similar petty abuses played a significant role in triggering some of the major customs and impressment riots. Antagonism to the *Maidstone*, attacked at Newport in early 1765, apparently rose in part from the contempt shown private shipmasters who boarded the royal vessel to pay back wages to men impressed from their ships. These masters were, it was reported, "used in such a Manner as it would be no Credit to his Majesty's Officers to relate." Others who went on board the ship to deliver chests and bedding to impressed seamen supposedly "had their Boats turn'd adrift, and themselves put under Confinement, and detained all Night." Captain Reid of the *Liberty*, whose ship was destroyed in 1769, had "behaved more like a pirate, than like one appointed or commissioned to protect our trade," the *New London Gazette* complained. He fired on outward-bound vessels and fishing boats, impounded and detained vessels headed in toward the customhouse at great cost to their owners, and, it was claimed, allowed his crew to engage in minor annoyances, such as cutting down a flag flying in New London on Election Day. Complaints against Lieutenant Dudingston of the *Gaspée* went back to 1769 when a Marylander, David Bevan, asserted that while innocently fishing on the Delaware River he was hauled on board the sloop and beaten. In April 1772, crew members of the *Gaspée* had stopped on Gould Island, the *New London Gazette* complained, and cut down thirty to forty "fine walnut trees" that their owner valued highly.[19]

American complaints were distinct from those of English-

18. *New London Gaz.*, May 14 and 18, 1773.

19. "O.G." in *Newport Mercury* (R.I.), June 10, 1765; *New London Gaz.*, September 22, 1769; Bevan's statement in *Va. Gaz.* (Rind), July 27, 1769, and *New London Gaz.*, July 21, 1769.

men only in that they took on a new gravity, for in the colonies the abuses of British officials were those of an external power. By their arrogance and arbitrariness, these bearers of the King's commission helped effect "an estrangement of the Affections of the People from the Authority under which they act."[20] The tendency was recognized throughout the decade before independence by concerned colonists, who regularly warned British authorities of the need to constrain Crown agents if the Anglo-American rift was to be healed.[21]

[II]

The persistence of popular uprisings and also their character and influence can be explained in part by the character of Anglo-American law enforcement procedures. There were no professional police forces in the eighteenth century. Instead, the power of government depended upon traditional institutions like the "hue and cry," by which the community in general rose to apprehend felons. The "hue and cry" dated back to the Middle Ages, when it had represented a form of summary justice similar to modern lynch law. By the eighteenth century magistrates turned most often, however, to the *posse commitatus*, literally the "power of the country," but meaning in practice all able-bodied men whom a sheriff might call upon to assist him. Where greater and more organized support was needed, magistrates could call out the militia. Both the *posse* and the militia drew upon local men, including many of the same persons who participated in extra-legal uprisings. This meant that insurrections could naturally assume the manner of a lawful institution, as insurgents acted by habit with relative restraint and responsibility. On the other hand, the militia institutionalized the practice of forcible popular coercion and thus made the formation of extra-

20. Joseph Reed to the president of Congress, October 21, 1779, in Hazard *et al.*, eds., *Pa. Archives*, VII, 762.

21. Stephen Sayre to Lord Dartmouth, December 13, 1766, Dartmouth Papers, William Salt Library, Stafford, England, D 1778/2/258; Joseph Reed to Dartmouth, April 4, 1774, in William B. Reed, *Life and Correspondence of Joseph Reed* (Philadelphia, 1847), I, 56–7.

legal crowds more natural, so that J. R. Western has called the militia "a relic of the bad old days," and hailed its passing as "a step towards . . . bringing civilization and humanity into our [English] political life."[22]

These law enforcement mechanisms, of course, left magistrates virtually helpless whenever a large segment of the population was immediately involved in the disorder, or when the community had a strong sympathy for the rioters. The Boston militia's failure to act in the Stamp Act riots, which was repeated in nearly all the North American colonies, recapitulated a similar refusal during the Knowles riot of 1747.[23] If the mob's sympathizers were confined to a single locality, the governor could try to call out the militias of surrounding areas, as Massachusetts Governor Shirley began to do in 1747, and as was successfully done to suppress the North Carolina Regulators in 1771.[24] In the case of sudden uprisings, however, these peace-keeping mechanisms were at best partially effective since they required time to assemble strength, which often in fact made the effort wholly pointless.

When the disorder continued and the militia either failed to appear or proved insufficient, there was, of course, the army, which was used periodically in the eighteenth century

22. Frederick Pollock and Frederic W. Maitland, *The History of English Law before the Time of Edward I* (Cambridge, Eng., 1968 [orig. pub., 1895]), II, 578–80; William Blackstone, *Commentaries on the Laws of England* (Philadelphia, 1771), IV, 290–1. John Shy, *Toward Lexington: The Role of the British Army in the Coming of the American Revolution* (Princeton, 1965), 40. J. R. Western, *The English Militia in the Eighteenth Century* (London, 1965), 74.

23. See Shirley's explanation for the militia's failure to act (the militiamen sympathized with the rioters) in a letter to the Lords of Trade, December 1, 1747, Lincoln, *Shirley Correspondence*, I, 417–18. The English militia was also unreliable. It worked well against invasions and unpopular rebellions, but was less likely to support the government when official orders "clashed with the desires of the citizens" or when it was ordered to protect unpopular minorities. Sir Robert Walpole believed "that if called on to suppress smuggling, protect the turnpikes, or enforce the gin act, the militia would take the wrong side." In Western, *English Militia*, 72–3.

24. Shirley to Josiah Willard, November 19, 1747, in Lincoln, *Shirley Correspondence*, I, 407. A bounty was apparently necessary to induce men to join the militia that marched against the Regulators. See *N.C. Col. Recs.*, VII, xxix, xxxi.

against rioters in England and Scotland. Even in America, peacetime garrisons tended to be placed where they might serve to maintain law and order. But since all Englishmen shared a fear of standing armies, the deployment of troops had always to be a sensitive and carefully limited recourse. Military and civil spheres of authority were rigidly separated, as was clear to Sir Jeffery Amherst, who refused to use soldiers against anti-military rioters at Philadelphia in 1759 and 1760 because that function was "entirely foreign to their command and belongs of right to none but the civil power." In fact, troops could be used against British subjects, as in the suppression of civil disorder, only upon the request of local magistrates. This institutional inhibition carried if anything more weight in the colonies. There, royal governors had quickly lost their right to declare martial law without the consent of the provincial councils, which were, again, usually filled with local men.[25]

For all practical purposes, then, when a large political unit such as an entire town or colony condoned an act of mass force, problems were raised "almost insoluble without rending the whole fabric of English law." Nor was the situation confined to the colonies. In England no technique for maintaining order was found before the nineteenth century, if then. Certainly by the 1770's no acceptable solution had been found— neither by the colonists nor "anyone in London, Paris, or Rome, either," as Carl Bridenbaugh has put it. Even to farsighted contemporaries like John Adams, the weakness of authority was an inescapable aspect of the social order that necessarily conditioned the way rulers could act. "It is vain to expect or hope to carry on government against the universal bent and genius of the people," he wrote; "we may whimper and whine as much as we will, but nature made it impossible when she made man."[26]

---

25. Shy, *Toward Lexington*, 39–40, 44, 47, 74. Amherst quoted in J. C. Long, *Lord Jeffrey Amherst* (New York, 1933), 124. Evarts B. Greene, *The Provisional Governor in the English Colonies of North America* (New York, 1898), 111-12, 115, 116.

26. Shy, *Toward Lexington*, 44; Clark, *Making of Victorian England*, 58–62; Carl Bridenbaugh, *Cities in Revolt* (New York, 1964), 297; Adams, *Works of John Adams*, IV, 74–5, and V, 209.

The mechanisms for enforcing public order were rendered still more fragile since the distinction between legal and illegal applications of mass force was precise in theory, but sometimes indistinguishable in practice. The English common law prohibited riot, defined as an uprising of three or more persons who performed what Blackstone called an "unlawful act of violence" for a private purpose. If the act was never carried out or attempted, the offense became unlawful assembly; if some effort was made toward its execution, rout; and if the purpose of the uprising was public rather than private—tearing down whorehouses, for example, or destroying all enclosures rather than just those personally affecting the insurgents—the offense became treason, since it constituted a usurpation of the King's function, a "levying war against the King." The precise legal offense lay not so much in the purpose of the uprising as in its use of force and violence, "wherein the Law does not allow the Use of such Force." Such unlawful assumptions of force were carefully distinguished by commentators upon the common law from other occasions on which the law authorized a use of popular force. It was, for example, legal for popular force to be used by a sheriff, a constable, "or perhaps even . . . a private Person" who assembled "a competent Number of People, in Order with Force to suppress Rebels, or Enemies, or Rioters"; also for a justice of the peace to raise the *posse* when opposed in detaining lands, or for Crown officers to raise "a Power as may effectually enable them to over-power any . . . Resistance" in the execution of the King's writs.[27]

In certain situations, these distinctions offered at best a very uncertain guide as to who did or who did not exert force lawfully. Should a *posse* exert more force than was necessary to overcome overt resistance, for example, its members acted illegally and were indictable for riot. Moreover, if different officials supported each side in a confrontation, or if the legality of the act officials were attempting to enforce was itself disputed, the decision as to who were or were not

27. William Hawkins, *A Treatise of the Pleas of the Crown* (London, 1716), I, 155–9; Blackstone, *Commentaries*, IV, 146–7; Edward Coke, *The Third Part of the Institutes of the Laws of England* (London, 1797), 176.

rioters was largely subjective. Impressment is a good example, since the legality of the practice in North American waters was disputable between 1713 and 1775. Even British authorities disagreed on the issue. Among those who believed impressment in general was lawful, disagreement was still possible as to whether or not the full consent of the governor and council was necessary before impressment could be carried on within a given province.[28] Because of these ambiguities, it was possible to view the press gangs as "rioters" for trying, *en masse*, to perpetrate an unlawful act of violence. The local townsmen who opposed the press might then be considered lawful defenders of the public welfare, acting much as they would in a *posse*. In 1770, John Adams cited opposition to press gangs who acted without warrants as an example of the lawful use of force; and when the sloop of war *Hornet* swept into Norfolk, Virginia, in 1767 with a "bloody riotous plan . . . to impress seamen, without consulting the Mayor, or any other magistrate," the offense was charged to the pressmen. Roused by the watchman, who called out "*a riot by man of war's men*," the inhabitants rose to back the magistrates, and secured not only the release of the impressed men but also the imprisonment of ten members of the press gang. The ship's captain, on the other hand, condemned the townsmen as "Rioters." Ambiguity was present, too, in Newport's *St. John* clash, which involved both impressment and criminal action on the part of royal seamen and culminated with Newporters firing on the King's ship. The Privy Council in England promptly classified the incident as a riot, but the Rhode Island governor's report maintained that "the people meant nothing but to assist [the magistrates] in apprehending the Offenders" on the vessel, and impudently suggested that "their Conduct be honored with his Majesty's royal Approbation."[29]

28. Dora Mae Clark, "The Impressment of Seamen in the American Colonies," *Essays in Colonial History Presented to Charles McLean Andrews* (New Haven, 1931), 198–224; "Manning the Royal Navy," 178–9.

29. L. Kinvin Wroth and Hiller B. Zobel, eds., *Legal Papers of John Adams* (Cambridge, Mass., 1965), III, 253. Account of Norfolk incident by George Abyvon, September 5, 1767, in *Va. Gaz.* (Purdie

Enforcement of the White Pine Acts was similarly open to legal dispute. The acts seemed to violate both the Massachusetts and Connecticut charters; the meaning of provisions exempting trees growing within townships (Act of 1722) and those which were the property of private persons (Act of 1729) was contested, and royal officials tended to work on the basis of interpretations of the laws that Bernhard Knollenberg has called far-fetched and, in one case, "utterly untenable." The Exeter, New Hampshire, "riot" of 1734, for example, answered an attempt of the surveyor to seize boards on the argument that the authorization to seize logs from allegedly illegally felled white pine trees in the Act of 1722 included an authorization to seize processed lumber. As a result, although the surveyors' reports "give the impression that the New Englanders were an utterly lawless lot . . . in many if not most cases they were standing for what they believed, with reason, were their legal and equitable rights in trees growing on their own lands."[30]

Occasions open to such conflicting interpretations were rare. For the most part, members of a mob clearly acted without the sanction of law. That ambiguous cases did arise, however, indicates that legitimacy and illegitimacy, *posse*s and rioters, represented poles on a single spectrum. Even where their relationship to the law was doubtful, moreover, popular uprisings benefited from a certain presumptive acceptability that was founded in part on colonial experience with mass action. In words that could be drawn almost verbatim from John Locke or other English authors of similar convictions, colonial writers assumed a certain moderation and purposefulness among insurgents. "Tho' innocent Persons may sometimes suffer in popular Tumults," observed a 1768 writer in the *New York Journal*, "yet the general Resentment of the People is principally directed according to Justice, and the greatest Delinquent feels it most." More important, upheavals

----

and Dixon), October 1, 1767; Capt. Morgan quoted in Lemisch, "Jack Tar," 391. Munro, *Acts of the Privy Council, Colonial Series*, VI, 374; Gov. Samuel Ward to Treasury lords, October 23, 1765, Ward Mss., RIHS, Box I, 58.

30. Knollenberg, *Origin*, 122–30; Albion, *Forests and Sea Power*, 255–8.

constituted only occasional interruptions in well-governed societies. "Good Laws and good Rulers will always be obey'd
and respected"; "the Experience of all Ages proves, that Mankind are much more likely to submit to bad Laws and wicked
Rulers, than to resist good ones." "Mobs and Tumults," it
was often said, "never happen but thro' Oppression and a
scandalous Abuse of Power."[31]

In the hands of Locke, such remarks constituted relatively
inert statements of fact. Colonial writers, however, often
turned these pronouncements on their heads such that instances of popular disorder became *prima facie* indictments
not of the people, but of authority. In 1747, for example, New
Jersey land rioters argued that "from their Numbers, Violences, and unlawful Actions" it was "to be inferred that . . .
they are wronged & oppressed, or else they would never *rebell*
agt. the Laws." When the people of any government become
turbulent and uneasy, a New York writer said in 1770, it is
always "a certain Sign of Maladministration." Even when disorders were not directly focused against government, they
provided "strong proofs that something is much amiss in the
state," as William Samuel Johnson put it; that—in Samuel
Adams's words—the "wheels of government" were "some-
where clogged." Americans who used this argument against
Britain in the 1760's continued to depend upon it two decades
later, when they reacted to Shay's Rebellion by seeking out
the public "Disease" in their own independent governments
that was indicated by the "Spirit of Licentiousness" in Massachusetts.[32]

Popular turbulence seemed to follow so naturally from in-
adequacies of government that riots and rebellions were often
described with similes from the physical world. In 1770, John

---

31. *N.Y. Jour.*, August 18, 1768 (summarizing arguments from the
British press), and *N.Y. Jour.*, *Supplement* January 4, 1770.

32. "A State of Facts Concerning the Riots . . . in New Jersey,"
N.J. Col. Docs., VII, 215; *N.Y. Jour.*, *Supplement* January 4, 1770;
Johnson to William Pitkin, April 29, 1768, MHS *Colls.*, 5th Ser., IX
(Boston, 1885), 275; Adams as "Determinus" in *Boston Gaz.*, August
8, 1768, and Harry A. Cushing, ed., *The Writings of Samuel Adams*
(New York, 1904–8), I, 237; John Jay to Thomas Jefferson, October
27, 1786, in Julian Boyd, ed., *The Papers of Thomas Jefferson*
(Princeton, 1950–   ), X, 488.

Adams said that there were "Church-quakes and state-quakes in the moral and political world, as well as earth-quakes, storms and tempests in the physical." Two years earlier, a writer in the *New York Journal* had likened popular tumults to "Thunder Gusts," which "do more Good than Harm." Thomas Jefferson continued the imagery in the 1780's, particularly with his famous statement that he "liked a little rebellion now and then," for it was like "a storm in the atmosphere." It was, moreover, because of the "imperfection of all things in this world" that John Adams found it vain to try to found a government totally free of tumultuousness. In effect, disorder was an integral, even predictable part of life on earth.[33]

If popular uprisings occurred "in all governments at all times," they were nonetheless most prevalent in free governments. Tyrants imposed order and submission upon their subjects by force. Only under free governments were the people "nervous," spirited, ready and able to react against unjust provocations. As such, popular insurrections could be interpreted as "Symptoms of a strong and healthy Constitution" even while they indicated some lesser shortcoming in administration. It would be futile, Josiah Quincy, Jr., said in 1770, to expect "that pacific, timid, obsequious, and servile temper, so predominant in more despotic governments," from those who lived under free British institutions. From "our happy constitution," he claimed, there resulted as "very natural Effects" an "impatience of injuries, and a strong resentment of insults."[34]

33. Adams in Wroth and Zobel, eds., *Adams Legal Papers*, III, 249–50; *N.Y. Jour.*, *Supplement* August 18, 1768; Jefferson to Abigail Adams, February 22, 1787, in Boyd, *Jefferson Papers*, XI, 174. Adams, *Works of John Adams*, IV, 77, 80.

34. Quincy's address to the jury in the soldiers' trial after the "Boston Massacre" in Josiah Quincy, *Memoir of the Life of Josiah Quincy, Junior, of Massachusetts Bay, 1744–1775*, ed. Eliza Susan Quincy (3d edn., Boston, 1875), 46. See also the claim of the Massachusetts House of Representatives that "a People accustomed to the Freedom of the English Constitution" could not be expected to remain patient while "under the Hand of Tyranny and arbitrary Power," in its reply to an address of Gov. Hutchinson of April 1770, *Boston Gaz.*, April 30, and *N.Y. Jour.*, May 10, 1770.

Occasional manifestations of this popular spirit were in fact "an evil . . . productive of good": they clearly brought popular feelings—particularly those of the mob—to bear on public authority; and, as Thomas Jefferson argued most cogently in 1787, they tended to hold rulers "to the true principles of their institutions" and so provided "a medicine necessary for the sound health of government." Thus, members of the British House of Lords could seriously argue that "rioting is an essential part of our constitution." Even the conservative Thomas Hutchinson remarked in 1768 that "Mobs, a sort of them at least, are constitutional."[35]

There were, however, distinct limits to colonial toleration of upheavals. It was always understood that insofar as uprisings abandoned their moderation and purposefulness, insofar as they ceased to be curative forces in society and threatened "running to such excesses, as will overturn the whole system of government," "strong discouragements" had to be provided against them. This desire to maintain the orderly rule of law led legislatures in England and the colonies to pass anti-riot statutes and to make strong efforts—in the words of a 1753 Massachusetts law—to discountenance "a mobbish temper and spirit in . . . the inhabitants," that would oppose "all government and order."[36]

Such laws were usually passed in response to immediate crises. The English Riot Act of 1714 was passed when disorder threatened to disrupt the accession of George I; a Connecticut Act of 1722 followed a rash of incidents over land title in Hartford County; the Massachusetts Act of 1751

35. Jefferson to William Stephen Smith, November 13, 1787, in Boyd, *Jefferson Papers*, XII, 356; Jefferson to Edward Carrington, January 16, 1787, and to James Madison, January 30, 1787, *ibid.*, XI, 49, 92–3. Taylor's remarks in "History of Violence," *The Listener*, CXXIX (1968), 701 ("Members of the House of Lords . . . said . . . if the people really don't like something, then they wreck our carriages and tear off our wigs and throw stones through the windows of our town-houses. And this is an essential thing to have if you are going to have a free country"). Hutchinson to (John or Robert) Grant, July 27, 1768, MA, XXVI, 317.

36. *N.Y. Jour.*, *Supplement* January 4, 1770; Adams in Wroth and Zobel, *Adams Legal Papers*, III, 250; *Acts and Resolves of the Province of Massachusetts Bay*, III (Boston, 1878), 647 (Chapter 18 of the Province Laws, 1752–3).

answered "several tumultuous assemblies" over the currency issue. The New Jersey legislature passed an act in 1747 during that colony's protracted land riots; Pennsylvania's Riot Act of 1764 was inspired by the Paxton Boys; North Carolina's of 1771 by the Regulators; New York's of 1774 by the "land wars" in Charlotte and Albany counties.[37] Always the acts specified that the magistrates were to depend upon the *posse* in enforcing their provisions, and in North Carolina on the militia as well. They differed over the number of people who had to remain "unlawfully, riotously, and tumultuously assembled together, to the Disturbance of the Publick Peace" for one hour after the reading of a prescribed proclamation before becoming judicable under the act. Some colonies specified lesser punishments than the death penalty provided for in the English act, but the American statutes were not in general more "liberal" than the British. Two of them so violated elementary judicial rights that they were subsequently condemned: North Carolina's by Britain, and New York's Act of 1774 by a later, revolutionary state legislature.[38]

In one important respect, however, the English Riot Act was reformed. Each colonial riot law except that of Connecticut was enacted for only one to three years, whereas the British law was perpetual. By this provision, colonial legislators avoided the shortcoming which, it was said, was "more likely to introduce arbitrary *Power* than even an *Army* itself," because a riot act without termination meant that "in all future time" by "reading a Proclamation" the Crown had the power of "hanging up their Subjects wholesale, or of picking

---

37. *The Statutes at Large* [of Great Britain], V (London, 1786), 4–6; Charles J. Hoadly, ed., *The Public Records of the Colony of Connecticut*, VI (Hartford, 1872), 346–8 for the law, and also 332–3, 341–8; *Acts and Resolves of the Province of Massachusetts Bay*, III, 544–6 for Riot Act of 1751, and also Hutchinson, *History of the Province of Massachusetts Bay*, III, 6–7; "A State of Facts Concerning the Riots . . . in New Jersey," *N.J. Col. Docs.*, VII, 211–12, 221–2; *The Statutes at Large of Pennsylvania*, VI (no place, 1899), 325–8; *N.C. Col. Recs.*, VIII, 481–6; *Laws of the Colony of New York, Passed in the Years 1774 and 1775* (Albany, 1888), 38–43.

38. Additional instructions to Gov. Josiah Martin in *N.C. Col. Recs.*, VIII, 515–16, and *Laws of the State of New York*, I (Albany, 1886), 20.

out Those, to whom they have the greatest Dislike."[39] A perpetual riot act would also reduce the flexibility of legislatures,
such as was exercised by the Massachusetts Assembly in April
1770, when it refused to renew the colony's riot act because
under current circumstances any augmentation of the civil
magistrate's powers seemed dangerous.

Even in discouraging popular disorder, then, colonial
legislators seemed as intent upon preventing any perversion
of the forces of law and order by established authorities as
with chastising insurgents. As such, the measures enacted by
them to deal with insurrections were shaped by their experience with and understanding of popular uprisings. Since
turbulence indicated above all some shortcoming in government, it was never to be met by increasing the authorities'
power of suppression. It was "far less dangerous to the Freedom of a State" to allow "the laws to be trampled upon, by
the licence among the rabble . . . than to dispence with their
force by an act of power." Uprisings were to be answered by
reform, by attacking the "disease"—to use John Jay's term
of 1786—that lay behind them rather than by suppressing
its "Symptoms." And ultimately, as William Samuel Johnson observed in 1768, "the only effectual way to prevent them
is to govern with wisdom, justice, and moderation."[40]

39. *The Craftsman*, VI (London, 1731), 263–4.

40. *N.Y. Jour.*, *Supplement* January 4, 1770; Jay to Jefferson, October 27, 1786, in Boyd, *Jefferson Papers*, X, 488; Johnson to Pitkin,
July 23, 1768, MHS *Colls.*, 5th Ser., IX, 294–5.

CHAPTER TWO

---◆◆◆---

AN IDEOLOGY
OF RESISTANCE AND
RESTRAINT

THE COLONIST'S ATTITUDES toward civil uprisings were part of a broader Anglo-American political tradition. In the course of the eighteenth century, colonists became increasingly interested in the idea of seventeenth-century English revolutionaries such as John Milton, Algernon Sidney, John Locke, and the later writers who carried on and developed this tradition—Robert Molesworth; John, Lord Somers; the Anglican bishop Benjamin Hoadly; John Trenchard and Thomas Gordon, whose essays, published together as *Cato's Letters*, were a classic for many Americans; the Scottish philosopher Francis Hutcheson; and the celebrated English historian of the 1760's and 1770's, Catharine Macaulay.[1] By the 1760's, this "Real Whig" or "Commonwealthman" tradition provided a strong unifying element, between colonists North and South. It offered, too, a corpus of ideas about public authority and popular political responsibilities that shaped the American revolutionary movement.

Spokesmen for this English revolutionary tradition were distinguished in the eighteenth century above all by their outspoken defense of the people's right to rise up against their rulers, which they supported in traditional contractual

1. Caroline Robbins, *The Eighteenth-Century Commonwealthman* (Cambridge, Mass., 1959); Bernard Bailyn, *Pamphlets of the American Revolution*, I (Cambridge, Mass., 1965), 28–37.

terms. Government was created by the people to promote the public welfare. If magistrates failed to honor that trust, they automatically forfeited their powers back to the people, who were free and even obliged to reclaim political authority. The people could do so, moreover, in acts of limited resistance, intended to nullify only isolated wrongful acts of the magistrates, or ultimately in revolution, which denied the continued legitimacy of the established government as a whole.

To stress the potential for revolution and disorder in these ideas, however, distorts not only the structure of late-seventeenth- and eighteenth-century Radical Whig thought, but also its influence on America. More than ever by the 1760's, Whig arguments for resistance and revolution rested on a firm commitment to an idealized version of the British regime and embodied an almost conservative desire to prevent it from further change or decay. The fundamental values of the Radical Whigs were realized most fully in a well-ordered free society, such that obedience to the law was stressed as much or more than occasional resistance to it. Moreover, while eighteenth-century Whig writers stood ready to challenge anyone who denied the people's right of revolution, they still sought to limit and even defer violence by a series of preconditions that were ever more carefully defined between Milton and mid-eighteenth-century writers like Hutcheson.

Naturally, the Real Whigs' justification of resistance could reinforce the colonists' tendency to condone uprisings where authorities were unresponsive to public needs. In fact, however, the Whigs' contrary emphasis on order and restraint counteracted any tendency toward a too-ready resort to force. In this way, Whiggism tempered the use of violence in the colonies, particularly during the eleven years before independence. The need to reconcile the impulse toward resistance with the injunction to restraint became, in fact, one of the central intellectual and practical problems of the American revolutionary movement.

[I]

A major reason for the emphasis on order and restraint among the Real Whigs lay in the fact that their model of revolutionary achievement was in the past. The Revolution of 1688–9 was for them the central event in Britain's history; and the English constitution that was settled in its wake became, for English writers and colonists alike, "undoubtedly the most desirable and complete form [of government] that the good fortune of man has hitherto produced or their wit been capable of contriving," "the Work of Ages which is the Envy and Admiration of the Universe, the Glory of the English Nation."[2] Bishop Hoadly argued that the Real Whigs were in fact the staunchest defenders of England's eighteenth-century establishment, the legitimacy of which rested on the people's right to replace tyrannical monarchs as practiced in 1688. The effective threat of disorder came primarily from the other end of the political spectrum: from the Jacobites and high Tories who advocated unlimited submission to authority, or at best passive obedience to unlawful edicts. Jacobite principles made the Glorious Revolution "a damnable Rebellion and Usurpation," the reigning monarch "a Rebel and Usurper"; and their uprisings for the Pretender in 1715 and 1745 gave the England of the first two Georges its most serious threats of upheaval.[3]

Since the Real Whigs were linked most fundamentally by their preocupation with a liberty that they understood to be almost synonymous with restraint, they were an unlikely party of disorder. They defined liberty for members of a political society as, briefly, an absolute freedom in all actions that concerned themselves alone. An individual could be protected from encroachments on his freedom of action on the part of other ordinary citizens by the rule of just laws, which was the end he sought in entering political society; but he had to be protected, too, from usurpations and arbitrary exactions on the part of men entrusted with the execution of law. Here was the peculiar glory of the English constitution: rulers as well as ruled were subjected to the rule of law;

2. Thomas Gordon, *The Works of Tacitus* (2nd edn., London, 1737), III, xxi; John Holt in *N.Y. Jour.*, September 1, 1774.

3. See, for example, *The Works of Benjamin Hoadly*, *D.D.*, ed. John Hoadly (London, 1773), II, 99, 365. The erratic italics added in this edition of Hoadly's works have been omitted in all quotations from it. John, Lord Somers, *The Judgment of Whole Kingdoms and Nations* (Philadelphia, 1773), para. 120, p. 102; Robbins, *Eighteenth-Century Commonwealthman*, 8.

none were given scope for arbitrary action that could endanger the liberty of others. English governmental institutions had apparently achieved this important result by their
much-praised "balancing" of King, nobles, and people, so
that each was restrained by the others. As a result, there was
no other civilized nation in the world—as Thomas Gordon
observed—"where the malice of men in Power has less scope
than here, or fewer opportunities of distressing or destroying
such as they dislike."[4]

Hoadly, then, could justly protest against accusations that
he sought "Licentiousness," a "taking off the Bridle of Laws";
rather, he had been pleading "for a Liberty terminated and
guarded by Laws."[5] Liberty, moreover, was far from an
abstract ideal divorced from material considerations for the
bishop and his intellectual partisans. Liberty was closely tied
to material prosperity in the real world, for only in free states
was every man guaranteed "his Right to enjoy the Fruit of his
Labour, Art and Industry as far as by it he hurts not the
Society." Only in free states could trade prosper, cities grow,
population increase: "Let the People alone and they will take
Care of themselves and do it best." Under tyrannies with
"perpetual Uncertainties, or rather certain Oppressions, no
Men will embark large Stocks and extensive Talents for
Business," so industry and commerce withered. Liberty was
in effect synonymous with the public welfare in the most
immediate sense, and the conclusion seemed upheld by history.
"Compare any free state with any other that is not free,"
wrote Thomas Gordon. "Compare England with France,
Holland with Denmark; or the seven Provinces under the
States, with the same seven Provinces under Philip the
second; you will find in these and every other instance, that
happiness and wretchedness are the exact tallies to Liberty and
bondage."[6]

4. John Trenchard and Thomas Gordon, *Cato's Letters* (6th edn.,
London, 1755), II, 245; Gordon, *Works of Tacitus*, III, xxi–xxii, and
Bailyn, *Pamphlets*, I, 45–53.

5. Hoadly, *Works of Benjamin Hoadly*, II, 365.

6. Trenchard and Gordon, *Cato's Letters*, II, 247, 249, 271, and
III, 56–8; Gordon, *Works of Tacitus*, I, 114. Also Algernon Sidney,
Discourses Concerning Government (London, 1763 [orig. pub., 1698]),
preface to first edition.

Yet because the Whigs justified resistance and revolution, their opponents constantly accused them of advocating disorder and forced them to refute the charge. A readiness on the part of the people to resist, they argued, discouraged usurpations and made disorder less likely. Seditions and rebellions were more frequently caused, Hutcheson wrote, by "the opposite doctrines giving unbounded licence to vicious rulers." If princes knew their abuses would encounter resistance, said Thomas Gordon, they would never encroach; and for Hoadly, too, a universal accord on the right of resistance "would entirely prevent the very beginnings of evil." It was the doctrine of nonresistance in the Turks' religion that had caused their enslavement, according to *Cato's Letters*; and Robert Molesworth in his *Account of Denmark* (1694) warned that "the Doctrine of a blind Obedience, in what Religion soever it be found . . . is the Destruction of the Liberty . . . of any Nation." In short, passivity on the part of subjects irresistibly tempted princes to seize arbitrary power, and this just as invariably induced disorder. "All disputes about right," Sidney wrote, "naturally end in force when justice is denied." There was a further effective curb on license implicit in any defense of the right of resistance, Hoadly claimed, for "he that tells [men] the Liberty they may take, warns them against taking more." Finally, spokesmen for resistance could not be responsible if men misapplied their principles. Evil men "disposed to public Disturbances" would find excuses in any case.[7]

The right of resistance and revolution was emphasized in Real Whig writings in good part because it was contested. Sidney wrote to refute Robert Filmer, Hoadly against Henry Sacheverell and Bishop Francis Atterbury; and Hoadly's American admirer Jonathan Mayhew preached his noted "Discourse on Unlimited Submission" for the same reason Milton had written *Eikonoklastes* a century earlier—to

7. Francis Hutcheson, *A System of Moral Philosophy in Three Books* (London, 1755), II, 279; Gordon, *Works of Tacitus*, I, 128; Robert Molesworth, *An Account of Denmark* (4th edn., London, 1738), 165; Sidney, *Discourses*, 417; Hoadly, *Works of Benjamin Hoadly*, 48, 365, 22; and John Locke, "Second Treatise of Government," in *Two Treatises of Government*, ed. Peter Laslett (Cambridge, Eng., 1960), para. 224, pp. 432–3.

counteract those who would make Charles I a martyr, for-
getting the people's right to deal severely with kings who
violate their trust. By the structure of their argument and
their commitment to law, however, the Whigs were forced to
lay equal or even greater emphasis upon submission and
obedience. Submission had to be stressed because resistance
was its converse: resistance turned on a violation of those
very functions of the magistrate—the support of law and the
protection of the public welfare—which in normal times
underlay obedience. "The same Rule which obliges us to
yield Obedience to the good Magistrate, who is the Minister of
God," Lord Somers observed, " . . . does equally oblige us not
to obey those who make themselves the Ministers of the
Devil." Even Jonathan Mayhew, the liberal minister of
Boston, who emphasized resistance as a religious obligation,
began his "Discourse" by observing that "Obedience to the
civil magistrate is a Christian duty," and concluded by telling
his listeners "government is *sacred* and not to be *trifled* with,"
and that under their current mild English government they
should be "contented and dutiful," leading "*quiet* and *peaceable*" lives. "Disobedience to civil rulers in the due exercise of
their authority is not merely a *political sin* but an heinous
offense against God and religion."[8]

For all writers in this Whig tradition, then, obedience to
lawful rulers was obligatory, as central to "liberty" as resistance to unlawful magistrates. Moreover, the right of
resistance was not simply asserted, but examined, and limitations were imposed upon it. The recourse to forceful resistance
—"disorder" in the language of its opponents—was especially
subject to restraining conditions. Never, in the first place, was
force to be an initial resort. "All due means of redress" short
of force, in Milton's phrase, were to be tried. "Where the
injured Party may be relieved, and his damages repaired
by Appeal to the Law, there can be no pretence for Force,"
Locke wrote. On this point the "war-like" Sidney was even
more emphatic: only "if the lusts of those who are too strong
for the tribunals of justice, cannot be otherwise restrained

8. Somers, *Judgment*, para. 111, pp. 95–6; Mayhew's "Discourse
Concerning Unlimited Submission and Nonresistance to the Higher
Powers," orig. pub., Boston, 1750, in Bailyn, *Pamphlets*, I, 220–1, 247.

than by sedition, tumults and war," were "those seditions, tumults, and wars . . . justified by the laws of God and man." "Gentle ways," he said, "are first to be used, and it is best if the work can be done by them, but it must not be left undone if they fail." Such had been the case in 1688 when, Mayhew pointed out, "there was no rational hope of redress in any other way" than revolution, and "Resistance was absolutely necessary in order to preserve the nation from slavery, misery, and ruin." Similarly, Thomas Gordon showed, the Romans had no alternative to tyrannicide against Caesar.⁹

Nor could forceful resistance to authority be justified by casual errors or private immoralities on the part of the governors. Indulgence was always necessary for "such imprudence or mistakes of rulers as subjects must have expected in any fallible mortals." It was not upon every shortcoming, Hutcheson argued, that governors forfeited their right to govern. If "in the main" they "answer the *End* of their *Office*, with respect to the *Body* of the Governed," even though guilty of "many personal Vices, or of some Acts of Injustice of a private nature," Hoadly emphasized, "Public Good requires the continuance of Allegiance." Mayhew, too, said that no government could function if resistance were legitimate when states were not administered "in the best manner possible," or even when they were "very ill managed." Such a principle would "throw all things into confusion and anarchy."¹⁰

Private individuals were forbidden to take force against their rulers either for malice or because of private injuries,

9. *Complete Prose Works of John Milton*, III (New Haven, 1962), 228; Locke, "Second Treatise," para. 207, p. 421; Sidney, *Discourses*, 174, 434; Mayhew, "Discourse," in Bailyn, *Pamphlets*, I, 241; Gordon, *Works of Tacitus*, I, 75, 79.

Milton, in the subtitle to "The Tenure of Kings and Magistrates," suggested that lawful procedures might effect the deposition and even death of a tyrant, thus avoiding force altogether. The tract promised to prove "That it is Lawfull, and hath been held so through all Ages, for any who have the Power, to call to account a Tyrant, or wicked KING, and after due conviction, to depose, and put him to death; *if the ordinary* MAGISTRATE *have neglected or deny'd to doe it.*" Reprinted in *Complete Prose Works of John Milton*, III, opposite 188 [italics mine].

10. Hutcheson, *System of Moral Philosophy*, II, 269, 270; Hoadly, *Works of Benjamin Hoadly*, II, 294; Mayhew, "Discourse," in Bailyn, *Pamphlets*, I, 237 n.

even if no redress for their grievances were afforded by the regularly constituted government. Explicitly, Somers said "it is not lawful for a few Persons to oppose their Prince"; and even Sidney wrote with disgust of "a sort of sedition, tumult, and war, proceeding from malice, which is always detestable, aiming only at the satisfaction of private lust, without regard to the public good." If private judgment was given full reign, and the prince could be resisted "as often as any one shall find himself aggrieved, and but imagine he has not Right done him," Locke said, all politics would be unhinged and overturned, "and instead of Government and Order leave nothing but Anarchy and Confusion." Hutcheson was somewhat more willing to grant a technical right to resist private injuries at the hand of the ruler, but in the end he, too, counseled against implementing that right. If a prince was generally faithful to his trust, but possessed with "some groundless prejudice or violent anger against any private subject, and aiming at his destruction without any just cause," Hutcheson hypothesized, then no one could obey his orders in that regard and remain innocent. The King's servants should suffer punishment rather than execute the orders, and the innocent object of the King's wrath "would have a right to all violent methods of defence, even against the prince in person, were he to regard only the right of the prince against him." Yet "for the sake of his country, not to deprive it of a prince in the main good, or expose it to any great evils which might ensue upon his death," it might be the subject's duty instead to emigrate "or to be a martyr for his country's interest, when he cannot escape by flight." Hoadly came to the same conclusion with more certainty. If any private individual or party of men "should think or speak of Resistance and Opposition, whilst all things, At Home and Abroad, are managed with sufficient regard to the Constitution and Interest of this Nation merely because they have not all the favour they could desire," he wrote, "they act in manifest Contradiction" to the doctrine of resistance as he taught it, "and are so far from being justified, that they are condemned by it."[11]

11. Somers, *Judgment*, para. 186, p. 145; Sidney, *Discourses*, 181; Locke, "Second Treatise," para. 203, p. 419; Hutcheson, *System of Moral Philosophy*, II, 344–5; Hoadly, *Works of Benjamin Hoadly*,

By the mid-eighteenth century, then, it was an almost fore-
gone conclusion that there could be no just revolution to
reform a government already adequate. Earlier writers had
been less hesitant in justifying revolution—Milton, for example, claimed the people could choose or reject, retain or
dispose of their King, *"though no Tyrant,* merely by the
liberty and right of free born Men, to be governed as seems
to them best," and Sidney tended toward the same view. But
by the early eighteenth century, Lord Somers wrote that the
people were forbidden to interfere even with the inheritance
of the Crown except on "just and urgent causes," when "the
Justice thereof is plain," and Hoadly explicitly denied that
"Subjects may rise up in Arms against their Governours . . . in
order to make Alterations in what is good and tolerable
already." Practicality as well as principle led John Trenchard
to agree. "No man of Sense and Fortune," wrote the man
whose ideals inclined more toward a republic than the monarchy under which he lived, "will venture the Happiness which
he is in full Possession of" for "imaginary Visions." In short,
for eighteenth-century Real Whigs, "revolution principles"
sanctified only defensive revolution.[12]

In the end, the people would move against their governors
only when "the Mischief be grown general," and the tyranny
or "Designs of the Rulers become notorious." And not just a
few individuals, but the "Body of the People" had to feel
concerned. What proportion of society qualified as the "Body of
the People"? Jonathan Mayhew referred to unanimous up-

II, 52. See also Andrew Eliot, *A Sermon Preached Before His Ex-
cellency Francis Bernard . . . May 29th, 1765* (London [orig. pub.,
Boston], 1766), 35; and [Stephen Johnson], *Some Important Observations, Occasioned by . . . The Public Fast, Ordered by Authority,
December 18th, A.D. 1765* (Newport, 1766), 27. "It is true, the best
constituted governments in the world are imperfect; some injuries may
befall some particular subjects, which cannot be remedied.—In such
cases there is no help, they must be patiently and peaceably borne; still
the bonds of our allegiance and obedience continue firm, unshaken, and
indispensible." The situation was, however, different, Johnson said,
"when the fundamental rights of the community are invaded."
    12. *Complete Prose Works of John Milton,* III, 206; Sidney, *Dis-
courses,* 413; Somers, *Judgment,* para. 83, p. 74; Hoadly, *Works of
Benjamin Hoadly,* II, 37; Trenchard and Gordon, *Cato's Letters,*
III, 120.

risings, but more often writers spoke of a vaguer "whole people who are the Publick," or the body of the people acting in their "public Authority," indicating a broad consensus involving all ranks of society. But even when a revolutionary consensus did exist, caution was absolutely requisite. Hoadly, who spoke of "the People" and "Public Society" because these were "the most Universal Words that could be chosen," refused to condone "the lawfulness of redressing Grievances, even in the whole Body of the Subjects, before it be certainly true that their Governours have consented and agreed to enslave them, and make them miserable; and that the Happiness of the Public Society cannot be preserved, or secured without it." It was only after "a long train of Abuses, Prevarications, and Artifices, all tending the same way," wrote Locke, and making the "design visible to the People," that they would "rouze themselves, and endeavour to put the rule into such hands, which may secure to them the ends for which Government was at first erected."[13]

13. Somers, *Judgment*, paras. 83 and 186, pp. 74, 145; Adams's quotations from Pufendorf's *Law of Nature and Nations* in Charles F. Adams, ed., *The Works of John Adams* (Boston, 1850–6), IV, 82; Mayhew, "Discourse," in Bailyn, *Pamphlets*, I, 237–8; Trenchard and Gordon, *Cato's Letters*, I, 86, 87, and II, 246. Locke, "Second Treatise," para. 225, p. 433; Sidney, *Discourses*, 413; Hoadly, *Works of Benjamin Hoadly*, II, 36; Hutcheson, *System of Moral Philosophy*, II, 273.
    Locke's formulation of the people's role in judging government differed from that of other writers. See "Second Treatise," para. 168, pp. 397–8: there can be no judge on earth between the people and an executive or legislative power that sets out to enslave them. The people cannot themselves become the judge of their cause. Yet they have "by a Law antecedent and paramount to all positive Laws of men, reserv'd that ultimate Determination to themselves, which belongs to all Mankind, where there lies no Appeal on Earth, *viz.* to judge whether they have just Cause to make their Appeal to Heaven." This formulation would make no material difference in the conduct of an injured people, however. While Locke reserved to God the judgment of the rightness of each side's cause, still *"every Man"* was *"Judge* for himself . . . whether another hath put himself into a State of War with him, and whether he should appeal to the Supreme Judge." See paras. 241 and 230, pp. 445, 435–6. In effect, then, the "appeal to Heaven" for Locke was the taking up of arms against a usurping authority, the outcome of the contest then being in the hands of God.
    See also *Cato's Letters*, II, 217–18, for a slightly different use of the "appeal to heaven," in effect an appeal to one's own conscience:

The effective judgment as to the trend of the magistrate's actions, as well as the decision to resort to force against the state, rested, then, with the mass of the people. This was fitting not only from the fiduciary character of public office, but also from the nature of the decision to be made. Resistance and revolution did not normally depend upon a technical legal judgment. English law was "so ambiguous, perplext, and intricate, that it is hard to know when it is broken," wrote Sidney. "In all the public contests we have had, men of good judgment and integrity have followed both parties." Moreover, rulers were permitted, even by Whig writers, a certain prerogative power, a power to act outside or beyond the law for the public good. Since the public good was thus the ultimate measurement of the King's conduct, a resort to popular judgment was natural. "It is certain," "Cato" wrote, "that the whole People, who are the Publick, are the best Judges, whether things go ill or well with the public." Nor were the criteria necessarily subtle since the public welfare brought tangible benefits. "Every Cobbler can judge, as well as a Statesman, whether he can sit peacefully in his stall, whether he is paid for his Work; whether the Market where he buys his Victuals be well provided; and whether a Dragoon, or a Parish-Officer, comes to him for his Taxes, if he pay any." The Boston clergyman Andrew Eliot echoed these words in May 1765 when he wrote that "Men cannot but perceive when they enjoy their rights and privileges; when they sit at quiet under their own vines and fig-trees, and there is none to make them afraid."[14]

In the view of Real Whig writers, this resort to public judgment was itself an effective curb on disorder. Universally they agreed that the people were slow to complain, that they would "bear a great deal before they will involve themselves

---

"Where no Judge is nor can be appointed, every Man must be his own; that is, when there is no stated Judge upon Earth, we must have Recourse to Heaven, and obey the Will of Heaven, by declaring ourselves on that which we think the juster Side."

14. Sidney, *Discourses*, 418, 438; and on prerogative, Locke, "Second Treatise," paras. 159–67, pp. 393–8. Trenchard and Gordon, *Cato's Letters*, I, 87; Hoadly, *Works of Benjamin Hoadly*, II, 61; Eliot, *A Sermon Preached*, 36–7.

in Tumults and Wars," and were never turbulent "unless seduced or oppressed," but often bore "a thousand hardships before they return one." Moreover, once they did act *en masse*, the people moved cautiously and foreswore extensive revamping of institutions. Through all the revolutions in English history, Locke noted, the people kept returning "to our old Legislative of King, Lords and Commons." Nor did the people deal with tyrants as severely as tyrants dealt with them. They were gentle, not revengeful, showing "mercy where they have found none."[15]

Finally, even when all the major conditions necessary for a just resort to force were present—when all peaceful means of redress had failed, when the ruler's abuses were so patent that the general public was convinced of his despotic intentions—still insurrection might not be justified, according to some writers, because it was imprudent. An account had to be taken of the chances of success, and some balance struck between the evils possibly arising from violence and those inherent in continued submission. When the "advantages hoped from the change, are not great enough to overballance some terrible mischiefs to be feared in a civil war," Hutcheson wrote, "the subjects may be sacredly bound, in duty to their country, to defer their designs to some more convenient opportunity," and meanwhile "continue in obedience." Moreover, resistance had to bear some relationship to the threat that provoked it. Benjamin Hoadly stressed that the degree of force justly invoked had to be measured and no excesses condoned. Only that degree of opposition "necessary for the Public Good," he thought, "ought to be defended."[16]

These considerations of prudence and measure provoked another question of fundamental significance for Americans from 1765 to 1776. Could one justly exert force not to overturn government, but to prevent isolated exertions of unlawful power? In *The Tenure of Kings and Magistrates* (1649)

15. Trenchard and Gordon, *Cato's Letters*, III, 257; Gordon, *Works of Tacitus*, III, 173–5, 179; also Mayhew, "Discourse," in Bailyn, *Pamphlets*, I, 237 n. Somers, *Judgment*, para. 186, p. 145; Locke, "Second Treatise," paras. 223, 225, pp. 432–3.

16. Hutcheson, *System of Moral Philosophy*, II, 277; Hoadly, *Works of Benjamin Hoadly*, II, 71.

Milton denied the possibility of such selective resistance: authority was integral, and any rising against it was *ipso facto* revolutionary, "an absolute renouncing both of Supremacy and Allegiance." A few decades later Whig writers arrived at a different conclusion. Both Milton and Sidney agreed that a man could justly disobey an unjust command; but Milton said he must then accept the penalties for disobedience, while Sidney explicitly denied that obligation. Moreover, for Sidney the public could justly rise to resist such commands while retaining their allegiance to the government as a whole: there had to be a way of proceeding "extrajudicially" against all who transgressed the laws when "judicial" methods failed, Sidney wrote, not to dissolve the government, but to preserve the laws. For Locke, too, a resistance of public abuses from their first appearance, before they grew grave enough to threaten the whole structure of the state, was necessary to avert the need for revolution. To tell men they must watch submissively until governmental power was wholly misappropriated was, for him, "to bid [men] first to be Slaves, and then to take care of their liberty; and when their Chains are on, tell them they may act like Freemen."[17]

Although normally designed to prevent revolution, limited forceful resistance also had an important function in confrontations with authority that would ultimately conclude in revolution. It let citizens "jealous" of their political liberty avoid Milton's unpalatable extremes of total submission or premature revolution while taking the necessary time to study the ruler's design, to see if indeed he was determined to set up his private interest in opposition to the public good. It was then a way to defer revolution, and to assure that when revolution was finally decided upon, that decision could be as careful and deliberated as it ought to be. So necessary was this concept of limited resistance to the Whig traditions as it evolved that Francis Hutcheson, who wrote a half century after Sidney, justified resisting not only lawless magistrates but unjust laws themselves. Where legislation was "notoriously unjust and oppressive toward great numbers," where the people were united and had a good chance of success—

17. *Complete Prose Works of John Milton*, III, 228; Sidney, *Discourses*, 180, 345; Locke, "Second Treatise," para. 220, p. 429.

again the prudence factor—they had "a right to compel the legislator by force to rescind such unjust decrees."[18]

For Englishmen, the distinction between limited forceful resistance and revolution was easily drawn: the first proceeded against acts of the King's officers, the second against the monarch himself. As "Cato" wrote, the sovereign's office lay "in being the publick Guardian of the publick Safety. . . . He can do no Wrong himself. . . . Every Act of his must be lawful, because all unlawful Acts are not his." By convention, then, the state in the person of the King remained above controversy. Opposition was directed against his officers "whilst the ligaments of the Constitution are preserved entire," and complaints remained of a limited character. Always, Locke wrote, "opposition may be made to the illegal Acts of any inferior Officer" or others comissioned by the King; but "notwithstanding such Resistance, the King's Person and Authority are still both secured, and so no danger to *Governor or Government.*" Only when the constitution was evaded, Parliament not allowed to meet or courts to sit, and force used against the people such as "dissolves all Relation," so that revolution had already become reality, could the people refuse allegiance to the monarch.[19]

It should be noted, too, that justified resistance and revolution never technically confronted authority, according to Whig formulations: instead, the people opposed men who pretended to retain an authority forfeited by their own unlawful efforts. Should a magistrate act unlawfully, Locke said, he "ceases in that to be a Magistrate, and acting without Authority, may be opposed" like any other private person "who by force invades the Right of another." Charles I and James II, for example, "unkinged" themselves before the people rose against them, so the people had opposed only a private person, a usurper who tried to exercise an authority he no longer held. In such cases, the ex-rulers were the rebels: "they are the Traitors," Lord Somers wrote, "who design and pursue the Subversion of [the constitution]; they are the Rebels that go about to overthrow the Government of their Country,

18. Hutcheson, *System of Moral Philosophy*, II, 346.
19. Trenchard and Gordon, *Cato's Letters*, I, 92–4; Locke, "Second Treatise," paras. 205–6, pp. 420–1.

whereas such as seek to Support and defend it are the truly
loyal Persons."[20]

Given all the legalistic distinctions and all the cautions
against premature resistance and revolution, could one call
forceful opposition to government "legal"? Certainly, the
ordinary course of law" could not provide for revolution. As
New York's *Independent Reflector* pointed out, revolution was
justified only where there was "a total Subversion of the
Constitution, which is a Case the Laws of England could
never suppose, nor consequently provide for . . . it would be
a most palpable Absurdity in any Government, to make a
Law which could only take Place when that Government is
dissolved." Still, revolution was not illegal, but was justified
by what Blackstone called "first principles," or the *Independent Reflector* termed a "moral and legal political Legality,"
and was further sanctified by its appearances in English history, thus becoming a part of that "noble pile," the British
constitution. Revolution was more properly extra-legal or
"without law" for those "*extraordinary*" occasions when posi-
tive law "proves too weak a defence against the violence of
fraud or oppression," an "extra-ordinary Remedy, not contrary
to the Spirit and Design of the Law, but allowable on Account
of its unavoidable Imperfection and Defectibility."[21]

Yet, despite all the safeguards, did not this setting aside
of law and resort to mass action involve a threat of disorder
and even anarchy—a threat as dangerous in its way, and as
tyrannic, as the rule of the most absolute king? In the end,
Sidney admitted the charge but still insisted that "the peace
may be broken upon just grounds, and it may be neither a

20. Locke, "Second Treatise," paras. 202 and 226, pp. 418–19, 433;
also Sidney, *Discourses*, 176; "a legal magistrate who takes upon him
. . . to exercise a power the law does not give" is "in that respect . . .
a private man." Mayhew, "Discourse," in Bailyn, *Pamphlets*, I, 242,
on Charles I; and Trenchard and Gordon, *Cato's Letters*, I, 94, on
Richard II and James II. Somers, *Judgment*, paras. 143 and 4, pp.
118–19 and 16.

21. William Livingston, *The Independent Reflector*, ed. Milton
Klein (Cambridge, Mass., 1963), especially 320–3; William Black-
stone, *Commentaries on the Laws of England* (Philadelphia, 1771),
I, 245, 250–1. On the legal status of revolution see also Pauline Maier,
"Revolutionary Violence and the Relevance of History," *Journal of
Interdisciplinary History*, II (1971), 127–8.

crime nor infamy to do it." To argue from the danger of
disorder that no resistance should be allowed was for Locke
patently absurd. "If the innocent honest Man must quietly
quit all he has for Peace sake, to him who lay violent hands
upon it," the world's peace would be "Maintained only for
the benefit of Robbers and Oppressors." What was important,
given the imperfection of the human condition, Sidney argued,
was to choose alternatives with "the most tolerable incon-
veniences"; and it was "much better, that the irregularities
and excesses of a prince should be restrained or suppressed,
than that whole nations should perish by them." Even anarchy
could be a prudent choice over tyranny: the former would,
Thomas Gordon wrote, "do less harm, and is likely to end
sooner. All tumults are in their nature, and must be, short
in duration, must soon subside, or settle into some order. But
Tyranny may last for ages, and go on destroying, till at last
it has left nothing to destroy." Moreover, improvements could
be effected by revolution—as by that of 1688—whereas there
was no hope of improvement from continued submission.[22]

Anarchy was not, in any case, integral to the nature of
resistance; its incidence was "purely accidental." And in the
final reckoning, those would-be despots who provoked the
people were answerable for whatever excesses the mob committed. Effective responsibility for preventing anarchic behavior rested, however, on the popular leaders. They alone
could possess and encourage in others the "prudence" with
which, Hoadly wrote, confusion might be prevented.[23] Those
nurtured in this Whig ideology were obliged to be the most
careful of revolutionaries, since their justification lay as much
in their restraint as in their vigilance and activism. Revolution in Whig theory was as much to be regretted as gloried in.

[II]

The restrictions placed upon extra-legal action did not make
it any the less necessary in Real Whig thought. True, the
resort to force was confined to exceptional occasions, but a

22. Sidney, *Discourses*, 414, 417; Locke, "Second Treatise," para.
228, pp. 434–5; Gordon, *Works of Tacitus*, III, 107; Trenchard and
Gordon, *Cato's Letters*, I, 191–2.
23. Hoadly, *Works of Benjamin Hoadly*, II, 54.

constant readiness to implement it against unlawful power
was requisite for a free society. Most Englishmen would have
justified revolution against tyranny; what made the Real
Whigs extraordinary in the eighteenth century, and what
spurred the criticism that forced them constantly to defend
their views, was just this belief in the constant necessity of
resistance. The need, as they saw it, sprang from a fundamental human selfishness that led any man entrusted with
authority to seek to expand his power and overrun its lawful
limits. The victim was always liberty, which depended on
law and restraint. Certainly institutional limitations, such as
the laws that bound rulers and ruled, or the checks on power
built into the English constitution, were essential. But even
the English constitution, like the liberty it protected, was
delicate. It could not be preserved in passivity; constant
vigilance was necessary, since power "warms, scorches, or
destroys, according as it is watched, provoked, or increased."
Thus in the end it was the political jealousy of the English
people, who simply "will never suffer" or endure absolute
power, as much as England's institutions, that preserved
English liberty.[24]

From the late seventeenth century, it was again and again
stressed that resistance had to be brought to bear against the
very first abuses of power. The least attempt upon public
liberty was alarming; "if it is suffered once, it will be apt to
be repeated often; a few repetitions create a habit; habit
claims proscription and right." And as always, tyranny was
"much easier to prevent than to cure."[25] On the other hand,
it was necessary to judge charitably the human faults of the
magistrate, to be cautious and even hesitant before refusing
submission to his rule. How could one reconcile these two
injunctions? How avoid both dangerous delay and precipitous
disobedience?

Here again the Real Whigs offered guidance. They suggested, in fact, an elaborate canon for judging which actions
of a ruler portended tyranny and must thus necessarily be

24. Bailyn, *Pamphlets*, I, 38–53; Trenchard and Gordon, *Cato's
Letters*, I, 192.
25. Gordon, *Works of Tacitus*, I, 128. Also Hutcheson, *System of
Moral Philosophy*, II, 343–4; and Locke, "Second Treatise," para.
220, p. 429.

resisted in the earliest stages. With enthusiasm they turned
to history: to that of France, of Denmark, of England as
told by the Whiggish Paul de Rapin-Thoyras or later by
Catharine Macaulay, or to the history of Rome, especially as
related in Thomas Gordon's translations of Tacitus and
Sallust, conveniently prefaced by long discourses in which
Gordon drew out the lessons of his texts. For Real Whigs,
history had a twofold use. It presented prototypical tyrants,
such as Caesar, Caligula, Nero, or England's own Stuart
kings, in whose stories appeared common omens that had
presaged their tyrannies, warning signs that might be recognized and combatted should they reappear. Let us study the
Romans, Gordon recommended, so we may "avoid the Rocks
upon which they have suffered Shipwreck, and set up Buoys
and Sea-marks to warn and guide Posterity." History also
offered heroes in the fight against absolutism, models for
latter-day patriots: Cicero, Cato, Brutus; John Eliot, John
Hampden, or others among England's "illustrious ancestors"
who "with the hazard and even the loss of their lives, attacked
the formidable pretensions of the Steward family, and set
up the banners of Liberty against a tyranny which had been
established for . . . more than one hundred and fifty years."[26]

Corruption was the most important indication of danger.
With corruption, potential tyrants could undermine their
people's civic virtue, and encourage a readiness to "bear with
. . . Tameness . . . the Yoke of Servitude." In its broadest
sense, "corruption" meant merely the pursuit of private interest at public cost: "a Deviation," Gordon wrote in his
commentaries on Sallust, "from our Duty to the Public, upon
private Motives." It was corruption that had spelled Rome's
downfall as voters and legislators sold their support to the
highest bidder, and the public became willing to trade their
Spartan vigilance for sloth and ease, "shews," and luxury.
This decline of virtue accompanied Rome's rise to opulence.
At first having "no Trade, no Money, no Room or Materials
for Luxury," the Romans were naturally temperate and

26. Bailyn, *Pamphlets*, I, 21–3 on the classics; Trenchard and
Gordon, *Cato's Letters*, I, 121–2, and Catharine Macaulay, *The History
of England from the Accession of James I to the Elevation of the
House of Hanover*, I (2nd edn., London, 1766), ix.

frugal, and "Liberty was their great passion." But with
luxury came lust for more, as "they first grew less Virtuous,
then Vicious, then Abandoned." Nor was the pattern Rome's
alone. It was, Thomas Gordon philosophized, "the Course and
Fate . . . of Men." "The same Causes will invariably produce
the same Effects," the New York *Independent Reflector* repeated in June 1753; "and that Luxury is the Harbinger of a
dying State, is a Truth too obvious to require the Formality
of Proof."[27]

Other more specific policies that augured misfortune for a
free state were also identified and publicized. As a "Service
to the World," John Trenchard listed various measures taken
by corrupt ministers in neighboring countries to enslave the
people, so as to illustrate "what Methods may be hereafter
taken to undo others." Such traitors might, like Sejanus,
isolate the prince from his people, making him dependent
upon ministerial "misrepresentations" for his knowledge of
affairs; they might engage the country in ridiculous, expensive wars to keep men's minds under "constant Fears and
Alarms," depriving them of "Leisure and Inclination to look
into publick Miscarriages," then negotiate peace treaties that
"deliver up the Strongholds of their Country, or its Colonies
for Trade, to open Enemies, suspected Friends, or dangerous
Neighbours." They would prefer "worthless and wicked
Men" for public posts "without any Regard to the Qualifications for those Employments, or indeed to any Qualifications
at all but as they contribute to their Designs, and show a
stupid Alacrity to do what they are bid." And they would
"by all practicable Means of Oppression, provoke the
People to Disaffection; and then make that Disaffection an
Argument for new Oppression . . . and for keeping up
Troops."[28]

Trenchard's list by no means exhausted the danger signs.
Any student of England's history, particularly of the Stuart

27. Trenchard and Gordon, *Cato's Letters*, I, 117, 203, 206; Thomas
Gordon, *The Works of Sallust* (London, 1744), 93, 98. Livingston,
Independent Reflector, 257. On corruption and the fall of Rome, see
especially Gordon's "Discourse VI," in *Works of Sallust*, 87–116, and
Cato's Letters, nos. 18 and 27, in I, 117–23, 202–10.

28. *Cato's Letters*, I, 111–17, and II, 262–3.

period, could list other policies tending toward repression. Would-be tyrants might levy taxes without popular consent, or interfere with Parliament. They might establish arbitrary courts or otherwise upset the normal course of justice, dispensing, of course, with juries wherever possible. They often promoted Roman Catholicism, which supposedly encouraged a servile submission to authority; they interfered with the press. Above all, rulers wanting arbitrary power would seek standing armies—a final sign that they could not rely on public support through the militia, that the goals of authority were no longer those of the people.

[III]

Just as English Real Whig writers absorbed themselves in elaborating the portents of tyranny, so, too, the colonists took up the task. Their newspapers regularly discussed the subject in the mid-eighteenth century; and where American essays were not forthcoming—or because they seemed unnecessary—the paper often reprinted verbatim appropriate tracts by "Cato" and other Englishmen.[29] But as American interest in England's "revolution principles" increased, those ideas slowly retreated into obsolescence for the most influential Englishmen. It was symptomatic of this change that Sir William Blackstone tried to explain away Locke's fundamental assertion that "there remains . . . inherent in the people supreme power to remove or alter the legislative, when they find the legislative act contrary to the trust reposed in them." However just this may be "in theory," the jurist wrote in early editions of his *Commentaries on the Law of England*, "we cannot adopt it, nor argue from it, under any dispensation or government at present actually existing." His statements reflected the effect of a century of complex change in England. Blackstone had to reconcile traditional English notions of limited government with his more modern belief that "so long . . . as the English constitution lasts . . . the power of parliament is absolute and without control." He did this, in effect, by resigning revolutionary beliefs to the

29. Bernard Bailyn, *The Origins of American Politics* (New York, 1970), 139–48.

purer realm of philosophy, denying that the people in real life had the right to resist a legislative power that abused its trust—denying, in effect, the notion that public officials *ipso facto* surrendered legal authority by violating their trust. For Blackstone and many other contemporary Englishmen, that conception had become otiose by the mid-eighteenth century. Parliament had, in effect, replaced the people as the repository of sovereignty.[30]

English efforts to distinguish political theory from practice were questioned in America, most notably on the part of some who rose to prominence in America's revolutionary movement; and their response dramatized the divergent ideological tendencies of England and her North American colonies. When Josiah Quincy, Jr., came across Blackstone's statement, he asked in the margin "whether a conclusion can be just in theory, that will not bear adoption in practice." John Adams, too, was dumfounded when he encountered an assertion that "revolution principles" were "noble and True" but "the application of them to particular cases is wild and utopian." "How they can be in general true, and not applicable to particular cases, I cannot comprehend," he wrote. "I thought their being true in general was because they were applicable in most particular cases." For Adams, "revolution principles" were hardly anachronistic, but "the principles of nature and eternal reason" upon which "the whole government over us now stands."[31] Jonathan Mayhew testified that this literal acceptance of the right of resistance and revolution prevailed generally in New England, and later a South Carolinian explained that Americans had come to a conviction of the virtue of resistance "through the honest impressions of education, and notions derived from old story-books, whipt into them when they were boys perhaps." Even some schoolbooks spread the doctrine: the *South Carolina Gazette* once quoted a "Mr. Guthrie's Geographical Grammar," in

30. Blackstone discussed in Josiah Quincy, Jr., *Reports of Cases Argued and Adjudged in the Superior Court of Judicature of the Province of Massachusetts Bay, between 1761 and 1772*, ed. Samuel M. Quincy (Boston, 1865), 526–7, *n.* 26. Thomas Gordon also defended parliamentary supremacy on at least one occasion: see his *Works of Sallust*, 201–2.

31. *Ibid.*, Adams, *Works of John Adams*, IV, 15.

which a French citizen advised an Englishman to "think
NOTHING . . . TOO DEAR" to maintain his rights, even to
venturing his "LIFE and ESTATE, rather than basely and
foolishly submit to that ABJECT CONDITION" to which the
French had been reduced.[32]

But when such colonists moved from theory to action, when
they assumed leadership, as they saw it, in defending liberty
against offending rulers, their revolutionary tradition proved
to be as much a burden as a guide. It called on men to resist
unlawful exertions of power—when their cause was just they
would be doing "a necessary duty to themselves and posterity
by making all the violent efforts . . . necessary to accom-
plish a change"; it would in fact be "highly criminal" to
shrink the call.[33] But contentiousness had to be restrained.
Before any force or violence could be justly invoked, contenders had to try all peaceful avenues to redress. They had
to assess carefully the actions of their government and ascer-
tain whether or not they were designed for the public good.
Should they decide this critical question in the negative,
American leaders could not rely on a revolutionary élite but
had to rouse a broad popular movement; and then, while
exercising at best an extra-legal authority over an inflamed
populace, they would have to avoid anarchy, to effect an
"orderly" revolution.

The challenge was imposing—more difficult than the young
John Adams could realize in 1765 when he rejoiced in the
opportunities given Americans by oppression. They could
become "Brookes, Hampdens, Vanes, Seldens, Miltons, Ned-
hams, Harringtons, Nevilles, Sidneys, Lockes."[34] Still, in
the period of conflict the Americans' success as revolutionaries compared favorably with Adams's heroes largely because of their full response to both sides of the Whig injunction: to resist and to restrain disorder, to revolt but to
prevent anarchy.

32. Mayhew to Thomas Hollis, March 19, 1761, in Bernhard
Knollenberg, ed., "Thomas Hollis and Jonathan Mayhew. Their
Correspondence, 1759–1766," MHS *Procs.*, LXIX (1947–50), 118;
S.C. Gaz., June 2, 1766, and June 13, 1774.

33. Hutcheson, *System of Moral Philosophy*, II, 274; Mayhew,
"Discourse," in Bailyn, *Pamphlets*, I, 238.

34. "Dissertation on the Canon and the Feudal Law," in Adams,
Works of John Adams, III, 463.

PART TWO

RESISTANCE

CHAPTER THREE

---∙◦⬥◦∙---

THE STAMP ACT
RIOTS AND ORDERED
RESISTANCE,
1765

IN RETROSPECT, colonial resistance to the Stamp Act seems to have been natural, even predictable. American writers characterized the Stamp Act as an entering wedge, a "Trojan Horse . . ⸱ big with exorbitant Mischiefs." It threatened uncontrollable confiscation of colonists' property by Parliament and, as the *Newport Mercury* claimed, could "deprive us of all our invaluable charter rights and privileges, drain us suddenly of our cash, occasion an entire stagnation of trade, discourage every kind of industry, and involve us in the most abject slavery."[1] From the first announcement of the Stamp Act, royal officials reported, the colonial press was "crammed" with this kind of "Treason" until—and on this the governors were virtually unanimous—all colonists, regardless of rank, disapproved of the act.[2] In short, the Stamp

1. *Pa. Jour.*, September 5, 1765; *Newport Mercury* (R.I.), October 28, 1765. The Stamp Act, which was finally enacted on March 22, 1765, placed stamp duties upon a series of colonial legal documents, papers, almanacs, newspapers, and newspaper advertisements to help finance British military expenses in America. The duties or taxes had to be paid in gold or silver, and violations of the act could be tried in admiralty as well as common law courts. See Merrill Jensen, *The Founding of a Nation: A History of the American Revolution, 1763–1776* (New York, 1968), 65.

2. On the role of newspapers: General Thomas Gage to Lieutenant Governor Cadwallader Colden, New York, August 31, 1765, in *The*

Act seems to have been an easy mark, as likely to draw the implacable resistance of the colonial mob as was, say, Britain's impressment effort.

At the time, however, the Stamp Act's fate was less clear. When contemporaries recalled the colonists' earliest reactions to the act, their most poignant memory was of a drawn-out "silent Consternation." Jonathan Mayhew remembered that some colonists were driven to despondency, while "even the wise and good men, tho' equally against the measure, could not . . . agree what was to be done." Although "ready to do any thing or everything to obtain relief," yet they knew not "what, when, where, how."[3] Discontent immediately greeted news of the Stamp Act in Boston, Thomas Hutchinson remembered; however, "there was no other expectation . . . than that the duty would be paid and the Act submitted to," and several persons who by March 1766 were "for dying rather than submit to it were then making interests with the distributor for places for themselves or friends." As late as October 6, 1765, Charles Thomson, the future "Sam Adams of Philadelphia," was forced to admit that he and his fellows had "not yet determined whether we will ever suffer the Act

---

Letters and Papers of Cadwallader Colden, VII, NYHS *Colls. for 1923* (New York, 1923), 57–8; Colden to Conway, September 23, 1765, *N.Y. Col. Docs.*, VII, 759; John Hughes to Stamp Commissioners, Philadelphia, October 12, 1765, *Pa. Jour.*, *Supplement* September 4, 1766, and HLRO Main Papers, January 14, 1766. Colonial unanimity: Gov. Francis Bernard to the Earl of Halifax, August 22, 1765, in The Papers of Sir Francis Bernard, IV, 146, HUL; Gov. Benning Wentworth to Secretary of State Henry S. Conway, Portsmouth, N.H., October 5, 1765, PRO, CO 5/934, ff. 52–3, and to Charles Lowndes, January 10, 1766, PRO, Treas. 1/452; Gov. Samuel Ward to Treasury Lords, Newport, December 26, 1765, PRO, Treas. 1/441; John Robinson to Commissioners of Customs, R.I., August 28, 1765, PRO, Treas. 1/442 (Officers were exposed to the fury "not of a trifling Mob, but of a whole Country"); John Hughes letter of September 8, 1765, extract, PRO, Treas. 1/442 (A frenzy or madness has seized people "of all Ranks"); Gov. Horatio Sharpe to Lord Baltimore, Annapolis, December 24, 1765, *Correspondence of Governor Horatio Sharpe*: III, *1761–1771*, in *Archives of Maryland*, XIV (Baltimore, 1895), 257, and earlier letters, such as that to Gage, September 6, p. 222.

3. Jonathan Mayhew, *The Snare Broken* (Boston, 1766), 17–18, 40; letter to printer, *N.Y. Gaz.*, November 7, 1765.

to take place here or not"; and in Charleston, South Carolina, Peter Timothy—whose radicalism through the next decade finally made him secretary of the Charleston Committee of Safety—apparently intended to pay the stamp duty for his *South Carolina Gazette*.[4]

In the end, of course, the Americans resisted, and the Stamp Act was effectively nullified, except for a brief exceptional interlude in Georgia. But the decision to resist, announced in August by the first Stamp Act riots, represented only a start in overcoming the colonists' original uncertainty and yearning for guidance. Almost immediately after the outbreak of mob activity, radicals undertook a painstaking elaboration of resistance strategy. Colonists consciously retreated from mere ad hoc violence to an ordered opposition, as criteria of purpose and constraint were applied to extralegal crowd action. In short, if during July 1765 it seemed possible, even probable, that the Stamp Act would be executed, in August the colonists decided to resist; and by September, efforts were under way to define how that resistance should be carried out—efforts largely completed by November and December 1765. This elaboration of the guidelines for resistance shaped all subsequent colonial opposition to objectionable imperial claims on into the Revolutionary War.

[I]

The Stamp Act seemed like a "frightful Dream" to one colonial observer because there was no apparent possibility of escape. American petitions against the act's passage had been spurned by Parliament, and thereafter "every Avenue to Elusion" seemed "barred up with a tenfold Guard" such

4. Thomas Hutchinson, "A Summary of the disorders in Massachusetts Province proceeding from an apprehension that the Act of Parliament called the stamp act deprives the people of their natural rights," MA, XXVI, 180; Hutchinson to Thomas Pownall, Boston, March 8, 1766 ("not sent"), *ibid.*, 202. John Hughes to Stamp Commissioners, Philadelphia, October 12, 1765, HLRO Main Papers, January 14, 1766. Announcement of Robert Wells and Peter Timothy, October 15, in *S.C. Gaz.*, October 19, 1765.

that "Slavery, with all its terrible Train, fenced us in on every Side."[5] On August 14, 1765, a mode of escape finally emerged. Early that morning an effigy of Andrew Oliver, the designated stamp distributor for Massachusetts, appeared on the future "Liberty Tree" in Boston's South End. In the evening a large crowd paraded the effigy, leveled a small building on Oliver's Dock reputed to be the future Stamp Office, then burned the effigy while a smaller contingent attacked the stampman's home. As a result of these events and signs of further violence the next day, Oliver announced on August 15 that he was asking the Treasury to be excused from executing his new office.[6]

The solution was infectious. Without distributors the Stamp Act could not go into effect, so the coercion of stampmen seemed rational, even efficient. It was "the most effectual and most decent Method of preventing the Execution of a Statute"; it struck "the Axe into the Root of the Tree."[7] "Our Brethren in Boston have indeared themselves more than ever to all the colonies in America," claimed a letter in the *New York Gazette* which was promptly reprinted in Philadelphia and Portsmouth, and which hoped that "the Noble Example . . . will be unanimously follow'd by all the Colonies." By August 20, Newporters were preparing effigies; their demonstration took place on August 27, and two days later their stampman renounced his office. Meanwhile, distributors in New Jersey and New York "voluntarily" resigned— moves they were later forced to confirm publicly; and the

5. Letter to printer, *N.Y. Gaz.*, November 7, 1765.
6. Interpretations and narrative details of the August 14 uprising used here are based upon: *Boston Gaz.*, *Supplement* August 19, 1765; Hutchinson to unnamed correspondent, Milton, August 16, 1765, MA, XXVI, 145a, b; Bernard to Halifax, Castle William, August 15, Bernard Papers IV, 137–44; Andrew Oliver to Thomas Whately, Boston, August 20, 1765, PRO, Treas. 1/439, and to Waterhouse (a neighbor), PRO, PC 1/51, Bundle 2 (54a). In discussing these events, the word "resign" can be used only with some distortion, since the stampmen's "resignations" were often qualified, and the stampmen themselves rarely considered their public "resignations" final.
7. John Dickinson's Anti-Stamp Act broadside, November 1765, in Paul Leicester Ford, ed., *The Writings of John Dickinson: I, Political Writings, 1764–1774*, in *Memoirs of the Historical Society of Pennsylvania*, XIV (Philadelphia, 1895), 201–5.

Maryland distributor, Zachariah Hood, fled to New York in panic after being hanged in effigy on August 29 and seeing his warehouse "pulled down" by a mob of three to four hundred men on September 2. Gradually, all the other colonies followed suit. The New Hampshire distributor was forced to resign first in Boston when he arrived from England on September 12, and later at Portsmouth; Jared Ingersoll had to step down in Connecticut on September 18; and by the end of October mass uprisings, real· or threatened, won stampmen's resignations in Pennsylvania, Delaware, Virginia, and South Carolina. In November, North Carolina followed; and before the year was out New Yorkers 'forced Hood's resignation for Maryland. Only in Georgia did the stampman avoid the humiliation of resignation.[8]

Even where there were no stampmen available, the new spirit was manifest. Mock trials for the stamps and stamp-

8. Reaction to Boston: "G." in *N.Y. Gaz.*, August 29; *Pa. Jour.*, September 5, and *Portsmouth Mercury* (N.H.), September 9, 1765; also "Colonus," *Prov. Gaz.*, August 24. Newport: see note 12. New York: Stampman James McEvers to Barlow Trecothick, New York, August 1765 and August 26, 1765, PRO, Treas. 1/439, and McEvers to Colden, *N.Y. Col. Docs.*, VII, 761. New Jersey: Gov. William Franklin to Benjamin Franklin, Burlington, September 7, 1765, enclosing Stampman William Coxe to Gov. Franklin, Philadelphia, September 3, 1765, PRO, Treas. 1/442. Maryland: Gov. Sharpe to Halifax, Annapolis, September 5, 1765, *Archives of Maryland*, XIV, 221, and *S.C. Gaz.*, October 5, 1765. New Hampshire: *Portsmouth Mercury*, September 16, 23. Connecticut: Jared Ingersoll's account, September 23, in *Conn. Gaz.*, September 27, 1765, and Franklin B. Dexter, ed., "A Selection from the Correspondence and Miscellaneous Papers of Jared Ingersoll," *Papers of the New Haven Colony Historical Society*, IX (New Haven, 1918), 341–9. Pennsylvania: *Pa. Jour.*, October 10, 1765, and John Hughes to Stamp Commissioners, October 12, in HLRO Main Papers, January 14, 1766, and *Pa. Jour.*, *Supplement* September 4, 1766. Hughes also mentions the threatened Delaware uprising. Virginia: Gov. Fauquier's letters to the Lords of Trade in PRO, CO 5/1331. Charleston: *S.C. Gaz.*, October 31, 1765, and Caleb Lloyd and George Saxby to Stamp Commissioners, Charleston, October 31, 1765, HLRO Main Papers, January 14, 1766. North Carolina: *N.C. Col. Recs.*, VII, 123–5, and *Pa. Jour.*, *Supplement* January 2, 1766. Hood at New York: *N.Y. Gaz.*, December 5, 1765. There is an excellent summary of Georgia events in W. W. Abbot, *The Royal Governors of Georgia, 1754–1775* (Chapel Hill, 1959), 105–22.

men were held, "funerals" for Liberty staged, or effigies of
the stampmen, the Devil, and of Lord Bute, who was said
to be behind the Stamp Act, were paraded.[9] Citizens' attitudes
toward stampmen changed dramatically. "When it was
known first here that I was Nominated [stamp distributor],"
James McEvers reported from New York in mid-August,
"People in General Seem[ed] Pleas'd that I had it in Preference to a Stranger." But suddenly McEvers found the
office "attended with . . . Disagreeable and Dangerous Consequences." In Rhode Island Augustus Johnston had a
similar experience, as did Jared Ingersoll in Connecticut.[10]
The press, too, now suggested violence, which it had not done
before August 14.[11] The *New York Gazette* reported on August 22 that the New Jersey stampman had been denied the
rent of a house unless he would insure it against being pulled
down or damaged, then asked "Whether it would not be
prudent for all the Stamp Officers to insure their Houses." In
the August 24 *Providence Gazette Extraordinary*, one writer
described Jared Ingersoll as a man who had betrayed the
Connecticut people "Judas like, for a little ungodly Gain." It
could be "no Matter of Surprize" that "the Vengeance of an

9. These pageants took place throughout the continent: in New
London (where even the children cried at the stampman's effigy, "There
hangs a Traitor . . . an Enemy of his Country"), Norwich, Lebanon,
Windham, West Haven, Fairfield, and Milford, Connecticut; in Provi-
dence, Rhode Island; Baltimore, Elk Ridge, and Frederick Town,
Maryland; in Portsmouth, New Hampshire, and also Duplin and the
Isle of Shoals; in Cross Creek, Newbern, Duplin, and Wilmington,
North Carolina. Even the Nova Scotia distributor was hung in effigy
near Halifax. See *Conn. Gaz.*, September 6 and 13 and November 22,
1765, and January 31, 1766; letter from Providence in *N.Y. Gaz.*, Sep-
tember 12; account of Maryland incidents in *Boston Gaz.*, *Supplement*
September 23; *Portsmouth Mercury*, September 16; *N.C. Col. Recs.*,
VII, 123–5, and *Pa. Jour.*, October 31, 1765.

10. James McEvers to Barlow Trecothick, New York, August 1765,
PRO, Treas. 1/439; Augustus Johnston in *Newport Mercury*, October
21, 1765; Jared Ingersoll to Stamp Commissioners, New Haven, November 2, 1765, in Dexter, "Ingersoll Papers," 354.

11. The most explicit earlier suggestions of mob violence were in
accounts of rioting in London. See, for example, *Boston Gaz.*, August
5, 1765. The *Boston Gaz.*, *Supplement* for August 19, claimed that the
American insurgents were only copying "the example set them by
their brethren at home."

abused People should fall on the Heads of such base Parricides."

The violence thus encouraged too easily became abusive. In Boston, twelve days after the Stamp Act riot of August 14 another uprising threatened or ransacked the homes of four royal officials connected with the vice-admiralty court or customs establishment, then destroyed the house of Lieutenant Governor Thomas Hutchinson. Similarly, an orderly effigy demonstration at Newport on August 27 was succeeded by several days of serious rioting. Insurgents destroyed the homes of two members of the royalist Newport Junto—who had taken on the defense of parliamentary right, and so had been effigized with the stampman; threatened Stampman Augustus Johnston's home so as to coerce him into promising not to execute his office without the townsmen's consent; and forced customsmen—against whom antagonism had grown during the previous year of hostile confrontations—to take refuge aboard the King's ship *Cygnet* in Newport Harbor. Finally, the situation descended to anarchy as the mob turned to marauding under the leadership of a twenty-one-year-old transient, John Webber, whom local magistrates supposedly tried to buy off with clothes, money, "everything he would have."[12]

---

12. Boston, August 26: *Boston Gaz.*, September 2, 1765; Gov. Bernard to Halifax, Castle William, August 31, 1765, Bernard Papers, IV, 149–52; Hutchinson to Richard Jackson, Boston, August 30, 1765, in MA, XXVI, 146–7, and George Anderson, "Ebenezer Mackintosh: Stamp Act Rioter and Patriot," CSM *Pubs.*, XXVI (*Trans.* 1924–6), 32–4. Newport: Thomas Moffatt's "Minutes" of the riots, in the Chalmers Papers, Rhode Island, NYPL; John Robinson to Customs Commissioners, Rhode Island, August 28, 1765 (with enclosed statements of four customs and naval officers) and September 5, 1765, PRO, Treas. 1/442; Augustus Johnston to Stamp Commissioners, Newport, August 31, 1765, PRO, Treas. 1/439; testimony of Moffatt and Martin Howard before the Parliamentary Committee on American Papers, in BM Add. Mss., 33030 (Newcastle), f. 78–84; *Newport Mercury*, September 2, 1765; letter from Newport in *Boston Gaz.*, September 2; *Portsmouth Mercury*, September 9; and *Pa. Jour.*, September 12. Several documents on the riots are in *R.I. Col. Recs.* VI, especially 453–7; and see also Capt. Charles Leslie to the Admiralty and to Admiral Lord Colville, Rhode Island, August 29 and 30, in Joseph Redington, ed., *Calendar of Home Office Papers of the Reign of George III, 1760*

Different groups of people were responsible for the successive phases of these uprisings. The effigies that inaugu-
rated the events of August 14 in Boston were prepared by
the "Loyal Nine," a social club of respectable merchants and
tradesmen that later became the town's organized Sons of
Liberty. There were, moreover, some forty to fifty "respectable people" in the crowd that gathered in the evening,
whether "decently dressed," as Hutchinson said, or "disguised
with trousers and Jackets on," as Governor Francis Bernard
claimed. These sought to limit violence: after the "stamp
office" was leveled, the crowd's leaders "gave directions to
carry the image to fort hill being near Mr. O[liver's] and
then burn it," as Hutchinson reported, "but to do no damage
to his dwelling home." The proceedings of August 26 were
instead "a scene of riot, drunkenness, profaneness and rob-
bery." This second uprising was not in fact a Stamp Act
riot: both the testimony of Hutchinson and Bernard and the
mob's peculiar interest in its victims' papers indicate that it
was inspired by a group of merchants who feared they had
been named in a set of recent depositions about smuggling.
In short, as the governor put it, "private resentments against
persons in Office work'd themselves in and endeavoured to
execute themselves under the Mask of the Publick Cause."[13]

(Oct.)–1765, I (London, 1878), 609–11. A useful secondary account
can be found in David S. Lovejoy, *Rhode Island Politics and the
American Revolution, 1760–1776* (Providence, 1958), 100–13.

Several documents interpret August 27 differently. Moffatt claimed
that day's peacefulness marked a defeat for the demonstration's organizers, who had passed out "strong drink in plenty with Cheshire
cheese and other incitements to intemperance [and] riot." Robinson
said peace reigned only because all the mob's targets had left town.
But Augustus Johnston—whose account is preferred here because he
knew the community better and his account was less biased—testified
that the malice of August 27 was directed wholly toward the day's
effigies. When he returned to town on the twenty-eighth he expected
no further disturbances. It was, incidentally, he who finally apprehended Webber and brought the rioting to a close.

13. Loyal Nine: William Gordon, *The History of the Rise, Progress,
and Establishment of the Independence of the United States of
America* (London, 1788), I, 175, and Henry Bass to Samuel P. Savage,
Boston, December 19, 1765, MHS *Procs.*, XLIV (1910–11), 688–9.
Bernard to Halifax, Boston, August 16 and 31, 1765, Bernard Papers,
IV, 142, 149–51; Hutchinson to unnamed correspondent, Milton,

Similarly at Newport, the effigies for the orderly August 27
demonstration were prepared by future Sons of Liberty William Ellery and Robert Crooks, along with Samuel Vernon.
Disorder first set in the next day due to a "private Pique"
between a local man and the collector of customs. Soon the
organizers of the twenty-seventh found themselves insulted by
Webber and, like the magistrates with whom they were
associated, incapable of stemming the continued rioting.[14]

Where resistance to the Stamp Act was at issue, the uprisings of August 1765 demonstrated a remarkable political
extremism on the part of colonial crowds. Everywhere, "followers" proved more ready than their "leaders" to use force
so as to assure that the Stamp Act would not go into effect.
"The better sort are for defending [English liberties] . . . by
all lawful means in their power," Thomas Hutchinson ex-

Mass., August 16, 1765, MA, XXVI, 145; Thomas Hutchinson, *His-
tory of the Province of Massachusetts Bay*, ed. Lawrence S. Mayo
(Cambridge, 1936), III, 87–9, and Andrew Eliot to Thomas Hollis,
August 27, 1765, MHS *Colls.*, 4th Ser., IV (Boston, 1858), 406–7.

This type of riot was not unique. In March 1766, for example, a
band of men in Scarborough, Maine, used the pretext that one Richard King was a prospective stampman to break into his home and
destroy the records of debts owed King by the rioters. See the records
of King v. Steward in L. Kinvin Wroth and Hiller B. Zobel, eds.,
Legal Papers of John Adams (Cambridge, 1965), I, 106–40.

14. See especially Moffatt, "Minutes," in Chalmers Papers; Charles
Leslie to Admiralty and Admiral Lord Colville, Rhode Island, August
29 and 30, 1765, in Redington, ed., *Calendar of Home Office Papers*,
I, 610–11; Johnston to Stamp Commissioners, Newport, August 31,
1765, PRO, Treas. 1/439.

The connection of Vernon et al. with Webber is obscure. On first
being apprehended, Webber claimed, according to Johnston, "that he
was betrayed by the very people who first set him to work." It is
unclear whether he meant more than that his own violence had been
given direction by the effigies of August 27. If the organizers of August 27 had planned to raise a riot, it seems unlikely that they would
have turned to a newcomer, with no established influence over the
local "rabble." In fact, it is questionable whether Webber ever held
the influence he claimed to exercise over the rioters of August 28 and
29. In his testimony before a parliamentary committee, Martin Howard
named as "principal ring Leader of the Mob" not Webber but Samuel
Crandall, who, it seems, was mainly concerned with coercing the
customs officers and who had no discernible tie with Vernon's coterie.
See Howard's testimony in BM Add. Mss., 33030 (Newcastle) ff. 83–4.

plained perceptively, "and the most abandoned say they will
do it *putas aut nefas*"—at any cost. In Boston, even the mob
of August 14 went further than their leaders desired in
coercing Andrew Oliver, attacking not only his "Stamp
Office" but his private home as well; the next day it was less
ready than its leaders to accept a nebulous statement of
"resignation" from Oliver, and was persuaded to disperse only
with difficulty. In Newport, the mob of August 28 went
beyond the organized effigy-burning of the previous day and
issued direct threats in an effort to secure Augustus Johnston's resignation; later it, too, was dissatisfied with a mere
promise not to accept the stamp distributorship, and forced
Johnston to appear before it a second time and swear to his
earlier pledge.[15]

The experience of most popular leaders and the lesson
they derived from the uprisings of 1765 were personified in
the plight of Boston's radical minister Jonathan Mayhew. On
August 25—eleven days after the first Stamp Act riot—
Mayhew preached an apparently standard sermon on Liberty,
emphasizing, it seems, the injunctions to resistance more
than those to restraint, and mentioning rumors that persons
in the colonies had encouraged passage of the Stamp Act "for
the sake of present gain." Not even this observation was
startling—it had been made many times in the newspapers.
But subsequently Mayhew was blamed for inciting the August 26 attack on Thomas Hutchinson's home, which, Mayhew
wrote, he abhorred from his soul. Finally, he concluded that
it had been "a very unfortunate time to preach a sermon . . .
to show the importance of Liberty, when the people were
. . . so generally apprehensive of . . . losing it." It was
more appropriate, he came to think, as did so many of the
popular leaders who shared his outlook, "to moderate and
pacify than to risk exciting so sensitive a people."[16]

---

15. Hutchinson to Thomas Pownall, Boston, August 31, 1765, MA,
XXVI, 149; Bernard to Halifax, August 16, 1765, Bernard Papers,
IV, 141–2; Augustus Johnston to Stamp Commissioners, Newport,
August 31, 1765, PRO, Treas. 1/439.
16. Citations and account in Charles W. Akers, *Called unto Liberty:
A Life of Jonathan Mayhew, 1720–1766* (Cambridge, Mass., 1964),
202–7. Also Mayhew to Richard Clarke, September 3, 1765, cited in

[II]

By September it was increasingly clear that the resort to violence in Boston and Newport had been politically counter-productive. Rather than contribute to the repeal of the Stamp Act, it seemed to alienate support and so to "hurt the good Cause." According to a writer in the *Constitutional Courant*, that single-issue newspaper produced in New Jersey from articles too extreme for the regular press, such excesses were likely to "startle men . . . accustomed to venerate and obey lawful authority . . . and to make them doubt the justice of the cause attended with such direful consequences."[17] The impulse toward caution and restraint was reinforced in mid-September by news that the ministry of George Grenville, which was responsible for the Stamp Act, had fallen. This announcement, Thomas Hutchinson wrote, "tended more to peace and quiet" in Massachusetts "than any thing in the power of the governor, or of any authority within the province." Earlier uprisings had been necessary because Grenville's "tyrannical and oppressive" ministry had "industriously concealed from the People of Britain all those Writings and Representations that were likely to expose the Injustices as well as the pernicious and fatal Tendency of their Projects respecting the Liberties and Trade of these Colonies." But now legal channels of redress were reopened. "You have no need to have recourse to *violent* methods any longer," the colonists were told; "The channel is now open to the ear and heart of the best of KINGS: Rely upon it, he will hear you, and his PARLIAMENT will enable him to redress you." Reports arrived from the Mother Country that the new ministry was determined to relieve colonial commerce as well as repeal the Stamp Act. Gradually, it became clear that continued violence only thwarted these hopeful trends. The colonists' opposition to the Stamp Act was "highly approved" among Englishmen,

---

Douglas Adair and John A. Schutz, eds., *Peter Oliver's Origin and Progress of the American Rebellion* (Stanford, 1961), 53, *n.* 11.

17. *Constitutional Courant* in CSM *Pubs.*, XI (*Trans.*, 1906–7), 428.

private letters indicated, "except the acts of violence,—the destruction and plunder of private property."[18]

These developments awoke an intense and widespread reflection on the whole question of popular force. In no way was the colonists' decision to resist the Stamp Act repudiated; rather, it was justified and strengthened. The Americans' earlier indecision, which amounted to a *de facto* passivity, seemed in fact to have helped bring the act upon them: the Grenville ministry "must have thought us Americans all a parcel of Apes and very tame Apes, too," Charleston's Christopher Gadsden decided, "or they never would have ventured on such a hateful, baneful expedient." Even with a new ministry, and with all signs pointing to a repeal of the Stamp Act, resistance could not be safely abandoned. The opportunity to shift the tax burden from electors in England to the Americans was, it seemed, too inviting for any ministry to repudiate easily. "When ministers are grasping at power," "Philolutherus" reminded *New York Gazette* readers in December, "they never give over their wicked projects, till they utterly despair of their success." The "most effectual way to procure a repeal . . . is to shew them that nothing will ever execute it, but down right force. This will make them despair of ever executing it at all."[19]

But an acceptance of resistance did not mean giving *carte blanche* to all insurrections. There were, it was understood, just and unjust uprisings; and from the start Boston's upheavals of August 14 and 26 were seen as prototypes of the acceptable and unacceptable uses of mass force. The coercion of Andrew Oliver was approved by Bostonians, Governor Bernard reported, "as a necessary Declaration of their Resolution not to Submitt to the Stamp Act; and even the cruel Treatment of him and his Family is justified by the con-

18. Hutchinson, *History of the Province of Massachusetts Bay*, III, 93; *Boston Gaz.*, *Supplement* September 16, 1765, and "Britannus Americanus," in *Boston Gaz.*, November 4, 1765; *Newport Mercury*, September 23, 1765, and New York intelligence in *ibid.*, February 24, 1766.

19. Gadsden to Capt. Burden, February 20, 1766, in Gadsden to James Pearson, February 20, 1766, Dartmouth Papers, D 1778/2/169, William Salt Library, Stafford, England; *N.Y. Gaz.*, *Extraordinary* December 27, 1765. See also John Dickinson's November broadside in Ford, *Dickinson Writings*, I, 201–5.

sequences the frightening him into a Resignation." But if "the body of the people favoured the whole proceedings" on August 14 "except the attack upon [Oliver's] dwelling house," after August 26, the *Boston Gazette* reported, "every Face was gloomy." It was only "in some extraordinary Cases" that "the Cause of Liberty requires an extraordinary Spirit to support it." The two uprisings, the *Gazette* suggested, proceeded "from very different Motives, as their conduct was evidently different." The "pulling down Houses and robbing Persons of their Substance . . . when any suppos'd Injuries can be redress'd by Law" was "utterly inconsistent with the first Principles of Government, and subversive of the glorious Cause."[20]

Boston's law enforcement mechanisms reflected these different attitudes. On August 14 efforts to raise the militia were abortive, and on the fifteenth the selectmen refused even to reinforce the night watch. On August 27, however, the Boston Town Meeting condemned the previous day's rioters and called on magistrates to "use their utmost agreeable to Law to suppress the like disorders for the future"; the selectmen called out the fire companies to keep the peace; the governor and council ordered the militia officers of Roxbury and Charlestown to keep a constant guard, and Boston volunteers doubled the Company of Cadets. "It seems as if the People only were capable of restoring Peace," Oliver commented; but he noted, too, "how carefully the Town of Boston and of Charlestown . . . in their Votes . . . keep out of sight the first Riot, which was aimed immediately at the Stamps." The distinction was remembered, too, in future years, when the Boston Sons of Liberty commemorated the anniversary of August 14. As in August 1766, they took care to toast (number thirteen) "Detestation to the villainous Proceedings of the 26th of August last."[21]

20. Bernard to Halifax, Castle William, August 31, 1765, Bernard Papers, IV, 154–5; Hutchinson to William Bollan, MA, XXVI, 151; *Boston Gaz.*, September 2, 1765, and Eliot to Hollis, Boston, August 27, 1765, MHS *Colls.*, 4th Ser., IV, 406–7.

21. Hutchinson to unnamed correspondent, Milton, Mass., August 16, 1765, MA, XXVI, 145a; Hutchinson, *History of the Province of Massachusetts Bay*, III, 87, 90–1. Oliver to Thomas Whately, Boston, September 2, 1765, PRO, Treas. 1/439; *Reps. R. C. C. B.*, XVI, 152, and XX, 174; *New London Gaz.*, August 22, 1766.

Outside Boston, initial accounts of the August 26 riot tended to group it with the earlier uprising; but as the differences became known disapproval became general. After the people at West Haven, Connecticut, tried and executed an effigy of the Stamp Act, the radical *Connecticut Gazette* emphasized that "through the whole of this Raree show, no unlawful Disorder happened, as was the Case in the last truly deplorable and truly detestable Riot in Boston"; and even the *Constitutional Courant*, which was not above threatening those stampmen who had not yet resigned, deplored the excessive "late violences" at both Boston and Newport.[22]

Finally, radical writers went beyond the specific events of August and elaborated the distinctions between just and unjust popular uprisings in traditional theoretical terms. The basic right of the people to resist oppressive authority—or, as Jonathan Mayhew more aptly put it, "to take the administration of government in some respects into their own hands"—was reasserted. But this right became operative only in causes "very plain and very important to the publick," such that "the whole Body of the People . . . unite and determine as one Man." Never was the defense of liberty to be confused with licentiousness, "an immoral or unreasonable Disobedience to . . . proper, merciful and just Laws." Just uprisings could occur, moreover, only when the "ordinary Methods of proceeding" had failed to win redress. Finally, a certain prudence had to be exercised: the people had to ask "whether the Evils imposed . . . by those they have entrusted with the Administration of publick Affairs, is greater than they would suffer from the Dissolution or Suspension of Government in its usual Forms."[23]

On all of these accounts, it was said, the colonists' resistance to the Stamp Act—that is, the insurrections patterned on the one in Boston on August 14, 1765—were justified. As a letter to the *South Carolina Gazette* explained, the colonies had already tried the "constitutional method" of redress, but their petitions had been rejected. With the Stamp Act near

22. *Conn. Gaz.*, September 13, 1765; *Constitutional Courant* in CSM *Pubs.*, XI (*Trans.* 1906–7), 428.

23. Mayhew, *Snare Broken*, 42; *N.Y. Gaz.*, November 14, 1765; *Boston Gaz.*, December 2, 1765.

the point of being executed, "the people, who had trusted to
their representatives while there was a possibility of their
being of service," became "terrified at the prospect of future
slavery," and simply "prevented the officers from enforcing
the Act." In late 1765, Samuel Adams cautiously ventured

> that if the whole People of the [British] Nation had
> thought their essential unalienable Rights . . .
> [were] invaded by an Act of Parliam[en]t, which
> is really the Opinion which the whole People of,
> America have of the Stamp Act . . . in such a
> Case, after taking all *legal* Steps to obtain redress
> *to no Purpose*, the *whole People of England* would
> have taken the same Steps and *justifyd themselves*.

Under the circumstances of 1765, the resort to direct action was in fact prudent, the *Newport Mercury* indicated on
October 21, for "a fixed and strenuous Opposition to this
unconstitutional Law cannot reduce us to Distress any Way
adequate to that of its Operation." No doubt, the South
Carolina writer admitted, the Mother Country could ruin
the colonies if she "exerted her force." Still, it was better "to
perish in that ruin" than to live to see their children subjected to "the daring insults of every son of Mars," or "to
behold their country reduced to that desart which their
fathers found it."[24]

Traditional criteria for just popular uprisings were repeated not only to justify the colonists' resistance to the
Stamp Act; they served also to specify the limits of just
resistance, to articulate guidelines for future action. In the
context of late 1765, more was needed here than tradition
offered: directives were required not only as to when, but
how limited forceful resistance ought to be exerted. No
treatise on that subject won universal acceptance during the
Stamp Act period, but the essential elements of colonial
thought on the subject on into the 1770's were succinctly
summarized in a set of directives for all participants in just

24. *S.C. Gaz.*, June 2, 1766; Samuel Adams to John Smith, Boston,
"20th 1765," in Harry Alonzo Cushing, ed., *The Writings of Samuel
Adams* (New York, 1904–8), I, 59–60.

popular uprisings—"especially those that act as Leaders and Directors"—published in the *New York* and *Boston Gazette*s in November and December 1765. Leaders and followers were enjoined to remember always that they sought to win a redress of grievances, not to occasion new ones. "No innocent Person, nor any upon bare Suspicion, without sufficient Evidence, should receive the least Injury." They should recall "that while they are thus collected, they act as a supreme, uncontrollable Power, from which there is [no] Appeal, where Trial, Sentence and Execution succeed each other almost instantaneously," so they were "in Honour bound to take Care, that they do no Injustice, nor suffer it to be done by others, lest they disgrace their Power, and the Cause which occasioned its Collection." In fact, "the Obligation upon them to do Justice is no less than it was upon the Magistrates, while Power was in their Hands." Since such extraordinary measures were to be confined to "weighty Matters of general Concernment and Complaint as could not be redressed by the ordinary Forms of Proceeding," insurgents must avoid "the mixing any other Matters of less general Concernment or Consequence" with the central cause. The greatest care was necessary "to keep an undisciplined irregular Multitude from running into mischievous Extravagancies." Finally, the leaders and members of mass assemblies were advised that "as soon as the grand Design of their Meeting" was "fully answer'd, and security given that the Stamp Act shall not be executed," they were "immediately to dissolve—and let Government go on in its usual Forms."[25]

[III]

The lessons learned at Boston and Newport were applied already on September 18, 1765, when five hundred to a thousand men gathered in Connecticut to force the resignation of Stampman Jared Ingersoll. Again, the contrast between the moderacy of the crowd's spokesmen and the extremism of the masses was manifest; but participants had been carefully

25. *N.Y. Gaz.*, November 14, and *Boston Gaz.*, December 2, 1765.

organized beforehand into a volunteer army whose "commandant" skillfully restrained all suggestions of violence. In Boston, Lieutenant Governor Hutchinson could well wonder "if such a public regular assembly can be called a mob."[26] Philadelphia's method of securing John Hughes's resignation in early October was similarly ordered. A mass meeting of several thousands was held at the State House, but only a carefully selected delegation of seven men was sent to confront the stampman. When Hughes refused to sign any resignation, the angry crowd was persuaded to give him time to reconsider. Later, William Bradford's *Pennsylvania Journal* rejoiced with "cool thinking people" that the affair had been successfully concluded without "any unnecessary acts of violence."[27] "No outrages whatever were committed" except for a few broken windows at Stampman George Saxby's house during Charleston's Stamp Act crisis of October 18–27, according to the *South Carolina Gazette*. Even Henry Laurens, who was visited by Charleston's Stamp Act mob, found it "amazing that such a number of men many of them heated with liquor and all armed with cutlasses and clubs did not do one penny damage to my garden . . . and not 15/ damage to my fence, gate, or house."[28]

The worst apparent threat of anarchy in late 1765 occurred at New York in early November. The uprising there was not aimed at the New York stampman, who had resigned soon after hearing of Oliver's fate in Boston. But several years' growing suspicion of Lieutenant Governor Cadwallader Colden had culminated in a widespread belief that he intended to enforce the Stamp Act by force of arms. The rumor was strengthened by Colden's reinforcement of Fort George and by the arrogant boasting of Major Thomas James of the Royal Artillery that the stamps would be

26. Ingersoll's account in *Conn. Gaz.*, September 27, 1765, and Dexter, "Ingersoll Papers," 341–9; account from Hartford in *Boston Gaz.*, September 30, 1765. Hutchinson to Thomas Pownall, [Boston? September or October 1765,] MA, XXVI, 157.

27. *Pa. Jour.*, October 10, 1765.

28. *S.C. Gaz.*, October 31, 1765; Laurens to Joseph Brown, October 28, 1765, quoted in David D. Wallace, *The Life of Henry Laurens* (New York, 1915), 119. A good secondary account is Richard Walsh, *Charleston's Sons of Liberty* (Columbia, 1959), 36–8.

crammed down New Yorkers' throats by a handful of men. Events in New York on November 1 resembled those in Boston on August 14. At first, an orderly crowd paraded effigies of Colden through the streets. Before the pageants were burned, a proclamation was issued "that no stones should be thrown, no Windows broken, no Injury offered to any one." In Boston at this juncture a contingent of the crowd had broken off to attack Oliver's house; in New York, sections of the mob left to destroy Colden's prized coach and sleigh, and to demolish the elegantly furnished home of Mayor James with a thoroughness unparalleled even in Boston. Threats of a mass attack on the Fort continued for several days, instituting a "General Terror" in which several observers feared the onset of a major rebellion and civil war.[29]

The situation was intrinsically more volatile in New York than at Boston, where years of celebrating Pope's Day had organized the crowd into two relatively settled contingents, the North and South End mobs. By contrast, New York's Stamp Act mob was composed of a series of separate and very different small parties, which were apparently most strongly influenced by sea captains, most of whom were

29. On the New York riots, see Robert R. Livingston to General Robert Monckton, November 8, 1765, MHS *Colls.*, 4th Ser., X (Boston, 1871), 559–67; G. D. Skull, ed., *The Montresor Journals*, NYHS *Colls. for 1881* (New York, 1882), 327–40; *N.Y. Gaz.*, November 7, 1765; Major James's testimony before the Parliamentary Committee on American Papers, BM Add. Mss., 33030 (Newcastle), f. 84–6; General Thomas Gage's accounts, particularly his letters of November 4 and 8 to H. S. Conway, in Clarence E. Carter, ed., *The Correspondence of General Thomas Gage* (New Haven, 1931), I, 70–3, with the enclosures of his November 4 letter in PRO, CO 5/83; and relevant documents, especially letters of Colden, in *N.Y. Col. Docs.*, VII, *Colden's Letters and Papers*, VII, and *The Colden Letter Books*, II, 1765–75, NYHS *Colls. for 1877* (New York, 1878). The fullest secondary account is in Roger Champagne, "The Sons of Liberty and the Aristocracy in New York Politics, 1765–1790," unpublished Ph.D. dissertation, University of Wisconsin, 1960, especially pp. 64–5, 67–77.
    Suspicions of Colden went back to his support of the Crown's prerogative in two judicial controversies of the 1760's, one on judges' tenure and another, still heatedly agitated in 1765, on the finality of jury decisions. See Milton M. Klein, "Prelude to Revolution in New York: Jury Trials and Judicial Tenure," *W. M. Q.*, XVII (1960), 439–62.

"highly enflam'd" by the Stamp Act.[30] What local leadership
was exerted over this fragmented mob was probably in the
hands of Isaac Sears, Marinus Willett, John Lamb, and
others who were emerging as New York's Sons of Liberty.
Willett and Lamb, it has been claimed, prepared the placards
used on November 1; and, according to a knowledgeable
eighteenth-century historian, Sears urged the mob on November 2 to continue agitating until the province's stamps
were safely removed from Fort George and Colden's control.
Once the stamps were entrusted to local magistrates, however, the mob quickly dispersed and the influential sea captains, who were akin to those "rough men of the Waterfront"
Sears and Lamb, joined in a public appeal for restraint
to show "that we have Conduct as well as Courage," and
"prove that we have acted, not as a Mob, but as Friends to
Liberty."[31]

Still, the violence at New York was becoming anachronistic, and Major James's was the last in a series of houses
"pulled down" during the Stamp Act crisis. The trend of the
times was apparent in the extraordinary efforts being taken
to maintain the peace in Boston, where violence seemed particularly threatened due to the proximity of November 1 and
5, marking respectively the day the Stamp Act was to go into
effect and Pope's Day. During the last week of October, Governor Bernard reported, "Two Gentlemen, called the richest
Merchants in this Town" entertained the leaders of the North
and South End mobs to "establish and confirm" an alliance
first effected on August 14 so as to keep the town in peace.
The influential mob leader and potential rabblerouser Ebenezer Mackintosh "was employed with his Corps to keep the
Peace and prevent mischief," a function he filled so well on
November 1 and 5 that even the governor had to admit "the
greatest order was observed." Each day began with the parad-

30. Livingston to Monckton, November 8, 1765, MHS *Colls.*, 4th
Ser., X, 559–67. Also Gage to Conway, New York, November 4 and
December 21, 1765, in Carter, *Gage Correspondence*, I, 71, 79.

31. See Howard Thomas's undocumented assertions in *Marinus
Willett: Soldier Patriot* (New York, 1954), 23; also Gordon, *History*,
I, 186. Champagne, "Sons of Liberty," 13; appeal for peace, posted
in New York Coffee House on November 6, in Colden, *Letters and
Papers*, VII, 91.

ing of effigies, which were destroyed early in the afternoon
so that "the Town might be perfectly quiet before Night."
"General" Mackintosh presided in a blue and gold uniform,
wearing a gold-laced hat and carrying a rattan cane and a
speaking trumpet to proclaim his orders. His officers, marked
by their laced hats and "wands," allowed no allegedly dis-
order-prone Negroes to join the 2000 paraders, and none but
the officers were allowed to carry any stick or offensive
weapon. Mackintosh walked arm-in-arm with Colonel William
Brattle, a councillor and leading merchant, who "compli-
mented him on the order he kept, and told him his Post was
one of the highest in the Government." Business was conducted, the *Boston Gazette* commented, in the "most regular
Manner," and disorder prevented "as could hardly be expected
among a Concourse of several Thousand People."[32]

The new emphasis on avoiding "mischievous Extravagances" was apparent, too, when a mock funeral was announced at Newport for North American Liberty, scheduled
to succumb at midnight on October 31. The notice invited
all the old man's "true Sons," but asked Bastard-kin to stay
away. "His Children inform the whole World," the announcement warned, "that they will take proper Notice of every
Motion of Disorder and Riot, either before, at, or after the
Funeral, and prosecute the Offenders." Meanwhile, a writer
in the *Newport Mercury* called on colonists to "be cautious
and circumspect, lest we disgrace the glorious cause we are
embarked in." "It always behoves us to conduct [ourselves]
like Men actuated, not by private Spleen, or mad Licentiousness, but by rational Principles," a letter in the next *Mercury*

32. Bernard to John Pownall, Castle William, November 1, 5, and
26, 1765, in Bernard Papers, V, 18–23, 43–6; Bernard to H. S. Conway, Boston, November 25, 1765, *ibid.*, IV, 172–3. Bernard at first
feared that the newly united mob would serve as a private army
"against the kings officers and government"; but other accounts indicate it was designed simply to keep the peace. See Hutchinson to
Benjamin Franklin, November 18, 1766, MA, XXVI, 174; a junction
of mobs "is thought to be the only way to preserve the town from
further outrages." Also *Boston Gaz.*, November 4 and 11. On the
11th, the *Gazette* said that the mob leaders and their assistants had
"engaged upon their Honor no Mischiefs should arise by their Means;
and that they would prevent any Disorders, on the 5th." The mobs'
union was later celebrated at a "Union Feast" attended by some two
hundred people, including some eminent Bostonians.

concluded; and the "Decency with which the FUNERAL OF LIBERTY was conducted" gave the "strongest Assurance" of the Newporters' "manly, sensible Behavior on any future Exhibition." In Portsmouth, New Hampshire, a November 1 demonstration was similarly conducted "with the utmost Decency." So, too, were rites in Middletown, Connecticut, where some eight hundred people were said to have taken part in ceremonies execrating effigies of Bute, Grenville, and the Devil, and in Frederick Town, New Jersey, where a funeral was held for the Stamp Act on November 30. Accounts of almost every colonial public assembly came to be characterized by the same final sentence, "the whole was conducted with decency and decorum."[33]

The movement away from overt violence was also clear in the efforts made to resume normal commercial and governmental activity in late 1765 and early 1766. Colonists had at first resigned themselves to forsaking activities for which stamps were required after November 1, but soon strong arguments were made for a resumption of business as usual. Some advocates, such as Philadelphia's John Dickinson, stressed ideological and political considerations. To suspend business was "nearly the same Acknowledgment of the Validity of the Stamp Act, and of its legal Obligations upon you, as if you use the Papers"; moreover, the cessation of business would convince London that the colonists were "intimidated to the utmost Degree," and make repeal of the Stamp Act less likely. Others were moved by practical considerations: the losses to merchants whose ships would be bound in port, or the danger to the peace of towns like Charleston where large numbers of sailors had arrived after November 1 and began "to grow licentious."[34]

Business as usual never became as generally accepted a

33. *Newport Mercury, Supplement* for October 28, and November 4, 1765; *Portsmouth Mercury,* November 4; *Conn. Gaz.,* November 15, and *Pa. Jour.,* December 26, 1765.

34. Dickinson's broadside in Ford, *Dickinson Writings,* I, 201–5; "Philolutherus," *N.Y. Gaz.,* December 27, 1765. Collector and Comptroller of Philadelphia to Customs Commissioners, December 1, 1765, Stowe Mss., 264, ff. 73–4, BM; Charles Stuart to Customs Commissioners, Philadephia, December 7, 1765, PRO, Treas. 1/452; Gov. William Bull to Conway, Charleston, February 6, 1766, PRO, CO 5/390, ff. 66–7.

policy as the coercion of stampmen. It was an issue that separated the spirited from the timid; nonetheless, although popular coercion was used in implementing the policy, violence was limited. Governor Bernard charged vaguely that customs officers opened Boston port only after it was known "that the two Mob Captains had fixed upon a day for rising." In Philadelphia, customs officials yielded not because there was an immediate threat, but because they felt that ultimately "people will not sit quiet and see their Interests suffer, and perhaps Ruin brought upon themselves and Families, when they have it in their power to redress themselves." The New London, Connecticut, "respectable populace" threatened their customs officers only with lawsuits for any damages suffered by merchants should the customhouse continue to refuse issuing clearances on unstamped paper. Cape Fear, North Carolina, was indeed opened to commerce by a carefully organized crowd of nearly seven hundred men, most of whom were armed. But the *North Carolina Gazette* could at least boast of the crowd's orderliness and sobriety, and the newspaper recommended the occasion as "worthy the imitation of all the Sons of Liberty throughout the Continent."[35]

In seeking the opening of courts, colonists again avoided violence. The *Pennsylvania Journal*'s "Phileleutherus" characteristically disavowed "riots and tumults," but also argued that "it can be no breach of the laws of nature nor of our country for people to assemble together peaceably" and demand that the courts remain active. In fact, the people most often worked through established governmental channels. In September, the Rhode Island Assembly asked all colony officials to "proceed in the Execution of their respective Offices . . . as usual," and indemnified them against any penalities stemming from such conduct. The unofficial instructions to New York City's assembly members drafted in

35. Bernard to Lords of Trade, Boston, January 10, 1766, Bernard Papers, IV, 185; Collector and Comptroller of Philadelphia to Customs Commissioners, December 1, 1765, Stowe Mss., 264, ff. 73–4, BM; Duncan Stewart (Collector of New London) to John Temple, December 19, 1765, PRO, Treas. 1/452; *N.C. Col. Recs.*, VII, especially newspaper extracts 168a–f, and Tryon to Conway, February 25, 1766, 169–74.

November by, it was said, the hard core of that city's Stamp Act opposition, called for a legislative sanction behind "business as usual." Salaries should be authorized for government officials, the instructions suggested, only if the officers would execute their duties on unstamped paper. In Boston, the town meeting sought the opening of courts first by a memorial to the governor and council, and later through the assembly. Even where one man blocked the resumption of court activity, as did the clerk of South Carolina's Superior Court, he was not mobbed nor was his property destroyed as had been the fate of the stampmen.[36]

The methods of coercing Stamp Act supporters became, in effect, refined. After the violence of August, a threat was often as effective as a mob; but even the character of threats underwent a transformation. The rough ultimatums of August and early September occasionally recurred—as in February 1766, when the inhabitants of Elizabeth-Town, New Jersey, vowed that "the first Person that either distributes [or takes] out a Stamped Paper, shall be hung . . . without Judge or Jury." And when a group of "respectable" Virginians decided to extract a public recantation from stamp supporter Archibald Ritchie, they went so far with anonymous threats to his life and property that one organizer feared "the man will arrive to such a state of despondency as to hang or drown himself and we shall be deprived of the Satisfaction of seeing the Wretch . . . mortified."[37] But particularly in the North, where development of the resistance was more advanced, threats were moderated from violent punishment to ostracism of Stamp Act supporters. The freemen of Essex County, New Jersey, for example, declared on October 25 that they would have "no Communication with any such Per-

36. *Pa. Jour., Supplement* February 6, 1766; *R.I. Col. Recs.*, VII, 451–2; *N.Y. Gaz.*, November 28, 1765; Bernard to Lords of Trade, Boston, January 10, 1766, Bernard Papers, IV, 185–6; and Gov. Bull to Treasury Commissioners, May 3, 1766, PRO, Treas. 1/445. The South Carolina clerk was only fined, and the governor suspended even the fine until he could receive instructions from England.

37. *N.Y. Gaz.*, February 27, 1766; Richard Parker to Richard Henry Lee, February 23, 1766; Lee Family Papers, UVa, available in Paul P. Hoffman, ed., "Lee Family Papers, 1742–1795," University of Virginia microfilm (Charlottesville, 1966), Roll 1.

son, nor speak to them on any Occasion, unless it be to inform them of their Vileness." The language might remain extravagant: let the man who would receive a stamp "be branded with eternal infamy and reproach," a letter in the *Newport Mercury* and *Pennsylvania Journal* enjoined; "let him be alone in the world—let him wish to associate with the wild beasts of some dark, loathsome cave." But even then the real punishment was to come from "a self-condemnation, [from the realization] that he has been instrumental in bringing slavery upon his country," not from the blows of his countrymen.[38]

This retreat from violence to ostracism signaled a new awareness that the "enemies of liberty" themselves had rights. "Let us not . . . while we are opposing an act, which we think . . . destructive of our rights, liberties, and estates, be guilty of so glaring an inconsistency, as to injure the rights and property of a fellow subject," a writer counseled *Newport Mercury* readers on October 28. "Let us not, by offering any violence to him or his property, give a wound to liberty itself. . . . But heap upon him all the contempt he will deserve; exclude him from every office of honour and trust in the government; and forever hold him in the utmost detestation and abhorrence."

The notion that boycotts could be substituted for colonial violence was reflected, too, in the method Americans finally settled upon for securing the repeal of the Stamp Act in England—nonimportation. Already in August 1764, some Boston merchants tried to counteract the economic effects of the Sugar Act[39] by reducing luxury imports from England, above all mourning clothes and the gloves traditionally given out at funerals. These fledgling efforts were systematized in September 1765 and thereafter nonimportation associations were organized in other commercial centers. A selective em-

38. *N.J. Col. Docs.*, XXIV, 671–2; *Pa. Jour.*, November 28, and *Newport Mercury*, *Supplement* October 28, 1765.

39. The Sugar Act, or Revenue Act of 1764, revised old duties on imports into the colonies, set up new ones, revised customs procedures affecting colonial trade, and changed regulations for adjudicating customs offenses. For a full description, see Jensen, *Founding of a Nation*, 47–51.

bargo could be carried on, one writer estimated, for three or four years; and even a shorter abstention could seriously dislocate those sectors of the British economy dependent on the colonial trade, and so induce agitation within the Mother Country for colonial redress. Reports from merchants in England indicated that this policy had already had considerable success by mid-1765.[40]

For Americans this meant that nonimportation could constitute an effective substitute for domestic violence: opposition could retreat from the streets to the spinning wheel. Colonial newspapers reported fully the riots American nonimportation had encouraged across the Atlantic, particularly those of weavers, glovemakers and other manufacturers, news of which arrived in August 1765. If the giving up of mourning had contributed "not a little to the ou[s]ting [of] the most detested and injudicious of M[iniste]rs that ever sat at the English Helm," asked a writer in the *Boston Gazette*, "what may we not expect from a full and general Execution of this Plan?" A writer in the *New York Gazette* estimated that a total boycott could reduce to a "starving condition" and political fury some million British workers, who "depend entirely on their commerce with the colonies for their daily bread."[41] And John Adams, as "Humphry Ploughjogger," wrote in the October 14 *Boston Gazette*, "I'de rather the Spittlefield weavers should pull down all the houses in old England, and knock the brains out of all the wicked men there, than this country should lose their liberty." If it were houses in old England that were pulled down and brains on the other side of the ocean that were knocked in, at least American violence could not be blamed. England would only be paying the price of her own unconstitutional legislation.

Within their own borders, then, the "men of America" had gone far to restrain those offensive "*men of Belial*" who had cloaked "their rapacious violences with the pretext of zeal for

---

40. Arthur M. Schlesinger, *The Colonial Merchants and the American Revolution, 1763–1776* (New York, 1957), 63–4, 76–82. On the aims of nonimportation: *Pa. Jour.*, *Supplement* January 2, 1766, and "Libertas et Natale Solum," *N.Y. Gaz.*, September 12, 1765.

41. *Boston Gaz.*, November 25, 1765; "Philolutherus," *N.Y. Gaz.*, December 27, 1765.

liberty," most dramatically in the events of August at Boston and Newport. When colonists looked back on the Stamp Act crisis, this repression of disorder seemed more important than its appearance. Though the spirit of liberty had "at first . . . burst forth in a tumultuous Torrent of disorderly Rage," William Goddard wrote in his *Providence Gazette*, gradually "it . . . acquired Consistency and Form, advanced toward Order and Regularity, and was directed by Judgment and Design. It restrained the Impulses of mistaken Zeal, prevented and suppressed Tumults and Disorders, and protected the private Property even of those whose Indiscretion had made them the Objects of Public Resentment."[42] The colonial leaders had become preoccupied with a dual concern, combined in the strategy of "ordered resistance"—a strategy soon to be adopted fully by the Sons of Liberty organizations the radicals formed, and to appear triumphantly vindicated with the Stamp Act's repeal.

42. Mayhew, *Snare Broken*, 7, 20, 44; *Prov. Gaz.*, August 23, 1766.

CHAPTER FOUR

THE INTERCOLONIAL
SONS OF LIBERTY AND
ORGANIZED RESISTANCE,
1765–1766

ONLY AFTER THE COLONISTS' OPPOSITION to the Stamp Act was well under way did an organized resistance movement emerge.[1] Rudimentary glimpses of informal intercolonial collaboration, were apparent in the early fall of 1765. In August, for example, some Bostonians wrote a letter encouraging Newporters to force their stampman into resigning.[2] But the emergence of organized local resistance groups and their often simultaneous merger into an intercolonial organization of a new type and significance began only in the closing months of 1765, and never really caught on until February 1766.

This newly organized group, called the "Sons of Liberty," rarely, if ever, went beyond trends of colonial action already apparent before it appeared. Yet by institutionalizing the colonists' new commitment to resistance of a defined type, and by implementing it with a new type of organization, the Sons of Liberty durably established a pattern for future opposition to

1. This is a common pattern with mass movements. See "Natural History of Social Movements," in Carl A. Dawson and Werner E. Gettys, *An Introduction to Sociology* (New York, 1929), 787–804, which uses the model of Methodism in England.

2. Augustus Johnston to Stamp Commissioners, Newport, August 31, 1765, PRO, Treas. 1/439.

Britain. Equally important, the Sons of Liberty demonstrated how limited in scope the agitation of 1765–6 was, how devoted even the most determined Stamp Act opponents were to the basic fabric of established government—in a word, how fundamentally the Americans' assumptions and beliefs would have to change before resistance could become revolution.

[I]

The idea of regularizing intercolonial cooperation against the Stamp Act sprang up independently in several widely separated colonies, but the most intense organizational effort began and remained centered in New York. It was there on either October 31 or November 6 that a meeting of some type—either an organized gathering in Burns's Coffee House or another less structured assembly "in the Fields"—appointed a committee to correspond with the other colonies. The new group included Isaac Sears and four others who would be outstanding Sons of Liberty: John Lamb, Gershom Mott, William Wiley, and Thomas Robinson. By late November, Alexander Colden indicated that such a committee was in operation, and that it had already established contacts outside New York. "The Sons of Liberty of this place have wrote to Philadelphia," he informed his father, "that if they do not make Hugh[e]s resign as fully as the other Distributors . . . [t]hey will disown them and hold no longer Correspondence with them."[3]

A more formal organization gradually spread through New England, starting in late December when two New York representatives, Gershom Mott and Hugh Hughes—the brother of Stampman John Hughes—visited New London and negotiated a written alliance between the New York and

3. Accounts of the New York meeting in Isaac Q. Leake, *Memoir of the Life and Times of General John Lamb* (Albany, 1857), 14, and William Gordon, *The History of the Rise, Progress, and Establishment of the Independence of the United States of America* (London, 1788), I, 186–7. Postscript to Colden letter in *The Letters and Papers of Cadwallader Colden*: VII, *1765–1775*, in NYHS *Colls. for 1923* (New York, 1923), 95. Roger Champagne, "The Military Association of the Sons of Liberty," *The New-York Historical Society Quarterly*, XLI (1957), 338–50.

Connecticut Sons of Liberty.[4] In January, the Sons' organization within Manhattan was formalized and correspondence was established with the Sons of Liberty in Boston and Albany.[5] Initiatives in February brought contacts with several Massachusetts towns outside Boston, while the Portsmouth, New Hampshire, Sons of Liberty entered the alliance.[6] In March, Providence's Sons of Liberty sent out proposals for a correspondence union to New York, Newport, and New Hampshire; and by early April, 1766, Newport—excluded by oversight from New York's organizational effort—had accepted Providence's offer and also been absorbed into the New York–based correspondence circuit.[7] While these criss-crossing efforts solidified forces to the north and west, the New York Sons turned their attention to other communities within their own colony and, more important, to the colonies farther south. On February 14, they sent out

4. Gordon, *History*, I, 195–8; Gov. Francis Bernard to H. S. Conway, Boston, January 19, 1766, with annexed narrative, in *The Fitch Papers*: II, *January 1759–May 1766*, in *Collections of the Connecticut Historical Society* XVIII (Hartford, 1920), 384–6. Bernard says the New Yorkers arrived on December 31, but the Gordon account and the text of the agreement (available also in Belknap Papers, 61.c.109, MHS) dates it December 25.

5. New York Sons' resolves of January 7 in *N.Y. Gaz.*, January 9, 1766; Major [John] Durkee to Isaac Sears, Norwich, Connecticut, February 10, 1766, including letter from the Boston Sons, January 27, and Albany Sons of Liberty to Joseph Allicocke and Isaac Sears, January 15, 1766, John Lamb Papers, NYHS.

6. Gordon, *History*, I, 199; Boston Sons to New Hampshire, February 3, Belknap Papers, and New Hampshire answer of February 8, 1766, Belknap Papers, 61.c.112 and 61.c.115. On February 10, the Boston Sons wrote that they were writing "to all the Towns in the Province to know their Dispositions," and on February 13 said that several towns had already expressed approval of the Sons of Liberty's Union. (To New Hampshire, Belknap Papers, 61.c.114 and 61.c.115.) For an example of these early Boston circulars, see Sons of Liberty to John Adams, Boston, February 5, 1766, in Charles F. Adams, ed., *The Works of John Adams* (Boston, 1850–6), II, 183–4.

7. Providence circular to New Hampshire Sons, with cover letter, March 24, Belknap Papers, 61.c.120, 61.c.121; to the New York Sons, March 19, Lamb Papers; to Newport, March 20, RIHS Mss., XII, f. 64, and the Newporters' answer of April 2, 1766, RIHS Mss., XII, f. 66. On Newport, see also New York to Boston Sons, April 2, 1766, Lamb Papers.

a circular calling on recipients "to assemble as many of the true Sons of Liberty as you possibly can . . . and propose an Association in order to form an union of the Colonies in Imitation of our Brethren in Connecticut, Boston, &c." The Albany Sons—who were already bound under a carefully framed "constitution"—forwarded the circular to Schenectady, then set about fitting their internal organization to the New York pattern. Resolutions were adopted that followed closely those passed at New York in January; a committee of correspondence was chosen, and arrangements were made for regular meetings of a general committee—a process echoed in the Long Island communities of Oyster Bay and Huntington.[8] In a response to New York dated February 15, the Philadelphia Sons of Liberty explained that their numbers were hitherto few, "as unfortunate Dissentions in Provincial Politics keeps us rather a divided people," and that they had found no reason in the past so much as to appoint a committee to represent them; but they, too, promised to organize immediately. Associations of the Sons of Liberty soon flowered in New Jersey and Maryland, where efforts were made not only to establish correspondences with other colonies but to consolidate organizations on the township, county, and colony level.[9] Sons of Liberty were also organized at Norfolk, Virginia, on March 31, prompted, it seems, by the example of

8. New York circular, February 14, 1766, in the papers of William Legge, Earl of Dartmouth, D 1778/2/165, William Salt Library, Stafford, England. The text is also in the proceedings of the Albany Sons of Liberty Committee, March 3, 1766, in *The American Historian, and Quarterly Genealogical Record*, ed. The Historical Society, Schenectady, N.Y., I (1876), 151–2. Albany "constitution" and letter to Schenectady, in *ibid.*, 145–57, 153. Oyster Bay to New York Sons, February 22, 1766, and results of a meeting at Huntington, N.Y., February 24, 1766, Lamb Papers.

9. Philadelphia to New York Sons, February 15, 1766, Lamb Papers. New Jersey: Henry Bicker to Isaac Sears and company, New Brunswick, N.J., February 23, 1766; Gershom Mott and Mr. Phillips, Trenton, N.J., February 28, and Upper Freehold to New York Sons, April 28, 1766, Lamb Papers. Also accounts of proceedings in *N.Y. Gaz.*, March 6, and *Newport Mercury*, March 24, 1766, and *N.J. Col. Docs.*, 63–4, 71–3, 108–11. Maryland: Baltimore Sons to New York, March 8, 1766, Lamb Papers, and account of Baltimore meeting of February 24, which asked other counties to organize, *Pa. Jour.*, March 20, 1766.

colonies to the north.[10] The New Yorkers hoped that their circular would unite the colonies "as far as South Carolina," but it is doubtful whether their letter of February or another of early April ever reached Charleston. But there, as Christopher Gadsden wrote in mid-April, 1766, a similar North Carolina Association formed in February was attracting great interest. The radical South Carolinians, moreover, carried on a *de facto* relationship with sympathetic Georgians that was much on the pattern of the New York plan.[11]

This delayed but widespread emergence of an organized intercolonial resistance movement has been obscured to some extent by its adoption of the name "Sons of Liberty." Long before 1765 the term had been used in a generic sense. The prefix "sons of" came easily to men accustomed to masonic lodges and other fraternal clubs; but the whole term "sons of liberty" enjoyed special connotations for eighteenth-century Americans. It indicated an awareness of being "born free," as the heirs of free institutions hard-won by their fathers in England and America, which they, like faithful sons, should maintain. The term "sons of freedom" was used interchangeably with "sons of liberty": "our worthy ancestors . . . having felt the effects of tyranny . . . fled . . . to seek shelter beneath the peaceful wing of liberty," an article in the *Boston Evening Post* once proclaimed; hence the colonists were "the sons of noble freedom." The concept thus designated a fervent

10. Norfolk account in *Va. Gaz.* (Purdie and Dixon), April 4, 1766; Governor Francis Fauquier to Lords of Trade, Williamsburg, April 7, 1766, and enclosure, J. Morgan to Fauquier, *Hornet* in Hamptons Road, April 5, 1766, PRO, CO 5/1331, ff. 76–8. Morgan said that one event prompting the organization was "Mr. Paul Loyel coming from the Northward having declared, that notwithstanding the Virginians were the first who attempted to oppose the Stamp Act [they] were now become mute and persilanimous while the people of the other colonies asserted their rights like sons of Liberty which he likewise behove them to do."

11. Boston to New Hampshire Sons, March 14, 1766, Belknap Papers, 61.c.119; Gadsden to [William] S. Johnson, Charleston, April 16, 1766, in Richard Walsh, ed., *The Writings of Christopher Gadsden, 1746–1805* (Columbia, 1966), 72. The North Carolina association he mentions was probably that formed at Wilmington on February 18; see *N.C. Col. Recs.*, VII, 168c–d. On the South Carolinians' role in encouraging Georgians' opposition, see W. W. Abbot, *The Royal Governors of Georgia, 1754–1775* (Chapel Hill, 1959), 116–20.

patriotism, as the *South Carolina Gazette* indicated when it casually referred to "every *Son of Liberty*, or loyal Subject of his Majesty, and true Friend to the English Constitution."[12] It was in this descriptive sense that the term appeared in some Connecticut documents of the 1750's discovered by the nineteenth-century historian J. H. Trumbull.[13] And it was in the same rhetorical, descriptive sense that Isaac Barré used the epithet in Parliament in early 1765.[14] Nor did the generic sense of "sons of liberty" wither after 1765: it continued to serve as a label for those who were ready to defend their rights however necessary, whether in England, America, Ireland, or anywhere else men jealous of freedom should appear.

Once the danger of the Stamp Act for American liberty was defined, however, "sons of liberty" took on a more specific connotation for colonists. By late 1765, it referred generally to all who opposed the Stamp Act. As such, a group of New Jersey lawyers who decided to suspend work rather than purchase stamps were at first called "sons of liberty"; and the people in Lebanon, Connecticut, who staged an anti–Stamp Act demonstration in August 1765, spoke of the ardent love for liberty in her "most virtuous sons." Even the Stamp Act "rioters" on the Island of St. Christopher acted, it was said, "like true-born sons of Britain fired with Liberty."[15] Groups

12. *Boston Evening Post* article in *Prov. Gaz.*, April 11, 1767, and also August 24, 1765; article from *S.C. Gaz.*, March 11, reprinted in *N.Y. Gaz.*, March 27, 1766.

13. J. Hammond Trumbull, "Sons of Liberty in 1755," *The New Englander*, XXXV (1876), 299–313, especially 308. Trumbull, however, thought the term denoted an organization prefiguring those of 1765–6.

14. Barré said the behavior of British officials in America "on many occasions, has caused the blood of those [colonial] sons of LIBERTY to recoil within them." His sense of the term was clear on another occasion, when he said the colonists were "as truly loyal . . . as any Subjects of the King, But a People jealous of their Liberties, and who will vindicate them, if they should be violated." Speeches in *S.C. Gaz.*, July 20, 1765; *Boston Gaz.*, May 27, 1765; and *Prov. Gaz.*, August 24, 1765.

15. Champagne, "Military Association," 339; Edmund S. and Helen M. Morgan, *The Stamp Act Crisis* (New York, 1963), 251. *Boston Gaz.*, October 14 and September 9, 1765; item from *St. Christopher Gazette* (Brit. W. I.) in *Pa. Jour.*, November 21, 1765.

of such sons of liberty had in fact to be recognizably present in the colonies before the organized intercolonial Sons of Liberty could emerge, for the associations formed under that name never pretended to create "sons of liberty," but merely to organize those already existing. Thus New York's February 14 circular addressed to the South called on its readers "by the Sacred Name of Liberty, and the regard you owe the British Constitution" to "assemble as many of the true sons of Liberty as you possibly can," as if the category was pre-existent. A call for the organization of New Haven County issued from Wallingford, Connecticut, in January was couched in similar terms.[16]

There were organized resistance associations within some colonies before the intercolonial Sons of Liberty movement got under way; but even these local groupings crystallized only two or three months after the first Stamp Act riots and then, to add to the terminological confusion, did not always call themselves Sons of Liberty. The colony most completely organized was Connecticut, and there the future Sons emerged under the name of the "respectable populace." Efforts in Connecticut began in early November, as was the case in New York. On November 11, a meeting at Windham laid out organizational plans that reached complete fruition on March 25, 1766, when delegates from a majority of Connecticut towns met at Hartford and approved several proposals, including a continued correspondence with the other colonies.[17] In Newport, Rhode Island, too, a broadside of October 1765 spoke of a meeting of the *"respectable Populace"* that had set up a committee of thirty to make sure no stamps were landed from the *Cygnet* and had further resolved that no customs officers or merchants should use the stamps. By December, however, a letter published in the *Newport Mercury* indicated that a group called the "Sons of Liberty" had been meeting in that town, and it was under the name "Sons of Liberty"

---

16. For New York circular, see *n.* 8 above; Wallingford meeting, January 13, in *Conn. Gaz.*, January 24, 1766.

17. *Conn. Gaz.*, December 6, 1765 (Windham), April 5, 1766 (Hartford). On the Connecticut organization, see Lawrence Gipson, *Jared Ingersoll* (New Haven, 1920), 195–221, and Oscar Zeichner, *Connecticut's Years of Controversy, 1750–1776* (Chapel Hill, 1949), 62–4, 72–4.

that demonstrations were staged in February and early March, 1766.[18] One of the first communities to organize Sons of Liberty was Savannah, Georgia, where, ironically, the Sons were the most successfully divided and dispirited by the royal governor. Already in late October, Governor Wright reported, "the Sons of Liberty began to have Private Cabals and Meetings, and I was Informed that many had Signed an association to oppose and Prevent the distribution of the Stamp't Papers and the act from taking effect."[19]

Occasionally, the formation of a local Sons of Liberty organization was spurred by a specific event rather than the suggestion of another community. In Albany, the Sons of Liberty first crystallized in an effort to prevent the appointment of a local deputy to the colony's stamp collector. In North Carolina, organization became necessary after customs officials in Cape Fear started seizing vessels with unstamped clearances. The people of several towns assembled at Wilmington on February 18 and entered an association that was not formally entitled the Sons of Liberty, but which was the equivalent of organizations being formed to the north. The associated brethren then proceeded to force the port and colony courts open. Similarly in Virginia, when Archibald Ritchie, a merchant, declared publicly that he would clear his vessels on stamped paper and that he knew where to get it, "a number of gentlemen" met at Leedstown on February 27, chose a committee to "regulate their plan of proceedings," then formally entered an association very similar to that of the Sons of Liberty elsewhere in the colonies.[20]

18. *Newport Mercury*, October 21, 1765 ("Piece found, Yesterday . . ."), December 30, 1765 (letter by "A Son of Liberty"), and March 24, 1766 (account of episode in March). Account of February 26 demonstration in *Boston Gaz.*, March 10, 1766. Ezra Stiles also referred to a March 28 meeting as one of "the Sons of Liberty in Newport." Stiles, "Stamp Act Notebook," 22, Ezra Stiles Papers, Beinecke Library, Yale University, New Haven, Connecticut.

19. Wright to Conway, Savannah, January 31, 1766, PRO, CO 5/658, ff. 112–15; Abbott, *Royal Governors of Georgia*, 106–16.

20. Beverly McAnear, "The Albany Stamp Act Riots," *W. M. Q.*, IV (1947), 486; *N.C. Col. Recs.*, VII, 168a–f; Virginia news in *Conn. Gaz.*, April 19, 1766, and Westmoreland Resolutions of February 27, 1766, in Richard B. Harwell, ed., *The Committees of Safety of Westmoreland and Fincastle . . .* (Richmond, 1956), 99–102. For back-

Often those individuals attracted to the Sons of Liberty had been previously united on the town or province level in some social, civic, or religious organization. The idea that New York's Sons of Liberty grew out of the older Whig Club has long since been discarded,[21] but a good portion of those in Albany belonged to the local volunteer fire company and the Dutch Reformed Church. In Charleston, many of the Sons of Liberty were already joined in several organizations, including Christopher Gadsden's Artillery Company and the Fellowship Society. As a result these "inveterate joiners," as their historian has called them, found it unnecessary to organize a separate Sons of Liberty, and resisted the Stamp Act under the title of the Charleston Fire Company. The Fire Company made clear its position as Charleston's Sons of Liberty on March 1, 1766, when it directed that its resolutions be "made publick, That the firm Sentiments of the Loyalty of this Company may be known to their Brethren Sons of Liberty in America and to the Latest Posterity."[22]

In Boston, a social club called the "Loyal Nine" prepared the effigies exhibited on August 14 and also coerced Andrew Oliver into publicly renouncing his office a second time in December, after rumors circulated that he had taken up his commission as stamp distributor. Only in December, however, did the group begin issuing public announcements as the Sons of Liberty. John Adams called this group the "Sons of Liberty" when he visited one of its meetings on January 15, 1766, held "at their own Apartment in Hanover Square, near

---

ground of the Virginia affair, see letters to Richard Henry Lee from Samuel Washington, February 22, and Richard Parker, February 23, Lee Family Papers, UVa, available in Paul P. Hoffman, ed., "Lee Family Papers, 1742–1795," University of Virginia microfilm (Charlottesville, 1966), Roll 1. John C. Matthews, "Two Men on a Tax: Richard Henry Lee, Archibald Ritchie, and the Stamp Act," in Darrett Rutman, ed., *The Old Dominion* (Charlottesville, 1964), 96–108.

21. Dorothy Dillon, *The New York Triumvirate* (New York, 1949), p. 95, *n*. 21.

22. McAnear, "Albany Stamp Act Riots," 490–1; Richard Walsh, *Charleston's Sons of Liberty* (Columbia, 1959), 30–3, 38–9; resolutions of the Charleston Fire Company, March 1, among enclosures in Wright to Conway, Savannah, March 10, 1766, PRO, CO 5/658, ff. 133, 134; *Newport Mercury*, March 31, 1766.

the Tree of Liberty," which was a small compting room in Chase and Speakman's Distillery. That the nine members mentioned by Adams, and later by the eighteenth-century historian William Gordon, completed the list of Sons of Liberty in Boston is improbable; but the Loyal Nine clearly constituted the backbone of the Boston Sons in 1765–6. The Sons' correspondence, for example, was to be addressed to the printers Edes and Gill, and Benjamin Edes was one of the original members of the Nine.[23]

Connecticut's opposition to the Stamp Act seemed to grow out of a series of earlier groups "originating with the N[ew] London Society—thence matamorphisd [sic] into the Faction for paper Emissions on Loan, thence into N[ew] Light, into the Susquehannah and Delaware Factions—into Orthodoxy," and finally against the stamp duty, as Killingworth's Benjamin Gale put it. The correlation of militant opposition to the Stamp Act with the New Light faction in Connecticut politics and with men involved in the Susquehannah Company, both centering in the colony's eastern counties, was particularly striking. By the time the organized Sons of Liberty began to crystallize, however, agitation was expanding beyond the eastern counties of Connecticut: already in mid-December 1765, Eliphalet Dyer wrote William Samuel Johnson in the west that "the fire is broke out in your part of the Country," and before repeal Sons of Liberty had been organized even in Litchfield County, in the colony's extreme northwest.[24]

The officers and committee members of the Sons of Liberty were drawn almost entirely from the middle and upper ranks of colonial society. The committee at Newport, Ezra Stiles recorded, "contained some Gentlemen of the first Figure in Town for opulence, Sense and Politeness"; in North Carolina, the Cape Fear Sons were led by "one of the wealthiest of the gentlemen and freeholders" of the region, Cornelius Harnett; in Virginia, the Westmoreland County Association, formed

23. Henry Bass to Samuel P. Savage, Boston, December 19, 1765, in MHS *Procs.*, XLIV (1910–11), 688–9; L. H. Butterfield, ed., *Diary and Autobiography of John Adams* (New York, 1964): I, *Diary 1755–1770*, 294. For membership in the Loyal Nine, see Appendix.

24. Gale quoted in Zeichner, *Connecticut's Years of Controversy*, 52; Dyer on 63, and also 73.

at Leedstown in February 1766, was organized by Richard Henry Lee and signed by members of several major Virginia families, including the Lees and Washingtons; while in Charleston the Sons of Liberty tended to coincide with mechanics' organizations. Charleston's artisans or "mechanics" were not, however, common wage earners but men of some substance, either sole or co-proprietors of their businesses, who were themselves preoccupied with the problems of hiring or purchasing the labor of others. Over half of them did well enough to invest in town lots or, more often, plantation land. New York's leaders, too, were involved in small but respectable independent business ventures. Isaac Sears, who apparently headed the radical nucleus, was the son of a Connecticut oyster catcher. As a boy he had peddled shellfish through the countryside. After making a name for himself as a privateer in the Seven Years' War, he was able to set up his own modest importing business. John Lamb, too, was a captain and merchant, and in fact the majority of those New York radicals once analyzed by Herbert Morais were merchants. Although men like Sears and Lamb were not part of New York's landed aristocracy, nor particularly "polite," they approximated in economic position both the independent tradesmen who made up Boston's Loyal Nine and Newport's more prominent and dignified Sons of Liberty.[25]

As older groups became metamorphosized into resistance cadres, however, their social bases were consciously broadened. Under the terms of England's revolutionary tradition resistance, like revolution, had to emerge from the "Body of the People," the whole of political society, involving all of its social or economic subdivisions. Occasionally it was said that "the people" included only men of property, but "property" was often broadly construed, such that the term included at least all free white males, however great or humble their

25. Stiles, "Stamp Act Notebook"; R. D. W. Connors, *Cornelius Harnett* (Raleigh, 1909), 46–7; on Virginia, see *n.* 20 above. Walsh, *Charleston's Sons of Liberty*, 15–18, 22–5; biographies of Lamb and Sears in Roger Champagne, "The Sons of Liberty and the Aristocracy in New York Politics, 1765–1790," unpublished Ph.D. dissertation, University of Wisconsin, 1960, 11–13; and Thomas Jones, *History of New York, during the Revolutionary War*, II (New York, 1879), 340–3. See also Appendix.

material possessions. Even the destitute, it was sometimes said, had a property in their freedom.[26] This means that more modern conceptions of revolution as class movements are inadequate for understanding the colonists' particular political concerns. The problem faced between 1765 and 1776 was analogous in fact to that later encountered in ratifying the constitutions framed for the newly independent American states. Just as those new charters were to be adopted under the broadest franchise possible, preferably one without a property requirement, since the people as a whole had to contract into government, similarly the dissolution of established authority—even in a limited sphere, such as pertained to the Stamp Act—had to be based upon a broad popular agreement.

The central preoccupation of the Sons of Liberty, and later of the revolutionary movement in general, was then with winning a mass base, with converting the population at large into sons of liberty. This concern can be seen in the Sons' reliance upon mass meetings, such as those "in the Fields" in New York, or at Portsmouth in February 1766. Every effort was made to attract all elements of the population, and afterwards sympathetic newspapers liked to announce that inhabitants of "all ranks and condition" had attended. After the February meeting in Portsmouth, it was proudly reported that "the Principall inhabitants of this and the Neighbouring Towns . . . were assembled on the occasion." Yet men whose rank in colonial society was defined by British honors and appointments remained generally (although not always) absent from the Sons' ranks. This deficiency could be dismissed by deriding such men as bought out, the "pensioned part" of the population, as Christopher Gadsden once said.[27]

The adherence of large segments of the lower classes of colonial society—in particular wage earners, such as shop assistants or seamen—was, however, more essential. Thus the Newport Sons' committee, "the most respectable . . . on this Continent," especially valued the comradeship of Major

26. Editor's comments in *N.Y. Jour.*, August 18, 1774, and Gadsden's statement in Walsh, *Charleston's Sons of Liberty*, 53–4.

27. Gadsden to F. Pearson, February 13, 1766, Dartmouth Papers, D 1778/2/169.

Charles Spooner "from among the middling and lower Life."
"He was very necessary," Ezra Stiles explained, "and perhaps
as important as any Man of the Com[m]ittee, as they without
him would not have had so intirely the Confidence of the
Populace." Here, too, lay the special advantage of the New
York leaders' background, for it created less labored links
with the "lower Life." Although themselves middle-class
"merchants on the make," men like Sears and Lamb had won
their way up toward success in the rough life of the sea. They
perhaps enjoyed a special authority within New York waterfront society by virtue of their success at the tars' own game;
moreover, they occasionally enjoyed other special social con-
nections with New York's seamen. Sears, for example, had
married the daughter of Jasper Drake, who ran a popular
alehouse for New York sailors and vagabonds. This advantage of day-to-day contact with the local masses was shared
by Connecticut's Israel Putnam and John Durkee, both of
whom operated popular inns, and by Charleston's master
mechanics or Boston's tradesmen, who worked under the
same roof, side by side with their workmen.[28]

This need to involve the "Body of the People" shaped pro-
cedural aspects of the Sons' intercolonial organization. It
meant the Sons could act as a secret organization only to a
limited extent. True, they established a private communications network after some "Villin" had "Brouk open" a letter
from Sears to Connecticut in late January or early February
1766, and it was one of their most impressive achievements.
Immediately after receiving the once-opened letter, the New
Yorkers advised the Connecticut Sons to be "Very Cautious"
in choosing men by whom their correspondence was carried;
and when they drafted their February 14 circular to the South,
the New Yorkers asked specifically that letters be carried "by
a true Son of Liberty." Gradually, communications routes
became established. Letters from New York northward were
sent through Connecticut to Rhode Island and Boston, and
from Boston to Portsmouth; southward, New York wrote
directly to Philadelphia and several towns in New Jersey and,
through Philadelphia, to Baltimore. From Maryland, letters

28. Stiles, "Stamp Act Notebook"; Champagne, "Sons of Liberty,"
13; Jones, *History of New York*, II, 340.

were to be forwarded further south. Charles Thomson later explained that this system offered exceptional speed in spreading news, since the carriers' zeal "was a spur to their industry." But it also protected the privacy of the radicals' correspondence, and thus shielded the more active Sons from prosecution, fear of which they acknowledged in occasional resolves.[29]

Secrecy was hardly a dominating preoccupation of the Sons of Liberty, however. When letters carefully carried from town to town by trusted members finally reached their destination, they were sometimes read and, as again at Portsmouth in February 1766, discussed in a large, well-advertised public meeting. Even in negotiating military plans, the Sons seemed to spurn secrecy. Negotiations at New London in late December were held in a public tavern, Governor Bernard reported, and so little care taken that one of those present told of the transactions "in open company" at Boston. Another "professed Agent from Connecticut," who came to Boston to coordinate efforts against the Stamp Act, was "so open and unreserved in his negotiation" that even the credulous Bernard could not believe he was charged with "so dangerous a commission as concerting the raising of men."[30]

On balance, the Sons appeared far more anxious to communicate their activities than to hide them from the public, as is evidenced by their readiness to publish accounts of their meetings. When the Windham meeting of November 11, 1765, elaborated plans for the organization of Connecticut's Sons of Liberty, it explicitly instructed local groups to "publish their proceedings in the *New London Gazette*." Publication of proceedings was prescribed equally clearly by the Sons in Rhode Island, and the New York Sons, too, took care that the resolutions of towns like Huntington, Long Island, were published "for the good of the Common Cause." The

29. Durkee to Sears, February 10, and New York to Connecticut Sons, February 20, 1766, Lamb Papers; for New York February 14 circular, see *n.* 8 above. Thomson to David Ramsay, November 4, 1789, "The Papers of Charles Thomson, Secretary of the Continental Congress," NYHS *Colls. for 1878* (New York, 1879), 219. On fear of prosecution, see especially Albany "constitution," *The American Historian*, I (1876), 146.

30. Bernard to Gov. Henry Moore, Boston, February 23, 1766, BM Add. Mss., 22679, f. 9, 10.

purpose of such publication, the Woodbridge, New Jersey, Sons of Liberty explained, was not "to Dictate to our neighbouring Towns or Counties . . . but only to communicate our Sentiments for them to improve upon."[31]

In effect, the newspapers continued to serve as a forum for the formation of policy and remained the prime vehicle of uniting the population. Thus the special significance of printers' membership in the Sons of Liberty. Benjamin Edes of the *Boston Gazette* was a member of the Loyal Nine. The printer of the *Providence Gazette*, William Goddard, was on the Sons' correspondence committee in Providence, as was Samuel Hall, printer of the *Newport Mercury*, in Newport. William Bradford, printer of the *Pennsylvania Journal*, is perhaps the only Philadelphian whose link with the intercolonial Sons of Liberty can be clearly documented.[32] The papers of these patriot printers served as more than a means of publishing news of interest to like-minded readers or of "propagandizing" radical policies. Long after the Sons of Liberty of 1765–6 were dissolved, these papers and others like them—John Holt's *New York Gazette* or *New York Journal*, Peter Timothy's *South Carolina Gazette*, Isaiah Thomas's *Massachusetts Spy*—remained a forum for public discussion. Over the next decade, they reflected the evolution of radical Americans' conceptions of Great Britain and of the colonies' relationship to her.

[I I]

By the time the Sons of Liberty emerged, royal officials were already complaining that their authority had disintegrated.

31. *Conn. Gaz.*, December 6, 1765 (Windham meeting); Newport Sons' resolution of April 2, RIHS Mss., XII, f. 66; New York Sons' committee to Nathaniel Williams, March 7, 1766, Lamb Papers; Woodbridge statement, February 1766, *N.J. Col. Docs.*, XXV, 42.

32. Boston to New Hampshire Sons, February 3, 1766, Belknap Papers 61.c.110; Goddard's name in Providence to New Hampshire Sons, March 24, 1766, *ibid.*, 61.c.120; and, for Hall's membership, Newport committee to Providence committee, April 4, 1766, RIHS Mss., XII, f. 67. Bradford to New York Sons, February 15, 1766, Lamb Papers.

Militias had either refused to answer royal governors' calls for support or were so clearly behind the mobs that it seemed foolhardy to muster them,[33] and local magistrates had often proved similarly useless.[34] As early as August 22, with only one uprising behind him, Governor Bernard viewed with alarm his "present defenceless State" and reported to England that he was a mere "nominal governor," "a prisoner at large . . . wholly in the Power of the People." By late September, he feared that soon even "the appearance of Government will cease; as the real Authority has ever since the first riot." On November 2, Jared Ingersoll in Connecticut wrote that "no one dares and few in power are disposed to punish any violences that are offered to the Authority of the [Stamp] Act," that "all the springs of Government are broken and nothing but Anarchy and Confusion appear in Prospect," while New York's Lieutenant Governor Cadwallader Colden told customs officers that he had "no power beyond the Fort," where he was pent up "expecting every Evening to be attacked by the Mob." Even Georgia's Governor James Wright complained to England that he had "the greatest Mortification to see the Reins of Government nearly hoisted out of my Hands, His Majesties authority Insulted, and the Civil power obstructed."[35] Such conditions fostered an illusion that the Sons

33. Bernard to Lords of Trade, August 22, 1765, PRO, CO 5/891, 551–5; Sharpe to Halifax, Annapolis, September 5, 1765, in William H. Browne, ed., *Correspondence of Governor Horatio Sharpe*: III, *1761–1771*, in *Archives of Maryland*, XIV (Baltimore, 1895), 221; Wentworth to Conway, Portsmouth, February 20, 1765, PRO, CO 5/934, ff. 54–5; Wright to Conway, Savannah, February 7, 1766, PRO, CO 5/658, f. 116.

34. See, for example, John Hughes to customs officers Swift, Barclay, and Gaine, November 5, 1765, PRO, Treas. 1/441; Capt. Charles Leslie to Colville, Rhode Island, September 5, 1765, PRO, Adm. 1/482; Tryon to Conway, February 25, 1766, *N.C. Col. Recs.*, VII, 174.

35. Bernard to Lords of Trade, August 22, 1765, PRO, CO 5/891, 551–5, and Bernard to Conway, September 28, 1765, PRO, CO 5/755, 323–7; Ingersoll to Thomas Whately, November 2, 1765, in Franklin B. Dexter, ed., "A Selection from the Correspondence and Miscellaneous Papers of Jared Ingersoll," *Papers of the New Haven Colony Historical Society*, IX (1918), 352. Collector and Comptroller of Customs at New York to Customs Commissioners, November 4, 1765, PRO, Treas. 1/442, and Wright to Conway, Savannah, January 31, 1766, PRO, CO 5/658, ff. 112–13.

of Liberty constituted a revolutionary movement, grasping for power: Thomas Hutchinson commented in March 1766, for example, that "the authority of every colony is in the hands of the sons of liberty." This juncture of events was not peculiar to America. As Hannah Arendt has suggested, proto-revolutionary movements often display a superficial aura of power and success when they first emerge because they enter a power vacuum.[36]

In fact, however, the purposes of the Sons of Liberty were carefully delimited. They sought to constrain authority and to act for the community only in areas affected by the Stamp Act. They insisted that the Stamp Act not be executed; but even here the organization simply institutionalized trends already apparent in earlier colonial resistance to the act. Where necessary, the Sons of Liberty took on the responsibility for coercing Stamp Act supporters or officers: In February 1766, for example, the Westmoreland County associators promised to go "to any Extremity, not only to prevent the Success" of any attempt against Virginians' fundamental rights "but to stigmatize and punish the Offender," whom they would regard as "the most dangerous Enemy of the Community." The Sons of Liberty assumed leadership, too, of the effort to effect a full resumption of "business as usual" lest, as the Lyme, Connecticut, Sons of Liberty put it, "the delay of business will be construed as implicit acknowledgement of the validity of the Stamp Act." New York's Sons advocated the opening of ports and the issuing of unstamped clearances from November 1765; New London customs officers conformed after being waited upon by the "respectable populace"; and it was primarily to open Cape Fear for shipping that the North Carolina Association was formed. Continuously, meetings demanded "that every Officer in the Colony duly execute the Trust reposed in him" despite the unavailability of stamps; and in Maryland and New Jersey, soon after their formation the Sons of Liberty waited on lawyers and court officials to encourage their proceeding as normal. Often—as again in New London, as well as New York, Bal-

36. Hutchinson to Thomas Pownall, Boston, March 8, 1766, third version, MA, XXVI, 215; Hannah Arendt, *On Revolution* (New York, 1965), 112.

timore, or Sussex, New Jersey—the Sons of Liberty promised to protect government officers from any punishment for disregarding the act.[37]

The Sons of Liberty were ready to answer in kind any effort to enforce the Stamp Act by military action. They vowed repeatedly that they would "not . . . be enslaved by any power on Earth, without opposing force to force."[38] The necessity of coordinating the various colonies' military efforts provided a major impulse toward intercolonial organization, but military organization was not a constant preoccupation of the Sons. Instead, military plans were made or forgotten as the threat of British force seemed imminent or unlikely. The original agreement negotiated at New London between the New York and Connecticut Sons of Liberty in December 1765 was prompted by a report that troops were being sent from England to force American submission to the Stamp Act, and that New York would probably be the first attacked. The written text included an agreement "to march with the utmost dispatch, at their own proper costs and expense, on the first proper notice (which must be signified to them by at least six of the sons of liberty) with their whole force if required . . . to the relief of those that shall, are, or may be in danger from the *stamp act*." Massachusetts

37. Harwell, *Committees of Safety*, 99–100; Lyme Sons of Liberty in *Conn. Gaz.*, January 24, 1766. Duncan Stewart to John Temple, New London, December 19, 1765, PRO, Treas. 1/452; *N.C. Col. Recs.*, VII, 168a–f; account of Baltimore County Sons' meeting, February 24, in *Pa. Jour.*, March 20, 1766; "Proceedings of the Sons of Liberty, March 1, 1766," in Leake, *John Lamb*, 3–4, and *N.J. Col. Docs.*, XXV, 30–1. Protection: resolutions of New York, January 7, *N.Y. Gaz.*, January 9, 1766; New London, December 10, *Conn. Gaz.*, December 27, 1765; Fairfield, Conn., *ibid.*, February 14; Sussex County and Upper Freehold, N.J., *N.J. Col. Docs.*, XXV, 109, 111. Charleston differed somewhat here, with radicals favoring the opening of courts but hoping that, by keeping the port closed, they could pressure the owners of British ships into supporting repeal of the Stamp Act. See Gadsden to William S. Johnson, April 16, 1766, in Walsh, *Gadsden Writings*, 73.

38. On New York circular, February 14, see *n.* 8 above. Also New Hampshire to Boston Sons, February 11, 1766, Belknap Papers, 61.c.112; Freehold, N.J., resolutions, April 2, 1766, *N.J. Col. Docs.*, XXV, 72; New York to Connecticut Sons, February 20, 1766, Lamb Papers.

and New Hampshire entered the Sons' union on the basis of this New London text, but New York's February 14 circular to the South made no mention of a formal military association. The circular spoke generally of opposing force to force, but the newly organized Sons of Liberty were asked to pass only such resolutions as they themselves considered "most efficacious for the preservation of Liberty and perfecting our union." The New London agreement was, however, revived in early April after alarming reports again arrived. Parliament had decided to enforce the Stamp Act and was sending forty-five men-of-war for the task, it was said; Lord Mansfield had ruled in favor of the Stamp Act's legality and, moreover, the Americans' defender, William Pitt, had been sent to the Tower. In a letter of April 3 to Baltimore, the New York Sons urged that the New London text be forwarded "to all the southern governments, with as much dispatch as possible, for we know not how soon we may be put to the test." The effort was nipped in the bud: on April 5, Baltimore answered with news of the Stamp Act's repeal.[39]

The Military Association of the Sons of Liberty indicated to what lengths the colonial radicals were willing to go in resisting the Stamp Act; but even this extreme measure served only to systematize a trend apparent before the organization's first appearance. Already on October 23 Ezra Stiles wrote that three-quarters of Connecticut's men were said to be "ready to take up their Arms for their Liberties: to which they no more question their Right than to their Lands." "Men of Eighty are ready to gird the sword," he reported, and "the very Boys as well as the hardy Rustic are full of fire and at half a Word ready to fight." The colony's leading men were "obliged to throw cold Water, and to use the utmost Address to extinguish and prevent the Flames breaking out." Joseph Allicocke, a prominent New York Son of Liberty, also seemed to think the colonists would march without formal alliances. On November 21—a full month before the New London negotiations—he claimed that a "respectable

39. Bernard to Conway, January 19, 1766, *Fitch Papers*, II, 384–6; on New York circular, see *n*. 8 above; news of early April, 1766, in Stiles, "Stamp Act Notebook," 24; New York to Baltimore Sons, April 3, and Baltimore's answer, April 5, 1766, Lamb Papers.

Body" of New York "Liberty Boys" would have "filed off to the Southward" had rumors of Philadelphia's accepting stamps proven true. Moreover, they would have been reinforced by "a noble Possy of Jersey Folks, besides a succeeding junction of Eastern Lads." His estimates were fully shared by Major Thomas James, who left the colonies in early November, 1765, when the Sons of Liberty's organization was at best rudimentary. "There can be assembled in New York and the Jerseys 50,000 Fighting Men," James told a parliamentary committee, and he had heard that "if any small [British] Force had been used there would have been a General Resistance."[40]

Through all their proceedings the Sons of Liberty insisted that they intended to uphold, not overturn, the established government. We "are not attempting any change of Government," the New Yorkers wrote to the Albany Sons, "—only a preservation of the Constitution." Saving the constitution required that they resist the Stamp Act; but the functioning of government beyond the Stamp Act's enforcement was to be left unimpaired. In effect, the Sons of Liberty were faced with a dual obligation, as Silas Downer of Providence explained: it was essential "that on the one Hand we do not yield the Garden of God, and our Birthrights to the Sons of Ambition, and on the other that . . . in a day of Darkness and Difficulty, we do keep up by all Means in our Power as much of civil Government as all Mankind have ever found absolutely necessary for . . . the purposes of social Life."[41]

By late 1765 the second of Downer's concerns, that of maintaining civil government, seemed the most pressing, and appeared sometimes to obsess the Sons of Liberty as much

40. Stiles to Benjamin Ellery, New Haven, October 23, 1765, Stiles Papers; Allicocke to Lamb, New York, November 21, 1765, Lamb Papers; and James's testimony in BM Add. Mss., 33030 (Newcastle), 84–6. South Carolina Governor Thomas Boone in a letter from New York to Lord Rockingham, November 8, 1765, also noted the Americans' readiness to fight if Britain should try to enforce the Stamp Act with arms. Rockingham Papers, RI-522, Central Library, Sheffield, England.

41. New York to Albany Sons, April 3, 1766, *The American Historian*, I (1876), 148; Downer to New York Sons, Providence, July 21, 1766, RIHS, Peck Mss., III, 3.

or more than that of resisting the Stamp Act. In Baltimore County, for example, the organization dedicated itself to both "the maintenance of order and protection of American Liberty"; and in Annapolis, the Sons of Liberty resolved that they would support and defend to the utmost of their power the established form of government, and that they would aid the civil authorities in executing all laws to which they had assented through their representatives. This excluded support of the Stamp Act as clearly as did the signers of Virginia's Westmoreland Association when they promised "to preserve the Laws, the Peace and good Order of this Colony as far as is consistent with the Preservation of our Constitutional Rights and Liberty." The meeting at Windham, Connecticut, that laid the groundwork for the Sons of Liberty's intra-colony organization there also dedicated itself to the maintenance of government and order; and, just as the Annapolis Sons promised to "suppress all Riots or unlawful Assemblies, tending to the Disturbance of the Public Tranquility, or the Injury of any Individual in his Person or Property," the Sons in Milford, Connecticut, declared their "greatest abhorrence" of lawlessness, and promised to "assist and support the Civil Magistrates in preserving the publick Peace and good Order of this Colony." The Newport Sons of Liberty also declared their determination "to discourage and discountenance all tumultuary and riotous Proceedings, to maintain the Laws, and to preserve Peace and good Order," while the Sons in Piscataway, New Jersey, promised to behave peacefully "in all Cases" and to use their influence more broadly to "Preserve the publick Peace."[42]

Such a goal required that the Sons continue earlier efforts to restrain the possible violence of extra-legal gatherings. Military discipline could contribute to this end, as it had in September 1765 when Connecticut's Jared Ingersoll was forced to resign his commission by a crowd in military formation, and to some extent also at Leedstown, Virginia, where

---

42. *Pa. Jour.*, March 20, 1766; Annapolis resolves in *N.Y. Gaz.*, April 24, 1766; Westmoreland resolves in Harwell, *Committees of Safety*, 99; *Conn. Gaz.*, December 6, 1765, and April 5, 1766; *Newport Mercury*, April 7, 1766; and Piscataway resolves, March 27, 1766, in *N.J. Col. Docs.*, XXV, 63.

a stamp supporter was visited in February 1766 by associators rigidly arranged two abreast in a formation that extended through the town's streets. More often, the Sons turned toward the civil procedures of the state as a model in designing restraints upon extra-legal action. The decision to invoke direct popular coercion of Stamp Act supporters was recognized as a serious one: never were accusations to be accepted, the Litchfield, Connecticut, Sons decided, except "upon the fullest, clearest, and most undeniable Evidence." The innocent were to be protected: on January 7, 1766, the New York Sons resolved against "publishing or propagating any Thing tending to cast an Odium on any Society or Body of Men, or on the private Character of any Person, farther than as he was a Promoter or Abettor of the *Stamp Act*." The Albany Sons of Liberty tried to guarantee respect for such guidelines by an institutional check on mass action: they would countenance no disturbances of the public tranquillity or private peace of any individual, the Sons agreed, without the advice and consent of their president and a majority of their executive committee, or of persons appointed by those officers to lead the membership. Finally, coercion was to be carried out with a calmness and a dignity similar to that of normal, legal judicial proceedings. A delegation sent by the Woodbridge, New Jersey, Sons of Liberty to their stampman was strictly instructed, for example, "that whether said Mr. [William] Coxe resign his commission . . . or not, you do treat him with that complaisance and decorum becoming a gentleman of honour."[43]

Rather than usurp the powers of local magistrates, the Sons of Liberty often worked closely with the regular government of their towns. This was particularly clear in Connecticut where, according to some witnesses, "Ninety Nine Hundredths of the Colony" supported the organization, and where the town meeting offered a lawful vehicle for popular action.

43. Litchfield resolves in Alain C. White, *The History of the Town of Litchfield, Connecticut, 1720–1920* (Litchfield, 1920), 66, 68; New York resolutions in *N.Y. Gaz.*, January 9, 1766; sections A. 3. and A. 5. of Albany "constitution," *The American Historian*, I (1876), 145–6; Woodbridge proceedings, December 28, 1765, in *N.J. Col. Docs.*, XXV, 7.

In many cases, in fact, the Sons acted in a traditional manner as voluntary associations supporting policies officially approved in town meeting. Norwich citizens, for instance, "unanimously agreed . . . in full town meeting . . . that the [town] clerk proceed in all matters relating to his office as usual,—And that the town will save him harmless from all damages that he may sustain thereby." A Wallingford town meeting, assembling on the same day although apparently separately from the Sons of Liberty, imposed a twenty-shilling fine on any inhabitant introducing or using stamped paper. One newspaper account claimed that even New Haven—supposedly a conservative stronghold—had agreed in town meeting that the Stamp Act was unconstitutional "and therefore not binding on the Conscience," and that the courts, magistrates, justices, and other legal practitioners should proceed in business as usual, without stamps.[44] Nor was there any effort to overturn provincial institutions. When the Connecticut Sons found themselves at odds with their governor, who swore to execute the Stamp Act, and with those councillors who supported him, they fought these opponents peacefully and lawfully at the ballot box, nominating their own candidates in what was then an extraordinary political device, a political convention.[45] One of the main grievances of the Virginia Sons of Liberty was the dissolution of their assembly, which they defended as the source of legitimate taxation: both the Westmoreland associators and the Norfolk Sons of Liberty condemned all who would use stamped papers "*unless authorized by the General Assembly.*"[46]

Where disorder was threatened beyond that entailed by the Stamp Act opposition, or where the ability of established magistrates to keep the peace was in doubt, the Sons of Liberty backed their resolutions to assist the civil magistrates

44. Norwich Town Meeting quoted in Frances M. Caulkins, *History of Norwich, Connecticut* (Hartford, 1866), 365; Wallingford meeting reported in *Conn. Gaz.*, January 24, 1766; letter on New Haven Town Meeting of February 3 in *ibid.*, February 7, 1766, and Zara Jones Powers, ed., *New Haven Town Records, 1684–1769, Ancient Town Records*, III (New Haven, 1962), 785–6.

45. Zeichner, *Connecticut's Years of Controversy*, 72–5.

46. Merrill Jensen, *The Founding of a Nation* (Oxford, 1968), 139; *Va. Gaz.* (Purdie and Dixon), April 4, 1766.

with action. In Charleston, it was the Sons of Liberty who dragged disorderly sailors to jail in late 1765. In New York, the Sons' leader, Isaac Sears, cooperated with the royal governor and local magistrates to maintain order in late November, 1765, and the following February the local Sons of Liberty went to great lengths to prevent violence when two merchants purchased stamped customs bonds.[47] Such efforts lay behind the claim made in a May 1766 *Boston Gazette* that the "Sons of Liberty have all along born Testimony against the Violence at first committed by a Rabble, and have distinguished themselves in maintaining Order and a due and regular Execution of the Laws of the Land." "The whole Tendency of the Opposition," the Providence Sons of Liberty claimed, "hathe been in support of good Order and Civility."[48]

[III]

Insofar as the Stamp Act agitation called into question any established authority, it was that of Great Britain. But the only British jurisdiction questioned for the time was that of imposing the Stamp Act. Beyond that area the loyalty of the Sons of Liberty was intact. "Allegiance and the strictest Loyalty is due from the People of the British American Colonies to our Lawful and Most Gracious Sovereign King George the Third," the Newport Sons of Liberty resolved on April 2, 1766; and later they declared that they not only supported "the present happy Establishment of the Protestant Succession in the Illustrious House of Hanover," but they entertained "a strong Sense of the Superior Excellence of the

47. Extract of letter from Charleston, *Boston Gaz.*, *Supplement* January 27, 1766; G. D. Skull, ed., *The Montresor Journals*, NYHS *Colls. for 1881* (New York, 1882), 340; John Holt to Mrs. Benjamin Franklin, February 15, 1766, quoted at length in Morgan, *Stamp Act Crisis*, 250–1. The Sons first tried to deal with the merchants privately, but news of this leaked out and a crowd of 5000 gathered. The Sons then attempted to moderate the mob's anger, but finally found it necessary to side with the merchants against "those of the inferior Sort, who delight in mischief merely for its own sake."

48. *Boston Gaz.*, May 5, 1766; Providence to Boston Sons, Providence, April 16, 1766, RIHS Mss. XII, f. 69.

English Constitution to that of any other Form of Government upon Earth."[49]

Organization had become necessary, the Providence Sons of Liberty claimed, only to support the King's government in the colonies "according to its true form and original texture" against "unjust force and usurpation."[50] But for some Americans these forces of usurpation had a long history. From the 1750's, Americans in England had complained of the "unbounded licentiousness and utter disregard of virtue" in England that seemed to threaten Britain's freedom. This corruption was not new: in Maryland the elder Charles Carroll traced it back to the minority of Robert Walpole, and Newport's Ezra Stiles to the reign of Charles II. In the early 1760's, political events had seemed to indicate that the danger to British liberty was ever more imminent. The replacement of William Pitt, who was admired as a man of "strict Temperance and Frugality," by John, Earl of Bute, who bore the family name of Stuart, was foreboding enough. Then almost immediately Bute concluded the "inglorious" Peace of 1763, conceding, it was thought, too much to France. And worse yet, Bute followed his diplomatic ventures with a domestic excise tax on cider, which entailed a host of new excise commissioners armed with extraordinary prerogative powers, reminiscent of a thankfully bygone era of onerous state power.[51]

Government policies for America also awoke suspicion. Britain's decision to maintain a standing army in the colonies after the Peace of 1763 aroused comment, as did the specter of an American Anglican bishopric, for which plans were reported seriously under way in 1763. What would prevent ecclesiastical courts from following the miter across the ocean? And had not the bishops proven the most ready supporters of Stuart tyranny? Fears of episcopacy were compounded by rumors about the growth of English Catholicism,

49. RIHS Mss., XII, f. 66.

50. Providence to New York Sons, March 24, 1766, Belknap Papers, 61.c.121.

51. Bernard Bailyn, *The Ideological Origins of the American Revolution* (Cambridge, Mass., 1967), 86–92, and the historical narrative in Stiles, "Stamp Act Notebook," 1–15.

which seemed to Boston's Jonathan Mayhew "as great, perhaps . . . as in the reign of Charles or James the second."
Thus it was that the Stamp Act, "a Matter of such prodigious
Consequence, that it must have made an entire Alteration in
the system of Government, throughout the English Dominions," was considered to be in all probability part of a scheme
"more than four Years in growing to Maturity."[52]

Rather than implicate Britain in general in such an attempt
upon American freedom, however, the colonists preferred to
focus their suspicions upon the Grenville ministry that had
drafted the Stamp Act and secured its passage. This distrust
lingered even after Grenville fell from office. In February
1766, the Boston Sons of Liberty were seething with contempt for those "Ministers of the Crown" who were "insidious and inveterate Enemies to his Majesty" and "directed
by no other View than to subvert the Brittish Constitution and
to alienate the Affections of his Majesties faithfull Subjects
in America from his Person and Government." And in April
1766, the Norwich, Connecticut, Sons wrote of their determination "to Risk even our Lives and fortunes in Defending
. . . our Just writes [sic] and Liberties against a Wicked
and trechirus Ministry" which was possessed, the New
Yorkers later said, by "an Unbridged thirst of Dominion."
Loss of office did not necessarily mean loss of influence; and
the possibility remained as late as April, the New York Sons
wrote, that they might yet "be put to the test by that pack
of infernal rascals, Granville [Grenville] and his minions."[53]

British agents in the colonies were also implicated in the
scheme, although during the Stamp Act conflict they were
rarely credited with deep-set maliciousness. Their acts could
be explained by natural, almost institutionalized bureaucratic
tendencies. "Our English Proverb says, *a Place is a continual
Bribe*," the *Boston Gazette* said; ". . . how seldom do we find

52. Jonathan Mayhew, *Popish Idolatry: A Discourse Delivered in
. . . Cambridge . . . May 8, 1765* (Boston, 1765), 50, and *Remarks
on an Anonymous Tract* (London, 1765 [orig. pub., Boston, 1764]),
72–7. *Prov. Gaz.*, August 30, 1766.

53. Boston to New Hampshire Sons, February 13, 1766, Belknap
Papers, 61.c.115; Norwich to Providence Sons, April 12, 1766, RIHS
Mss., XII, f. 68; New York to Providence Sons, April 2, 1766, Lamb
Papers; New York to Baltimore Sons, April 3, 1766, in Leake, *John
Lamb*, 19.

a Man who holds a Place dependent on the Crown, who does
not use all his Influence in Support of the Measures of the
Ministry, however repugnant to Reason and Justice, even
. . . where the most sacred Interests of his Country are concerned." It was unfortunate that Parliament had to rely for
knowledge of the colonies on "the Governors of the Colony,
and other Officers of the Crown, their own Agents," who were,
Samuel Adams feared, too often "captivated by the Smiles
of the Great," or else upon "transient Persons who perhaps
were seeking some profitable Employment."⁵⁴

Even for those who projected a more deep-seated scheme
against American liberties, the King was never implicated.
"We cannot entertain the least suspicion of the paternal affection of our present gracious Sovereign," the Portsmouth Sons
of Liberty wrote in April 1766. Instead, they declared their
dependence upon him "for security from the progress of that
lawless power which certain Enemies of Britain and of Liberty
have artfully attempted to establish." Was not George III
of the "Illustrious House of Hanover," which owed its right
to rule to the Glorious Revolution of 1688, the current heir
of the "Protestant Succession" that had overturned the tyranny
of the Catholic Stuarts? *"He glories in being King of freemen,
and not of slaves,"* "Philoleutherus" wrote in the *Constitutional Courant.* Nothing, the New York Sons of Liberty
claimed, tended more to reinforce the King's authority and
dignity "than a scrupulous Maintenance of all our inherent
rights as British subjects," since there was "more real Dignity
in ruling Freemen than Slaves." Hence resolutions never to
submit to the Stamp Act could be seen as "the most pleas-
ing and convincing proofs of . . . Attachment both to . . .
King and Country—." And as for the King, as the *Courant*
put it, "to shew that we are freemen . . . cannot displease,
but must endear us to him."⁵⁵

For some, the King would have become the ultimate vic-

54. Article from the *York* [England] *Gazette* in *Boston Gaz.*, September 30, 1765; Samuel Adams to John Smith, Boston, "20th 1765,"
in Harry A. Cushing, ed., *The Writings of Samuel Adams* (Boston,
1904–8), I, 57.

55. Portsmouth to Providence Sons, April 10, 1766, Belknap Papers,
61.c.122; *Constitutional Courant* in CSM *Pubs.*, XI (*Trans.*, 1906–7),
426; New York to Middletown, N.J., Sons, April 10, 1766, Lamb
Papers.

tim of whatever conspiracies were afoot. The enemies of
Britain and liberty, it was sometimes said, consisted of England's perennial foes, the French, and their ward, the Stuart
Pretender. Suspicions existed as early as June 1765: along
with the news that the Stamp Act had passed, *Boston Gazette*
readers were told that "French Agents and French Monies
are employed to set on foot Measures that may have a Tendency to alienate the Affections of the Colonies from their
Mother Country," so as to create a situation in which the
French might recover the lands they had lost in the Seven
Years' War. The next February, Christopher Gadsden wrote
that he had always looked upon the Stamp Act "as a Jacobiti-
cal Scheme to alienate the affections of us Americans."[56]

To judge by both their public resolutions and private
correspondence, loyalty to the King was the most significant
bond linking the intercolonial Sons of Liberty. Always, even
in the Military Association signed at New London, the Sons
began by declaring their "most unshaken faith and true
allegiance to his Majesty King *George* the Third." The
Portsmouth Sons of Liberty entered the Connecticut–New
York alliance because, they said, "the same principles of true
Loyalty to his Majesty" resided in their breasts. On this
basis the Bostonians welcomed their accession, as did the
Connecticut Sons of Liberty, who wrote to Portsmouth, "we
rejoyce with a Joy inexpressible, to find you actuated by the
Just Principles of true Loyalty to his Majesty King George."
Moreover, insofar as the colonists' "Spirit of Opposition to
all Arbitrary Measures destructive of the British Constitution" countered French schemes to dismember the empire, it
tended to prevent American independence. The Boston Sons
of Liberty hoped, too, that their opposition to the Stamp Act
would convince the Mother Country that she ought to re-
establish the colonists' rights and privileges, and raise her
child "so that when it comes to be Old, it may not depart from
her."[57]

---

56. *Boston Gaz.*, June 3, 1765; Gadsden to Capt. Burden, February
20, 1766, Dartmouth Papers, D 1778/2/169, and also to William S.
Johnson, Charleston, April 16, 1766, in Walsh, *Gadsden Writings*,
72–4.

57. New London Association in Gordon, *History*, I, 196; Portsmouth
to Boston Sons, February 8, Boston to Portsmouth Sons, February 13;

The conclusion was favorable to Britain. The Parliament and King, who had passed and sanctioned the Stamp Act, had been misled, perhaps by French agents, but more likely by biased British officeholders. "We cherish the most unfeigned loyalty to our rightful sovereign; we have a high veneration for the British parliament," the *Constitutional Courant* had said. "But the wisest of kings may be misled," being dependent for information upon persons "whose interest it is to represent all things to them in false lights; so that it is rather to be admired that they are not oftener misled than they are." Parliaments, too, were "liable to mistakes," even to the extent of taking steps "which, if persisted in, would soon unhinge the whole constitution." The theory had been used to explain the Sugar Act: it was "probable," the *Boston Gazette* speculated in May 1765, "that a certain great Ass[em]bly has been . . . carried away with . . . idle and false Reports" of the potential yield of those new trade regulations, "and so led into Measures, which in the End will prove very detrimental to Great-Britain, as well as her Colonies." After the Stamp Act was passed, the Sons of Liberty referred again to "Parliamentary Error" and spoke of "undeceiving" the King. And just as the Sugar Act did not change the *Boston Gazette*'s faith in the fundamental "Wisdom and Goodness of Parliament," so the assumption continued through 1765 and 1766 that when Parliament discovered that it had been misled on the Stamp Act it would remedy its error. In times past, the Massachusetts General Court claimed, those "zealous advocates for the constitution" in Parliament would compare their acts to Magna Charta, and if any disconsonance was found, repeal their acts. "We have the same confidence in the rectitude of the present parliament."[58]

This discrimination—blaming the King's servants for the Americans' grievances while acquitting the Parliament and,

Connecticut to Portsmouth Sons, March 3, and Boston to Portsmouth Sons, February 10, 1766, in Belknap Papers, 61.c.112, 115, 118, 114.

58. *Constitutional Courant* in CSM *Pubs.*, XI (*Trans.*, 1906–7), 425; *Boston Gaz.*, May 20, 1765; Connecticut to Portsmouth Sons, Norwich, March 3, 1766, Belknap Papers, 61.c.118 ("we need not enlarge upon this Parliamentary Error . . ."), and, on the King, especially Albany to New York Sons, May 24, 1766, Lamb Papers. Also *Boston Gaz.*, January 14, 1765, and, quoting the General Court, October 28, 1765.

with even greater rhetorical emphasis, the King—made the Stamp Act agitation a classic instance of limited forceful resistance. The fundamental authority of the state, as embodied in the monarch, was not contested; and the distinction between this authority and that of individual malefactors was consciously drawn. Should any stamped papers find their way into Connecticut, the Litchfield County Sons of Liberty convention declared, they should be preserved untouched "for His Majesty." In March 1766, the New York Sons of Liberty were angered at one Lieutenant Hallam of His Majesty's ship *Garland*, who had compared the Sons' activities to those of the Scots in 1745. Should Hallam "meet the Resentment of an undeservedly provoked People," it would be his own seeking, they announced. But "while he makes an Assylum of His Majesty's Ship he will be safe; as the SONS OF LIBERTY would to a man join in preserving the Property of their Sovereign, and . . . would carefully avoid every Step that may have a Tendency to any Act of Disloyalty."[59]

Given their fundamental confidence in the British government, the Sons of Liberty not only sought repeal but confidently expected it. When John Adams visited the Loyal Nine on January 15, 1766, he "heard nothing but such Conversation as passes at all Clubbs among Gentlemen about the Times. No Plotts, no Machinations," but instead the Nine "Chose a Committee to make Preparations for grand Rejoicings upon the Arrival of the News of a Repeal of the Stamp Act." For Adams, such confidence seemed premature—"I wish they mayn't be disappointed," he commented. Even while concerting their union with the New Hampshire Sons in mid-February, the Bostonians wrote of "favourable Accounts" from England indicating that the King would relieve his American subjects, restore their rights, "and frustrate the pernicious Designs of false Politicks"; and in Norwich, Connecticut, too, the Sons of Liberty exulted in the "favourable Hope . . . of speedy Deliverance from our Tyrannical Oppression." In Charleston, Christopher Gadsden, in his own special style, expressed the same expectation. "Our affection to our *dear* Mother Country tis impossible to alienate and

59. White, *History of Litchfield*, 68; letter in *N.Y. Gaz.*, March 27, 1768.

turn into absolute hatred all at once," he wrote an English correspondent; "we have therefore generally flattered ourselves that as the Stamp Act was . . . very precipitately and inconsiderately enter'd into[,] your Bowels would again Yearn over us as Brethren and Nature compel you to . . . repeal the dreadful Sentence."[60]

Not even adverse rumors in April undermined this confidence. Although on April 4 the Bostonians forwarded to Providence reports that Britain had decided to enforce the act, they also expressed hopes that they could "congratulate you before the middle of next Week that our most gracious Sovereign has been pleas'd to relieve his American Subjects" of oppression and restore their rights and privileges. A congress of Sons of Liberty proposed by the New Yorkers in April was to be held only if Great Britain should finally decide to enforce the Stamp Act; and even Boston's more modest proposal for a "Union of Writers" was so phrased that the news of repeal made it seem as unnecessary as the congress. The writers' union, which was originally to continue indefinitely, was meant "to prevent the Cunning and Artifice of some designing Men who perhaps may attempt some other Method . . . to enslave us" once the Stamp Act was defeated and colonial unity dissolved. The New York Sons endorsed the plan to prevent the colonies from falling "an easy prey to our common enemy, viz. a Corrupt Ministry."[61]

When news of repeal at first arrived, it seemed part of so total a reform that no such lurking suspicions could be justified. Not only was the Stamp Act repealed, it was soon learned, but also the English Cider Act, sometimes seen as England's domestic counterpart of the Stamp Act. Moreover, it was said that the Acts of Trade relating to America would be reconsidered "and all Grievances removed." On June 13, the London merchants announced not only that legislation to

60. Butterfield, *Adams Diary*, I, 294; Boston to New Hampshire Sons, February 13, and Connecticut to New Hampshire Sons, March 3, 1766, Belknap Papers, 61.c.115, 118; Gadsden to Capt. Burden, February 20, 1766, Dartmouth Papers, D 1778/2/169.

61. Boston letter in RIHS Mss., XII, f. 67; New York to Boston Sons, April 2, 1766, Lamb Papers; Boston to Providence Sons, April 4, 1766, RIHS Mss., XII, f. 67.

repeal certain duties and create free ports in Jamaica and Dominica had been passed on the "liberal principles of reciprocal advantage" that the colonies had advocated, but that steps were being taken on "a scheme for a general paper currency through America, which has been proposed to the administration." The Rhode Islanders were told by their agent "that every Grievance" of which they had complained was "Absolutely and totally removed."[62]

The tidings indicated that America had friends in the British government, such as William Pitt "and the noble band of PATRIOTS who joined him in Support of the Cause of America," who understood the colonists' effort. "They insisted," the *Pennsylvania Journal* reported, "that we had shewn a Spirit of *Liberty*, not of Sedition, that we had not the most distant Thoughts of assuming an Independency on our Parent Country." Pitt had gone so far as to say he rejoiced that America had resisted, since "Three millions of people, so dead to all the feelings of liberty as voluntarily to consent to be slaves, would have been fit instruments to make slaves of the rest." "Friends to America" were "very powerful," Ezra Stiles noted, "and disposed to assist us to the utmost of their Ability"; and even more significant, the greater part of Britain seemed to share in the colonies' triumph. "The People of G[reat] Britain and Ireland, the Ministry, the Parliament, King, Lords and Commons, have all approved our Cause, have stood in Defence of our just Rights, and repeal'd the oppressive Acts," John Holt announced in his newly renamed *New York Journal*. And their assent made it all the more certain that the acts had been originally passed "by Means of Surprise and Misrepresentation, and therefore ought to be ascribed wholly to a Faction, not to the People or Legislature of Great-Britain, who have deliver'd us from Oppression, and preserved us from Slavery and Ruin." The downfall of Grenville was apparently complete, and his

62. *S.C. Gaz.*, June 16, 1766; Stiles, "Stamp Act Notebook," 42; London merchants' letter, June 13, in *Newport Mercury*, September 1, 1766; Joseph Sherwood to Governor and Company of Rhode Island, [England,] May 15, 1766, in Gertrude Selwyn Kimball, ed., *The Correspondence of the Colonial Governors of Rhode Island, 1723–1775*, II (Boston and New York, 1903), 384.

principles, too, it seemed, had been "sufficiently canvassed" and discarded, such that it could be hoped "there never may be Occasion to agitate such Matters again."[63]

Once these reports had arrived, the New York Sons of Liberty publicly announced that they had "the greatest inducements to believe, that the Colonies will never more be threaten'd with such a Fetter, as an Act so mischievously calculated to bereave its Inhabitants of their darling *Liberty*." Among the people, William Brattle wrote Lord Dartmouth on June 4, "the only contention . . . is who hath the greatest gratitude" for repeal. It was the Sons of Liberty who spread the news by their carefully organized communication routes,[64]

63. "American MONITOR," No. 1, *Pa. Jour.*, May 8, 1766; Pitt reported in *Newport Mercury*, May 5, 1766; Stiles, "Stamp Act Notebook," John Holt in *N.Y. Gaz.*, May 29, 1766.

64. New York circular, May 31, 1766, and Brattle letter in Dartmouth Papers, D 1778/2/202, 205.

The news of repeal first arrived in Maryland and was sent north along Sons of Liberty communications channels in two successive waves. The first began in late March when a vessel from Cork brought a letter from London of late January that prematurely announced "every Thing relating to the Affairs of America" had been settled and the Stamp Act repealed. This ship stopped at Oxford, whence the news was spread by "A Gentleman from Maryland" to Philadelphia, where John Lamb was visiting. Lamb sent the news north on March 24; it arrived in New York on the evening of the twenty-fifth and was forwarded to Jonathan Sturges at Fairfield, Connecticut, with the request that it be dispersed among his neighboring counties. (Sons of Liberty at New York to Sturges, March 25, 1766, Lamb Papers.) On March 29, the *Conn. Gaz.* at New Haven published Lamb's letter of the twenty-fourth. Ezra Stiles recorded in his "Stamp Act Notebook" (p. 24) that the news of repeal arrived in Newport on April 1. "The Sons of Liberty forwarded it in Twenty hours to New York from Philadelphia," he noted.

Another vessel, this one from London, arrived in Maryland in early April, bringing a letter from "Messrs. R. and I. Days, eminent merchants in London," who congratulated a Maryland correspondent on the Stamp Act's repeal, which, they wrote, "thanks to God is just now resolved here by a great majority in Parliament." The Baltimore Sons of Liberty immediately assembled and ordered their committee to send an express to Philadelphia, from which the news was to be forwarded to New York. (Baltimore to New York Sons, April 5, 1766, Lamb Papers, and Leake, *John Lamb*, 27.) The arrival of the Baltimore express on the previous Sunday was noted in the *Pennsylvania Journal* of April 10. The news reached New York, since Baltimore's

and they played a prominent part in the repeal celebrations
of 1766, just as they arranged the celebrations of its anniversary in many communities during the years to come.[65]
Always the pageants and the toasts at the repeal celebrations
stressed the colonists' exuberant loyalty to Great Britain;
and sometimes, as at Providence and Charleston, they were
held on the King's birthday.[66] Everywhere, stringent efforts
were made to organize the celebrations so as to prevent

---

letter survives among the Lamb Papers, and its arrival from "the
western Sons of Liberty" was noted in the *Connecticut Gazette*, April
12. Meanwhile, the Baltimore Sons' announcement arrived independently at Newport on April 12 by a ship from Philadelphia, and
was forwarded to Boston, where the Sons of Liberty sent Thomas
Edes to Portsmouth with the news on April 13. (Boston to Portsmouth Sons, April 13, 1766, Belknap Papers 61.c.123.) The news
was, then, sent from Baltimore to Portsmouth in a little over a week.
The news was contradicted, however, by a report that England had
decided to enforce the act. When final confirmation arrived in May,
the Sons of Liberty again spread the news. On May 17, Ezra Stiles
wrote in his "Stamp Act Notebook" (p. 30), "Glorious News of the
Repeal arrived here [at Newport] Yesterday XI.h.30' before Noon it
came to Boston by Mr. Hancocks Ship being the first Vessel sent last
fall without Stamps. The Sons of Lib[ert]y at Bo[ston] sent an Express to Sou[th], and Newport, w[hi]c[h] set off at I PM reached
Bristol Ferry at IIh. at night and arrived in Newport VIh.30' this
morning but concealed the News till the printer dispersed Hand Bills.
The Bells rang all Day. Royal Assent given 18 March." This account
was confirmed in the *Newport Mercury*, May 19. The Boston Sons of
Liberty also sent a "Confirmation of the Repeal of the Stamp Act," on
May 19, to the Portsmouth Sons (Belknap Papers, 61.c.127).
    65. See, for example, the account of repeal celebrations at Boston,
where selectmen set the date for celebrations but the "pageants" and
fireworks were arranged by the Sons of Liberty as a group and by
private individuals, especially John Hancock, in *Boston Gaz.*, May 26,
1766. In Newport, the Sons appointed the day and planned the celebrations: see *Newport Mercury*, May 19 and 26, 1766. In Philadelphia,
"an active son of liberty" announced the news of repeal, but the "inhabitants" organized the celebrations; see *Pa. Jour.*, May 22, 1766.
Christopher Gadsden's Artillery Company was prominent among the
Charleston celebrants: see *S.C. Gaz.*, June 9, 1766.
    66. *Prov. Gaz.*, August 9, 1766; *S.C. Gaz.*, June 9, 1766. See also
account of Boston celebrations, *Boston Gaz.*, May 26, 1766: "All was
Loyalty to the King, Blessings on the Parliament of Great-Britain,
Honour and Gratitude to the Present Ministry, and Love and Affection
to the Mother-Country."

disorder that might discredit America's "Friends at Home" who had "ventured to declare for us that we had Prudence enough to temper our Joy with Discretion on this Occasion."[67] "Any disorderly Behaviour would dishonour the Day, and disgrace the Government," a letter in the *Newport Mercury* announced. "Now [that] the detested Object of our Resentment is buried (never, I hope, to rise again) let us bury with it every animosity and cultivate Love and Friendship," that writer suggested, and "especially endeavour to conciliate and secure the Esteem and Affection of our Parent State—On this our Happiness greatly depends."[68]

With repeal, the Sons of Liberty movement dissolved, and nowhere more self-consciously and significantly than where it had begun—in New York. There the Sons embodied even more intensely the enthusiasm that characterized their fellows elsewhere, calling on their colleagues to "vie with each other" to find "who can with Decency be most thankful." "If hereafter any attempts should be made to deprive us of our invaluable Freedom, or Religious Rights," they promised "not [to] be backward in joining . . . with Hearts and Hands to oppose such Measures"; but they were confident that such an event "cannot happen in our Day." Whereupon this organization—the linchpin of continental union, the group that more than any other had created the intercolonial Sons of Liberty, and had most recently suggested a Sons' national congress and endorsed the Boston proposal for a "Union of

67. "American MONITOR," No. 1, *Pa. Jour.*, May 8, 1766, and letter from *Pa. Gaz.* reprinted in *Newport Mercury*, May 26, calling for "the avoidance of every Appearance of Indelecacy" in part as "INTEREST may demand it." London merchants had written the colonists that reports of American violence had made the work of gaining repeal more difficult. More violence, they warned, would mean America's friends "must certainly lose all power to serve you," and the Americans' "taxmasters" would probably be restored and "such a train of ill consequences follow" as would be easier for the colonists to imagine than the merchants to describe. See London Merchants' Committee to Abraham Redwood and other Newport merchants, in *Newport Mercury*, May 12, 1766.

68. *Newport Mercury*, May 26, 1766, and also account of Boston celebrations, *Boston Gaz.*, May 26: "every Thing" was conducted with "the utmost Decency and good Order, not a Reflection cast on any Character, nor the least Disorder during the whole Scene."

Writers"—voluntarily dissolved.[69] In a sense, their action represented a final act of compliance with the opposition directives published in Holt's *New York Gazette* the previous November: "as soon as the Grand Design of their Meeting is fully answer'd, and security given that the Stamp-Act shall not be executed," the extra-legal assemblies should "immediately . . . dissolve—and let Government go on in its usual Forms."[70] The Sons of Liberty had formed as an effort of limited forceful resistance, seeking, as they had vehemently declared, only to nullify the Stamp Act and defend their liberties. With repeal they had achieved their objective to most members' satisfaction, so the organization disbanded. On their terms, there was no reason why it should ever be revived.

69. A letter to Nicholas Ray, New York's representative on the London Merchants' Committee, October 10, 1766, announced "the dissolution of our society, which happened immediately upon the repeal of the Stamp Act." It was signed by six individuals—Isaac Sears, Edward Laight, Flores Bancker, John Lamb, Charles Nicoll, and Joseph Allicocke, "in behalf of the Sons of Liberty"; Leake, *John Lamb*, 36.

70. *N.Y. Gaz.*, November 14, 1765; *Boston Gaz.*, December 2, 1765.

CHAPTER FIVE

RESISTANCE
IN TRANSITION,
1767–1770

REPEAL OF THE STAMP ACT did not, of course, finally resolve the Anglo-American conflict. Colonial opposition reawoke in part over the New York Restraining Act, but above
all over the Townshend Revenue Act of 1767.[1] Never again,
however, did the Americans relapse to the consternation of
1765 when they had lamented that "no similar Examples from
former Times" existed to guide them.[2] Colonists now simply

1. Both laws posed threats to colonial assemblies. The Restraining
Act suspended the power of the New York Assembly until it complied with a Quartering Act of 1765, which required colonial legislatures to supply British troops within their provinces with specified
articles. Colonists argued that this amounted to a tax imposed by
Parliament, and was therefore as unacceptable as the Stamp Act. The
Townshend Revenue Act of 1767 was opposed because the new duties
it levied on tea, lead, paper, and painters' colors were also considered
taxes and because the revenue raised under the act would be used to
pay the salaries of provincial judges and other royal officials who had
previously been dependent upon provincial assemblies for their liveli-
hoods. Writs of assistance were, moreover, sanctioned by the Townshend Act, and these were considered another violation of English
liberty because they gave customs officials broad authority to search
for contraband on mere suspicion of wrongdoing. The Restraining
Act never went fully into effect, so opposition efforts were aimed
primarily at the Townshend Act.
2. Jonathan Mayhew, *The Snare Broken* (Boston, 1766), 17–18;
editor's comments in *N.Y. Gaz.*, November 28, 1765.

revived and developed the tactics first evolved during the Stamp Act crisis and articulated by the Sons of Liberty. It was clear that legitimate resistance must involve the body of the people, must prefer peaceful over violent forms of action, and must confine whatever force was necessary within defined limits. Yet even as these limitations upon agitation were honored, colonial resistance moved beyond the model of 1765–6 toward a more serious threat to British authority as nonimportation associations increasingly assumed the functions of civil government. The portents of revolution in the final months of the Townshend agitation reflected, moreover, an important corrosion of that ultimate faith in British rule which had characterized the Stamp Act resistance, and which had survived even into the opening years of opposition to the Townshend Act.

[I]

In 1766, Jonathan Mayhew already grasped the potential significance of the Stamp Act resistance. Should a similar occasion recur, he said, the colonists' "late experience and success will teach them how to act in order to obtain the redress of grievances." He referred to the peaceful methods gradually settled upon in the course of the Stamp Act agitation: "joint, manly and spirited, yet respectful and loyal petitioning," backed up by commercial sanctions. The strategy of petition and nonimportation reappeared a year later in John Dickinson's "Letters from a Farmer in Pennsylvania." First published between December 1767 and February 1768, the Farmer's Letters rallied colonists against the new British legislation and more than any other source defined guidelines for the Americans' subsequent opposition to Britain. All "excesses and outrages" were condemned by Dickinson in 1767 just as they had been in 1766 by Mayhew. To talk of defending rights as if they could be upheld only by arms or by riots and tumults was "as much out of the way," Dickinson said, "as if a man having a choice of several roads to reach his journey's end, should prefer the worst for no other reason but because it *is* the worst." Free men should be spirited, ready to maintain their rights; but such efforts should for the time be channeled into "constitutional methods of seeking Redress," such as petitions or nonimportation, modes of opposition proposed as conscious alternatives to violence.[3]

Accordingly, the colonists first petitioned Britain for relief from the Townshend Revenue Act. But during 1769, as it became clear that their petitions were unsuccessful, Americans gradually united behind nonimportation agreements similar to those already initiated in New England and New York. There were, however, significant local variations in the various nonimportation associations. In the Northern and middle colonies, merchants alone formed the covenant; while in the plantation colonies, which lacked so pre-eminent a commercial class, broader-based public bodies endorsed the agreements. A Williamsburg conclave of members of the House of Burgesses with various local traders and merchants concluded Virginia's nonimportation agreement of May 18, 1769, and North Carolina's agreement was similarly adopted the following November by an extra-legal meeting of assemblymen. Public meetings in Georgia and South Carolina endorsed nonimportation agreements, while Maryland's association of June 22, 1769, was adopted by a meeting of delegates from associations already formed in the various counties of that colony. The lists of goods proscribed for importation also varied from colony to colony, and in the South agreements tended to emphasize nonconsumption more than nonimportation.[4]

3. Mayhew, *Snare Broken*, 27, 34, 37–9; John Dickinson, "Letters from a Farmer in Pennsylvania," in Forrest McDonald, ed., *Empire and Nation* (Englewood Cliffs, N.J., 1962), 15–20. On the reception of the "Farmer's Letters," see David L. Jacobson, *John Dickinson and the Revolution in Pennsylvania 1764–1776* (Berkeley and Los Angeles, 1965), 55–7.

4. Charles M. Andrews, "The Boston Merchants and the Non-Importation Movement," CSM *Pubs.*, XIX (*Trans.* 1916–18), 215–21; Arthur M. Schlesinger, *The Colonial Merchants and the American Revolution* (New York, 1968), 104–49. The failure of previous petitions is noted, for example, in the preamble to the South Carolina Resolutions of July 22, 1769, in Andrews, "Boston Merchants," 218, and in Philadelphia to Boston merchants' committee, June 7, 1769, Sparks Mss., XLII, Vol. 7, p. 193, HUL.

Where the old Sons of Liberty organizations reappeared in 1769 and 1770, they did so as fervent supporters of nonimportation. The New York Sons of Liberty reorganized themselves in July 1769 to support the nonimportation agreement concluded there almost a year earlier. The Charleston mechanics, who had constituted that town's Sons of Liberty in 1765–6, spearheaded South Carolina's agreement along with their old spokesman Christopher Gadsden. These same groups, moreover, continued to champion nonimportation even after April 1770 when Parliament repealed all of the Townshend duties except that on tea. Cornelius Harnett reorganized the Sons of Liberty at Wilmington, North Carolina, in June 1770 to support the strict maintenance of the nonimportation agreement; and when New York merchants decided to resume importing in July, thus undermining the movement, they had to contend with the strenuous opposition of the Sons of Liberty, led by John Lamb, Isaac Sears, and now also Alexander McDougall.[5]

Nonimportation was thus the successor of the Stamp Act resistance. Besides the familiar names, continuity was evident in strategy, such as the nonimporters' concern for widening their base of support throughout the population. In the South, this goal was often explicit from the outset: Virginia's association of May 18, 1769, for example, invited "all Gentlemen, Merchants, Traders, and other Inhabitants of this Colony" to sign subscription lists. In the Northern colonies, however, the nonimportation associations only gradually involved the nonmercantile population. Massachusetts developments illustrated the slow widening of the movement. The original Boston agreement of March 1768 was drafted and signed only by merchants. In the fall of 1769, however, merchants circulated another subscription paper through the town, asking other inhabitants to pledge not to purchase goods imported

5. Roger J. Champagne, "The Sons of Liberty and the Aristocracy in New York Politics 1765–1790," unpublished Ph.D. dissertation, University of Wisconsin, 1960, 207, 249–75; broadside on New York Sons' July 7, 1769, meeting, Evans 11379; Richard Walsh, *Charleston's Sons of Liberty* (Columbia, 1959), 45–50; R. D. W. Connor, *Cornelius Harnett* (Raleigh, 1909), 55–8, and reports on the North Carolina Sons of Liberty in *S.C. Gaz.*, July 5 and August 9, 1770.

contrary to the association and to support patriotic traders. By December of that year, organizers were summoning "Merchants and all others who are any Ways concerned in, or connected with Trade," to assemblies which, the lieutenant governor reported, were "as numerous as a Town meeting and consisted of much the same sort of people." The merchants remained central in the movement, as Samuel Adams recognized in 1770 when he accepted a letter from Charleston to the Boston Sons of Liberty, but found it was meant for "the Trade," with which he was "not connected, but as an Auxiliary in their Nonimportation Agreement." These large public meetings afforded an opportunity, however, for non-merchants, such as those who were currently signing letters as the Boston Sons of Liberty, to thrust themselves into influence: men like Josiah Quincy, Jr., James Otis, Dr. Thomas Young, or Samuel Adams himself. Support for nonimportation also spread beyond Boston. By April 1770, Thomas Hutchinson estimated that the representatives of seven-eighths of the provincial towns favored the agreement, and that "the majority of every order of men in government" had united with "the body of the people" on that issue.[6]

Popularity meant that nonimporters could often work through established political institutions. The Boston Town Meeting, for example, not only took steps to encourage domestic manufacturing but proscribed men who violated the association. In other communities, too, lawful town meetings passed resolutions supporting the association. Even provincial legislatures intervened: the Connecticut, New Jersey, and New York assemblies all passed resolutions commending nonimportation supporters. Such action by official institutions naturally gave the ad hoc associations stronger claims to legitimacy.[7]

6. Virginia Association in Julian P. Boyd, ed., *The Papers of Thomas Jefferson*, I (Princeton, 1950), 29; notice for Boston meeting of December 28, 1769, and Lt. Gov. Thomas Hutchinson to Lord Hillsborough, January 24, April 27 and 19, 1770, in Sparks Manuscripts: X, Papers Relating to New England (henceforth "New England Papers"), III, ff. 61, 64, 79, 74, HUL; Samuel Adams to Peter Timothy, Boston, November 21, 1770, in Harry A. Cushing, ed., *The Writings of Samuel Adams* (New York, 1904–8), II, 64.

7. *Reps. R. C. C. B.*, XVI, 239–40, 264, 289–90, 297–8, and ac-

The effort to unite the people against Britain's "unconstitutional" legislation encouraged also the creation of popular institutions where none had previously existed. The virtues of the New England town meeting for "uniting the whole body of the people in the measures taken to oppose the Stamp Act induced other Provinces to imitate their example," Philadelphia's Charles Thomson later testified. Large public meetings provided important support for nonimportation in New York and Philadelphia. But the most striking effort to create in the resistance organization a surrogate for the New England town meeting emerged in Charleston, which remained unincorporated until 1783, hence had no central municipal institutions during the colonial period. What began there in 1768 as meetings of the "MECHANICS and many other inhabitants of this town" to encourage South Carolina's entrance into the nonimportation movement grew through the absorption of other economic groups until it emerged in September 1769 as a "General Meeting of INHABITANTS . . . at LIBERTY TREE" not only to discuss measures for the "strict Observance" of the nonimportation resolutions but, further, "to consider of other Matters for the General Good." In 1770, the South Carolinians sought to hold meetings as "*full* . . . as possible" so that their resolutions could be announced as "*the Sense of the Whole Body.*"[8]

At the outset of the nonimportation effort, economic considerations encouraged widespread participation. A commercial depression afflicted the continent. Colonists suffered in part from a scarcity of hard currency, which, they said, had been drained from America by customs payments. New Englanders were particularly aware that trade law reform and economic retrenchment were necessary for recovery. In the South, nonimportation conferred an additional benefit, as

---

count of October 4, 1769, meeting in New England Papers, III, f. 37. Andrews, "Boston Merchants," 206, 213–14, 234–6; Schlesinger, *Colonial Merchants*, 125.

8. Thomson to David Ramsay, New York, November 4, 1786, in "The Papers of Charles Thomson," NYHS *Colls. for 1878* (New York, 1879), 218–19. Walsh, *Charleston's Sons of Liberty*, 45–50; and for a particularly graphic picture of the evolution of the Charleston meeting, *S.C. Gaz.*, June 8, 29, July 6, 13, 27, and August 31, 1769.

George Washington understood, for it gave debt-ridden planters an honorable excuse for cutting back upon extravagant display.⁹ Meanwhile merchants could use the curtailment of imports to reduce their inventories of less desirable goods. Yet by late 1769 it had become clear that the association involved—as the town of Abington, Massachusetts, expressed it—"self-denial and public virtue" more than self-indulgence. Even artisans, who might have gained by the new emphasis upon domestic manufacturing, frequently suffered. Too often their trades depended upon imported materials, while occasional public efforts to support American manufacturing were for the most part limited to the production of essential articles such as paper or cloth.¹⁰

The enduring arguments for nonimportation were, then, above all political. It offered the "wisest and only peaceable method" for Americans to recover their liberty, one, moreover, that was legal and seemed to promise success. As during the Stamp Act crisis, colonists argued that economic retrenchment would awaken the attention of British traders such that "they would see, they would feel, the oppressions we groan under, and exert themselves to procure Us redress." Nonimportation might also result in large masses of unemployed Englishmen who, were the Americans' grievances not redressed, "would raise such a disturbance at home as would endanger the heads and necks of those great men who were the promoters of them." In short, if nonimportation was strictly observed, it was said, it could not help but be effectual.¹¹

9. Andrews, "Boston Merchants," 181–9; Washington to George Mason, Mount Vernon, April 5, 1769, in John C. Fitzpatrick, ed., *The Writings of George Washington* (Washington, 1931–44), II, 502–3.

10. Abington quoted in Andrews, "Boston Merchants," 214, *n*. 1. Note, for example, Thomas Hutchinson's observation that local tradesmen were "destitute of works" but still ardent for nonimportation, in a letter to Hillsborough, January 24, 1770, New England Papers, III, f. 64. For a portrait of one artisan's plight, see Richard Walsh, "Edmund Egan—Charleston's Rebel Brewer," *South Carolina Historical Magazine*, XVI (1955), 200–4.

11. "A Member of the GENERAL COMMITTEE" [John Mackenzie] and "A Member of the Assembly . . ." [Christopher Gadsden] in William Henry Drayton, *Letters of Freeman* (London, 1771), 111, 141–2; George Mason to George Washington, April 5, 1769, in Kate Mason

The claims for effectiveness were never disproven in the period through 1770. The movement's disintegration indicated only that any future nonimportation association would have to be more carefully designed—preferably with one identical plan for all the colonies—and less dependent upon the merchants than its predecessor. Even though the associations of 1768–70 were "drawn up in a hurry and formed upon erroneous principles," they had, it was said, forced the partial repeal of the Townshend duties. Total relief, it was insisted, could have been won had nonimportation been persisted in a little longer. Hence there was justification enough for the Continental Congress to revive the policy in 1774.[12]

The notion that nonimportation afforded a peaceful and legal means to redress did, however, come into question. Proponents considered nonimportation peaceful in that it was nonviolent. But force was not condemned in general; even the docile John Dickinson considered the resort to forceful resistance in 1765, when there was no alternative but submission to the Stamp Act, "prudent and glorious." Admittedly, force was "always to be the very last means thought of, when every things else fails," and as of 1768 and 1769 it seemed possible to avoid it. Furthermore, the political liabilities of violence continued to be stressed; forcible resistance and other acts "contrary to the strictest peace and good order" would be "productive only of the greatest misery and confusion" and do "infinitely more mischief than good," as Christopher Gadsden emphasized. The Americans' problem, Dickinson said,

---

Rowland, *The Life of George Mason* (New York, 1892), I, 142; "Narrative of Occurrences at Boston" for April 20, 1770, New England Papers, III, f. 76.

12. "Cato," "Landowner," "A Farmer," and "Issacher" in *New London Gaz.*, October 5, 26, and November 2, 1770, and February 8, 1771. "Libertas et Natale Solum," *S.C. Gaz.*, *Supplement* August 20, 1770; George Mason to a young relative in England, Virginia, December 6, 1770, in Rowland, *George Mason*, I, 148–9. London informants encouraged this view: see William Palfrey's journal entry, March 20, 1771, in John G. Palfrey, "Life of William Palfrey," in Jared Sparks, ed., *The Library of American Biography*, 2nd Ser., VII (Boston, 1845), 376, and Henry Marchant to Ezra Stiles, London, September 5, 1771, in Ezra Stiles Papers, Beinecke Library, Yale University, New Haven, Connecticut.

was like that of "pushing a Vessel against a strong stream. Over hasty zeal, will infallibly hurt us; and on the other hand, if we indolently intermit our efforts for a moment, we shall be hurried down the current."[13]

Once again, as during the Stamp Act period, those who ignored or violated the patriotic agreements were coerced by social and economic boycotts which became harsher as the movement itself gained strength and intensity. The original Boston merchants' agreement of March 1768 provided only that signatories would "give a constant preference" to subscribers in making purchases. Such a mild proscription quickly gave way in New York to a total boycott of merchants who failed to honor the association, and within two years several associations also branded importers as enemies to their country, who should be treated with contempt. In January 1770, the Bostonians themselves voted to withhold "for ever hereafter . . . not only all commercial Dealings, but every Act and Office of Common Civility" from four men who had proven "obstinate and inveterate Enemies to their Country." Smaller communities followed—ostracism of nonimportation opponents was endorsed, for example, in Lancaster, Pennsylvania, where supporters of the agreement promised "never [to] have any fellowship or correspondence" with people who purchased or imported British goods contrary to the association and to "publish his or their names to the world . . . as a lasting monument of infamy." Whole colonies might be indicted: when Georgia failed to enforce its agreement, patriots in Charleston resolved that the colony ought "to be amputated from the rest of their brethren, as a rotten part that might spread a dangerous infection"; and attempts in Providence and Newport to withdraw from the agreement in May 1770 were cut short after New York, Philadelphia, and Boston imposed an

13. Dickinson, "Farmer's Letters," in McDonald, *Empire and Nation*, 16; [Gadsden] in Drayton, *Letters of Freeman*, 132, and as "Pro Grege et Rege" in *S.C. Gaz.*, June 22, 1769, and Richard Walsh, ed., *The Writings of Christopher Gadsden 1746–1805* (Columbia, 1966), 81. See also Mason to Richard Henry Lee, June 7, 1770, in Rowland, *George Mason*, I, 144 ("we must avoid even the appearance of violence"). Dickinson to Richard Henry Lee, January 16, 1769, in Richard Henry Lee, *Memoir of the Life of Richard Henry Lee* (Philadelphia, 1825), I, 69.

absolute boycott on Rhode Island merchants. A mass of resolutions to boycott New York was also passed after that city finally defected from the movement in 1770.[14]

The architects of nonimportation hoped that the movement could remain peaceful and still be effective. By publishing the names of those who violated the agreement or patronized violators as enemies of their country and greeting them with "every mark of infamy and reproach," Virginia's George Mason argued, associators could effectively play upon men's "sense of shame and fear of reproach." Self-interest could also serve the association if the colony's principal people would "renounce all connection and commerce forever with such merchants, their agents and factors." The Maryland Association contained an elaborate provision against renting, selling, or allowing importers to use storehouses "or any kind of Place whatever, belonging to us" for selling, securing, or landing imported goods. In South Carolina, too, associators denied nonsubscribers the use of their wharves and refused to purchase their rice, indigo, or other plantation products. Economic sanctions alone were apparently effective there. Some association opponents were menaced, Lieutenant Governor William Bull reported; but when "after a little cool reflection" men submitted, it was not so much for fear of violence as of "a torrent of popular Opinion or perhaps resentment." A public opponent of the agreement, William Wragg, also admitted that those who were "indirectly forced to subscribe" were impelled by economic pressure. Their refusal to conform, he claimed, "must have made them useless members of society and objects of charity." More direct intimidation came only from the "indiscreet Zeal" of individuals and was by no means characteristic of the nonimporters as a whole.[15]

Nonviolence was rarely if ever a passive achievement. In Boston, active efforts to contain popular exuberance were as

14. Andrews, "Boston Merchants," 201, 207, 212, 219, and 220, *n.* 3; Boston resolutions, January 23, 1770, in New England Papers, III, f. 62.

15. Mason to Richard Henry Lee, June 7, 1770, in Rowland, *George Mason*, I, 144; Maryland Association, June 22, 1769, in *Maryland Historical Magazine*, III (Baltimore, 1908), 147; Bull to Hillsborough, Charleston, March 6 and October 20, 1770, PRO, CO 5/393, ff. 22, 119; Wragg in Drayton, *Letters of Freeman*, 205.

necessary as they had been during the Stamp Act agitation. As early as 1767, Thomas Hutchinson understood that those who had been "very forward" in promoting the tumults of 1765 had decided to use other means against the Townshend duties. Mobbish incidents were successfully avoided that year, even when the new American customs commissioners, appointed as part of Charles Townshend's reorganization of the customs service, happened to arrive in the midst of Pope's Day celebrations. An incendiary letter found posted on Liberty Tree was answered in town meeting by James Otis, a Son of Liberty. "To insult and tear each other in pieces was to act like madmen," Otis argued. Bostonians should behave like men and use the "proper and legal measures to obtain redress," that is, "humble and dutiful petitions and remonstrances,", which would "sooner or later be heard and meet with success, if supported by justice and reason." During the reign of Charles I, he claimed, Englishmen waited fifteen years for their petitions to be heard before resorting to force. And during the Glorious Revolution of 1688, "there were no tumults or disorder." Even "when the whole city of London was in motion, only a single silver spoon was stolen," and the people so resented that lapse that they hanged the thief. "Let this be the language of all," articles in the *Boston Gazette* pleaded: "no mobs, no confusions, no tumults." The cause of liberty was not to be disgraced "by a single rash step, for constitutional methods are the best. . . ."[16]

The efforts of Boston leaders to maintain peace continued into 1768. Effigies that appeared on Liberty Tree the morning of March 18—the anniversary of the Stamp Act's repeal—were taken down by William Speakman, Thomas Crafts, and John Avery, Jr. Crafts and Avery had been members of the Loyal Nine, which had met in Speakman's distillery. Rumors of an insurrection had circulated for days beforehand, Hutchinson wrote, but because the "Sons of Liberty

16. Hutchinson to unnamed correspondent, Boston, July 18, 1767, MA, XXVI, 281; letter of Ann Hulton, London, December 17, 1767, in Ann Hulton, *Letters of a Loyalist Lady* (Cambridge, 1927), 8. Richard Frothingham, *Life and Times of Joseph Warren* (Boston, 1865), 37–9, footnote, 38–9, for report of Otis's speech, and 32–3 for quotations from the *Boston Gazette*.

. . . declared there should be no Riots, we had only such a mob as we have long been used to the 5 of November and other Holidays." The people were told "that application had been made for the repeal of the Act of Parliament establishing the Commissioners, and it was best to stay till they saw the Success of this Application."[17] In September, signs of an insurrection appeared again, this time to fend off the imminent occupation of Boston by royal troops. But the uprising never materialized—in part perhaps because of James Otis's efforts at an important Boston Town Meeting of September 12–13, which voted to call a convention of towns to consult upon measures for the "peace and safety" of the King's subjects in Massachusetts.[18] Again a year later, when a mob seemed intent upon revenging a brutal beating of Otis by a group of royalists, it was turned back by radicals who called out, "No violence, or you'll hurt the cause."[19]

When violence did break out—in June 1768 during the *Liberty* riot—it was not a result of nonimportation. The incident culminated weeks of mounting tension over impressment between townsmen and the King's ship *Romney*, and was sparked off by the customsmen's method in seizing John Hancock's sloop *Liberty*. From the outset, leading Bostonians tried to stop the disorder. A mob pelting the comptroller's house with stones withdrew "by the advice of some prudent

17. Anne Rowe Cunningham, ed., *Letters and Diary of John Rowe, Boston Merchant* (Boston, 1903), 156–7; Hutchinson to Richard Jackson, Boston, March 23, 1768, MA, XXVI, 295–6.

18. This interpretation of the September 12–13, 1768, Boston Town Meeting was argued persuasively in Frothingham, *Joseph Warren*, 80–8. It is certainly more probable, given available evidence and the context of Boston events, than the theory that Otis and his colleagues were trying to raise an insurrection, as was argued most recently in Hiller Zobel, *The Boston Massacre* (New York, 1970), 90–2. The appearance of a tar barrel on Beacon Hill had raised fears of an insurrection. Otis apparently tried to undercut any such schemes by saying the resort to force might be necessary in the future, but should be deferred at present. See account of his speech in New England Papers, II, f. 81: "in case Great Britain was not dispos'd to redress their Grievances after proper applications, the Inhabitants had *then* nothing more to do, but gird the Sword to the Thigh, and shoulder the Musquet." Italics mine.

19. Quoted in Zobel, *Boston Massacre*, 151.

gentlemen that interposed"; and as the crowd burned a pleasure boat belonging to the customs collector, Joseph Harrison, "some gentlemen who had influence" with the mob —allegedly John Hancock, Samuel Adams, and Joseph Warren—persuaded the rioters to disperse. Danger over the weekend was minimal, due to the Sabbath; but an uprising threatened for Monday night was averted by "printed tickets . . . put up in different quarters notifying the Sons of Liberty to meet . . . to consult what was proper to be done . . . to preserve peace and Order and maintain their Rights &c." Within the week William Molineux, the radical nonimportation supporter, wrote a letter of sympathy to Harrison, blaming the collector's losses upon a local minority of "such Sort of People" as inhabited "Every Great City perhaps in the World." The destruction of Harrison's pleasure boat was possibly even a "lucky Incident" in "Directing their minds . . . from Greater Evils."[20]

The *Liberty* riot resembled in this respect both the Boston Massacre of March 5, 1770, and the *Gaspée* affair at Rhode Island in 1772. All three incidents were exploited by radical spokesmen as dramatic illustrations of some British threat to American welfare or liberty: impressment, the danger of a standing army, in time of peace, or the use of an executive commission, such as was established to investigate the *Gaspée*'s destruction, for judicial functions. But the rioting itself was never defended. The Massachusetts Provincial Council refused to justify the *Liberty* riot; the burning of the *Gaspée* was termed an "illegal proceeding" by patriot historian Mercy Otis Warren; and the massacre riot, as Josiah Quincy, Jr., testified, was justified by no one. In later years, John Adams blamed the massacre upon some unnamed townsmen who, he claimed, had tried for weeks to excite incidents between citizens and soldiers, but the local Sons of Liberty were clearly not involved

20. *Prov. Gaz.*, June 25, 1768; Frothingham, *Joseph Warren*, 57–61; George G. Wolkins, "The Seizure of John Hancock's Sloop 'Liberty,'" MHS *Procs.*, LV (1921–2), 239–84, especially 255, quoting Bernard, and 254, quoting Richard Harrison. Molineux to Harrison, June 15, 1768, New England Papers, III, f. 1. Hutchinson to Richard Jackson, June 16 and 18, 1768, MA, XXVI, 310–12. See also Mercy Warren, *History of the Rise, Progress, and Termination of the American Revolution*, I (Boston, 1805), 60.

in any planning for March 5. The group's secretary, William Palfrey, was as surprised and confused as his colleague Adams when the riot broke out. Other Sons of Liberty, particularly Richard Palmes, Andrew Cazneau, and Thomas Young, publicly urged the disorderly crowds to desist from acts of violence and to go home.[21]

Although violence was everywhere curtailed, coercion was not universally eschewed. Fear of mob reprisals forced Simon Cooley to confess his political sins and vow to honor the association at New York in July 1769, and a scaffold erected near Liberty Tree brought the submission of a jeweler, Thomas Richardson, in September. In June 1770, a New York mob seized and burned three barrels of goods stored by the local committee for an association violator, David Hills.' Until then, however, threats had been sufficient to avert actual violence in New York. On September 21, 1769, a notice in the *New York Journal* recommended New York's "Method of proceeding with [nonimportation] Delinquents" to the Bostonians. "It would have a more powerful Effect in reducing . . . such Culprits to Reason," the notice claimed, "than the most convincing Arguments that could be used."[22]

About the time this notice appeared the Bostonians, it seems, began to use more forceful methods against importing merchants. One observer complained in October 1769 that the means taken to induce compliance were "really infamous." The nonsubscribers, he thought, were "in real danger of their Lives. Their property was actually unsafe, their Signs, Doors and Windows were daub'd over in the Night time with every

21. *Reps. R. C. C. B.*, XVI, 308–9; Warren, *History*, I, 180 and, on the massacre, 94, 101; Stiles to Rev. Elihu Spencer, Newport, February 16, 1773, in Franklin B. Dexter, ed., *The Literary Diary of Ezra Stiles* (New York, 1901), I, 349 ("No one justifies the burning of the Gaspee"). Quincy in L. Kinvin Wroth and Hiller B. Zobel, eds., *Legal Papers of John Adams* (New York, 1968), III, 228–30; Palfrey to John Wilkes, March 13, 1770, MHS *Procs.*, VI (Boston, 1863), 480; Charles F. Adams, ed., *The Works of John Adams* (Boston, 1850–6), II, 229–30. On the Sons of Liberty during the massacre, see Pauline Maier, "Revolutionary Violence and the Relevance of History," *Journal of Interdisciplinary History*, II (1971), 123–5.

22. *N.Y. Jour.*, July 20, 27, and September 21, 1769; and July 5, 1770, for notice of committee meeting as to Hills.

kind of Filth, and one of them particularly had his person treated in the same manner."[23] On October 28, the crowd turned against John Mein, publisher of the *Boston Chronicle* and leading opponent of the association, whom impending social stigma and economic ruin had failed to silence. Mein was first attacked by ten to twelve persons "of some considerable Rank," including merchant Edward Davis, Captain Francis Dashwood, nonimportation chieftain William Molineux, and a tailor, Thomas Marshal, the lieutenant colonel of the Boston militia regiment, all four of whom had been associated with the Sons of Liberty. Later, these assailants were joined by a mob of over a thousand persons which had gathered earlier to tar and feather a suspected customs informer. Mein received an ugly wound from an iron shovel swung by Marshal, but managed to escape into the guardhouse, where he was shielded by royal troops.[24]

In December, Lieutenant Governor Hutchinson reported that the province was "in a very calm state" although "discontents" continued in Boston. Then, in January, a group of merchants that included Hutchinson's sons Elisha and Thomas, Jr., decided to resume the sale of imported goods. The entire association was brought into peril and agitation revived. Association meetings voted to visit the offenders *en masse*, but these official visits were, as Hutchinson admitted, "without any degree of tumult." Committees were chosen before each visit, and the crowd normally marched to the offender's house with great order, then remained outside the gate while its leaders negotiated with its host. Recalcitrance

23. George Mason to Joseph Harrison, Boston, October 20, 1769, and extract of a letter from Nathaniel Rogers, Boston, October 23, 1769, in New England Papers, III, ff. 40, 44. Rogers claimed that his house had twice been "besmeared" (with dung) and that he had finally acquiesced in the demands of the associators only "from principles of self-preservation."

24. Mason to unnamed correspondent, Boston, October 28, 1769, and Mein to Harrison, Boston, November 5, 1769, in *ibid.*, ff. 47, 51. The assailants' names were compared with "An Alphabetical List of the Sons of Liberty who Dined at Liberty Tree, Dorchester, Aug. 14, 1769," MHS *Procs.*, XI (1869–70), 140–2. See also John E. Alden, "John Mein: Scourge of Patriots, CSM *Pubs.*, XXXIV (*Trans.* 1937–42), 571–99.

on the part of the importers did not automatically bring violent reprisals. When William Jackson refused to comply with the associators' demands on January 17, 1770, for example, William Molineux simply announced that it was "beneath the dignity of this Committee to be parlied with in the streets," "turn'd about," and marched his retinue back to Faneuil Hall.[25]

With the failure of peaceful mass pressure, more virulent forms of mob pressure were again revived. On three successive Thursdays—February 8, 15, and 22—signs and effigies mysteriously appeared pointing out "importers," particularly William Jackson and Theophilus Lillie. Crowds of boys and country people gathered, for it was marketing day, when schools were closed. Customers were intimidated from entering proscribed shops and sometimes pelted with dirt. During those weeks, importers' signs were defaced and their windows broken or "besmeared . . . with tar & feathers." On each occasion, efforts to remove the "importer" signs were repulsed: on the eighth, Jackson was turned back by "a Number of Idle people . . . standing by, with Clubs and sticks in their Hands"; soldiers who made a similar effort on the fifteenth were "beat of[f] and some of them much Hurt"; and finally, on the twenty-second, an attempt to remove an effigy over Lillie's door by Ebenezer Richardson, an ex-customs informer who was considered particularly obnoxious in Boston, resulted in bloodshed. Richardson was chased to his nearby home and besieged by a rock-throwing crowd until he fired shots into the street, hitting an eleven-year-old boy, Christopher Sneider. At that the crowd seized Richardson, dragged him through the streets, and some tried "to put a rope about his Neck and . . . execute him themselves."[26]

Even within this surge of violence the hand of restraint was apparent. A line was usually drawn at lesser forms of

25. Hutchinson to Hillsborough, Boston, December 1, 1769, and January 24, 1770, New England Papers, III, ff. 58, 64; letter from Boston, January 29, in *N.Y. Jour.*, March 1, 1770; "Journal of Transactions at Boston" for January 17, 1770, New England Papers, III, f. 55.

26. Extract of a letter from Boston, March 14, 1770, and "Narrative of Proceedings at Boston," New England Papers, III, ff. 69, 70, 71.

harassment: window breaking, the "besmearing" of signs, suggestions of impending violence. More serious crimes were sometimes avoided almost by luck: two men who resembled Mein were attacked in an alley and nearly killed before their true identities were discovered, and an apparent effort to burn Jackson's store failed. On other occasions, leaders intervened to curtail violence and to protect the persons of their enemies. In June 1770, for example, a mob was dissuaded from tarring and feathering Patrick McMasters when it became clear that he could not survive the ordeal. More important, Richardson was saved from his would-be murderers by William Molineux, who was probably responsible for turning the crowd against importers in the first place. Molineux in fact personified the ambiguity that persisted even in the extremes of Boston radicalism. He was the arch demagogue of nonimportation, believed to be "the first Leader of Dirty Matters," whose violence was a divisive factor even within the nonimportation movement in 1770; yet it was he who saved Richardson and also consoled Joseph Harrison after the *Liberty* riot. There were limits on the violence Molineux endorsed, and those limits were not wholly subjective. In January 1770, it was said, he claimed he would kill with his own hands every person who presumed to open imported goods—"were it not for the law."[27]

Basic to Molineux's behavior there was, it seems, a dis-

27. John Fleming to John Mein, Castle William, July 1, 1770, extract, New England Papers, IV, f. 5; Zobel, *Boston Massacre*, 233–4. Molineux: Cunningham, *Diary of John Rowe*, 286; "Narrative of Proceedings at Boston" for February 8 and January 12, 1770, New England Papers, III, ff. 70, 55; Hutchinson to Gen. Thomas Gage, February 25, 1770, and to Bernard, February 28, March 1 and 2, 1770, MA, XXVI, 445, 448, 450–1.
  It is not certain that the crowd would have killed Richardson without Molineux's intervention. On a similar occasion four years later, when efforts to restrain the mob failed, customsman John Malcom was tarred and feathered, carted to the gallows, and threatened with being hanged unless he renounced his royal commission and swore "never [to] hold another inconsistent with the liberties of his country." He refused, but gave in later when the mob threatened to cut his ears off—as if he believed it might follow through on that lesser threat but not on the more serious. See *Mass. Spy*, January 27, 1774, in CSM *Pubs.*, XXXIV (*Trans.*, 1937–42), 443–5.

tinction drawn between violence and coercion. While the destruction of persons and property was condemned as criminal, the resort to lesser forms of harassment for political purposes might be justifiable under criteria of collective necessity. Once force was used against importers, however, the immediate legality of nonimportation came increasingly into question. From the outset, proponents argued that the associations were lawful because their aims were lawful: no statute required colonists to purchase imported goods or to patronize importing merchants and their supporters. Local justices of the peace therefore denied Lieutenant Governor Hutchinson's claim that the association's meetings in Boston involved a "breach of law" unless—as the justices said in January 1770—"there should be something more disorderly than yet had been." If, however, the associations could be linked with illegal violence, all members would be in grave danger: since, as Hutchinson warned in January 1770, "their professed design [was] to reform the law by effecting the repeal of the revenue acts"—a public aim, beyond their personal grievances—"any violence from any of the inferior people who were among them would in my opinion involve them all in the guilt of high treason."[28]

The warning was not lost on those association participants who had all along taken care to avoid any connection with acts outside the law. Their concern was clear in the way mass visits to importers were carefully organized in January 1770. Nor was there any overt link between the association and the mob scenes that followed in February: well before the "importer" signs appeared, one contemporary reported, the "Committee of Inspection stopt their Visitations, and seem'd to have given the matter Intirely up." Indicative, too, of the associators' concern for legality was a heated debate at their meeting on January 18, 1770. Josiah Quincy, Jr., a radical lawyer and member of the Sons of Liberty, asserted that a proposed visit to Elisha and Thomas Hutchinson, Jr., who lived with the lieutenant governor, would itself constitute an act of treason. He was answered by Molineux and Samuel Adams, who argued that the visit would be legal because it

28. Hutchinson to Hillsborough, January 24, 1770, New England Papers, III, f. 64.

concerned only the sons, not their father, and sought only to persuade them to honor an earlier promise to abide by the nonimportation agreement. When Quincy persisted, Molineux carried the day by pleading that the effort was essential to maintain the association, the colonists' only way of winning redress. Ironically, the association's consequent confrontation with the lieutenant governor consisted largely of a sullen discussion of technical points of law that recapitulated in large part the earlier debate within the association.[29]

Some opponents argued that this careful effort to keep the association itself uncontaminated by illegal action was inconsequential. Even without violence, men like William Henry Drayton and William Wragg contended in South Carolina, the association was illegal in that it constituted an unlawful confederacy. In a confederacy, Drayton claimed, "there must be a voluntary combination by bonds or promises," such as were made by the nonimportation subscribers; "the combination must be to do damage to an innocent man"; and "there must be an unjust revenge intended," as was specified in the last section of the South Carolina agreement, which called for the ostracism of men who, Drayton stressed, were "innocent of having violated the laws of their country." " 'Tis injurious to deprive men of the benefits of society, where no law has been transgressed," Wragg added, noting that the nonimportation resolutions "forbid those who have associated themselves, to purchase from non-subscribers, tho' they have transgressed no law." In Massachusetts, Thomas Hutchinson was apparently thinking along the same lines, although his conclusions were more cautious. Nonimportation meetings had "no foundation in law," he noted, and "their proceedings, though without any degree of tumult, in going in a great body to two or three persons . . . and demanding of them a compliance with their agreement was altogether unwarrantable."[30]

29. "Narrative of Proceedings at Boston" for early February, 1770; "Journal of Transactions at Boston" for January 18, and letter by George Mason, Boston, January 24, 1770, in *ibid.*, ff. 70, 55–6, 63. Letter from Boston, January 29, in *N.Y. Jour.*, March 1, 1770.

30. [Drayton] and Wragg in Drayton, *Letters of Freeman*, 101–2, 204; Hutchinson to Hillsborough, January 24, 1770, New England Papers, III, f. 64.

In effect, Drayton and Wragg charged the nonimporters with conspiracy, a crime in common law that had changed dramatically in meaning since the early seventeenth century.[31] Its applicability to nonimportation was disputable. The essential issue was whether or not men could be guilty of conspiracy when the act they concerted upon, that is, the withholding of patronage or social intercourse from a third party, was not itself unlawful. Throughout the eighteenth century the feeling persisted that criminal conspiracy could occur in such a case, but the inclination of lawyers was never authenticated in court. Judges occasionally seemed to affirm the existence of such a crime, as in the case of the Journeymen Tailors, 1721, when the court declared that "a conspiracy of any kind is illegal, tho' the matter about which they conspired might have been lawful . . . if they had not conspired to do it." These pronouncements were, however, *obiter dicta*, unnecessary for the decisions actually made, and so did not gain the force of precedent. As late as 1873, a leading authority on the English law of criminal conspiracies concluded that the authorities "strongly favour the view that a combination to injure a private person (otherwise than by fraud) is not as a general rule criminal unless criminal means are to be used."[32]

31. The crime of conspiracy originally consisted only in a "confederacy or alliance for the false and malicious promotion of indictments and pleas," as outlawed in an Ordinance of Conspirators of 1305 (33 Edward I). There was a technical distinction between conspiracy and confederacy: conspiracy referred to combinations for false and malicious indictments, confederacy to combinations for maintenance, that is, "an unauthorized and officious interference in a suit in which the offender has no interest, to assist one of the parties to it, against the other." The evolution of the modern notion of conspiracy dates from the early seventeenth century. See R[obert] S. Wright, *The Law of Criminal Conspiracies and Agreements* (London, 1873), 5–6, 15, and *passim* on the evolution of the law; and Henry C. Black, *Black's Law Dictionary* (St. Paul, 1968), 1106, 368.

32. Wright, *Law of Criminal Conspiracies*, 53, 41. See also 37–43 "on Combination to injure Individuals (otherwise than by Fraud)," and 50–5 on whether "a combination to coerce a man's freedom in respect of the bestowal of his industry or capital, by means which would not be punishable apart from combination, is a criminal conspiracy 'at common law.' " In the latter category, again, most prosecutions involved conspiracies to commit some act outlawed by statute.

Here, in fact, lay much of the problem for royal officials. In South Carolina, where the deference of the lower to the higher social orders remained strong, Drayton's undocumented arguments and casual use of Latin induced at least one opponent to bow before his learning and knowledge of the law. But in Massachusetts, where every man thought himself a lawyer, Thomas Hutchinson's suggestion that the nonimportation combinations were unlawful confederacies was simply rejected. And Hutchinson himself seemed at times to admit that the law was with his opponents. "The Combinations against importing," he wrote in November 1769, ". . . are Subversive of government, and yet are justifiable as legal." Before authority could be stabilized, he came to understand, Parliament would have to pass a statute outlawing the nonimportation agreements.[33]

When British officials explored the possibility of prosecuting Boston's leaders, they found that they had to prove the crime of treason, not conspiracy. Not only was treason a more established offense, but an act passed in the thirty-fifth year of the reign of Henry VIII was the only extant law under which crimes committed in America might be tried in England, and that act did not cover offenses inferior to treason. Trial in England was considered advisable because the widespread involvement of both judges and prospective jurors in the American agitation seemed to make convictions unlikely in

---

The only possible exceptions are "probably of a later date than 1797" (55).

Nineteenth-century Irish leaders were sometimes tried for seditious conspiracy. It is noteworthy, however, that conspiracy was not charged in political or seditious cases until well after American independence was established. The first such case was probably that of Redhead Yorke in 1795 (25 State Trials, 1003). See Sir James F. Stephen, *A History of the Criminal Law of England* (London, 1883), II, 377–80. Nor could the American leaders be charged with sedition alone, since no such crime existed in English law. Seditious offenses were prosecuted on into the nineteenth century as seditious words, seditious libels, or seditious conspiracies. *Ibid.*, 298.

33. Hutchinson to Hillsborough, Boston, November 11, 1769, in New England Papers III, f. 63; Schlesinger, *Colonial Merchants*, 172. See also the statement of a pro-British merchant, April 1770, in Zobel, *Boston Massacre*, 227: "Until Parliament makes provision for the punishment of the confederacies, all will be ineffectual."

colonial courts. As of November 1768, however, the Tudor statute was still inapplicable to the Bostonians, according to the British attorney general and solicitor general, because no overt acts of treason had yet been proven. The threat of trial in England did, however, make Americans particularly anxious to show that justice could still be won in Massachusetts, that Boston was not in fact a lawless city. It was under the shadow of these legal developments that two leading members of the Sons of Liberty, John Adams and Josiah Quincy, Jr., undertook the defense of the King's soldiers accused of murder after the Boston Massacre. Quincy was "advised and urged" to assume the task, he assured his father, "by an Adams, a Hancock, a Molineux, a Cushing, a Henshaw, a Pemberton, a Warren, a Cooper, and a Phillips"—all prominent supporters of the American cause.[34]

The colonists' concern for acting within the law indicated a continued respect for British institutions. Like the Sons of Liberty during the Stamp Act crisis, the nonimporters insisted that their opposition to British authority was limited. The various associations usually provided for their own dissolution once the Townshend Revenue Act was repealed. An effort by Boston to extend the agreements to work for the repeal of earlier revenue acts as well, particularly that of 1764, failed completely. Even where royal control faced the greatest resistance, at Boston, the ligaments of British authority were loosened in only limited areas. "In other matters which have no relation to this dispute between the Kingdom and the Colonies," Hutchinson wrote as late as February 28, 1770, "Government retains its vigour and the administration of it is attended with no unusual difficulty."[35]

Nonetheless, by 1770 the American agitation had clearly reached a stage of seriousness far beyond that of three years earlier. Escalation was marked by the increasing severity of reprisals: from mild economic boycotts, through public ad-

---

34. Zobel, *Boston Massacre*, 86, 92, 109; Josiah Quincy, Jr., to his father, Boston, March 26, 1770, in Josiah Quincy, *Memoir of the Life of Josiah Quincy, Jun[ior]*, ed. Eliza S. Quincy (3rd edn., Boston, 1875), 28.

35. Schlesinger, *Colonial Merchants*, 131–3; Hutchinson to Hillsborough, MA, XXVI, 447.

vertisements of importers as "enemies of their country" who deserved the contempt of their countrymen, to the violence of Boston, which was itself an act of desperation. The town's disorder, Hutchinson testified, came from a "general disposition . . . to favour the measures of the Merchants as the *only means* to preserve the Rights of the people and bring about the Repeal of the Revenue Acts and other Acts called unconstitutional." Desperation appeared, too, in the Boston Association's hesitant decision of January 1770 to risk illegality in visiting the Hutchinsons because it was essential to the agreement, the only remaining way to redress, and in the South Carolinians' espousal of "constitutional" arguments against William Henry Drayton's accusations. Whenever government used the authority delegated to it by the people so as to threaten the safety of society, it was said, the people had "a right to resist and reduce it within its proper bounds." A studied conviction that America was in a situation of "extreme Danger" lay behind the Marylanders' decision to enforce the association with strictness in 1770, and for Christopher Gadsden the colonists were "visibly on the very brink of a steep precipice" as early as June 1769, such that "nothing but GOD's blessing on our own immediate Prudence, Union and Firmness, can prevent our being plunged headlong . . . into *irrecoverable* ruin and distress."[36]

The inflamed rhetoric, the assertions that Parliament's unconstitutional acts justified colonial resistance, were reminiscent of the Stamp Act crisis. But even while precautions were taken to maintain the general framework of legal authority, resistance to the Townshend duties became a more serious threat to British authority than that to the Stamp Act. By nature, nonimportation committed partisans to a wider share of administrative responsibilities than had been exercised by the Sons of Liberty of 1765–6. In short, the associations increasingly exercised functions normally reserved to a sovereign state. Committees regularly demanded the right to inspect

36. *Ibid.*, italics mine; [Mackenzie] in Drayton, *Letters of Freeman*, 110; "The Case of the Good Intent," *Maryland Historical Magazine*, III (1908), 154, 157; Gadsden, "To the Planters, Mechanics, and Freeholders of . . . South Carolina," June 22, 1769, in Walsh, *Gadsden Writings*, 77.

merchants' invoices and papers, to judge the guilt of suspected violators of the association, and to impose sanctions against the unyielding. These responsibilities were undertaken with great seriousness: the complex issues raised by the arrival of the *Good Intent* at Annapolis in early 1770, for example, were adjudicated by a special committee from three Maryland counties that collected masses of evidence and testimony before issuing a decision based upon the text of the association. Occasionally—as again in Maryland—the association tried to regulate prices so as to prevent anyone from taking advantage of the scarcity of goods. In Maryland, then, or Virginia, as much as in Massachusetts, the association's proceedings were carried on "in as formal a manner as in a body corporate legally assembled and . . . established by the Constitution."[37]

As the number of adherents increased, and nonimporters could claim to speak for the body of the people, the various associations came to serve as social compacts, analogous to the formal constitutions that would be set up by the various colonies in the mid-1770's. The Virginia Association of June 1770, for example, outlined the structure and procedures of that colony's enforcement mechanisms. It took the form of a solemn agreement or compact among the subscribers—described simply as "his Majesty's most dutiful and loyal subjects of *Virginia*"—to adhere to its provisions, which were "binding on all and each" of them. Although their sphere of activity was limited, within that sphere the associations had, as Drayton charged in South Carolina, set up a new legislative power.[38]

On the fringes of the movement, moreover, this assumption of power was conscious, and its legitimacy was rigorously defended. In April 1770, Boston's committeemen were said to be "calling people before them who they said had spoke disrespectfully of that body, and obliging them to make the proper concessions, nobody daring to resist their almighty power." The New York committee similarly resented the

37. "Case of the Good Intent," *Maryland Historical Magazine*, III (1908), 141–57, 240–56, 342–63; Hutchinson quoted in Schlesinger, *Colonial Merchants*, 163.

38. Virginia Association in Boyd, *Jefferson Papers*, I, 43–6; [Drayton] in Drayton, *Letters of Freeman*, 119.

mob's destruction of David Hills's stored goods as a "high insult" to its authority, as if that authority was established and to be respected like that of a legal government. Boston's Thomas Young was even accused of saying in January 1770 that "it was high time for the people to take the Government into their own hands."[39]

Rhetoric also revealed this *de facto* assumption of authority. At Boston, royalist observers complained, merchants' meetings sometimes referred to themselves as "The Board of Trade," while goods imported contrary to the association were called "contraband." Tea from Holland could "lawfully be sold" in Boston, Thomas Hutchinson complained, but it was considered "a high crime to sell any from England"; and one local radical, Benjamin Kent, supposedly accused those who violated the association of "High Treason against the Majesty of the people." Similarly, at New York, nonimportation violator Simon Cooley was publicly labeled "a vile Disturber of the Peace, Police and good Order of this City." Such a man, it was said, "must not expect [that] the People with whom he lived in Society, would permit him with Impunity, to transgress and violate the Rules and Agreement they had entered into for their Welfare and Security. . . ."[40]

As committees increasingly assumed the right to speak and act for the people, the associations' right to coerce nonconformers seemed ever more justified. The personal rights of opponents were not denied, but put in perspective. "The hardships of particulars are not to be considered," Christopher Gadsden wrote, "when the good of the whole is the object in view; as evidently it is, in the case before us." Eighteenth-century political thought had never emphasized individual rights so much as the corporate rights of the community; and patriotism itself was said to involve at core a willingness to sacrifice private interest for the public good. As such non-

39. "Narrative of Occurrences at Boston," April 28, 1770, New England Papers, III, f. 77; New York Committee statement, June 26, 1770, in *N.Y. Jour.*, July 5, 1770, and "Journal of Transactions at Boston" for January 18 in New England Papers, III, f. 56.

40. "Narrative of Occurrences at Boston" for April 20 and Hutchinson to Hillsborough, Boston, April 27, 1770, New England Papers, III, ff. 76, 78; *N.Y. Jour.*, July 20, 27, 1769.

importation, with its demand of self-sacrifice for the general welfare, seemed to institutionalize public virtue: "the little conveniences and comforts of life," George Mason wrote, "when set in competition with our liberty, ought to be rejected, not with reluctance, but with pleasure." Importers were, then, in the words of Cornelius Harnett, men who lacked "virtue enough to resist the allurement of present gain," or as the Virginia Association of June 1770 put it, men who "preferred their own private emolument, by importing or selling articles prohibited by this association, to the destruction of the dearest rights of the people of this colony." To condemn nonimportation because it supposedly involved "infringing the right of others while . . . contending for liberty ourselves" was an "ill-founded" argument: "every member of society is in duty bound to contribute to the safety and good of the whole," Mason contended;

> and when the subject is of such importance as the liberty and happiness of a country, every inferior consideration, as well as the inconvenience of a few individuals, must give place to it; nor is this any hardship upon them as themselves and their posterity are to partake of the benefits resulting from it. Objections of the same kind might be made to the most useful civil institutions.

Samuel Adams similarly compared the authority of the non-importation supporters with that of regular institutions when he defended the Bostonians' actions against importer Patrick McMasters, who was banished from Boston by a mob in June 1770. In all states, Adams said, individuals were bound to act according to the common will of their fellow citizens or to leave. And in exceptional situations, like the present, the "will and pleasure of the society" was not "declared in its laws," but had to be imposed directly.[41]

41. [Gadsden] in Drayton, *Letters of Freeman*, 176; Mason to George Washington, April 5, 1770, and to Richard Henry Lee, June 7, 1770, in Rowland, *George Mason*, I, 141, 145; Harnett to Charleston Sons of Liberty, quoted in Connor, *Cornelius Harnett*, 57; Virginia Association in Boyd, *Jefferson Papers*, I, 43; Adams as "Determinus" in *Boston Gaz.*, January 8, 1770, and Cushing, *Writings of Samuel Adams*, II, 5.

[II]

For most royal observers, the careful legal distinctions that colonial leaders tried to maintain were of no significance. The associators' claim that nonimportation was lawful seemed at best a pretense. In Boston, the fanatical Tory Peter Oliver later claimed, inhabitants armed themselves with home-made "massy Clubs," since "Guns they imagined were Weapons of Death in the Eye of the Law, which the meanest of them was an Adept in; but Bludgeons were only Implements to beat out Brains with." Such constructions seemed only to circumvent the law.[42]

The colonists' goals seemed as culpable as their methods, for in the eyes of British officials all resistance to Parliament's authority was unjustifiable. Such rigidity was in part imposed by office: "officers of the Crown cannot Judge an Act of Parliament otherwise than to yield to it," Cadwallader Colden once said. But more fundamental political convictions reinforced the obligations of office. For Colden, or Thomas Hutchinson, or Pennsylvania's stamp distributor John Hughes, as for so many contemporary Englishmen, "to say an Act of Parliament is illegal seemed . . . a contradiction in Terms." Parliament was supreme; the Lords and Commons had become "the people"; it was Parliament which judged the legality even of its own acts, not the dispersed British population for whom it acted. The right of resistance was a historical anomaly, part of a doctrine once used against usurping monarchs, which in contemporary circumstances was inappropriate, even incomprehensible. When the *Boston Gazette* proposed to reprint the English Bill of Rights of 1689 and sections from Magna Charta, Governor Francis Bernard considered its action to be a telling proof of colonial sedition.[43] The colonists' constitutional defenses, in short, seemed as facetious as their legal

42. Douglas Adair and John A. Schutz, eds., *Peter Oliver's Origin and Progress of the American Rebellion* (San Marino, Cal., 1961), 89.

43. Colden to Major Thomas James, Springhill, May 1, 1766, *The Colden Letter Books*, II, NYHS *Colls. for 1877* (New York, 1878), 108–9; Hutchinson to Richard Jackson, Boston, June 4, 1765, MA, XXVI, 139; Hughes to Stamp Commissioners, November 2, 1765, PRO, Treas. 1/441. Bernard to Shelburne, August 24, 1767, and enclosures, PRO, CO 5/756, 185–91.

arguments. As a result, the Americans' painstaking distinction between just and unjust uprisings also became meaningless: all extra-legal uprisings were unjust.

The royal officials' insistence on the authority of Parliament and the Americans' criminality acquired particular shrillness and rigidity as they saw their own authority disintegrate. The failure of local magistrates and militias to support them during the Stamp Act period was not easily forgotten, particularly since the same situation was re-enacted during later incidents. Nor was the success of colonial political leaders in repressing or subduing violence of any consolation. Such authority was not their own; it was at the disposal of powers outside the legal British establishment, and as such seemed unreliable. Thus, even when Boston was quiet, customs officials complained that "the power was entirely in the hands of the leaders of the people and every one's security depended on their caprice." Such a displacement of authority appeared in itself essentially disorderly: insofar as bodies of men were allowed to assume "powers unwarrantable and illegal" to carry on their opposition to Parliament, everything seemed to be "tending to disorder and anarchy." Should the partisans of resistance utilize established agencies of government—the legislature, or town meeting for example—it made little difference, marking only a change of scene "from the Mob without Doors to the Mob within."[44]

As the dominant opinion in the colonies turned toward the radicals rather than toward London, royal officials had a ready explanation. They argued, as Thomas Jefferson later put it, "that the whole ferment has been raised and constantly kept up by a few principal men in every colony, and that it might be expected to subside in a short time either of itself, or by the assistance of a coercive power." The theory was readily adopted in England, where some Members of Parliament

44. Henry Hulton and William Burch to the Duke of Grafton, April 3, 1770, quoted in Oliver M. Dickerson, "The Commissioners of Customs and the 'Boston Massacre,'" *New England Quarterly*, XXVII (1954), 323; Thomas Hutchinson, *History of the Colony of Massachusetts Bay* (Cambridge, 1936), ed. Lawrence Shaw Mayo, III, 185; Adair and Schutz, *Peter Oliver's Origin of the American Rebellion*, 67.

clamored for the arrest and punishment of the principal troublemakers. The argument appealed also to the King, who considered Parliament's right to bind the colonists "in all cases whatsoever, as essential to the dignity of the crown, and a right appertaining to the state, which it was his duty to preserve entirely enviolate." He was therefore "greatly displeased" with colonial petitions and remonstrances that denied Parliament's absolute supremacy, and regretted that his subjects were so "misled"—again, by a handful of factious leaders. In retrospect this rhetoric of conspiracy, which the colonists themselves gradually adopted to explain England's actions, belied the gap between English and American political assumptions, for neither side could recognize the other as acting honestly upon legitimate principles different from its own. It indicated, too, a pervasive desire to interpret the other side's "defection" in terms as charitable as possible: since the King was "unwilling to Suppose that the Sentiments of his faithful Subjects in general . . . corresponded with the unwarrantable doctrines" in their petitions and remonstrances, he "imputed the same to the artifices of a few who seek to create groundless jealousy and distrust" and disturb peace and harmony with the Mother Country. At the time, however, the Crown's emphasis upon an American "faction" seemed a cruel reversal of reality, "the utmost efforts of the most intelligent people having been requisite and exerted to moderate the almost ungovernable fury of the people," as Jefferson noted.[45]

Sometimes haunted by fears for their own safety, conscious that the King's and Parliament's authority was at stake in their own persons, the governors and officials reverted to an old solution for their problems. Troops were necessary, not only to execute individual laws, but, as Georgia's Governor Wright wrote, to support His Majesty's authority from insults. On September 2, 1765, Cadwallader Colden suggested that New York needed a battalion; and by the following February even Governor Henry Moore, Colden's successor and critic,

45. Jefferson to William Small, draft, Virginia, May 7, 1775, in Boyd, *Jefferson Papers*, I, 166, *n.* 1; King's comments reported in Dartmouth to Franklin, Whitehall, June 2, 1773, New England Papers, IV, f. 38.

who had gone so far as to wear homespun in an effort to conciliate the colonists, reluctantly concluded "that nothing . . . but a superior Force will bring the people to a sense of their Duty." Of all the voices, however, Governor Bernard's sounded out most clearly and persistently. "Surely it is not known at Whitehall how weak and impotent the Authority of American Governors is in regard to Popular Tumults," he wrote Thomas Pownall on August 18, 1765; and he lamented the demise of independent companies which, he claimed, had previously protected some governors. "It is a shocking Thing that British Troops should be used against British Subjects," he admitted six days later, "but a defection of the Colonies is a greater Evil even to the Colonists." This call for soldiers became a standard theme, not only for governors, but for customs officials, particularly those on the American Board of Customs Commissioners, who arrived in November 1767 and within a year convinced London to send a contingent of troops—uncalled for by local officials—to Boston. In fact, the pleas continued *ad absurdum* into the 1770's, as when the sinecured surveyor of customs at Sassafras and Bohemia in Maryland wrote of the need for military forces, or the shady John Hatton in the Chesapeake called for a "ship of warr" to protect him.[46]

As early as the Stamp Act crisis, however, it seemed unlikely that troops could successfully remedy the officials' isolation. In part, the problem was a technical one of how many men Britain would engage in North America and where to locate them. The number of men General Gage could offer governors in 1765 was often so insufficient that the troops would have constituted a provocation more than a deterrent to insurrection; and Dr. Thomas Moffatt told a parliamentary

46. Wright to Conway, Savannah, January 31, 1766, PRO, CO 5/658, f. 114; Colden to Gage, September 2, 1765, *Colden Letter Books*, II, 30; Moore to Conway, New York, February 20, 1766, *N.Y. Col. Docs.*, VII, 810–11; Bernard to T[homas] Pownall, Castle William, August 18, 1765, and to Richard Jackson, Castle William, August 24, 1765, in Sparks Manuscripts, IV, The Papers of Sir Francis Bernard (henceforth "Bernard Papers"), IV, 13, 19–20, HUL. Robert S. Byrnes to Customs Commissioners, March 17, 1775, PRO, Treas. 1/513, and Hatton to Customs Commissioners, November 20, 1770, PRO, Treas. 1/476.

committee that it would have taken ten weeks to send troops into Rhode Island. Any military solution was compromised as well by ingrained beliefs and expectations. For colonists, a standing army signaled that the government was pursuing ends other than the good of the governed. Thus, rather than augmenting the government's authority, the use of troops encouraged additional suspicion and hostility. Already in September 1765, the New York Council advised Colden that it would be "more safe for the Government to shew a Confidence in the People, than to discover its distrust of them by Calling any assistance to the Civil Power"; and John Adams's Braintree Instructions also suggested "that any extraordinary and expensive Exertions would tend to exasperate the People and endanger the public Tranquility, rather than the contrary."[47] The wisdom in these warnings was illustrated at New York in late 1765, where Colden's reinforcement of Fort George in effect aggravated the riot he was preparing to meet. The same lesson was repeated there in late 1769 and early 1770, when the presence of royal troops proved useless for protecting importers, while repeated frays between soldiers and citizens finally culminated in the so-called Battle of Golden Hill in January 1770. Again at Boston, the royal troops which arrived in October 1768 proved useless for protecting nonimportation opponents such as John Mein: "in Ireland perhaps where the people have been long used to the military upon an apprehension only of violence from the populace" regular soldiers might have been used for Mein's protection, Hutchinson commented; but "in the present state of the colonies I could not think it so. . . ." The troops were finally withdrawn when their continued presence threatened to occasion a battle worse even than that of March 5, 1770.[48]

British suppositions also hindered any confident and effective use of troops against the colonists. Traditional ideas

47. Moffatt's testimony in BM Add. Mss., 33030 (Newcastle); New York Council minutes, September 7, 1765, in *The Letters and Papers of Cadwallader Colden*, VII, in NYHS *Colls. for 1923* (New York, 1923), 61, and also 62 for supporting testimony of the magistrates. Braintree Instructions in *Boston Gaz.*, October 14, 1765.

48. Champagne, "Sons of Liberty in New York," 225–31; Hutchinson to Hillsborough, November 11, 1769, MA, XXVI, 403.

about the proper role of the army in a free country were as vivid for military commanders like Sir/Jeffery Amherst or Thomas Gage as for John Adams, and even British ministers shared the Americans' misgivings. When Governor Wright of Georgia managed briefly to distribute stamps with the aid of regular troops, he earned not the thanks of his superiors but a word of admonition from Secretary of State Shelburne. Although it was necessary to protect the prerogatives of the Crown, Shelburne wrote, still "it is the Duty of His Majestys Governors so to conduct themselves as not to create groundless Jealousies or suggest Suspicion that they are capable of . . . wishing to restrain the just and decent Exercise of that Liberty which belongs to the People." "An Administration founded on large Principles of Public Good," the secretary wrote, "will give Dignity to Power [,] insure the Reverence and Affections of the Governed . . . and make it unnecessary to have recourse to lesser and more narrow Means of Government." The secretary's sentiments here were not far different from those of New York's radical printer John Holt. In commenting upon a letter that anticipated the day when mobs would be suppressed and a proper respect for the laws impressed upon "the lower rank," Holt said simply that *"Not force, but justice will do it."*[49]

Out of this impossibility of military rule arose in good part the peculiar conditions that gave the American Revolution its distinctive character. British authority could not be imposed upon an unwilling people. To be effective it had to be administered by men "reverenced and beloved by the people," as the *Boston Gazette* once said;[50] its power had to flow directly from the governed who, when the laws seemed to promote their welfare, would both obey and enforce them. As these conditions ceased to be true, royal authority disintegrated; imperial officials became incapable of restraining hostility and disorderly outbreaks. But simultaneously, the function of maintaining order was assumed by their opponents. Both sides shared a respect for orderly, lawful procedures; they differed in their definitions of order and their conceptions

49. Shelburne to Wright, Whitehall, September 22, 1766, PRO, CO 5/658, f. 143; *N.Y. Jour.*, July 13, 1769.

50. January 31, 1774.

of legitimacy. The colonists' progressive assumption of power paralleled their increasing conviction that Britain aspired to despotic power. Yet, ironically, it was not only British inability but also her remaining liberal traditions that prevented a simple forceful suppression of the American agitation.

[III]

The basic guidelines for American opposition to Britain were defined already during the Stamp Act crisis; but the nature of the Anglo-American conflict changed radically within the next decade. Signs of this transformation were already apparent in the nonimportation effort by 1770. The fixation of 1765–6 with buttressing British authority beyond the regions affected by the Stamp Act had to some extent been replaced by a conscious assumption of extra-legal political power. More important, the old Sons of Liberty's faith in Britain, her rulers and institutions had given way to a new desperation for American liberty, which was marked by a willingness to resort to ever more extreme methods to maintain the nonimportation association. By 1770, in short, the colonists had begun to advance along the road from resistance to revolution.

Disillusionment with Britain did not immediately follow the Declaratory Act of 1766, which asserted Parliament's sovereign right "to make Laws . . . to bind the Colonists and People of America . . . in all Cases whatsoever." Most colonists apparently interpreted the enactment as a face-saving device upon which Parliament did not intend to act. Colonists remained strongly confident of British justice in late 1767, when John Dickinson's "Letters from a Farmer in Pennsylvania" were readily accepted as expressing the views of his countrymen. In words strikingly like those of Jonathan Mayhew a year earlier, Dickinson stressed that the Americans had "an excellent prince" in whose "good dispositions they could confide"; they had a "generous, sensible and humane nation" to whom they could apply for redress from their newest grievances. Separation was the least desirable outcome of the conflict—"Torn from the body, to which we are united by religion, liberty, laws, affections, relation, language and commerce, we must bleed at every vein."[51]

Attitudes toward Britain changed, in short, most dramatically only after 1767. There were, however, a handful of colonists like the Providence Son of Liberty Silas Downer who viewed British actions pessimistically already in 1766. It could not be supposed, Downer asserted, that Parliament had repealed the Stamp Act because of any "Sensibility of Error or Mistake in taxing a People without the Shadow of a Representation" since it went on to declare that the King, Lords, and Commons could make laws to bind the colonies *"in all cases whatsoever."* Moreover, Parliament had hardly been "set right" by the Americans since it had treated the colonies' petitions with "Contempt and Indecency, without saying Wrath and Indignation . . . session after Session," using "nugatory arguments . . . infinitely unbecoming the Character and Dignity of Legislation . . . to get rid of them." Although he did credit "those few Sons of Liberty, in and out of Parliament, who were for the Repeal from Principles of Justice and a Regard to the Liberties of the Subject," they were, for Downer, unrepresentative of the Stamp Act's British opposition. Merchants trading with America solicited repeal "from Principles of Convenience to themselves," "utterly disclaiming" any of the principles on which the American opposition was built; while others favored the measure "the better to promote party Views, and for the maturing of some deep laid Scheme in political Craft and Juggle." "Is it not the avowed Policy of the whole Kingdom that we are to be restrained . . . in every Exertion for our continental Interest, if it should be judged to interfere in the least with their Systems of Wealth?" he asked. "Where then is their boasted Tenderness, their

51. Dickinson, "Farmer's Letters," in McDonald, *Empire and Nation*, 18–19. Compare to Jonathan Mayhew in *The Snare Broken*, 29: "Let us, as much as in us lies, cultivate harmony and brotherly love between our fellow subjects in Britain and ourselves. . . . There are no other people on earth, that so 'naturally care for us.' We are connected with them by the strongest ties; in some measure by *blood*. . . . We are strongly connected with them by a great commercial intercourse, by our common language, by our common religion as protestants, and by being subjects of the same King, whom God long preserve and prosper."

Magnanimity, and benevolent Intentions? . . . *In Nubibus, in
the Clouds*," he answered, "that is no where."[52]

Others came around to Downer's view: Samuel Adams in
Boston; William Goddard, still writing for the *Providence
Gazette* but now living in New York; Christopher Gadsden
in Charleston. By late 1766, despite "all that [had] been done
in favor of the Colonies," Goddard still found "too much Reason for Discontent and uneasy Apprehensions." Trade was still
halted, he complained, "or driven from its usual Channels,"
leaving it in a "languishing State"; but even more significant
was the "considerable Body of Regular Troops . . . stationed
among [the colonists] without any visible Occasion," and the
fact that some assemblies had been required to support them.
"If [the British] were sincere in any benevolent Intentions,"
Downer had asked, "would they be multiplying Crown Officers
amongst us, planting officers and Soldiers in every Corner of
the Country, contriving all Methods of draining us of every
Shilling of our Money. . . ?" In December 1766, Samuel Adams,
too, mentioned the new Quartering Act in a letter to Gadsden. It
required the governor and council of any province where His
Majesty's troops were stationed to supply them at the expense of
the province. Was this not taxing the colonists "as effectually as
the Stamp Act?" Adams asked. New Yorkers had had troops
stationed among them for several months; "perhaps I am cap-
tious," he said, "however I always looked upon a standing Army
especially in time of peace not only [as] a Disturbance but in
every respect dangerous to civil Community." The troops moreover had been employed against the civilian "rent rioters" in
rural New York—a subject of concern to radical observers.[53]

52. Downer to New York Sons of Liberty, Providence, July 21,
1766, RIHS, Peck Mss., III, 3.

53. Goddard's résumé of the Stamp Act crisis in *Prov. Gaz.*, September 13, 1766; Downer to New York Sons, Providence, July 21, 1766,
RIHS, Peck Mss., III, 3; Adams to Gadsden, Boston, December 11, 1766,
in Cushing, *Writings of Samuel Adams*, I, 108–11. Gadsden's sentiments
are known not from contemporary documents but from accounts of his
meeting with the Sons of Liberty in the fall of 1766 which were unfortunately written years later. See, for example, Joseph Johnson, *Traditions and Reminiscences Chiefly of the American Revolution in the
South* (Charleston, 1851), 28, 29.

Historians have to some extent been led astray by Capt. John

The conclusion of Downer and Adams was clear: repeal meant only an alteration, not an end, of the "evil designs" of 1765. As Downer put it, "WHAT COULD NOT BE BROUGHT TO PASS BY AN UNDISGUISED AND OPEN ATTACK UPON OUR LIBERTIES IS INTENDED TO BE DONE BY SECRET MACHINA-TIONS, BY ARTIFICE AND CUNNING." "The Stamp Act," Adams said, "was like the sword that Nero wished for, to have decollated the Roman People at a stroke, or like Job's Sea monster . . . 'who sinks a River, and who thirsts again.'" With uncanny accuracy, he suggested the next threat might come in the form of trade regulations. "Suppose for Instance," he asked Gadsden, "that some time hereafter under the Pre-text of Regulating Trade only, a revenue should be designed to be raised out of the Colonys, would it signify anything whether it be called a Stamp Act or an Act for the Regula-tion of the Trade of America?"[54]

Despite these dark conclusions, however, men such as Adams or Goddard badly wanted to share their countrymen's charitable assessment of the British government. Where was the danger? "None from His present Majesty and the Par-liam[en]t, in their Intention," Adams said. But again he stressed that "such is human Frailty that 'the best may err sometimes,'" especially as to colonies that were "remote from the national Parliam[en]t, and unrepresented." Even the acts of trade Adams projected would be passed only "thro the In-advertency of our friends or for want of suitable Intelligence from the Colonys," not from malevolence. For William

---

Montresor's snide remark that the Sons of Liberty were "great op-posers to these [anti-Rent] Rioters as they are of opinion no one is entitled to Riot but themselves." (G. D. Skull, ed., *The Montresor Journals*, NYHS *Colls. for 1881* [New York, 1882], 363.) Such an in-terpretation ignores the generally sympathetic response of the radical press to the Rent Rioters. See particularly a letter from a "gentleman in ——— to a Friend in Providence," *Prov. Gaz.*, August 9, 1766, and *N.Y. Jour.*, August 21, 1766. John Holt's reprinting of the letter and his refusal to apologize when criticized (*N.Y. Jour.*, September 18) also cast doubt on the so-called subserviency of the New York radicals to the landed aristocracy.

54. Downer to New York Sons, Providence, July 21, 1766, RIHS, Peck Mss., III, 3; Adams to Gadsden, Boston, December 11, 1766, Cushing, *Writings of Samuel Adams*, I, 109–10.

Goddard, like Downer, the Declaratory Act had "entirely destroyed the Merit of the Repeal," and showed that "the Parliament with the new Ministry . . . acted upon the same Principles as . . . the old," and claimed even more power than that sought through the Stamp Act "whenever *they* should think it expedient." But, against all the evidence he cited, and in the desire to think the best of England, Goddard's final conclusion was not unlike that of other Americans. "For the Honor of the new Ministry," he said, "we would impute all these strange Things to the Influence of the old."[55]

In assigning responsibility for continued "oppressive" policies, the colonists tended to accuse more familiar figures. "Much Danger lies here at Home," Downer warned, among men "who have it at Heart to enslave the People." For Downer, such figures apparently included all who held office and were thus naturally prone to extend their power. More often, writers followed the example of Isaac Barré, who in 1765 had denounced British officials sent to the colonies to prey upon the Americans, to spy out their liberties, "to misrepresent their actions." Newspapers of 1765 and 1766 continually repeated rumors that the Stamp Act had been proposed and promoted by British agents on the American continent.[56] With more reason, the Americans claimed that British officials presented colonial pleas and conduct in the least favorable way: "the body of these [Crown] Officers (who are generally Europeans) from one End of the Continent to the other," Ezra Stiles wrote, "take pains to condemn Americans in every Light and to dispise us to the dirt." Gradually, misrepresentations from "this side the water" became the entire explanation of British policy, as King and Parliament were allegedly led into ill-considered decisions by false information from the colonies. As "Britano Americanus" explained in the *New London Gazette* on October 9, 1767, the colonists were victimized by "a generation of vipers, sons of tyranny and oppression, venality and corruption," who lived among them and "for a paltry interest to themselves and a few debauched

55. *Ibid.*; *Prov. Gaz.*, September 6, 1766.

56. Barré speech in *Boston Gaz.*, *Supplement* May 27, 1765; and see report on London correspondence in *Prov. Gaz.*, August 24, 1765.

supporters and dependents, would . . . plunge millions into
inevitable destruction."[57]

At first, several scattered individuals were singled out for
attack. In 1764, Rhode Island's Governor Stephen Hopkins
complained that royal customs officials were misrepresenting
that colony. By 1765, fears centered on the Newport Junto.
In Charleston, South Carolina, Christopher Gadsden complained of misrepresentation at the hands of local Scottish
merchants. But after 1766, charges focused increasingly on
one man, Massachusetts's Governor Francis Bernard. Opposition to the governor from within the Bay Colony had pre-
dated the Stamp Act agitation, then intensified and spread
when Bernard asserted the absolute authority of Parliament
before the provincial assembly in September 1765 and recommended submission to the Stamp Act. His stance assumed significance for other colonies, too, when he was cited by a dissenting faction in the House of Lords to buttress its opposition to the Stamp Act's repeal: "We are of Opinion," the Lords
said, "that the total Repeal of that Law, especially while . . .
Resistance continues would (as Governor Bernard says in
their Intention) *make the Authority of Great Britain contemptible hereafter.*"[58]

After 1766, continued concern about Governor Bernard
was prompted by a new departure in his behavior. When

57. Stiles, "Stamp Act Notebook"; Rhode Island Assembly letters
of September 1768 in *Prov. Gaz.*, May 13, 1769; "Americanus," from
New Hampshire Gazette, in *S.C. Gaz.*, November 7, 1768; John Holt's
comments, in brackets, in *N.Y. Jour.*, May 21, 1767, and New York
Assembly's Address to Governor Moore, in *ibid.*, December 3, 1767;
letter to *Newport Mercury* from "A Friend to LIBERTY," reprinted in
Prov. Gaz., September 5, 1767.

58. Hopkins to Lord Halifax, August 15, 1765, PRO, CO 5/1280,
ff. 30–1; Gadsden to F. Pearson, February 13, 1766, in The Papers of
William Legge, Lord Dartmouth, D 1778/2/169, William Salt Library,
Stafford, England; Bernard's speech in Appendix C of Hutchinson,
History of the Province of Massachusetts Bay, III, 334–8; and, for the
reaction, see *Boston Gaz.*, September 30, 1765, April 28 and May 19,
1766; Ezra Stiles's indictment of Bernard in his "Stamp Act Notebook";
and William Goddard's rejection of favorable statements about Bernard
because "his own Speeches plainly . . . show the contrary," *Prov. Gaz.*,
September 6, 1766. Lords' resolutions as published in *Conn. Gaz.*, *Supplement* May 31, 1766.

his local political opposition, James Otis's "country party," exploited resentments of the Stamp Act period to increase its electoral following, Bernard refused to interpret its success as part of a local conflict that had begun before 1765. His earlier administration, Bernard inaccurately reported to England, had been marked by utmost harmony; Otis's campaign was not aimed merely at him, but at the royal authority he and his fellow officials embodied, and as such amounted to a continuation of the Stamp Act agitation.[59] The interpretation was purposeful: it was not he, Bernard, who had failed through personal errors to uphold his power in Massachusetts. Guilt rested rather on Otis and his "faction," who attacked him as the nearest spokesman for the Crown.

Still, the governor's political failure became apparent as the opposition won control of the assembly in 1766 and refused to return some of Bernard's supporters to the council, and as suspicions and recriminations increasingly robbed him of the authority and respect normally due to his office. For Bernard, defeat was particularly bitter. A man of humble background, lifted into the colonial service through the wife he fortunately won—a cousin of Lord Barrington—he had hoped to make his name and fortune in the colonies. From failure he first sought flight: if summoned to England, Bernard pleaded, he could fully inform the ministry on the colonial situation. When that alternative was refused, he instead returned to his pen. Bernard had already begun submitting to the Board of Trade and the secretary of state long reports so replete with detail and interpretation they naturally commanded attention. (Whenever the ministry submitted American correspondence to Parliament in the 1760's, the collections included a disproportionate number of Governor Bernard's letters.) Now encouraged by being cited in the House of Lords and praised by the ministry, Bernard found in his letters' influence in London a surrogate for the power he had lost in Massachusetts. Unfortunately, the governor distorted daily events. His misguided conviction that the "faction" had espoused violence as its primary method of opposition, for example, kept him from recognizing the radi-

59. Bernard to Shelburne, December 22, 1766, PRO, CO 5/755, 9–16.

cals' peace-keeping efforts as fully as could his lieutenant governor, Thomas Hutchinson. Equally dangerous, Bernard's elaborate accounts were sometimes built on insubstantial evidence, perhaps an inevitable outcome when an official submits his longest reports at a time when and even because he has become estranged from a wide range of observers and informants. When some of these letters were pirated from England and published by the Bostonians in 1769, they seemed so fully to confirm suspicions of the governor that they spelled an effective end to his usefulness in America.[60]

Long before his letters were published, however, Bernard's actions in Massachusetts spurred charges that he was misrepresenting the colonies. In a speech to the Massachusetts Assembly of May 1766, the governor blamed the Stamp Act agitation on a few private persons acting under "the borrowed Mask of patriotic Zeal," and he charged that their inflammatory efforts were continuing despite repeal. Since the Americans were currently waging an all-out campaign for peace and order to manifest their gratefulness to the Crown, the charge brought quick recriminations. For months there had been an "undisturbed Tranquility" in the province, the assembly answered; allegations to the contrary could come only from "Persons not well affected to this People," persons who had taken "all Occasions from the just Resentment of the People, to represent them as inflammatory, disaffected and disloyal." Immediately afterwards, both James Otis and William Brattle wrote to England to counteract any reports "that the Colonies are in the least disposed but to their duty and loyalty to the best of Kings."[61]

60. Portrait of Bernard in Edmund S. and Helen M. Morgan, *The Stamp Act Crisis* (New York, 1963), 19–35, especially 23–4. See also Bernard's letters to Shelburne, September 7 and 14, 1767, PRO, CO 5/756, 237–8, 243–5: on the seventh, he reported that efforts to revive nonimportation had failed, and analyzed the development exhaustively. Then, on the fourteenth, he admitted he had been in error, and built his speculations upon an observation that a recent *Boston Gazette* had been milder than usual.

61. Bernard's speech and Assembly's answer in *Boston Gaz.*, June 2 and 9, 1766. Otis to Conway, Boston, June 9, 1766, PRO, CO 5/755, 523–5; Brattle to Dartmouth, Boston, June 2, 1766, Dartmouth Papers, D 1778/2/205.

Events thereafter only reinforced suspicions of the governor. Bernard presented a recommendation from England that victims of the Stamp Act riots be compensated for their losses in such a fashion that the assembly refused to honor it, whereupon he reported the incident so unfavorably that the colony's agent in London, Dennis DeBerdt, immediately suspected that the account was "a slander on the Province." In the fall of 1766, fear of a riot prevented customs officials from breaking into merchant Daniel Malcom's house to search for smuggled goods. To Bostonians, the governor's effort to submit *ex parte* evidence on the incident was clearly designed "to cast a reflection on . . . the whole Town, as if they were Contemners of public Authority and Encouragers of Tumults and Riot." Again their fears were confirmed the next January, when DeBerdt wrote from London that "there are some among yourselves who delight to give false Representations of the Province."[62] Finally, in late 1767, Bernard showed the assembly a letter from Secretary of State Shelburne that in itself seemed to document what the colonists suspected, for Shelburne expressed the King's sorrow that ill-temper remained in Massachusetts Bay despite the Stamp Act's repeal. Misrepresentation remained a major complaint again in the letters protesting the Townshend duties which the Massachusetts Assembly adopted in January 1768. To DeBerdt the assembly claimed that the English government had been "grossly misinformed" as to the temper and behavior of the colony; and again it wrote Lord Shelburne of its fears "that the Colonies have been misrepresented to his Majesty's Ministers and the Parliament, as having an undutiful disposition . . . and a disaffection to the mother-kingdom."[63]

62. *Boston Gaz.*, June 9, 1765, and Boston news in *Prov. Gaz.*, November 30, 1766. DeBerdt to Thomas Cushing, London, August 6, 1766, in Albert Matthews, ed., *Letters of Dennys DeBerdt, 1757–1770* (Cambridge, Eng., 1911), 322. Malcom: Boston Town Committee to DeBerdt, extract, PRO, CO 5/755, 735–9, and depositions in PRO, Treas. 1/446 and 452, and CO 5/755. Printed version of DeBerdt to Otis (who was appointed by the town to write to the agent about the incident), London, January 10, 1767, PRO, CO 5/756, 135.

63. Hutchinson, *History of the Province of Massachusetts Bay*, III, 133–5; letters of January 12 and 15 in *Boston Gaz.*, April 4 and March 21, 1768.

But why should Bernard and his fellow royal officials misrepresent the colonists as factious, disposed to riot, disloyal? Certainly such reports put the officials' actions "in a more advantageous light," as an account in the *New York Journal* explained fully.[64] For Bostonians the motive appeared even more ominous. Was it not perhaps to justify military rule? During the Daniel Malcom affair, customs officials had already threatened the Bostonians with soldiers, and the impression that customs officers sought military reinforcement under the pretext of anarchy and disorder seemed verified by the *Romney*'s arrival in Boston Harbor after the minor incident of March 18, 1768. And had not the customsmen exacerbated the *Liberty* riot of June 1768, which led to the stationing of regular troops in the town the following October? For colonists this military build-up was unnecessary. Boston was not in a state of anarchy; incidents before the *Liberty* riot had been trivial, and even that more serious incident had been brought under control by the steady efforts of native Bostonians. Eventually, the British government came to much the same conclusion.[65]

64. *N.Y. Jour.*, *Supplement* June 18, 1768, for account by one "who had lived long in America . . ." from the London *Chronicle*: "Governors and other officers of the crown, even the little officers of the revenue sent from hence," mix accounts of "their own loyal and faithful conduct" with darker representations of the colonists to put their own conduct in a better light. Every good thing done by the provincial assemblies to promote the King's service happened as a result of the governor's influence. "And if through his own imprudence, or real want of capacity, any thing goes wrong, he is never at fault; the Assembly and the people are to bear all the blame;—they are factious . . . turbulent, disloyal, impatient of government, disrespectful to his *Majesty's Representative*—Then the custom-house officer represents the people as all inclined to *smuggling*," only French and Dutch goods would be used but for his "*extreme vigilance*," for which he deserves "a *larger salary*," etc.

65. See deposition of William Mackay, September 24, sworn October 20, 1766, on the Malcom affair, in PRO, CO 5/755, f. 743: "Mr. Hallowell told me this Affair wou'd be of bad Consequence to the Town and Province, that they must have a Regiment of Soldiers here to Assist them in doing their Duty, I told him if Soldiers were sent for, it wou'd be his Fault and not ours as we wanted none." John Shy, *Toward Lexington: The Role of the British Army in the Coming of the American Revolution* (Princeton, 1965), 298–301; and see also

In the immediate aftermath of the troops' arrival, colonists throughout the American continent with increasing unanimity indicted Crown officials in the Bay Colony. In October 1768, Pennsylvania Chief Justice William Allen wrote correspondents in England that "the gross Misrepresentations of Governor Bernard (who, was his true Character as well known with you as it is in America, would be little regarded) have very undeservedly inflamed the Nation." New Yorkers burned Bernard in effigy two months later, and as late as 1770 the Portsmouth Town Meeting blamed misrepresentation for America's grievances. "It is the Opinion of this Town," it resolved, "That our King, and many of the principal Men in the Nation, have been greatly deceived by the false and malicious Accounts sent from America by Governor Bernard, the Commissioners [of Customs] and other wicked designing Persons who expected to enrich themselves on the Spoils of America."[66]

A belief in misrepresentation was, however, insufficient to transform American opposition from resistance to revolution. Its implications were reformist, not revolutionary. To assuage conditions, Parliament need only do as the *New London Gazette*'s "Britano Americanus" recommended and "remove from . . . trust and confidence all such traiterous conspirators . . . all such despotic, arbitrary, corrupt and dangerous Tories . . . who, true *Iscariots*, would betray their master all his wide dominions for a pitiful post in some new excise office."[67] Moreover, misrepresentation absolved officials in

item from London *Chronicle*, April 22, 1769, quoted in Frothingham, *Joseph Warren*, 76: "I was at Boston last October [1768], and found that the patriot leaders of the opposition were much more concerned at any mobs that happened than the Government people. These last seemed pleased with them, as countenancing their representations,— the necessity of sending soldiers to keep them in order."

66. Allen to David and John Barclay, October 29, 1768, in Lewis Burd Walker, ed., *The Burd Papers*: [Vol. I,] *Extracts from Chief Justice William Allen's Letter Book* (n. p., 1897), 74. New York effigy-burning in Shy, *Toward Lexington*, 387; Portsmouth Town Meeting in Belknap Papers, 61.c.138, MHS, and see also "The Citizen," No. VIII, in *Pa. Jour.*, January 19, 1769.

67. *New London Gaz.*, October 9, 1769, and also Thomas Cushing (for a committee of the Boston Town Meeting) to Dennis DeBerdt,

London of any guilt for their actions. This was true for the
dispatch of troops to Boston; it apparently also freed Lord
Hillsborough of responsibility for his famous order to rescind
the Massachusetts circular letter of February 1768. Because
Hillsborough erroneously blamed the letter on a "thin House at
the end of the session" and because, unjustifiably, he found
it inflammatory, the colonial secretary must have acted on
false information. In September 1768, the Rhode Island
Assembly appealed to Hillsborough to act on his "Sense and
love of Liberty" in re-establishing harmony, despite the "secret Machinations" of men who "misrepresented and abused"
the dutiful Americans; and as late as November 14, 1768, a
letter in the *Boston Gazette* completely exonerated the secretary from any implications of wrongdoing. The protraction
of grievances was "not to be imputed to an unkind disposition
in Lord Hillsborough towards us," it said, "but altogether to
the malicious and false representations of an infamous faction
on this side the water."[68]

For the radical movement to become revolutionary, more
extreme conclusions were necessary. The Americans must
become convinced, as John Dickinson put it, that "mistake
or passion" could not explain Britain's wrong-headed actions.
It had to appear "UNDOUBTED that an inveterate resolution
is formed to annihilate the liberties of the governed," one
that involved the King, Parliament, and ministry as centrally
as their servants in the colonies. And to arrive at such a conclusion, colonists had to turn their eyes from their own
continent to London, to examine the actions of King, Parliament, and ministry. In that fact lay the truth of a statement
continually repeated by colonists during the frenetic days of

---

September 27, 1768, Dartmouth Papers, D 1778/2/289: "Nothing we
apprehend is wanting to restore a much desired harmony but for his
Majesty's Subjects on both sides the Atlantick fully to explain themselves to each other which is not likely to be done thro' the medium
of interested Men."

68. Hillsborough to Bernard, April 22, 1768, *Boston Gaz.*, July 4,
1768; Massachusetts Assembly to Hillsborough, June 30, 1768, in
ibid., July 18, 1768; Rhode Island Assembly letters in *Prov. Gaz.*,
May 13, 1769. Note also that one "Strip Mask" continued Hillsborough's defense in the November 21, 1768, *Boston Gaz.*

the Stamp Act crisis—that only Great Britain could force America toward independence.[69]

69. See Dickinson, "Farmer's Letters," in McDonald, *Empire and Nation*, 18, and Dickinson to William Pitt, Philadelphia, December 21, 1765, PRO, Chatham Papers, 30/8, Vol. 97; also Gadsden to F. Pearson, February 20, 1766, Dartmouth Papers, D 1778/2/169: "The King has not more loyal Subjects nor has all true English Men better and more staunch Friends than we native Americans"; "we desire to be knit together with you in the United Affection and Interest and it must be your own Fault if we are not lastingly so."

PART THREE

FROM RESISTANCE
TO REVOLUTION

CHAPTER SIX

———— ·⦿· ————

THE INTERNATIONAL
SONS OF LIBERTY AND
THE MINISTERIAL PLOT,
1768–1770

[I]

THE AMERICANS WERE NOT DEDICATED to overthrowing the King's authority at the outset of the Townshend agitation. Yet they were, in a sense, already world revolutionaries. Arthur Lee later summarized the far-reaching aspirations of contemporary radicalism. No man, he said, could be a sincere lover of liberty who was not in favor of communicating that blessing to all peoples: the "giving or restoring it, not only to our brethren of Scotland and Ireland, but even to France itself, were it in our power, is one of the principal articles of Whiggism." Appropriately, then, colonial observers were acutely interested whenever or wherever militant reform movements or insurrections broke out against repressive regimes—in Spain, France, Turkey, Poland. Their newspaper editors put together accounts from whatever fragmentary sources were available, frequently adding comments to celebrate the successes or lament the failures of the freedom fighters of their day, whom they called the "sons of liberty." The use of that term, which after 1765 was strongly associated with the Stamp Act agitation, was significant. Even the colonists' resistance to the Stamp Act, which would have taxed only Americans, was considered but one episode

in a worldwide struggle between liberty and despotism.[1]
This absorption in affairs outside their continent played a
central role in the colonists' own conversion from loyalty to
active revolution.

Certain revolutionaries or militant reformers were especially
compelling to Americans. In 1765–6, attention was drawn
to a Prince Heraclius of Georgia, who was leading an apparently successful fight against the Turks. More enduring
and significant was colonial interest in Pascal Paoli, whom
John Holt's *New York Journal* called "the greatest man on
earth," and in Paoli's followers, the "sons of liberty in Corsica," who for decades had opposed Genoese rule. Their
"glorious struggle," Holt claimed, was "extremely . . . interesting to every friend of liberty and the just rights of mankind."[2]

Nor did the British Empire lack its militants. In Ireland, a
group of patriots were struggling for a broad slate of constitutional reforms. Among these Irish "sons of liberty" Dr.
Charles Lucas, apothecary, editor of the *Freeman's Journal*,
and member of the Irish Parliament for Dublin, whose patriotic activities dated back to the 1740's, was apparently best
known to Americans. In London, John Wilkes had assumed
Liberty's cause by opposing general warrants, which were
issued at large and authorized the seizure of private papers.
America's involvement with all these causes was emphasized
by Silas Downer in 1768, when he dedicated Providence's
Liberty Tree *"in the name and behalf of all the true* SONS *of*
LIBERTY *in* America, Great-Britain, Ireland, Corsica, *or
wheresoever they may be dispersed throughout the world."*[3]

As of 1766, this camaraderie was one among victors. The
Stamp Act was repealed, Wilkes had won a court decision

1. See especially William Goddard's résumé of the Stamp Act
conflict in *Prov. Gaz.*, September 6, 1766.

2. *N.Y. Jour.*, June 11, 1767 (bracketed comment), *Supplement*
September 15, 1768, and August 6, 1767; letter from *London Chronicle*,
explaining Paoli's significance, in *New London Gaz.*, October 7, 1768.

3. Downer, as "a Son of Liberty," *Discourse, Delivered in Providence, in the Colony of Rhode Island, upon the 25th Day of July, 1768.
At the Dedication of the Tree of Liberty. . . .* (Providence, 1768); republished in *The Magazine of History* (New York), Extra Number 65,
XVI (1918), 309–24, especially 323–4.

that general warrants were illegal, and there were signs of change in Ireland that might work to the patriots' advantage. Indeed, it seemed to be "an Aera peculiarly favorable to Liberty in all Parts of the World."[4] Two years later, newer developments reinforced that conclusion: the Irish won Crown approval of a much-needed Octennial Act, Wilkes returned from exile and, in March 1768, was elected a Member of Parliament for Middlesex County.

But within the next four years, from 1768 to 1772, Wilkes, Paoli, the Irish, and the Americans all suffered serious reverses. Each of these defeats, moreover, viewed individually and in the aggregate, reflected directly on the British government, and led American radicals to reassess successively the British ministry, the Parliament, and finally the Crown itself, until they came to doubt the possibility of maintaining freedom under British rule. The period marked a turning of the way, the most crucial years in the prewar decade. Through the failure of radicals abroad the colonists themselves were pushed, clearly if reluctantly, onto the path toward revolution.

Colonial involvement with John Wilkes was closer than that with any other non-American "son of liberty." Interest dated back to the inception of the "Wilkes case" in 1763, when the English publicist was arrested on a general warrant for his famous *North Briton Number 45*, accused of seditious libel, and then chose to go into exile. Colonial enthusiasm revived with the patriot's return to England and his election to Parliament in 1768. "Wilkes and Liberty" were toasted from New England to South Carolina. Towns were named after him—such as Wilkes-Barre, Pennsylvania, settled in 1769 by the Connecticut Son of Liberty John Durkee—as were children, for instance, the Boston Son of Liberty Nathaniel Barber's son Wilkes. (Barber's other children were named Oliver Cromwell and Catharine Macaulay.) By 1770, gifts for Wilkes and substantial contributions to his cause were sent from several colonies, and that "great patriot" had correspondents in the West Indies, Virginia, Maryland, and, most important, in Boston, where the local Sons of Liberty

4. *Prov. Gaz.*, September 6, 1766.

sent off the first of several letters in June 1768. By then, the Boston Sons of Liberty were no longer the Loyal Nine of the Stamp Act days, but an organization of men more prominent to later ages, men who became the nucleus of the Massachusetts revolutionary movement: John Adams, Joseph Warren, Thomas Young, Benjamin Church, Benjamin Kent, James Otis, Samuel Adams, John Hancock, Richard Dana, Josiah Quincy, Jr., and the organization's secretary, William Palfrey, who carried on his own private correspondence with Wilkes.[5]

Why such enthusiasm for a man whom Benjamin Franklin, viewing the Wilkes agitation from London, characterized as "an outlaw . . . of bad personal character, not worth a farthing"? First of all, Wilkes was welcomed as an advocate of certain "generous and inflexible principles" already held by the colonists. Wilkes's sentiments were clearly of the Real Whig school. His personal library contained the books colonists studied and quoted, those of Trenchard, Gordon, Locke, Harrington, Molesworth, Sidney. His own printed works, such as his introduction to a projected history of England, or the *North Briton*, were replete with Whig sentiments that commended their author to like-minded observers in England and America.[6]

5. Oscar J. Harvey, "Wilkes-Barre's History," in *Wilkes-Barre . . . 1769–1906* (Wilkes-Barre, 1906), 19–20; and on Barber, Boston news of April 30 in *S.C. Gaz., Supplement* May 17, 1770. Wilkes's correspondence with Bostonians is available in George M. Elsey, ed., "John Wilkes and William Palfrey," CSM *Pubs.*, XXXIV (*Trans.*, 1937–42), 411–28; Worthington C. Ford, ed., "John Wilkes and Boston," MHS *Procs.*, XLVII (1913–14), 190–215; William V. Wells, *The Life and Public Service of Samuel Adams* (Boston, 1865), I, 377–8; John Gorham Palfrey, "Life of William Palfrey," in Jared Sparks, ed., *Library of American Biography*, 2nd Ser., VII (Boston, 1848), 358–62; MHS *Procs.*, VI (1862–3), 480–3. Some unpublished letters remain in the Palfrey Family Papers, HUL; and in BM Add. Mss., 30870, which also includes correspondence to Wilkes from Virginia and the West Indies.

6. Benjamin Franklin to William Franklin, London, April 16, 1768, in John Bigelow, ed., *Complete Works of Benjamin Franklin*, IV (New York, 1887), 149; Sons of Liberty to Wilkes, Boston, June 6, 1768, XLVII, 191. Catalogue of Wilkes's Library, 1764, in Guildhall Library, London.

Wilkes's political ideology, in fact, linked him with what remained of a Real Whig party in British politics—by the reign of George III a fringe group of the far left, whose members seemed increasingly eccentric, even anachronistic, to contemporaries of greater influence and sophistication. Thomas Hollis, who personified Whiggism for Samuel Johnson, seemed to Horace Walpole "a most excellent man, a most immaculate Whig, but as a simple a poor soul as ever existed," a man "formed to adorn a pure republic, not to shine in a depraved monarchy." By the late 1760's Catharine Macaulay, Hollis, and others of their persuasion had become obsessed with the steady erosion of British liberty at the hand, as they saw it, of a resurgent executive power. Whiggism and "the cause of Revolution"—that is, the maintenance of the constitutional balance achieved by the Glorious Revolution— were "everywhere ruining." With Wilkes's return from exile, prospects improved: for Hollis, Wilkes was a "wonderful man" who championed "with fortitude and magnanimity . . . the cause of a great, and yet free, though a sunken, falling people."[7]

Any unbalancing of the British constitution would, of course, affect all subjects of the Crown, whether at home or in the colonies. Thus it seemed significant that the American Stamp Tax had coincided with England's equally short-lived Cider Tax. Now issues in the Wilkes case echoed other American grievances. Wilkes's reputation as a champion of liberty in England stemmed in large part from his campaign against general warrants. In 1768, Americans were confronted with a similar issue in the guise of writs of assistance. Although the most famous writs of assistance controversy had been waged in Massachusetts in 1761, the issue was reopened when the Townshend Act authorized their use by customs officials in all the colonies and awoke opposition

---

7. Caroline Robbins, "The Strenuous Whig: Thomas Hollis of Lincoln's Inn," *W. M. Q.*, VII (1950), 407, 408–9, 410 (quoting Hollis); Walpole to the Rev. William Mason, London, April 7, 1780, in Paget Toynbee, ed., *The Letters of Horace Walpole*, XI (Oxford, 1904), 150; Horace Walpole, *Memoirs of the Reign of King George the Third* (New York, 1894), ed. G. F. Russell Barker, III, 220. Hollis to a friend, [1765,] in Francis Blackburne, ed., *Memoirs of Thomas Hollis, Esq.* (London, 1780), I, 289.

throughout the American continent.[8] This development coincided with Wilkes's return to political prominence. Thus it
was natural for Americans to look to Wilkes, the man who
had defeated general warrants in England, as a defender of
the whole constitutional cause.

John Dickinson's "Letters from a Farmer in Pennsylvania"
offered a common platform for both Wilkes and the Americans—and, in fact, the Irish as well. The Boston Sons of
Liberty included a copy of the "Farmer's Letters" with their
first letter to Wilkes, declaring flatly that "his sentiments are
ours." In reply, Wilkes thanked them and said the cause of
freedom was "perfectly understood" in Dickinson's tracts;
later, he claimed that the cause of liberty had never been so
ably argued in any place at any time. Meanwhile, extracts
from the "Farmer's Letters" applicable to Ireland were quickly
reprinted in Charles Lucas's *Freeman's Journal*, and thereafter continually reproduced as their popularity increased
among the Irish patriots.[9]

Wilkes's agreement with Dickinson's careful distinction
between liberty and licentiousness and with his insistence
that peaceful modes of resistance be exhausted before resorting to force, influenced Wilkes's conduct in ways that made
him congenial to the Americans. For the readers of colonial
papers, Wilkes was not the mob leader and demagogue often
pictured by historians, but a man who, like the colonial
leaders, was forced continually to enjoin his followers to
peace and order. Before the tumultuous Middlesex election
of March 1768, it was said, Wilkes distributed 40,000 hand-
bills asking "that all possible measures may be used to preserve peace and good order through the whole of the
approaching election . . . to convince the world, that liberty
is not joined to licentiousness." When violence nonetheless
broke out (owing, the newspapers hinted, to provocations

8. Oliver M. Dickerson, "Writs of Assistance as a Cause of the
Revolution," in Richard B. Morris, ed., *The Era of the American
Revolution* (New York, 1939), 40–75.

9. Sons of Liberty to Wilkes, June 6, 1768, and Wilkes's reply,
King's Bench Prison, July 19, 1768, MHS *Procs.*, XLVII, 191–2, and
London letter, January 19, in *S.C. Gaz.*, May 4, 1769. Michael Kraus,
"America and the Irish Revolutionary Movement in the Eighteenth
Century," in Morris, *Era of the American Revolution*, 336.

from his opponents), Wilkes placated the crowd, sent several of his committee to patrol the City and London's West End "to preserve peace and good order," and even commiserated with the riot's victims over the "outrageous and scandalous behaviour" that flowed from the "intemperate zeal of the populace." All of Wilkes's behavior seemed to follow the same pattern: colonists read of his leaning out of a window at the Three Tuns Tavern in Spitalfield, trying to disperse a crowd that had "rescued" him on his way to the King's Bench Prison, to which he was committed in the summer of 1768 for publishing the *North Briton Number 45* and an *Essay on Women.* When the mob came with pickaxes to level the prison walls, once more Wilkes asked them to disperse. Time and again he returned to his window, begging the crowd "not to commit any violence," telling them "that if they were his friends, the best way to shew it would be to depart to their respective homes." Finally, when his term was over and he was released, Wilkes went directly to Kent from the prison door to prevent disorder in London, while his followers staged a quiet and peaceful celebration much like those organized by their comrades in America. On both sides of the Atlantic, it seemed appropriate that the buttons given Wilkes by the manufacturers of Birmingham for distribution among the sons of liberty were decorated with an olive branch.[10]

Confidence in Wilkes's political principles and public conduct made criticism of his personal character, such as that raised by Franklin, irrelevant. Irregularities in his conduct were, Hollis said, "as spots in the sun." Moreover, the prosecution of Wilkes had nothing to do with his private life. "It should be remembered," an article in the *Boston Gazette* cautioned, "that if all which the most virulent of his enemies have alleged against him were true . . . it would not have the least weight as to the propriety or equity of any proceedings against him." And as a Rhode Island almanac put it,

10. Accounts of Wilkes's efforts for peace and order run through all the colonial papers. The above narrative draws particularly on *Prov. Gaz.*, May 28, June 4 and 11, and August 6, 1768; *N.Y. Jour.*, June 9, July 28, *Supplement* August 4, 1768, and June 21, 1770; *Pa. Jour.*, June 9, July 7, August 4, 1768; May 4, 1769 (Wilkes buttons), and August 2, 1770; *S.C. Gaz.*, July 18, 1768.

Whatever his fate may be, and however severely his enemies may arraign his private failings, it will never, can never be denied, that his steady opposition to illegal general warrants has been, and ever will be, of lasting benefit to the subjects of Great Britain; that, if he is not virtuous, he is a lover of virtue; and a friend to the civil and religious liberties of mankind; which we have no doubt of his displaying upon all future occasions, if he should sit in the House of Commons.[11]

The colonists hoped that Wilkes would be politically effective, proving *"one* of those incorruptibly *honest men* reserved by heaven to bless, and perhaps save a tottering Empire." Both newspapers and private letters from England continually assured the colonists that Wilkes's supporters included many men of substance as well as the mob, and that his party was strong in the Commons.[12] The main source of Wilkes's strength moreover lay in the City of London, whose merchants had helped the Americans win the Stamp Act's repeal in 1766. Now once again, in 1768, the colonists had many sympathetic London contacts in a position to link their cause with that of Wilkes. George Hayley, Wilkes's brother-in-law, was the commercial agent in England of Boston merchants John Hancock and William Palfrey. The Virginian William Lee, brother of Richard Henry and Francis Lightfoot Lee, and Stephen Sayre, a Princeton graduate and friend of New York's Isaac Sears, also dealt in the American trade in a partnership with the Massachusetts agent in Lon-

11. Hollis to friend, [1765,] in Blackburne, *Hollis Memoirs*, I, 289. *Boston Gaz.*, *Supplement* August 1, 1768; Abraham Weatherwise (pseud.), *The New England Town and Country Almanack . . . for . . . 1769* (Providence [1768]), [3].

12. Sons of Liberty to Wilkes, Boston, June 6, 1768, MHS *Procs.*, XLVII, 191. London news of May 4 in *Boston Gaz.*, *Supplement* August 1, 1768; Arthur Lee to one of his brothers in Virginia, in Richard Henry Lee, *Life of Arthur Lee, LL.D.* (Boston, 1829), I, 189 ("the party of Mr. Wilkes is strong in the house of Commons"). Even Franklin said if Wilkes had had a good character and George III a bad one, the King would have been turned off his throne. In R. W. Postgate, *That Devil Wilkes* (New York, 1929), 130–1.

don, Dennis DeBerdt. Sayre and William Lee, like another of his brothers, Arthur Lee, currently a law student in London, were Wilkes supporters and active in London politics. Sayre and William Lee became sheriffs; William Lee also became the first American alderman of the city, while Arthur Lee was an especially active member of Wilkes's organized followers, the Society of the Supporters of the Bill of Rights.[13]

Rather than saving British liberty by working within British political institutions, however, Wilkes was denied his seat in Parliament. And rather than win redress for the colonists, Wilkes by his failures added dimensions to their grievances that American problems alone might never have suggested.

[II]

In June 1768, when the Boston Sons of Liberty began their correspondence with Wilkes, the Americans already had serious complaints against the British government. The Stamp Act had been repealed, but other unpopular measures remained and new ones were enacted: the Quartering Act, the New York Restraining Act, the Townshend Revenue Act. Within the month, another major grievance was added when Lord Hillsborough's condemnation of the Massachusetts Assembly's circular letter became known. Dispatched to the twelve other colonies in February, the letter had summarized Massachusetts' opposition to recent British measures and

13. Sketches of Arthur and William Lee, and Stephen Sayre, in Francis Wharton, ed., *The Revolutionary Diplomatic Correspondence of the United States*, I (Washington, D.C., 1889), 515–53, 586–9, 614–19; Worthington C. Ford, ed., *Letters of William Lee* (Brooklyn, 1891), I, 5–65; and Palfrey, "William Palfrey," 343–4. Sayre's friendship with Sears was made public after he tried to get Sayre appointed as New York agent. See "Americanus," *N.Y. Jour.*, May 3 and June 14, 1770, and defense of Sears in *ibid.*, June 28, 1770. By the early 1770's Sayre was also a friend and correspondent of Ezra Stiles in Newport, who gave the Son of Liberty Henry Marchant a letter of introduction to Sayre. See Marchant to Stiles, May 14, 1772, and Sayre to Stiles, July 20, 1772, Ezra Stiles Papers, Beinecke Library, Yale University, New Haven, Connecticut. On Arthur Lee see Lee, *Arthur Lee*, I.

asked for intercolonial cooperation, particularly in petitioning for redress. The new American secretary called the letter dangerous and factious, "calculated to inflame the Minds" of the King's colonial subjects, "to promote an unwarrantable Combination, and to . . . subvert the true Principles of the Constitution." Moreover, he demanded that the Massachusetts Assembly rescind the letter or be dissolved, and that the other assemblies express "proper Resentment" or suffer prorogation and perhaps even dissolution.[14]

The Massachusetts Assembly rejected Hillsborough's demand by a vote of 92 to 17. Immediately, 92 became the American "patriotic number" and, to symbolize the colonists' new-found alliance with Wilkes, was constantly linked with the number 45. The Bostonians sent Wilkes two turtles, one weighing 45 pounds, the other 47, making a grand total of 92. In South Carolina, the Charleston mechanics met under their Liberty Tree, trimmed with 45 lights, toasted the "Massachusetts Ninety-two" before the lieutenant governor's house, then marched to the local tavern, where they put 45 bowls of punch on the table, 45 bottles of wine, and 92 glasses.[15] Despite the support of other colonies, however, the Massachusetts "patriotic vote" resulted in the General Court's dissolution. Massachusetts Bay remained without a legislature throughout the rest of that difficult year which in October saw the arrival of British troops in Boston.

Grievances were clearly at hand, but responsibility for them was ambiguous in mid-1768. Occasionally, the ministry was charged with full responsibility for British policy. The Maryland Assembly, for example, explained the whole effort against the Massachusetts circular letter as "an Attempt, in some of His Majesty's Ministers, to suppress all Communication of Sentiments between the Colonies, and to prevent the united Supplications of America from reaching the Royal Ear." Similarly, addresses read to Philadelphia public meetings in April and July 1768 argued that there was a willful design against American liberties, and that it emanated from England. But who in England was responsible? New Yorkers

14. Hillsborough to North American governors, April 21, 1768, PRO, CO 5/241, f. 28.

15. Palfrey to Wilkes, Boston, July 26, [1769,] MHS *Procs.*, XLVII, 206; *S.C. Gaz.*, October 3, 1768, and *Boston Gaz.*, November 7, 1768.

were told that responsibility for the Restraining Act lay not
in the ministry, but in its parliamentary opposition, led by
George Grenville. There was reason to think, a letter from
England said, that had the ministers been left to themselves
they "would gladly have let the Matter [of New York's response to the Quartering Act] sleep, and given the Colonies
some Time to recollect themselves, and to have come voluntarily into what is here called their Duty." The most pervasive view, however, was that the authorities in London were
the well-meaning victims of biased intelligence sent them by
Crown officials in the colonies. Granted that the ministry was
enforcing abusive measures, then, the question remained
whether it acted willfully or passively, from design or from
ignorance.[16] The Wilkes case dissipated this uncertainty.
When the ministry turned its efforts against Wilkes, its acts
could no longer be explained by parliamentary pressure nor,
most important, by false information from distant officials.

The tendency to indict the ministry grew stronger between
the fall of 1768 and the spring of 1769, and nowhere more
clearly than in Massachusetts, where ministerial innocence
had been most strongly asserted. Whereas in January 1768 the
Massachusetts Assembly, pleading false representation, had
directed its agent DeBerdt to "make known to His Majesty's
Ministers the sentiments of this House," by September the
Convention of Towns, although again asserting that the
colony had been greatly misrepresented, directed DeBerdt
to bypass the ministers and present its petition to the King
"*in person.*" In October 1768, the Boston Sons of Liberty still
chose to speak of the ministers as merely "inadequate." By
February 1769, however, William Palfrey referred to "ministerial despotism" being exerted in America; and in April, he
wrote of a "weak and wicked Administration," of "arbitrary
and despotic Ministers," who found "the three Kingdoms
[England, Scotland, and Ireland] too small a field for the
exercise of their rapacity," so they "extended their ravages to
America." A certainty "that the Ministry have formed a plan
for subjugating the Americans and that they are determined

16. Maryland Assembly in *N.Y. Jour., Supplement* July 9, 1768;
Pennsylvania "address," April 25, 1768, printed by William Bradford
as a handbill, and *Pa. Jour.*, July 4, 1768; *N.Y. Jour., Supplement*
September 10, 1767.

to persist in it" was expressed, too, by a committee of Philadelphia merchants in June 1769.[17]

This growing alienation was due to a peculiar confluence of events in England and America. Colonists had read detailed accounts of the "Massacre" at St. George's Fields on May 10, 1768, when royal troops had fired on a crowd assembled outside the King's Bench Prison hoping to catch a glimpse of Wilkes. One innocent young bystander, William Allen, was mistaken for a mob leader, pursued, and shot to death. Five or six rioters, it was reported, were killed and another fifteen wounded. Wilkes subsequently published a letter from Lord Weymouth to the chairman of the Lambeth Quarter Sessions promising troops would be ready if needed by local authorities. In an introduction Wilkes claimed that the letter, sent three weeks before the event, proved that the massacre had been planned in advance by the government. Meanwhile, Americans, too, feared a new governmental reliance on the military. On July 25, 1768, the *South Carolina Gazette* noted that its "Advices . . . intimate that the Government at Home seems more determined than ever that the Revenue Acts . . . shall be enforced," perhaps by force. When troops actually did move into Boston in October 1768, the event was readily seen as a piece with the use of a standing army against civilians in London. Wilkes expressed his "grief and indignation" at the ministry's ordering troops to Boston "as if it were the capital of a province belonging to our enemies, or in the possession of rebels." "Asiatic despotism does not," he claimed, "present a picture more odious in the eye of humanity."[18]

17. *Boston Gaz.*, April 4 and October 10, 1768; Sons of Liberty to Wilkes, October 5, 1768, and Palfrey to Wilkes, February 21, 1769. MHS *Procs.*, XLVII, 193, 197; and Palfrey to Wilkes, April 12, 1769, BM Add. Mss., 30870. Note also Joseph Warren's ambiguity in an April 13, 1769, letter to Wilkes, in MHS *Procs.*, XLVII, 199–200: he wrote of "repeated shocks of Ministerial Oppression" but also of a "weak Administration" and a "misguided Court." Philadelphia to Boston merchants' committee, June 7, 1769, Sparks Mss., XLII, Vol. 7 (Letters of the Philadelphia Merchants), pp. 192–4, HUL.

18. Accounts of the "Massacre" of St. George's Field in *S.C. Gaz.*, July 18; *Pa. Jour.*, *Postscript* July 28; *N.Y. Jour.*, August 4, and *Prov. Gaz.*, July 30, 1768. Wilkes's accusation in *Prov. Gaz.*, March 25,

The ministry was more deeply incriminated by its apparent inhumanity at another Middlesex election held at the town of Brentford on December 6. There the court candidate William Beauchamp Proctor sought to forestall the impending victory of John Glynn, a Wilkes supporter, by hiring a mob to exacerbate a riot. During the disorder George Clark, again an innocent bystander, was killed by two of these "hirelings," Edward McQuirk and Laurence Balfe. Afterwards, the newly elected Glynn labeled the proceedings a violent attack on "the last sacred privilege we have left," the freedom of a county election, an effort "to destroy those whom they [the ministry] could not corrupt."[19]

Judicial proceedings, too, seemed grossly partial toward supporters of the administration. From the outset, the "ministerial" proceedings against Wilkes were accused of irregularity. The *Boston Gazette* reported that Wilkes had been served a writ and bill of discovery so that if proceedings against him were upheld in court all his effects, "even the small pittance generously subscribed by his fellow subjects for discharging his debts," could be forfeited. If he won his days in court, it was said, he still would be required to establish "in an unusual way" his qualifications for the Commons, so as "to give him as much vexation and put him to as much expence as possible." The court refused to release Wilkes on bail, although the charges against him, according to one colonial paper, were "for misdemeanors of so dark a nature, that all the learning of a court has not yet been able to discover their extreme guilt to the understandings of the people." Yet at almost the same time it admitted to bail Donald Maclane, found guilty of willfully murdering William Allen at St. George's Fields, and the two soldiers who aided and abetted him. Wilkes was subsequently imprisoned and fined, and his petition to the Crown for clemency spurned.

1769. *S.C. Gaz.*, July 25, 1768; Wilkes to Sons of Liberty, March 30, 1769, MHS *Procs.*, XLVII, 198. London and Boston events were also linked by "Rusticus," who condemned the ministry, in *S.C. Gaz.*, October 3, 1768, and in a "Letter to Hillsborough," *Prov. Gaz.*, February 17, 1770.

19. *Prov. Gaz.*, March 11, 1769; O. A. Sherrard, *A Life of John Wilkes* (London, 1930), 197–8; George Rudé, *Wilkes and Liberty* (Oxford, 1962), 59–61.

Meanwhile McQuirk and Balfe, convicted at the Old Bailey of murder in the death of George Clark at the Brentford election, were pardoned. This pardon, Arthur Lee claimed, was based upon "a groundless and venal opinion of ten Surgeons, five of whom were placemen, that the blow did not appear to them the cause of the death." As a result, "not one person . . . suffered for that unparallel'd outrage."[20] Bostonians also complained of unequal justice in 1769. Civil and criminal prosecutions against inhabitants were pushed "with great rancor and rigor," William Palfrey claimed, while those against the troops and revenue officers were "frown'd upon and embarrass'd by every possible means."[21]

The rewarding of Crown spokesmen in the colonies also indicated that the ministers were more than passive victims of their biased intelligence. The baronetcy awarded to Francis Bernard in 1769, just as his hated letters were being republished in newspapers throughout the colonies, reminded a South Carolina critic that the "dirty wretches" who had used "their utmost endeavours to cram the late Stamp-Act down our throats" had been amply rewarded by Crown commissions in the courts or customs service. Condemnations of governors and customsmen for their biased accounts of colonial affairs continued. From 1769, however, the American officials were often referred to as "tools" of the ministry in London.[22]

When in January 1769 the colonists learned of the King's speech at the opening of Parliament on November 8, 1768,

20. *Boston Gaz.*, *Supplement* August 1, 1768, and April 24, 1769; *Prov. Gaz.*, April 28, 1770; *N.Y. Jour.*, August 4, and *S.C. Gaz.*, July 18, 1768; Arthur Lee to a brother, London, March 23, 1769, Arthur Lee Papers, HUL; available in Paul P. Hoffman, ed., "Lee Family Papers, 1742–1795," University of Virginia microfilm (Charlottesville, 1966), Roll I.

21. Palfrey to Wilkes, Boston, November 4 or 5, 1769, Palfrey Papers II, b, 89; also Palfrey's earlier letter to Wilkes, July 26, 1769, MHS *Procs.*, XLVII, 205. The royal soldiers, however, thought local justice was partial to the inhabitants: see Hiller B. Zobel, *The Boston Massacre* (New York, 1970), 135–44.

22. "A Planter," *S.C. Gaz.*, June 1, 1769; also *Pa. Jour.*, August 3, 1769, which noted after John Hughes was made collector of the Port of Piscataqua that "Now all the late Stamp Masters, except Z[achariah] H[oo]d, who used all their influence to enslave this country, are provided for by a ——— M[i]n[is]try." "Tools": Thomas Young to Wilkes, September 6, 1769, MHS *Procs.*, XLVII, 209, and letter in

with its reference to a "state of Disobedience to all Law and Government" in Massachusetts, and to a "Disposition to throw off their Dependence on *Great Britain*," they were further embittered. The Massachusetts General Court had assured the British government that accounts of disorder in Boston were exaggerated, and that its circular letter, far from being "factious" and designed to subvert the law, had been voted by a full House and represented the sentiments of the whole province. Furthermore, the letter represented a lawful application of the right of petition. The King's obvious disregard of the colonists' protests, as *North Briton Number 45* had long ago pointed out, could only be ascribed to the ministers who wrote it.[23]

News that the colonists received in March, April, and May 1769 strengthened their disenchantment with the ministry, and at the same time caused them to re-evaluate Parliament itself. In 1768, there had been little fundamental disillusionment with Westminster; hope remained strong that Parliament would remove America's current grievances just as it had earlier repealed the Stamp Act. Such hope, in fact, was implicit in the whole entente between Wilkes and the Americans as originally conceived: it was thought at first, as one pamphlet put it, that Wilkes would sit "amidst the great assembly of the people," where his abilities "will prove to the good of our country."[24] Optimism was further encouraged by the fact that Wilkes was to sit in a new Parliament, freshly elected in 1768. As "Rusticus" put it in the October 3, 1768, *South Carolina Gazette*, "God be praised, the house that laid these burthens on us is at an end; their power is over, and we may hope better things from their successors."

The new Parliament, however, not only endorsed the King's condemnations of Massachusetts, but asked that he take steps for "bringing to condign punishment the chief authors and instigators of the late disorders." The King, Parliament sug-

N.Y. Jour., April 12, 1770, which spoke of "the designs of wicked ministers, at home, and . . . the many tools of power, resident in the colonies."

23. *Boston Gaz.*, January 16, 1769; also letter from New York in *New London Gaz.*, January 20, 1769: They would see by the King's speech in the newspapers "how the Ministry drive on at home."

24. *Britannia's Intercession for the Deliverance of John Wilkes, Esq. from Persecution and Banishment* (6th edn., Boston, 1769), 10.

gested, should have the governor submit to England the names of the principal offenders and as much information as possible on the "treasons" committed within the past year, "in order that his Majesty may issue a special commission for enquiring of, hearing and determining the said offences within this realm" according to an act passed under Henry VIII. Letters from London informed Bostonians that the resolves were "drawn up by administration," and that Hillsborough even refused to accept from the Massachusetts agent Dennis De-Berdt papers and affidavits from Boston because they were not properly authorized and were "of too *trivial* a nature."[25]

In February, the House of Commons condemned Wilkes's censure of Lord Weymouth's letter as "an insolent, scandalous, and seditious libel, tending to a total subversion of all good order and legal government," and, upon a motion by the secretary of war, Lord Barrington, then expelled the Middlesex representative. "By my expulsion," Wilkes told his Middlesex electors, "the Ministry have . . . openly shewn that they entertain no scruple of violating the sacred Rights of the People, even in the most important case, that of having a Deputy nominated by themselves to the great Council of the nation." If through its control of Parliament the ministry could dictate whom the electors must not send to Parliament, he warned, it would soon dictate who shall be sent—a prediction that would shortly seem fulfilled—"and then the boasted constitution of England will be entirely torn up by the roots." In mid-April, Joseph Warren told Wilkes that his expulsion had "filled America with Grief." Wilkes's "inflexible Patriotism" and fortitude under "the repeated shocks of Ministerial Oppression" had, it seemed, won him the resentment of the "Enemies of Freedom," who were using their "whole Power to crush every Man who has Ability to discover and Firmness to pursue the national Welfare."[26]

25. Extracts of Lords' and Commons' proceedings in *Pa. Jour.,* March 23, April 27, 1769, and Boston news of March 27 in *Prov. Gaz.,* April 1, 1769.

26. *Prov. Gaz.,* March 25, 1769. J. Steven Watson, *The Reign of George III, 1760–1815* (Oxford, 1960), 136. Wilkes's statements in *Boston Gaz.,* April 10, and *S.C. Gaz.,* May 4, 1769. Joseph Warren to Wilkes, April 13, 1769, MHS *Procs.,* XLVII, 199–200.

As Wilkes returned to the polls at Brentford, and the Middlesex electors rallied a second, third, then fourth time to re-elect him to Parliament, the Americans watched with involvement: he might yet get into the House of Commons and make "a weak and wicked Administration . . . tremble at the name of *Wilkes*," he might yet save "the great System from dashing to pieces." "Our eyes are at present fixed on the county of Middlesex," Thomas Young wrote from Boston in July. Unknown to Young, however, Parliament had already chosen to seat Wilkes's opponent in the fourth Middlesex election, Henry Lawes Luttrell, despite Wilkes's having defeated him at the polls 1145 votes to 296. Later, Wilkes charged explicitly what was commonly inferred in mid-1769, that his expulsion and disqualification had been decided beforehand in the cabinet "and only brought to Parliament by the minister in order to go through the common forms."[27]

In effect, it became plain that Parliament was no longer an institution to which one could appeal against the ministry, but that the ministry and parliamentary majority were "the same Thing." Already in June 1769, Rhode Islanders were informed that the ministry had secured a majority in both houses of Parliament by the purposeful granting of places and pensions, and later statistics seemed to prove the assertion. By the Court Calendar, it was reported in early 1770, 192 Members of Parliament held Crown offices. Since the current pro-government majority was 261, only 69 remaining persons were "uncorrupted"—far fewer than the 188 opposition members. That the opposition constituted a majority of nonpensioned members, did not, of course, give it more legal power. The figures did, however, tarnish any remaining faith in the legislature as a whole. In London, even the relatively moderate Benjamin Franklin concluded by April 1769 that the colonists were no longer justified in speaking of the wisdom and justice of Parliament. A year later, a South Carolina writer found the "doctrine of *trusting* to the British parliament to do [Americans] justice"—respectable enough two years earlier—

27. Palfrey to Wilkes, April 12, 1769, BM Add. Mss., 30870; Sons of Liberty to Wilkes, June 6, 1768, and Young to Wilkes, July 6, 1769, MHS *Procs.*, XLVII, 191, 203; Wilkes to Middlesex Freeholders, April 18, 1770, in *Pa. Jour.*, June 7, and *N.Y. Jour.*, June 21, 1770.

a "monstrous and slavish doctrine," such that only those "dead to the dearest and most necessary rights and feelings of humanity, can be mean enough to submit to it."[28]

Simultaneous developments in Ireland and Corsica added impact to this dismaying trend in England and America. In Ireland, colonial observers followed particularly the efforts of a group of patriots who sought the recognition of rights and liberties already established in England and America. No Habeas Corpus Act existed in Ireland. Not only Catholics but, more disturbing, Protestant dissenters were disfranchised. The Irish Parliament included a large number of easily controlled borough seats, more even than those in the unreformed English Parliament, and could, moreover, sit for an entire reign: under George II thirty-three years elapsed between general elections. Its power was shackled by both Poyning's Law, which since 1494 had denied the Irish Parliament a right to initiate legislation, and by an English Declaratory Act of 1720 that formally enunciated the British Parliament's supreme power to bind the Irish kingdom and people, much like the American Declaratory Act of 1766. Irish judges still held their positions at the Crown's pleasure, making them subject to manipulation by royal officials. The Irish were also burdened with the cost of a pensions list that had more than doubled between 1755 and 1767, and the pensions for which they paid often rewarded services unrelated to Ireland or, perhaps worse, fed the system of official absenteeism and corruption. Yet it was not only England which stood in the way of the patriots' desire to liberalize Irish government. From about the 1730's, effective power rested in a group of "undertakers," parliamentary managers who "undertook" to shepherd government business through the Irish House of Commons in return for patronage and other personal advantages, and who had in time become more powerful than

28. London news of March 4, via Philadelphia, *N.Y. Jour.*, May 24, 1770; London letter in *Prov. Gaz.*, June 3, 1769; London news of February 17, *Pa. Jour.*, May 3, 1770. Benjamin Franklin to Samuel Cooper, April 27, 1769, BM Kings Mss., 204, and "A Resolutionist," *S.C. Gaz.*, July 19, 1770. The Philadelphia merchants were also convinced of the ministers' corrupt control of government: see Sparks Mss., XLII, Vol. 7, pp. 175–6.

the Crown-appointed lord lieutenant, whom they had origin-ally served.[29]

The arrival in 1767 of George Lord Viscount Townshend (brother of Charles Townshend, who originated America's Townshend duties) as lord lieutenant seemed to promise reform. Townshend's appointment represented an English ef-fort to regain power from the "undertakers," but one that might serve the Irish patriots' cause as well. Unlike many of his predecessors, Townshend was to reside in Ireland, which obviated the need for many appointments that had fed the undertakers' power. He was, moreover, authorized to promise that no new pensions would be granted, and to inform im-portant persons in Ireland that the Crown was ready to limit the duration of the Irish Parliament and to approve secure tenure for judges, a Habeas Corpus Act, and yet another measure favored by Irish patriots, a militia act. In his first speech from the throne, however, the new lord lieutenant made these commitments firmer than London was prepared to support. The Irish were granted an Octennial Act—which produced wild rejoicing and warm votes of thanks to the King—but other hopes came to nothing. The Irish Parliament's Habeas Corpus Bill was vetoed in England, as was its leg-islation to secure judges' tenure.[30]

Townshend's proffered concessions to Irish demands, it was suspected, were calculated primarily to win acceptance of a measure intensely desired by the King himself, the ex-pansion of the Irish army from 12,000 to 15,000 men. The lord lieutenant's efforts to secure the larger army increased the disillusionment of Irish patriots with him and his English superiors. Fear of standing armies was less intense in Ireland than in America or England, but still the Irish preferred a militia for use within Ireland. In any case, it was argued, the expansion would enable Britain to keep more troops in America "in order to crush the spirit of the colonies," with whom the

29. William E. Lecky, *A History of Ireland in the Eighteenth Cen-tury* (London, 1892), I, 192–9, and II, 60–2, 70–1, 211–12; J. C. Beckett, *The Making of Modern Ireland, 1603–1923* (New York, 1966), 51, 164, 190–1, 198–9.

30. Lecky, *Ireland*, II, 80–95; Beckett, *Making of Modern Ireland*, 198–9; London news in *Pa. Jour.*, April 28, 1768.

Irish patriots were sympathetic. In Parliament the patriots were joined by the old undertakers and their followers, who expected to be bought off from the opposition with places and pensions. As a result the Army Augmentation Bill failed in May 1768; and Parliament was dissolved. When the new Dublin Parliament assembled in October 1769, opposition to Townshend continued. Although the Army Augmentation Bill was eventually passed, the assembly did assert its right to originate money bills. In retaliation, Townshend prorogued the Parliament and set out to build his own court party with pensions and places either newly created or taken from the partisans of the old undertakers. Meanwhile, during the fourteen months before Parliament reassembled in February 1771, Ireland was torn by an intense popular agitation that in many ways paralleled those in England and America.[31]

Events in Corsica also seemed to fit the trend of events, and the cause of Corsica was one that awoke if anything more interest in the colonies than did that of Ireland. Here was a small nation that had held out for decades against Genoa, and whose devotion to liberty was announced in a rhetoric even more zealous and florid than that of the Americans. Colonial papers periodically republished the Corsicans' Manifesto of 1754, in which they promised to fight Genoa and any other European power entering the contest until all their strength was exhausted and then to rush voluntarily into the fire "rather than submit ourselves and posterity to the insupportable yoke of Genoese tyranny and slavery." Their success seemed to show that tyranny was "a mere Chimera," with "no Power but what Wickedness and Folly, Ignorance and Cowardice give it." "The Corsicans grow stronger and stronger," John Holt wrote in his *New York Journal*, and he judged this to be "a natural Consequence of Freedom." Praise of the Corsican cause became something which "cannot but be approved by all who deserve the Name of either Patriots or Englishmen," and Paoli and the Corsicans became models

31. Irish M.P. quoted in Kraus, "America and the Irish Revolutionary Movement," 338; Lecky, *Ireland*, II, 94–115; Beckett, *Making of Modern Ireland*, 200–20. See also Benjamin Franklin's description of Townshend quoted in James B. Nolan, *Benjamin Franklin in Scotland and Ireland* (Philadelphia, 1938), 147.

of virtue for mankind—"Not what you are, but what you ought to be":

> The *general Good*'s their Aim; no slavish Awe
> Marks Man from Man, but LIBERTY is LAW:
> No venal Senates public Credit drain,
> No King enslav'd by Creatures of his Reign.
> Of public Honours Merit is the Test,
> And those obtain them who deserve them best.
> In this vile Age, no Virtue now rever'd,
> No Gods like Patriot Prodigy appear'd,
> 'Till one small Spot (for in the ALMIGHTY's Book,
> The smallest Spot he will not overlook)
> Held forth the Wonder, to All Europe's Shame,
> Produc'd the Man—and PAOLI [was] his Name.[32]

In May 1768, the Genoese sold to France their title to Corsica, and the Corsican question became intertwined with British commercial and strategic interests. "Though Corsica, by itself, or dependent on its old master, is a kind of nothing, when plucked from the heart of Europe to be incorporated into France," Edmund Burke warned the Commons, "it becomes a serious object." France's interest in the island was seen as part of her quest for the whole Mediterranean, and Burke noted with alarm the expansion of the Bourbon family's power: "France extending forth its hands to Spain; Spain stretching out its long arms to France; Morocco, the old enemy of Spain, now in alliance with it; and Naples reaching out towards Morocco; a Prince of the same house at Parma, and Tuscanny now an accession to the family compact." Only Corsica's resistance prevented the formation of a "line of circumvallation round the Mediterranean, impenetrable to human force." Even an invasion of England might follow Corsica's fall. Well

---

32. Corsican manifesto in *Prov. Gaz.*, February 23, 1765, and again, slightly different, September 13, 1766. "Remarks and Reflections on our late Advices from Home," *N.Y. Jour.*, *Supplement* August 6, 1767, April 21, 1768, and Poet's Corner in *Supplement* November 17, 1768. For a general summary of American interest in the Corsican question, see George P. Anderson, "Pascal Paoli, An Inspiration to the Sons of Liberty," CSM *Pubs.*, XXVI (*Trans.*, 1924–6), 180–210.

might "Liberty," the supposed author of an "Address to her Britons, in Behalf of the Corsicans," remind Englishmen of the Cyclops' den where "The chosen few (a favorite repast), Were but preserv'd to be devour'd the last."[33]

Newspapers claimed that British officials in Paris had protested the anticipated French subordination of the island, and the dispatch of British squadrons was suggested. In August 1768, some colonists even read that Britain was organizing a European confederation for the Corsicans' defense; but in the end the British government did nothing. Even as French troops embarked, Americans hoped that "the bravery and virtue of [the Corsicans] (the admiration of the world) would still preserve them a free, and so a happy people." In London, James Boswell—the self-appointed spokesman for Corsica in England, and author of the popular *Account of Corsica* (1767)—collected contributions for the Corsican cause, and sent Paoli funds and a substantial supply of arms. Nevertheless, in August 1769 colonists learned "that the venerable and illustrious PAOLI, and his brave Adherents," after boldly disputing their ground inch by inch and covering their land with blood, were "entirely routed." Paoli refused to surrender and fled to the mountains, then to Leghorn (Livorno) and so to exile in England.[34]

Nor did military defeat prove the last disappointment for admirers of the "brave Corsicans." If British inaction had abetted his demise, Paoli traced defeat more directly to French bribery of some Corsican officers. Finally Paoli himself, "the greatest man on earth," proved corruptible. Accounts mul-

33. *Prov. Gaz.*, September 10, 1768 (London news, June 24), January 21, 1769 (Burke's remarks), and November 5, 1768 (Liberty's "Address"). Article from *London Chronicle* in *New London Gaz.*, October 7, 1768.

34. Reports of aid: *New London Gaz.*, October 28, 1768; *Prov. Gaz.*, September 10, 1768; and London news of June 10 in *N.Y. Jour.*, August 25, 1768. Frederick A. Pottle, *James Boswell, The Earlier Years, 1740–1769* (New York, 1966), 390, 396–7. Boswell's *Account of Corsica* was popular in America and had at least three printings in England. William Bradford, the old Son of Liberty, handled it in Philadelphia. See *ibid.*, 337–8, 357, and 'Anderson, "Paoli," 188. Defeat: London news of July 11 in *New London Gaz.*, September 8, 1769; Paoli's parting speech to his followers in London news, July 12, in *Pa. Jour.*, September 7, 1769.

tiplied of his visiting the Duke of Grafton, first lord of the Treasury, and attending royal levees until "the real character and principle of the Corsican chief" became "doubted amongst the patrons of liberty." He kept his distance from the current opposition, "even those who were the forwardest in promoting the subscription in favour of the Corsicans," and visited none of the city's heroes—neither Mrs. Macaulay, nor John Bingley, imprisoned for his continuation of the *North Briton*, nor Wilkes. Soon it was rumored that the ministry had purchased his passivity, a suggestion confirmed in late 1769 when colonists read that Paoli had been awarded a Crown pension of £1000 per year. By August 1770, a letter from London regretted the lot of "Poor Paoli," who was "quite lost since his arrival in England," his abject subservience to the Duke of Grafton and acceptance of a pension having "totally eclipsed the Fame of this wonderful chief."[35]

[III]

The impact of these and related events was of the greatest significance. Together, the ministry's actions seemed to betray an almost classical plan for the establishment of tyranny. All the harbingers of despotism enumerated by Real Whig writers were transformed into current policy. By late 1769 and early 1770, the outlines of the plot seemed clear; later events would only fill out the details and darken the lines so the design became apparent to a larger audience.

Corruption was everywhere, and forceful enough to buy off even the paragon Paoli. It existed most egregiously in Ireland, but even the British Parliament was controlled by placemen. Support for government was regularly bought or rewarded: after Bernard was rewarded with his baronetcy and the ex-stampmen were given commissions in the judicial or

35. Items on Paoli in *S.C. Gaz.*, *Additional Supplement* November 30, 1769, and pension announcement, *New London Gaz.*, December 22, 1769. The London letter is in *ibid.*, August 24, 1770, and *Pa. Jour.*, August 16, 1770. Paoli's name is included among Crown pensioners for 1779 in John Robinson's account books, BM Add. Mss., 37836, ff. 60, 62, 71.

customs service, Wilkes's erstwhile political opponent William Beauchamp Proctor was given a "genteel vacancy . . . as a reward for trouble and expence incurred during the Middlesex election." Appointments, like those of the Irish judges, were often revocable at pleasure, to ensure the incumbent's continued subserviency to the government. And the appointees—whose only qualification, it was said, was their enmity to the rights of their country—were of a low caliber, "abandon'd or contemptible characters," fit "to be made subservient and instrumental to the Designs of Baseless Malevolence and Folly," just as *Cato's Letters* had predicted a half century earlier. Corruption extended into ranks higher than that of the "swarms of searchers, tidewaiters, spies, and other underlings" in American ports after 1768. When Benjamin Hallowell was made a commissioner of customs, William Palfrey complained to Wilkes that he was "of no family and as ignorant and illiterate as the Duke of Cumberland," and was recommended for the post by Governor Bernard only because of "a mulish and blundering opposition to the Cause of liberty here." The problem was not only annoying in itself—John Dickinson compared it to being devoured by mice rather than a lion—but also ominous as to underlying British intentions. Palfrey, for example, saw the appointment of Hallowell as "an incontestable proof" of the ministers' "profound policy."[36]

With power won by corruption, the Ministry sought to subvert the legislative element of the constitution. The rights of legislatures, even the right of the people to be represented by men of their choosing answerable only to their constituents, were threatened in America, England, and Ireland. Reports from the new British colony of Grenada in the Windward Islands added to the concern for representative government. In 1769, the lieutenant governor admitted French Roman

36. London news of February 6 in *Pa. Jour.*, May 3, 1770. Letter to *ibid.* printed October 19, 1769; Palfrey to Wilkes, November 20, 1770, CSM *Pubs.*, XXIV (*Trans.*, 1937–42), 427, and see also his remarks on Jonathan Sewell's appointment as vice-admiralty judge in Palfrey to Wilkes, November 4 or 5, 1769, Palfrey Family Papers, II, b, 89, and BM Add. Mss., 30870. Dickinson as "Rusticus," November 27, 1773, in Paul L. Ford, ed., *The Writings of John Dickinson*, I, *Political Writings, 1764–1774. Memoirs of the Historical Society of Pennsylvania*, XIV (Philadelphia, 1895), 461.

Catholics into the Grenada assembly despite the Test Act, awakening the hostility of Protestants, who petitioned for a new parliamentary election and refused to pay taxes levied by their "unconstitutional" legislature. (John Wilkes's brother, Israel, who sat on the Grenada Court of Common Pleas, helped acquit one householder of nonpayment, showing "more true Patriotism," a witness said, in "defending the rights of the natural-born subjects, than his brother . . . ever did or ever will exhibit.") The new governor, William Leyborne, arrived, nonetheless, with instructions to admit Catholics to both legislature and bench and to change the assembly from an annual to perpetual body like the Irish Parliament before its recent Octennial Act. When the Grenada Council balked at admitting two Roman Catholic appointees, six out of eight members were summarily suspended.[37]

The Grenada episode raised the specter of government sympathy toward Roman Catholicism, and with it more memories of Stuart rule. In many ways, the government's efforts to establish regular government in Grenada by absorbing the old French settlers into public office, while making necessary alterations in traditional English procedure to accommodate them, forecast the Quebec Act of 1774, which became for many the strongest proof of despotism. But even the Grenada affair was not unprecedented. In 1769, the colonial newspapers reported, a Catholic priest had been settled at Halifax with a government salary of £100 a year to satisfy a request from the local Indians. "The M-n-stry at home I suppose," commented a letter to Boston from Nova Scotia, "have not so bad an opinion of that infamous religion as you and I have."[38]

Law itself apparently failed to restrain the ministers. Under their control, it seemed to be administered unequally, even suspended: by executive decree the Test Act was "dispensed with" for Grenadians—an action directly reminiscent of James II. The "irregular" proceedings against Wilkes, the revival of an old act of Henry VIII against the leaders of the Mas-

---

37. Summary of Grenada events in *Pa. Jour.*, January 30, February 6 and 13, 1772; John de Ponthieu to Wilkes, Grenada, October 10, 1769, BM Add. Mss., 30870.

38. Letter from Halifax, December 1, 1769, via Boston, in *N.Y. Jour.*, January 4, 1770; Blackburne, *Hollis Memoirs*, I, 430–1.

sachusetts "disorders," Parliament's suggestion that a "special commission of enquiries" be appointed to deal with the Massachusetts situation, all were seen as predecessors of the *Gaspée* commission of 1772, which similarly aroused bitter resentment. Like the ministry's tendency to proceed against opponents on the basis of "informations," thereby obviating the need for a grand jury indictment, or the establishment of vice-admiralty courts in America, these new commissions, too, indicated a governmental desire to undermine the importance of juries. Yet like the legislatures, juries brought the people into government as a counterweight to executive power. Given the many British efforts to get around the law, a Grenadian could well claim that their struggle was "a common one to all the Colonies." With "no Law to depend on," John de Ponthieu wrote Wilkes from the island, "we are certainly Slaves."[39]

The question of law was closely related to charter rights, which again had been abused by James II. Now charters seemed no more respected by British authorities than the rest of the law. The instructions of Grenada's first English governor, which established British government there in 1764 and extended the Test Act to the island, were regarded like a "constitution" or a charter. The instructions were no more revocable, the Grenadians claimed, than Magna Charta was revocable in England, yet they were summarily overridden. The ancient charter rights and privileged immunities of the City of London were also apparently ignored in the famous Printer's Case of 1770. Wilkes and the city magistrates had jailed a House of Commons messenger who, they claimed, violated London immunities by attempting to arrest a printer on the Commons' behalf within the city's bounds. But the Commons called for the magistrates, and went so far as to commit the lord mayor and a leading alderman, Richard Oliver, to the Tower. If London's magistrates could be imprisoned, Oliver commented, "the most distant part of the British dominions are as insecure . . . as the nearest." And in fact, Massachusetts already feared a violation of her charter, particularly in the Crown's effort to assume the salary of her

39. De Ponthieu to Wilkes, October 10, 1769, BM Add. Mss., 30870. See also definition of law by "Democritus" in *N.Y. Jour.*, July 19, 1770: "Little walls to fence in small rogues, over which great ones continually play leap frog."

governor.[40] Such efforts were followed by Lord North's East
India Company Act of 1773, which disfranchised the company's freemen and later its administration, "in order," it was
claimed, "to subject all their affairs"—and their extensive
patronage—"both at home and abroad, to the immediate power
and influence of the crown." "The example of the East India
Company may shew us," the American Stephen Sayre told
the city's livery in 1773, "that neither the faith of Parliaments,
nor the sanction of charters, is held sacred when violating
them may serve the purposes of corruption and arbitrary
power."[41]

By 1769, the ministry also seemed especially prone to use
troops against civilians—at St. George's Fields in London, as
at Boston in 1768. Its dependence on the army rather than the
militia was apparent in its intense effort to win an expansion
of the Irish army: proof to one Irishman of "a long-settled
scheme for establishing Despotism in every Part of the Kings
Dominions." By the spring of 1770, reports proliferated of
more intense military activity on Black Heath and Hownslow
Heath, with other English encampments "in agitation." The
expressed purpose was to deal with any rioting when Wilkes
was released from prison; but months later the London press
reported that patrols of horse guards had been appointed for
the Strand, Piccadilly, Holborn, and adjacent streets as "never
before in the Memory of the oldest Man."[42]

40. Oliver's statement of April 27, 1771, in *New London Gaz.*, July
5, 1771; Massachusetts Assembly to Benjamin Franklin, June 29,
1771, in Harry A. Cushing, ed., *The Writings of Samuel Adams*
(New York, 1904–8), II, 181. Thomas Young referred to "the Threats
of the British Ministry to take away the Massachusetts Charter" in a
speech at Boston: see *Boston Gaz.*, March 11, 1771.

41. *Prov. Gaz.*, August 14, 1773, and August 28, 1773 (Sayre statement). A group of dissenting members of the House of Lords also
condemned the East India Act as "part of a design, long since formed,
and never abandoned, for enlarging the influence of the Crown . . .
by the introduction of ministerial authority in the nomination to the
numerous lucrative employments, now in the gift of the Company":
report in *Pa. Jour.*, March 31, 1773. The full implications were de-
picted in an article from the *London Evening Post* reprinted in *Mass.
Spy*, April 22, 1773.

42. Dublin's *Freeman's Journal*, quoted in Kraus, "America and the
Irish Revolutionary Movement," 334; London news of March 21 in
N.Y. Jour., May 24, and *Pa. Jour.*, May 24, 1770; *N.Y. Jour.*, Sep-
tember 20, 1770.

This background of a growing official reliance on troops, with the sense of impending danger it evoked, explains the English opposition's readiness to champion the cause of the black Caribs of St. Vincent's Island in the West Indies. England had only a doubtful title to the Caribs' lands, it was said, but in 1772 she was theatening to remove them from their island by force. Suspicion of the project intensified when Grenada's hated Governor Leyborne was made "generalissimo" for the project. The resisting Caribs were readily admitted to the confraternity of freedom as men, Isaac Barré told Parliament, who were "fighting for Liberty," whom "every English heart must applaud." The *Boston Gazette* also found in the Caribs a model of virtue for Americans struggling "in the glorious Cause of Liberty."[43]

By early 1770, it seemed that every source of potential opposition to the "ministerial plan" was being stifled either by corruption or by direct repression. Wilkes was the most publicized victim in England, while across the ocean in September 1769 James Otis was cruelly beaten by British partisans. Even in Georgia, the newspapers claimed, a councillor was suspended by express Crown order with no cause assigned, "as he always . . . was a staunch and real friend to LIBERTY. . . ." "Some there are," the account reported, "who cannot avoid looking upon this suspension as a hint, what men of his stamp have to look for." And just as news arrived of the suspension of Grenada's councillors, the Whiggish Joseph Greenleaf lost his Massachusetts justiceship of the peace on a vague charge that he was "reputed to be concerned with Isaiah Thomas in printing and publishing" the radical *Massachusetts Spy*. London's lord mayor and Alderman Oliver were similarly attacked, as a New York poet put it, because they "dared to be just among a venal crew."[44]

43. December 1772 Parliamentary debates in *Pa. Jour.*, February 17, 1773; "Probus" to Dartmouth, London, January 4, in *Mass. Spy*, April 29, 1773; *Boston Gaz.*, June 6, 1774. Hillsborough's letter to Leyborne, April 18, 1772, in *Pa. Jour.*, June 16, 1773, suggests that the accusations were overdrawn. He sought subjection of the Caribs to the Crown, and forceful evacuation from the island was to be used only if all else failed.

44. Palfrey to Wilkes, Boston, September 9, 1769, MHS *Procs.*, XLVII, 210; Georgia incident reported, via Boston, in *Pa. Jour.*,

Nor was immunity granted to the press, that "great bulwark of the liberty of the people." Wilkes was imprisoned for publishing the *North Briton*, as was his successor, John Bingley. The ministry prosecuted the publishers of "Junius's" first letter to the King and Parliament moved against three printers who published the House of Commons's proceedings in 1770. Similarly, South Carolina's appointed upper House of Assembly moved against Thomas Powell, a printer of the *South Carolina Gazette*, for publishing their proceedings, citing as precedent the case of John Bingley and the *North Briton*. In New York, Alexander McDougall was prosecuted for publishing a radical pamphlet; in Massachusetts, Governor Bernard had attacked the *Boston Gazette* in 1768 only to be checked by the colony's assembly, and Governor Hutchinson prosecuted the *Massachusetts Spy* in 1771. The efforts of Hutchinson and the ministers in London were frustrated when juries failed to return indictments, but fears still lingered. The press was not yet safe, a London writer claimed in 1772: "Though *open* Attacks have failed, the design is not laid aside. . . . The plan now is to *bribe* or *buy up* the rights of the different papers, not only here in England, but in foreign countries. And when you have got them *all* into your hands, your subjects may be kept in as great ignorance as the French."[45]

Even the government's foreign policy and defense deployment could be fitted into this general interpretation of events. Its neglect of Corsica, with its tacit complicity in French expansion, could be traced back to Lord Bute. After his "infamous peace" of 1763, it was noted, a proclamation was issued from St. James's Palace forbidding British subjects to correspond with or aid the Corsican "malecontents." The peace itself was also undergoing re-examination, spurred in part by the accusations of one "Dr. Musgrave" that British negotiators had been "bought out" by the French. A letter

May 10, 1770. Items on Grenada and Greenleaf in *ibid.*, February 6, 1772. Greenleaf's account in *Mass. Spy*, December 5, 1771. *N.Y. Jour.*, June 6, 1771, on London magistrates.

45. *S.C. Gaz.*, September 2, 1773; *Pa. Jour.*, September 27, 1770 (London news of July 19), March 12, 1772 (Boston news), and August 12, 1772 ("Millions," from *St. James Chronicle* [London]).

to the colonies from London claimed in February 1770 that it was "a fact universally agreed to, that the last peace was purchased by enormous and extensive bribery; every tool had his finger in the sweetened pye."[46] After the Portsmouth Naval Yards burned in July 1770, rumors suggested arson at the hands of foreigners mysteriously connected with the British ministry. Within a year, the more extreme contributors to the English press linked the French and Spanish prime ministers in the affair, along with Bute and a handful of British Catholics. The tragedy became for at least one correspondent "a more infernal Scheme than the Popish Plot," for "blowing up both houses of Parliament . . . could soon have been repaired . . . but the destruction of the British Navy might have been fatal to the whole nation." The negotiated settlement accepted by the ministry after the Spanish governor took over Britain's outposts in the Falkland Islands seemed to represent another concession to the Catholic powers. Boston's William Palfrey called the settlement a "vile Composition," and even Lord Chatham thought there were "some important mysteries in the conduct of this affair."[47]

Although Americans tended to be more cautious than some Englishmen in attributing treasonable motives to the ministry, they, too, were concerned about its strategic decisions. The Boston Sons of Liberty rejected several drafts of a letter to Wilkes because rapidly developing local events made them obsolete; then in November 1769, the Sons commented most extensively on Britain's failure to defend Canada adequately since 1763. Why should so many ships be tied up supporting revenue officers along the settled American coast, especially when it was "much to be apprehended [that] the parties to the Family Compact are mediating some great blow"? Perhaps

46. "A short Narrative of a few interesting FACTS relating to CORSICA," *Prov. Gaz.*, November 4, 1769; London letter in *Pa. Jour.*, April 26, 1770.

47. Fire: *Prov. Gaz.*, October 6, 1770; *Pa. Jour.*, September 27, 1770. English rumors in *Prov. Gaz.*, November 9, 23, 1771, and January 25, 1772 ("The Whisperer LXXVI"), and *Mass. Spy*, Nov. 22, 1770 ("Craftsman"). London news, September 7, in *N.Y. Jour.*, November 14, 1771. Palfrey to John Hancock, London, February 4, 1771, Palfrey Family Papers, II, b, 34; and Chatham's speech to House of Lords reported in *Pa. Jour.*, February 14, 1771. Also "Junius" in *ibid.*, April 18, 1771.

the Corsican expedition itself was formed "but to whet [French] swords, and discipline the French slaves for the further carnage of sons of liberty. Where so likely to begin as in North America?"[48]

The very fact of domestic disorder confirmed the existence of official treachery. Efforts to restrain the population had been made by Wilkes in London as by the American radicals, and even Dublin's Liberty Boys were urged to avoid riotous acts. Yet periodic outbreaks of violence still occurred in America, especially between soldiers or customsmen and civilians. After 1760 Ireland, too, became subject to periodic waves of rural uprisings by groups known as the Whiteboys, Oakboys, or Hearts of Steel. In May 1768, almost unprecedented rioting broke out in the Dublin area, and after Viscount Townshend's dissolution of the Irish Parliament in December 1769, a "furious mob" was said to have assembled with several hundred left wounded or dead. Mob action in London, which was recurrent throughout the 1760's, reached a peak the day the lord mayor was committed to the Tower: Lord North was captured by the mob near the door of Parliament and so brutally treated that, accounts claimed, only a timely rescue saved his life.[49] Through it all the colonists recalled, with their counterparts in England, the classical edict that people were by nature placid and never rose in "Mobs and Tumults . . . but thro' Oppression and a scandalous Abuse of Power." As such, the "tumults and disturbances catching in the very bowels of the empire" by the early 1770's became themselves a testimony to the misrule of the empire's governors.[50]

48. Sons' letter in Palfrey, "William Palfrey," 360–2. The identical view is stated in Samuel Adams to Dennis DeBerdt, November 6, 1769, in Cushing, *Writings of Samuel Adams*, I, 446–7. Thomas Hollis speculated that the British might have desisted from supporting the Corsicans on the hope that France would similarly desist when Britain attempted the subjugation of America. (Blackburne, *Hollis Memoirs*, I, 180.)

49. Kraus, "America and the Irish Revolutionary Movement," 338; accounts of Irish rioting in *Pa. Jour.*, August 4, 1768, and April 19, 1770 ("Watchman IV"); Lecky, *Ireland*, II, 105–6. London riots: *N.Y. Jour.*, May 16, 1771; *New London Gaz.*, June 7 ("Freeholder") and 14, 1771.

50. *N.Y. Jour.*, *Supplement* August 11, 1768; also Massachusetts Assembly in *Prov. Gaz.*, May 5, 1770. "Centinel XV," *Mass. Spy*, October 3, 1771.

[IV]

As the "ministerial scheme" became more apparent, colonists were quick to interpret American events in terms of it. The New York case of Alexander McDougall, the "Wilkes of America," was symptomatic. The pamphlet McDougall published in December 1769, *To the Betrayed Inhabitants of the City and Colony of New York*, chastised the New York legislature for apparently bowing to Parliament's threat and conforming with the Quartering Act of 1765. But McDougall's frame of reference, and that of his supporters, was clearly London more than New York. The pamphlet spoke of the "minions of tyranny and despotism in the mother country and the colonies," who were "indefatigable in laying every snare that their malevolent and corrupt hearts can suggest, to enslave a free people." McDougall called on his countrymen to rouse and "imitate the noble example of the friends of liberty in England; who, rather than be enslaved, contend for their right." The aftermath seemed to prove further that the English and colonial causes were the same. The New York legislature's condemnation of McDougall's pamphlet recalled Hillsborough's denunciation of the Massachusetts circular letter and Parliament's condemnation of Wilkes's commentary on the "Massacre" of St. George's Fields. McDougall's pamphlet, the legislature charged, was "an infamous and scandalous Libel," calculated to inflame the minds of the people, "introductive of Anarchy and Confusion, and subversive of the Fundamental Principles of our happy Constitution." The legislature called on the lieutenant governor to seek out the author and commence prosecution. McDougall was arrested on the testimony of a government-paid informer, a printer, just as Wilkes had been. Moreover, like Wilkes, McDougall was charged with seditious libel. While in prison, McDougall issued elaborate statements "to the Freeholders, Freemen, and Inhabitants of the Colony of New-York," much as Wilkes had addressed the Middlesex freeholders. On his release from prison, again like Wilkes, he carefully enjoined the mass of his followers to observe the "greatest Decency and Order," and it was triumphantly noted that McDougall was accompanied home by 600 friends "without any Tumult or Noise."[51]

Soon observers remembered that the New York Assembly that condemned McDougall's pamphlet had also expelled one of its duly elected members, and New York's "aping of the conduct of a late corrupt Parliament and arbitrary abandoned Ministry" seemed almost complete. In celebrating the 1770 anniversary of the Stamp Act's repeal, Bostonians joined in a toast that "the pigmy Apes of Mr. Wilkes's Oppressors be confounded and defeated in their Attempts on the brave Captain McDougal." The *Boston Gazette* also noted that the proceedings against McDougall were printed on the forty-fifth page of the New York House of Assembly proceedings. Constantly, he was associated with the number 45: on February 14, "the Forty-fifth Day of the Year, forty-five Gentlemen . . . cordial Friends . . . of American Liberty, went in decent Procession to the New Gaol; and dined with [McDougall] on Forty-five Pounds of Beef Stakes, cut from a Bullock of Forty-five Months old." McDougall once received forty-five virgins who sang him forty-five songs: did it dilute the pleasure that the virgins, as one correspondent charged, were forty-five years old?[52]

Boston events also seemed to mirror London developments. When the Massachusetts governor attempted to call out royal troops against a local mob in 1769, William Palfrey accused him of trying to use a "trivial occasion . . . to repeat the Tragic scene of S[t.] Georges fields." The incident demonstrated, he wrote Wilkes, "that the life of a paltry Citizen is in the estimation of some of as little Value here as at Brentford or St. Georges Fields." Then, in February 1770, eleven-year-old

---

51. Alexander McDougall as "A Son of Liberty," "To the Betrayed Inhabitants of the City and Colony of New York," in E. B. O'Callaghan, ed., *The Documentary History of the State of New York*, III (Albany, 1850), 528–32. New York Assembly proceedings in *N.Y. Jour.*, February 15, 1770. McDougall's addresses of February 9 and 24 in *ibid.*, February 15 and *Supplement* March 8. *N.Y. Gaz.*, May 6, 1770.

52. "A Son of Liberty," *N.Y. Gaz.*, May 6, 1770; letter from Philadelphia to New York, March 27, 1770, in *N.Y. Jour.*, April 5, 1770, and *Prov. Gaz.*, April 21, 1770. Boston toasts in *ibid.*, April 28, 1770; *Boston Gaz.*, February 26, 1770; John C. Miller, *Origins of the American Revolution* (Boston, 1943), 306.

Christopher Sneider was shot and killed by Ebenezer Richardson during a Boston nonimportation incident. Sneider's funeral, which attracted hundreds of Bostonians, was patterned on that for the victim of the St. George's Field Massacre. A *Boston Gazette* article carefully related the incident to a long series of events from the past, spelling out its place in the history of the ministerial conspiracy, whose victims included McDougall, Otis, and now young Sneider as "the first, whose LIFE has been a Victim to the Cruelty and Rage of *Oppressors!*[53] The paper recalled the young victim of St. George's Field, and, despite the *Gazette*'s predictions to the contrary, Richardson's fate was also reminiscent of his English counterparts. Found guilty of murder by a Boston jury, he was granted a Crown pardon, and subsequently appointed to a "profitable office" in the Philadelphia customs service. Richardson never exercised his office, however, because Philadelphia proved "too hot" to hold this "Bird of Darkness."[54]

The Boston Massacre of March 1770 seemed to complete the parallel development of English and American events. "A more dreadful Tragedy has been acted by the Soldiery in King-Street, Boston, New-England, than was sometime since exhibited in St. George's Field, London, in Old England, which may serve instead of Beacons for both Countries," the *Boston Gazette* reported on March 12. Papers in London, too, including Bingley's *North Briton*, wrote of "oppressors . . . who delight in blood and murder," citing together "St. George's Fields, and the BUTCHERS at Boston." After the accused soldiers were released on bail, a New York writer

---

53. Palfrey to Wilkes, November 4 or 5, 1769, Palfrey Family Papers, II, b, 89, and BM Add. Mss., 30870. Thomas Hutchinson, *The History of the Colony and Province of Massachusetts Bay* (Cambridge, 1936), ed. Lawrence S. Mayo, III, 193–4; *Boston Gaz.*, February 26, 1770.

54. *Prov. Gaz.*, March 14 and 21, 1772, and May 29, 1773 (Boston news). A notice was printed in Philadelphia that enumerated Richardson's history and called on "all Lovers of Liberty, in this Province" to make "diligent search after the said RICHARDSON," then produce him, "tarred and feathered, at the Coffee House, there to expiate his sins against his country, by a public recantation." It included a description of Richardson, who was found, but made a hair-breadth escape into a woods. See *Pa. Jour.*, October 13 and 20, 1773.

claimed the court's leniency was based on the "System of Laws" of Lord Mansfield in London, "who admitted Bail to the ———— Murderers of ALLEN and CLARK, the former of which was murdered in St. George's Fields, the other at Brentford, in England." And when the Crown-appointed sheriff managed to pack the jury that decided the fate of Captain Thomas Preston, the soldiers' commander, his effort provided just another example of the government's disregard for law and customary judicial procedure.[55]

Such a reading of events was clearly one-sided, for it took into account neither the provocations of the patriots nor the needs of the Crown. The domination of the executive power that Whiggism so feared was apparently far more normal for English eighteenth-century politics than the "balanced" government idealized in constitutional thought, and it was, historians have stressed, essential to the well-working of English government. Political stability, J. H. Plumb has argued, demanded that the Crown tame parliamentary opposition and the anarchy implicit in local privileges, both traditional bastions of "English liberty," and political stability was the price of industrial and scientific development.[56] Such considerations, however, contribute little to understanding the evolving revolutionary mentality of Anglo-American radicals. For these men, events were evaluated against ominous parallels from England's past. And the cascading developments in the contemporary empire that recalled others under earlier tyrannies overshadowed whatever differences there were. That the soldiers involved in the Boston Massacre were acquitted and went free like those in London seemed, for example, significant, despite the inadequacy of the prosecution's case against them, which most radical Bostonians admitted.

The colonists' readiness to see particular events in terms

55. *N.Y. Jour.*, July 5 ("Portius" from *London Evening Post*) and May 3, 1770 (New York letter, April 21); *Prov. Gaz.*, June 30 ("Portius") and July 14, 1770 (*North Briton*, May 12, 1770). Palfrey's account of jury selection in letter to Wilkes, October 23–30, CSM *Pubs.*, XXXIV (*Trans.*, 1937–42), 425; also L. Kinvin Wroth and Hiller B. Zobel, eds., *Legal Papers of John Adams* (Cambridge, 1965), III, 17–19.

56. J. H. Plumb, *The Origins of Political Stability: England, 1675–1725* (Boston, 1967).

of a pervasive pattern also explains the almost uniformly sympathetic response of the radical press to the North Carolina Regulators, a group of Western insurgents who were defeated by Governor William Tryon in a military encounter at the Alamance in 1771. Writers began interpreting the affair, as they admitted, even before sufficient information had arrived from North Carolina for a "just opinion" to be formed: the very fact that the Regulators had resorted to arms indicated, it was said, that they "found themselves aggrieved, and had reason to despair of relief from any other quarter." Gradually, the Regulators emerged as a paradigm of the entire American resistance movement. Repeatedly they had sought legal redress, carefully complaining not of their form of government, "but [of] the abuses we suffer by those who are empowered to manage our affairs." Their leaders continually urged that they "do nothing rashly . . . nothing against the known laws of the land, that we appear not a faction endeavouring to overturn the system of government, but . . . free subjects by birth, endeavouring to recover our lost rights." But the Regulators were condemned as libelers, bills were brought against their leaders "for daring to complain." When one of their number, Herman Husbands, was "with difficulty" indicted by a grand jury, he was at first denied bail and treated in an "inhuman manner," while an official indicted on twenty counts was fined one penny, "carressed and favoured." Only after a "continued series of oppression, too heavy to be longer submitted to," did the Regulators take up arms, and then only reluctantly and defensively when Governor Tryon took the military initiative.[57]

57. The *Massachusetts Spy* was particularly full of articles supporting the Regulators in 1771: see, for example, "Leonidas" to Governor Tryon in issue of June 27 and again August 1; "Mucius Scaevola," June 27; "Humanus," July 25; "Benevolentior," August 15; "Centinel" X and XI, August 29 and September 5. Sympathy characterized other radical newspapers, too: see Boston's first assessment of the Regulators' cause, reprinted in *New London Gaz.*, July 26, 1771, and a local Connecticut or Rhode Island letter attacking Tryon in *ibid.*, August 9; sympathetic editorial analysis, in brackets, in *S.C. Gaz.*, August 8, which also republished another favorable piece from *Pa. Gazette* in the September 5, 1771, issue. Also italicized editorial comment in *Pa. Jour.*, July 11, letter from North Carolina and "To the PUBLIC" in *ibid.*, August 1 and 8, 1771; strongly sym-

To North Carolinians, this interpretation of events was dumfounding. Local radicals had supported the forceful suppression of the Regulators: Cornelius Harnett himself marched with Tryon in May 1771 to the battle of the Alamance, which broke the Regulators' strength. For men like Harnett, the Regulators represented a "licentious spirit" since they had resorted to force without exhausting the normal channels of redress. The provincial legislature, the radicals knew, was ready to grant relief. James Iredell even claimed that "a majority of the house are of regulating Principles." The Regulators constituted, in short, another unjust uprising that had to be suppressed before it injured the American cause in the Mother Country, where, it was feared, observers would not distinguish between the orderly resistance to the Townshend Act by the Sons of Liberty at Cape Fear and the violence of the Regulators.[58]

Yet when Carolinians protested the inaccuracy of accounts being published in the North and burned one news report, they only hardened their critics' attitudes. The *Massachusetts Spy* said the North Carolinians had acted "in humble imitation of [their] betters at home," giving "the poor harmless paper the same fate as the famed *North-Briton.*" Continually, radicals outside North Carolina linked the "planners, executors and vindicators of the St. George's-Fields, Brentford, Boston, and Alamance expeditions"; and as with the earlier incidents, the Regulators' fate could "fully prove . . . and evince what Englishmen may expect, unless they prevent it by some manly vigorous effort."[59]

---

pathetic editorial preface to letter on the Regulators' grievances in *Boston Gaz.*, June 24, 1771, and July 15, 1771, for report, via Newport, asking whether it was any longer possible "for any man, unless he possess the soul of a Cannibal, to wish success to an administration so corrupt, so absolutely void of humanity, and every christian virtue, as that of North-Carolina!!!" Finally, *Boston Gaz.*, July 22, September 9, 1771. Quoted passages from *Mass. Spy*, September 5, *Pa. Jour.*, August 8, and *S.C. Gaz.*, September 5, 1771.

58. R. D. W. Connor, *Cornelius Harnett* (Raleigh, 1909), 62–3, 66–7; James Iredell to John Harvey, December 21, 1770, and report of the North Carolina Assembly's Committee of Propositions and Grievances, January 2, 1771, in *N.C. Col. Recs.*, VIII, 270, 388–9.

59. "Centinel X," "Benevolentior," and "Centinel XI," in *Mass. Spy*, August 29 and 15, and September 5, 1771.

CHAPTER SEVEN

THE IMPLICATION
OF THE KING,
1770–1772

[I]

As THE NETWORK of common grievances throughout the empire became more evident, efforts by the various international sons of liberty seemed increasingly united. Any doubts were gone; all could agree, as the London *Public Advertiser* put it, that "the Cause of Liberty . . . is ONE COMMON CAUSE" because attacks, wherever made, were begun "by the *same Set of Men*, with the same Views, and the same illegal Violence." When Philadelphians celebrated Paoli's birthday in April 1769, they toasted not only his victory over the French and "The Spirit of Paoli to every American," but "The Friends of America and Corsica in Great Britain," including Wilkes and Middlesex County. That August the Boston Sons of Liberty toasted America and her sons of liberty, Wilkes and the colonies' friends in Great Britain, and "Speedy Deliverance to the illustrious PAOLI, and the brave Corsicans." They remembered, too, Dr. Charles Lucas and the Irish patriots.[1] Mutual support sometimes took more substantial forms: the Society of the Supporters of the Bill of Rights, organized in February 1769 to back Wilkes's cause,

1. London article reprinted in *Boston Gaz.*, May 8, 1769, and *Pa. Jour.*, May 18, 1769; *ibid.*, April 13, 1769; Boston toasts in *Prov. Gaz.*, August 26, 1769. See also connection of Ireland and America in toasts at New York and Boston celebrations of the anniversary of the Stamp Act's repeal in *N.Y. Jour.*, March 24 and 31, 1768.

contributed £2400 to Boswell's Corsica fund.[2] Bostonians contented themselves with toasting the generosity of such contributors to Paoli; yet they took care to send their version of the Boston Massacre not only to their agents and friends in England but to Dr. Lucas in Dublin, too.[3] Some Irishmen had, in fact, emphasized the interconnection of the American and Irish causes from early 1768, arguing that the chains being forged for America were first to be fitted in Ireland. Later they, too, associated American and Irish developments with those surrounding Wilkes in England, and they apparently sent aid to Paoli.[4]

The colonists' connection with Wilkes, however, remained closest of all, for he and his London fellows stood "in the Breach," as a committee of the South Carolina Assembly put it, "fronting the whole collected Fury of Ministerial Vengeance." In September 1769, William Palfrey assured Wilkes of the Boston Sons of Liberty's sympathy with him and their ardor against "the distresses brought by arbitrary Min-

2. Frederick A. Pottle, *James Boswell, The Earlier Years, 1740–1769* (New York, 1966), 390, 396–7; London news of May 5 in *Prov. Gaz.*, July 29, 1769, and translation of Paoli's letter to Barlow Trecothick and Samuel Vaughn, March 20, 1769, thanking them for their support, in *Pa. Jour.*, June 29, 1769.

3. *Prov. Gaz.*, August 26, 1769; *Reps. R. C. C. B.*, XVIII, 10, 46. Lucas published his reply in the *Freeman's Journal*. See Michael Kraus, "America and the Irish Revolutionary Movement in the Eighteenth Century," in Richard B. Morris, ed., *The Era of the American Revolution* (New York, 1939), 335.

4. *Ibid.*, 336–8, and the interesting book Irish patriots published as a testament to posterity of their efforts in the cause, *Baratariana* [i.e., Ireland], *A Select Collection of Fugitive Political Pieces Published during the Administration of Lord Townshend in Ireland* (3rd edn.; Dublin, 1777). It includes a series of letters dated January and February 1768, "From a Native of Baratariana, to his Friend in Pennsylvania," in which the argument that oppression in Ireland was a rehearsal for America is given. See 2, 9. Also, for connection with English events, v–viii. Benjamin Franklin also reported that the Irish supported the American cause warmly, "there being in many points a similarity in our Cases." To Samuel Cooper, London, April 27, 1769, and April 14, 1770, BM King's Mss., 204. See also Franklin's accounts of his 1771 visit to Ireland in a letter [to Thomas Cushing?] from London, January 13, 1772, PRO, CO 5/118, ff. 32–8, and James B. Nolan, *Benjamin Franklin in Scotland and Ireland, 1759–1771* (Philadelphia, 1938), 157.

isters upon Great Britain and her dependencies." In November, a committee of the Sons wrote to Wilkes: "We . . . too sensibly feel the loss of every right, liberty, and privilege, that can distinguish a freeman from a slave, not to sympathize in the most tender manner with you, in the conflict you have been so long engaged in." "Nothing less than an entire change of men and measures will ever regain the confidence of the Americans," Dr. Thomas Young wrote Wilkes in August. The next month his vehemence was even greater: "We have obtained such a thorough sense of the designs of your superlative ministry and their tools here," he declared, "that we are fully ripe for the execution of any plan that promises an effectual redress of our no longer supportable grievances." But the Americans still hoped the despots would fall as a result of agitation centered in England: "We long to hear of some thorough paroxism among you that may forward a crisis of the lingering disease," the doctor wrote. "Such corrupt humors hanging so long on the vitals, threaten the utter extinction of the animal heat."[5]

Unlike a year earlier, hope now centered on the King. The English, Americans, and even the Irish blamed the ministry for their grievances in 1769, but did not extend responsibility higher in the governmental hierarchy. Just as the Irish and Americans presumed the ministers innocent until events seemed to prove their guilt, they now joined English Whigs in arguing that the King was deceived by his advisors.[6]

5. South Carolina Committee to Robert Morris, Esq., Charleston, December 9, 1769, "Correspondence of Charles Garth," *South Carolina Historical Magazine*, XXXI (1930), 132, and account of meeting of the Bill of Rights Society, February 6, 1770, at which the letter was read, *Pa. Jour.*, Supplement April 26, 1770. Palfrey to Wilkes, September 9, 1769, MHS *Procs.*, XLVII (1913–14), 210; Sons of Liberty to Wilkes, November 4, 1769, in John G. Palfrey, "Life of William Palfrey," in Jared Sparks, ed., *Library of American Biography*, 2nd Ser., VII (Boston, 1848), 358–9; Young to Wilkes, August 3, September 6, 1769, MHS *Procs.*, XLVII, 207, 209–10.

6. There is some evidence that the Irish originally thought their problems stemmed from malevolence or misinformation originating within Ireland: see Letter III, "From a Native of Baratariana," January 23, 1768, in *Baratariana*, 21. By late 1769, however, they were blaming the ministry. Kraus, "America and the Irish Revolutionary Movement," 335.

Monarchical innocence became their working assumption: the King could do no wrong. His public acts, if considered oppressive, could be ascribed to his ministers. This hope had a theoretical basis as well as a tactical justification. George III's membership in the Hanover line of British kings, who were the beneficiaries of the Glorious Revolution and defenders of the Protestant succession, was emphasized in England, Ireland, and the colonies, just as it had been by the Sons of Liberty during the Stamp Act crisis. Wilkes himself, who had incurred the personal wrath of George III, scrupulously distinguished between the Crown and its ministers, professing his devotion to the King even while virulently attacking the ministry.

Appeals for redress, then, would have to bypass the ministers and be submitted to the King directly. A new wave of petitions to the King from American assemblies began after the Massachusetts circular letter incident and continued into 1769. In 1770, colonists read that the Irish Parliament was also preparing a petition to the King.[7] But colonial hopes for a "paroxism" in England were centered more directly on English petitions, particularly those of Middlesex County and the City of London's Livery, which not only could be presented by the petitioners directly to the King, but publicly linked England's cause with the colonies. The petitions attempted to educate the King as to the schemes of his ministers: "With great grief and sorrow," the Middlesex petition (as printed in the *Boston Gazette*) began, "we have long beheld the endeavours of certain evil-minded persons, who attempt to infuse into your royal mind, notions and opinions of the most dangerous and pernicious tendency." The min-

7. Several American petitions are printed in the newspapers: see *Pa. Jour.*, February 2, 1769 (Pennsylvania's of September 1768), May 25, 1769 (Virginia, May 1769), and *S.C. Gaz.*, January 5, 1769 (Georgia, December 1768) and February 9, 1769 (North Carolina, November 1768). On Irish petitions, *Pa. Jour.*, August 16, 1770, and *N.Y. Jour.*, March 7, 1771 (London news, November 27). Insofar as the colonists' efforts to circumvent the ministers and Parliament offended influential persons in England, it may have actually undercut their prospect of redress. See Michael G. Kammen, *A Rope of Sand, The Colonial Agents, British Politics, and the American Revolution* (Ithaca, 1968).

isters had introduced into the administration a "certain unlimited and indefinite discretionary power; to prevent which is
the sole aim of all our laws, and was the sole cause of all
those disturbances and revolutions, which formerly distracted
this unhappy country." The petition, like that of the London
livery, then proceeded to list such perversions of court power,
mentioning among other grievances the attempts to create a
standing army and infringements of judicial rights. "The
same discretion has been extended by the same evil counsellors to your Majesty's dominions in America," the petition
noted, "and has produced to our suffering fellow subjects in
that part of the world, grievances and apprehensions similar
to those of which we complain at home."[8] More specifically,
the London petition (as in the *South Carolina Gazette*) told
the King that his counsellors had "established numberless
u[ncon]sti[tutiona]l regulations and taxations in the colonies.
They have appointed civil law judges to try revenue causes,
and to be paid out of the condemnation money." After a series
of such contrivances, the ministers had "completed their design" by taking away the "right of election" in Middlesex
County.[9]

The Middlesex and London petitions did not, however, become the model for the deluge of petitions that followed.
These were patterned rather on the Westminster petition—
short, and limited mainly to the Middlesex election issue,
thus omitting any reference to America. As an article in the
South Carolina Gazette put it, such petitions aimed their ax
at the root of the tree; once the ministry was downed and
its subservient Parliament dissolved, the grievances in England, Ireland, and America would also disappear. Thus the
Americans read with joy that "private letters from almost
every county in England remark, that there is no other language to be heard, from highest to lowest, but petition, petition, petition!" As a recent historian has pointed out, over a
quarter of England's voters signed the petitions.[10]

8. *Boston Gaz.*, July 31, 1769; *Pa. Jour.*, August 10, 1769.
9. *S.C. Gaz.*, September 14, 1769.
10. *Ibid.*, November 14, September 14, 1769, and *Prov. Gaz.*, October 21, 1769 (London news, July 24). George Rudé, *Wilkes and
Liberty* (Oxford, 1962), 105.

The petition movement of late 1769 and 1770 represented a stage of critical importance. If the petitions failed to win the King's support, their defeat would strongly suggest that the entire British government, including the monarch, was intent on extending executive power at the cost of the constitution and British liberties. At its outset, the effort seemed hopeful of success. "Never was the ministerial party so much alarmed as at present," London sources indicated. "Things appear as if they would come to a speedy issue; for it would seem that the Ministers must either lose their heads, or take those of the Patriots."[11]

Realizing the issue at stake, colonists supported the English anti-ministerial forces with increased activity. As John Dickinson wrote Arthur Lee on November 25, 1769, nothing could advance the fight for liberty more than "joining our force to that of the public spirited men who are now asserting the rights of Englishmen, against those degenerated Englishmen who would destroy them."[12] The South Carolina Assembly echoed the same sentiment in December 1769, when it appropriated £10,500 (£1500 sterling) "for the support of the Just and constitutional Rights and Liberties of the People of Great Britain and America." The House's committee broadened the grant's goal when it claimed the money was to be used "in Defence of the Constitutional Rights of all the Subjects of the British Empire"; and it sent the whole sum to the "Gentlemen Supporters of the Bill of Rights," who were currently championing the petition movement, as the most effective way to achieve that end.[13] In response, the Bill of

11. *Pa. Jour.*, August 24 (London news, June 28) and December 7, 1769 (London letter, dated October 4). Also *S.C. Gaz.*, May 4 (London letter, February 7: "Things draw towards a crisis; the ministry blamed by all moderate men") and *Prov. Gaz.*, June 3, 1769 (London letter, February 6).

12. In Richard Henry Lee, *Life of Arthur Lee* (Boston, 1829), II, 298.

13. South Carolina Committee to Robert Morris, Charleston, December 9, 1769, "Garth Correspondence," 132-3. A letter of solicitation from the Supporters of the Bill of Rights had been sent directly to Christopher Gadsden. (See Robert Morris to Wilkes, Lincolns Inn, February 6, 1770, informing him of the receipt of the letter and grant "in consequence of the Circular Letter sent to Mr. Gadsden." BM,

Rights Society promised it would "ever consider the rights of
all our fellow subjects throughout the British empire in England, Scotland, Ireland, and America, as stones of one arch,
on which the happiness and security of the whole are founded."
That English and American rights were attacked "by the
same men, at the same time . . . will serve only to draw us
closer in one band of mutual friendship and support."[14]
Some Virginia patriots tried to send forty-five hogsheads of
tobacco to Wilkes as a "small acknowledgment for his suffer-
ings in the cause of liberty," and a group of Marylanders
sent him forty-five "curious hams" along with the same number of hogsheads of tobacco "as a grateful acknowledgment
for his having *smoked* the ministry so long." And in March
1769, it seems, a subscription for Wilkes was having considerable success in the Island of St. Christopher (now St.
Kitts).[15]

Even the nonimportation association, which so preoccupied
the Americans in 1769 and 1770, was often seen as an ad-
junct of the British petition movement, a phase of the constitutionalists' efforts in which the colonists could take a more
active part. If adhered to with determination, the nonimportation agreements, like the English petitions, could undermine

---

Add. Mss., 30871.) The appropriation was also encouraged by items
from London, such as that in *S.C. Gaz.*, May 11, 1769: "It is sur-
prizing what a change, for the better, in the complexion of the affairs
of Mr. Wilkes, the subscription in support of the public cause, at the
London tavern, has already brought about." Carolinians were later
assured by a London correspondent that their grant "will, in all Likelihood, be the best laid-out 1500 l. that ever was applied by you; for,
it has given a greater Shock to the mini[steria]l Operations, for binding Liberty in Fetters, than any one Act of the Americans since the
Stamp-Act bounced out of Pandora's Box." Letter of March 30 in
S.C. Gaz., *Supplement* May 17, 1770.

14. The letter of thanks was never received in South Carolina,
where the text was reprinted from the London press. *S.C. Gaz.*,
Continuation August 23, 1770.

15. Letter from Liverpool dated November 1, 1769, in *Va. Gaz.*
(Rind), January 11, 1770. The Virginia collection was never completed: George Mason letter, Virginia, December 6, 1770, in Kate M.
Rowland, *Life of George Mason, 1725–1792* (New York, 1892), I,
150. Items on Maryland in *Pa. Jour.*, January 4 and April 19, 1770.
I. Gardiner to Wilkes, Basseterre, Island of St. Christopher, March
26, 1769, BM Add. Mss., 30870.

"the very Existence of [the] present M-n-st-y" whose principles were so "diametrically opposite to the true Interest" of
Britain.[16] Letters from London, particularly from men in
Wilkes's circles like Arthur Lee, urged and supported the
establishment of nonimportation agreements, and examples
could be multiplied of instances such as one in Lexington,
Massachusetts, where young ladies assembled to spin American linen and cotton in a group of forty-five.[17] So closely
were the two efforts interrelated that when the New York
merchants suggested breaking the agreement in 1770, the
merchants and traders of Essex County, New Jersey, demanded that their brethren across the water be consulted, too,
for " 'Tis not our Cause only but theirs also, which is now
depending upon keeping or braking our Agreement."[18]

The petition movement, however, produced disappointments
almost from the start. When the Middlesex petition was
presented in May 1769 (to "avoid tumult, no more than seven
gentlemen went with it"), the King was "graciously pleased
to accept it," and received the patriotic petitioners "in a
manner that [did] the highest honour to the good sense of
our august Sovereign," the papers reported. But no answer
was given to it, nor to the London petition in July. In the
latter event the lord mayor made a presentation speech, "but
the King made no answer, and immediately turned about to
Baron Dieden, the Danish Minister, and delivered the petition
to the Lord in waiting."[19] It was quickly evident that the
petitions were producing no dramatic change. On December
28, 1769, a New York paper noted that there was "not the

16. London letter in *N.Y. Jour.*, May 24, 1770.

17. See, for example, Arthur Lee to one of his brothers, August 15,
1769, in Lee, *Arthur Lee*, I, 195; London letter of July 8 in *Pa. Jour.*,
September 7, and *Prov. Gaz.*, September 16, 1769; another, of March
11, in *S.C. Gaz.*, June 5. Also address to South Carolina planters,
mechanics, and freeholders, June 20, 1769, in *ibid.*, June 22, 1769,
which refers to the confidence in nonimportation of "all our friends in
Great-Britain."

18. To the Committee of Merchants in New York, Elizabethtown,
New Jersey, June 8, 1770, *N.J. Col. Docs.*, XXVII, 194. See also
South Carolina General Committee to the Connecticut Sons of Liberty,
April 25, 1770, in *New London Gaz.*, June 8, 1770.

19. *Prov. Gaz.*, August 5, 1769; *S.C. Gaz.*, September 14, 1769;
New London Gaz., September 8, 1769; *Pa. Jour.*, September 7, 1769.

least Appearance of a Design to repeal the Acts imposing a Duty upon Goods imported into America, or to change the Ministry, or dissolve the Parliament; tho' Petitions from all Parts of England for a Dissolution, either have been present[ed], or are preparing." A *North Briton* of October 28, the paper further claimed, had reported that it was "impossible to imagine any thing more cold, uncivil, or forbidding, than the Reception these Petitions have met with from the Sovereign, who has never vouchsafed a single Syllable to any of the Gentlemen, that have attended on these Occasions; hence we may absolutely despair of Success, at least for some Time."[20]

In 1770, the City of London presented remonstrances to the King protesting this inattention to the city's original petition. The response to these only fulfilled the premonitions of late 1769. Even when arranging a date to present their first remonstrance, the city's representatives faced harassment from the secretaries of state, then coldness from the King himself. After the city officials answered questions about the remonstrance's authentication, "his Majesty," as the *South Carolina Gazette* sarcastically reported, "was *most graciously* pleased to reply, in these *most gracious and condescending* words . . . '*I will consider of the answer you have given me.*'" A comment in the *Boston Gazette* was more direct, more virulent, and, like the *South Carolina Gazette*'s, indicated a new attitude toward George III: "Is this the virtuous the religious k[ing], who was to bring back the Golden Age, and to banish vice and impiety from the realm[?] How long is England to be the sport of Libertines and Tyrants[?]"[21] When the remonstrance itself was presented on March 14, the King—as the newspapers throughout America explained in detail—expressed his contempt directly. After hearing the petition, "his *Majesty* was pleased to *read* the following *most gracious* Answer," obviously prepared beforehand. "I shall always be ready . . . to listen to the Complaints of my Subjects," he began. "But it gives me great Concern to find, that any of them should have been so far misled as to offer me an

20. New York article reprinted in *Boston Gaz.*, January 8, 1770; *New London Gaz.*, January 12, 1770.

21. *S.C. Gaz.*, May 10, and *Boston Gaz.*, April 30, 1770.

Address and Remonstrance, the Contents of which I cannot
but consider as disrespectful to me, injurious to Parliament,
and irreconcileable to the Principles of the Constitution." Before leaving, the lord mayor and some of his entourage kissed
the King's hand, "after which, as they were withdrawing—
his Majesty instantly turned round to his Courtiers, and
laughed." The day's proceedings, including the text of the
city's remonstrance, a speech made by a city official, and the
King's "ignoble reply," were considered so important that
they were publicly read at a nonimportation meeting in
Boston on April 26. Some colonial newspapers appended to
their accounts a cryptic remark obviously copied from an
English paper: *"Nero fiddled while Rome was burning."*[22]

George III's response of March 1770 was, in effect, his
answer to all the remonstrances presented him in 1770 and
1771, and even on into the American war. Later in March,
Westminster presented a remonstrance, open, so the King
might look at it, but he refused, "turned his back on the
Gentlemen, and delivered it to the Lord in waiting, who
delivered it to another, who handed it to a groom, and he
carried it off."[23] When the City of London presented a second
remonstrance in May, the King said his sentiments continued
as they were before, and received without comment an im-
promptu plea by the lord mayor that the remonstrants not be
dismissed without some prospect of redress;[24] and in November
he received a third remonstrance with the reply "that he had
communicated his sentiments to them on the same subject
before, and could by no means comply with the prayer of
their Petition."[25] In July 1771, he explicitly told the city
remonstrants that he had "no less a thorough confidence in

22. *Pa. Jour.*, May 17, 1770; *Boston Gaz.*, May 14, 1770; *New
London Gaz.*, May 18, 1770; *Prov. Gaz.*, May 19, 1770; *S.C. Gaz.*,
May 17, 1770. "Narrative of Occurrences at Boston" for April 26,
Sparks Mss., X, Papers Relating to New England (henceforth "New
England Papers"), III, f. 77, HUL.

23. London news in *Pa. Jour.*, *Supplement* June 7, 1770; also *N.Y.
Jour.*, May 24; *Prov. Gaz.*, June 2, and *S.C. Gaz.*, May 24, 1770.

24. *N.Y. Jour.*, August 9; *Prov. Gaz.*, August 4; *New London Gaz.*,
August 3, and *Pa. Jour.*, August 9, 1770.

25. *Pa. Jour.*, February 14; *Prov. Gaz.*, February 2, and *N.Y. Jour.*,
January 31, 1771.

the loyalty and candour of [the Commons] than in the upright-
ness and fidelity of his ministers."[26]

Meanwhile, the Americans were receiving no better response to their petitions. But then could the Americans, "at
a thousand leagues distance from the throne," expect a more
favorable answer than the City of London, a letter in the
Massachusetts Spy asked two years later. "*Surely, no!*" And the
Irish, far from winning reforms, were given new grievances
which were more outrageous than the old and which further
underlined the common elements of their cause and America's.
In late 1771, by a majority the Irish Parliament voted down
a proposed reorganization of the Irish tax commission which,
it was said, sought only to create more unnecessary positions
to increase Crown patronage. The measure was nonetheless
put into effect by the Crown alone, and one of the new commissioners of excise was Sir Francis Bernard, "the tyrant of
New-England." In 1773, to complete the analogy, Ireland
was given a Stamp Act. "The only successful petition I can
recollect," the *North Briton* could comment, "is that of Mr.
Quirk, the murderer."[27]

[I I]

The failure of the petition movement pushed the opposition
efforts into a far more serious phase, not only because hope
of redress was undercut and communication between the
government and colonists impaired, but because the King
had become implicated in his ministers' policies. True, despite Lord North's announcement that the King had personally
drawn up his answers to the city and that they were only
approved of in council, one could still argue that the King
had acted under the influence of his ministers. This was the
lord mayor's interpretation of events, and also that of Chat-

26. *S.C. Gaz.*, September 24, and *New London Gaz.*, September 13,
1771. Also comment from London in *N.Y. Jour.*, October 3, 1771.

27. "Probus," *Mass. Spy*, September 12, 1771. Account of Irish proceedings in *Pa. Jour.*, March 26 and April 30, 1772; William E.
Lecky, *A History of Ireland in the Eighteenth Century* (London,
1892), II, 110–11, 113, 133; Kraus, "America and the Irish Revolutionary Movement," 338. *North Briton* in *Pa. Jour.*, January 4, 1770.

ham.[28] But in any case the King's answers to the Londoners⌐ meant, as "Junius" pointed out, that all the abuses remonstrated against were "confirm'd by the K[ing]'s decisive approbation." It became increasingly difficult to see him as passively innocent of government decisions. Could anyone of common sense deny that George III took a "personal and decisive" role against the Americans, "Candidus" asked in a February 1770 letter to the *New York Journal*? If Charles I, that "poor unhappy (yet as a private Man virtuous) Prince, acted by the Advice of his Favourites," did he not nonetheless thereby "take a personal Part against his People"? Whether or not the various violations of the constitution were committed "by the immediate order or direction of the King, is not material to determine," commented an English writer in "THE SCOURGE." "It is only necessary to say, it was not done without his knowledge, otherwise redress had been obtained from his hands; he is therefore deeply involved in the guilt of his ministers."[29] In 1772, another British writer claimed that the "delusion" of the King's weakness led Englishmen "to become prey to the cunning of a Prince of the Brunswick line"; and an article in the *New London Gazette* called the old maxim that the King can do no wrong "a grand absurdity."[30]

Observers in London were particularly ready to blame the King directly. In April 1772, Arthur Lee wrote Samuel Adams that the King personally selected his ministers from his court "as among *bad men the worst*. Their unequaled merit, in his eye, is that they *want everything*, and will *do any thing*." The next year he asserted "there is not an action" in George III's reign, "some few treacherous ones expected, but what manifest it to be his sole wish to be the tyrant of his people."[31]

28. Lord North to Parliament, in London news of March 20, *Pa. Jour.*, June 14, 1770; Lord Mayor's remarks in *ibid.*, *Postscript* May 7, 1770; report of Chatham's May 6 speech in *Prov. Gaz.*, July 7, 1770.

29. "Junius," *N.Y. Jour.*, May 24, 1770; "Candidus," *ibid.*, March 8, 1770; "The Scourge, I," *New London Gaz.*, June 21, and *Mass. Spy*, May 9, 1771.

30. "Millions," *Prov. Gaz.*, September 5, 1772; "A Dialogue," *New London Gaz.*, April 10, 1772.

31. Lee to Adams, April 7, 1772, Samuel Adams Papers, NYPL; Lee to Adams, June 11, 1773, in Lee, *Arthur Lee*, I, 231.

Some writers in the colonies followed suit, but the turning of American attitudes toward the King is better seen in other, more subtle statements. In 1767, the King was called the "darling of America"; and in 1768, colonists could still express their "entire confidence in his Majesty, who is ever attentive to the complaints of his subjects, and is ever ready to relieve their distress." But by 1771, assertions of the King's goodness were often hedged with tell-tale qualifications, such as those of "AN AMERICAN" writing an open letter to the King: "I view your Majesty as one of the greatest and best Princes on Earth, yet capable of becoming greater and wiser. The wisest and best men are very imperfect and the more shining their talents, the more capable of improvement." In 1768, the birthday of their "most gracious and beloved Sovereign" was celebrated by Charlestonians "with every demonstration of joy, affection, and gratitude, that the most loyal subjects could give." The next year fewer houses were illuminated, and "the people in general seemed . . . depressed in spirits. . . ." By 1770 there were apparently no illuminations.[32] Well might "PROBUS," addressing the King in the September 12, 1771, *Massachusetts Spy*, warn George III that should "a few more of your answers to the most reasonable and dutiful prayers of your distressed people, resemble what we have had, that personal affection which filled your empire will greatly diminish, if it does not become utterly extinct."

The ministers were still most often blamed for grievances, but these attributions were in many cases clearly tactical maneuvers, and not statements of conviction. "*Let* us avoid blaming the king," the "CENTINEL" said in the October 31, 1771, *Massachusetts Spy*, as if this were an act of concession. Since the King's answers to London were delivered from the throne, a writer in the *North Briton* similarly argued, "it *may* fairly, I think, be treated, like all other speeches from the

32. *N.Y. Jour.*, October 1, 1767 (statement from *Boston Evening Post*) and July 7, 1768 (letter of Virginia Burgesses, May 9, 1768). "An American," *Boston Gaz.*, December 16, 1771. Accounts of Charleston celebrations in *S.C. Gaz.*, June 6, 1768, June 8, 1769, and May 17 and June 7, 1770. By 1773, their celebration of the King's ascension to the throne emphasized more than anything else the splendor of the local artillery company. (*Ibid.*, November 1, 1773.)

throne, as the speech of the minister; and it is in this light . . .
I *propose* to consider it."[33] "Junius" maintained the same
fiction, as did, after his model, the American Stephen Sayre.[34]
The reason went back to classical Whig principles: to deny
the King's innocence of offenses so serious was to declare that
a revolution existed, that the authority of government itself,
as contained in the King, had been dissolved. The King could
not reject the united appeals of the British electors to the
throne, the *North Briton* explained. "For if he can, he is no
longer a limited, but an absolute monarch; and it will then
be lawful for you, by every means you can think of, to reduce
his power within the same precise and determined limits
within which it was originally placed." Thus even Samuel
Adams in Boston continued to blame the King's actions on
his ministers, for no one was ready to go further, as he wrote
in August 1770, "*at present.*"[35]

Despite such refinements, the outer fringes of the opposition
took on revolutionary or proto-revolutionary overtones by the
early 1770's. The original London petition had explicitly
declared that the King was the last resort for redress short
of God and, with the decline of hope in George III, recollec-
tions of the seventeenth century became more menacing.
George III was likened to Charles I, he was threatened
editorially with the fate of James II—"THE SCOURGE" in fact

---

33. *North Briton,* CLV, in *Pa. Jour., Supplement* May 24, 1770.
Italics mine.

34. "Junius's" distinctions were labored: "I confess that, as far as
his [the King's] personal behaviour, or the royal purity of his intentions is concerned, the truth of those declarations [to the London
remonstrants], which the minister has drawn up for his master, cannot
decently be disputed." But in all other respects, he said, they could
not be supported in argument or fact. (Letter of March 1770 in *N.Y.
Jour.,* May 24, 1770.) See also Sayre to Ezra Stiles, July 20, 1772:
"the *Best of Princes* had taken care to offend all his English subjects
by a uniform and studied Inattention which irritable men like myself
construe into more than Neglect and downright Insult—Observe;
when I speak of the Best of Princes, I mean to speak in the Language
of Junius." (Ezra Stiles Papers, Beinecke Library, Yale University,
New Haven, Conn.)

35. *North Briton,* in *Pa. Jour., Supplement* May 24, 1770; Adams
as "The Chatterer," in Harry A. Cushing, ed., *The Writings of
Samuel Adams* (New York, 1904–8), II, 35–7.

claimed that the current British situation was much worse than in 1688; a speaker in Parliament remembered the days of Cade, Wat Tyler, and Jack Straw, while "Junius" reminded the King that "the name of Stewart, of itself is . . . contemptible." "The Prince who imitates their conduct should be warned by their example; and . . . should remember, that as [his title to the Crown] was acquired by one revolution, it may be lost in another."[36]

The most virulent London publications called only for preparations for a future uprising, but some individuals in England were apparently ready for immediate action. After the King refused the first London remonstrance in March 1771, a mysterious figure was reported to have harangued a mob of 500 near the King's Bench Prison, "treasonably exciting them to take up arms against his M[ajesty] of whom he spoke in the most scurrilous and audacious terms," reading to the crowd the London remonstrance and the King's answer and making "most impudent and treasonable remarks thereon." Soon thereafter, a £1000 reward was offered for the author of "A PROPHECY" stuck up on St. James's Palace:

> A cold winter;—a mild spring;
> A bloody summer;—A DEAD ———.

The threat of open violence merged with reality in 1771 when the lord mayor was imprisoned: the London mob not only assaulted Lord North, but attacked and insulted the King. Papers reported that news of the lord mayor's imprisonment led to the gathering of large bodies of people in several parts of Devonshire, and that these "behaved in a very riotous manner, calling out *to arms!*" and declaring they would "at any time (if Gentlemen of distinction would head them) take

36. London petition in *Pa. Jour.*, September 7, 1769; "Candidus," *N.Y. Jour.*, March 8, 1880; "Whisperer XLIII" (from London) in *Mass. Spy*, March 14, 1771; "Cassius" (from *Connecticut Courant*), *Prov. Gaz.*, September 25, 1773; "The Scourge, I," *New London Gaz.*, June 21, 1771, and "Junius" in *Va. Gaz.* (Rind), *Supplement* March 8, 1770, quoted in Robert D. Meade, *Patrick Henry, Patriot in the Making* (Philadelphia and New York, 1957), 276. Also "Americanus," *New London Gaz.*, December 25, 1772; and *Pa. Jour.*, May 23, 1771.

up arms in defence of those Magistrates, who attempted to prevent the laws from being trampled under foot."[37]

In America, too, alternatives to force were being foreclosed. Colonists began to reject petitions as a way of opposing their grievances. In April 1772, a writer in the *New London Gazette* expressed hope that no more would be sent to England, as America had been tantalized and mocked long enough. In 1773, the *Massachusetts Spy* called petitioning "degrading." Were the colonists to "whine and cry for relief, when we have already tried it in vain?" George Washington asked in July 1774. For the Baltimore Committee of Correspondence the contempt with which American petitions were treated indicated strongly "that some thing more sensible than Supplication will best serve our Purpose." "When a spirit so hostile to general liberty prevails in those who have power at home . . . the idea of proceeding by petition and remonstrance is the most ridiculous idea that ever entered into weak heads," another writer declared in 1774; and for proof he again cited the failure of London's petitions and remonstrances. By 1775, indeed, the very suggestion that redress could be won through "loyal and constitutional applications" could seem "an insult to the understanding of mankind."[38]

Where continued petitioning was advocated, it was for its domestic effects[39] or because petitions, as John Wilkes himself

37. *Pa. Jour.*, May 17 and 24, 1770, and May 23 and 30, 1771.

38. "Dialogue between a RULER and a SUBJECT," *New London Gaz.*, April 10, 1772; "LOCKE to the American COLONIES," *Mass. Spy*, November 26, 1773; Washington to Bryan Fairfax, Mount Vernon, July 20, 1774, in John C. Fitzpatrick, ed., *The Writings of George Washington* (Washington, 1931–44), III, 232–3; Baltimore to Boston Committee, June 4, 1774, Purviance Papers, MS. 1394, MdHS; "ANGLUS AMERICANUS" to the citizens of New York, *Boston Gaz.*, August 1, and *Prov. Gaz.*, August 6, 1774; Westmoreland County, Virginia, Committee of Safety proceedings, May 23, 1775, in Richard B. Harwell, ed., *The Committees of Safety of Westmoreland and Fincastle . . .* (Richmond, 1956), 40.

39. This became particularly clear in 1775. See particularly letter from Philadelphia in the *Massachusetts Spy*, July 19, 1775: Although all intelligence from London says petitions will be of no avail, still the Congress intends to petition the King once more "under this idea, that if it should be rejected, those moderate people, who now keep back, will, when they find no hopes [but] in the success of a War . . .

put it, were "useless, altho' necessary forms." When the
Virginia burgesses petitioned in 1770, "they did not expect
this petition would produce any alteration in the conduct of
the British ministry," one Virginian explained, "but, they
intended it, as their protestation, never to submit silently, to
the power of the parliament to tax the colonies." Four years
later, Benjamin Franklin echoed the identical idea—that petitions let Americans declare their opposition to grievances,
but that, having no other effect, "tho called *Petitions* . . . they
are rather Remonstrances and *Protests*."[40] This new attitude
had its counterpart in England, too, where colonial agents
gave up for the time all hope "of prevailing by reason and
argument against such fixed, rooted prejudices and resentment," and resorted to figurehead actions, efforts that were
"merely official."[41]

Gone, too, was the tolerance and flexibility that allowed
all but a handful of Americans to accept even the Declaratory
Act with few misgivings in 1766. Suddenly, in the face of
"despotism . . . systematically pursued," no suspicious British
effort, however trivial in immediate consequence, could be
overlooked; each became an "essay to try the people's spirit."
Submission to any seemed tantamount to accepting the ultimate end of British policy—total political slavery. All issues
became total, involving not only the immediate right involved,
but all rights, all freedom. To allow a governor to be salaried

---

heartily unite with us in prosecuting it effectually." Also intercepted
letter to Massachusetts [from Arthur Lee?], September 2, 1775, PRO,
CO 5/40, ff. 17–20, where continued petitioning is advocated in part
because "the more your petitions are rejected, the more truly may you
say . . . justum est Bellum, ubi necessarium."

40. Wilkes to Palfrey, September 27, 1769, CSM *Pubs.*, XXXIV
(*Trans.*, 1937–42), 414–15; letter from gentleman in Virginia, June
30, in *S.C. Gaz.*, August 23, and *Pa. Jour.*, July 19, 1770. Franklin to
Cushing, London, April 2, 1775, PRO, CO 5/118, ff. 72, 73. See also
Arthur Lee to Samuel Adams, April 7, 1772, Samuel Adams Papers,
recommending "no meeting of Your Assembly should pass away,
without . . . a Petition to the Throne. . . . Reiterating Petitions, would
serve to shew both the King and his Ministers, that we are not sub-
dued to their yoke"; it would perplex and mortify them, "which if not
victory is yet—revenge."

41. Extract of London letter, July 12, in *Pa. Jour.*, September 20,
1770. Kammen, *Rope of Sand*, especially 226–40.

from England was to accept a "condition . . . more humiliating and miserable . . . than that of the people of England in the infamous reigns of the Stuarts"; and the Crown's decision to pay judges, too, became " THE FINISHING STROKE," making Americans "as compleat slaves as the inhabitants of Turkey or Japan." That "court of inquisition, more horrid than that of Spain and Portugal," the *Gaspée* Commission, made it "an absolute certainty, that . . . the state of an American subject . . . will soon be infinitely worse than that of a subject of . . . any . . . despotic power on earth," such that Americans became bound "to stand forth in the glorious cause of freedom" and "either prevent the fastening of the infernal chains . . . or nobly perish in the attempt!" If East Indian tea were landed before the Tea Act was repealed, colonists were warned, there would be "Nothing we possess, whether Lands, Houses, Cattle, Money, or any Thing else, which we can *then* call our own." The image of Americans standing on a precipice was particularly compelling. Extreme caution was simple prudence; their next step could always be fatal.[42]

This sense of imminent danger was reflected in the increased militancy of American nonimportation supporters in 1769 and 1770. The Bostonians' decision to use mob coercion against importers in February 1770 and also their later decision to force the return of imported goods to England correlated exactly, it was said, with the arrival of news or radical tracts from London. Similarly, a special committee of the Maryland Association cited at length the actions of King and Parliament during 1768 and 1769 to document the "extreme Danger" which, it indicated, lay behind its decision to uphold the nonimportation agreement with particular strictness in the case of the *Good Intent*.[43]

The extremist tendency within the nonimportation associa-

42. *Boston Gaz.*, November 2, 1772 ("An American"), August 31, 1772 ("An Elector, 1772"), October 7, 1771 (on governor's salary), October 19, 1772 ("Oliver Cromwell"), January 4, 1773 ("Americanus"), and October 5, 1772 ("The Whig-Proselyte"). "A Demonstration," *N.Y. Jour.*, December 23, 1773.

43. "Narrative of Proceedings at Boston" for February 7 and April 26, 1770, New England Papers, III, ff. 70, 77; "The Proceedings of the Committee," reproduced in "The Case of the Good Intent," *Maryland Historical Magazine*, III (1908), especially 141–57.

tion coincided, too, with a new interest in direct action and military preparation which in America, as in England, was particularly clear within the outer fringe of the opposition. Already in 1769, some Virginians had expressed surprise, August Miles wrote Wilkes, "that the conduct of your British (tho pensionary) House of Commons did not give birth to a revolt." By 1771 American papers, especially the *Massachusetts Spy*, reprinted London articles saying there was an "actual diss[olutio]n of gov[ernmen]t," and attempting to rouse the people "for the day . . . not far distant, when we must all stand forth and bravely attempt a restoration of our rights, or nobly die in the cause of freedom." Other articles of colonial origin echoed the idea, sometimes vehemently. By the spring of 1770, Thomas Hutchinson detected a growing popular conviction "of the necessity of the people's preparing to defend themselves and their Rights not by arguments and reasoning only but by Arms and open resistance." Such a feeling perhaps accounted for increased requests that he, as acting governor, put the militia on a more respectable footing. And when the Boston Town Meeting met in November 1772 to create its famous committee of correspondence, the gathering was "not so full as has sometimes been on Occasions of much less Importance," Samuel Adams admitted, "partly from the Opinion of some, that there was no method left to be taken but *the last*, which is also the Opinion of many in the Country." In 1770, Adams himself began proudly announcing "that our *young Men* begin to be ambitious of making themselves perfect Masters of the Art *military*."[44]

The exact purpose of military readiness in the eyes of radical leaders was sometimes ambiguous: Adams perhaps saw the existence of effective American troops as a means of increasing the colonists' bargaining power in negotiations with the Mother Country, should she go to war with Spain; and as late

44. Miles to Wilkes, August 10, 1769, BM Add. Mss., 30870; "Whisperer XLIII," from London, in *Mass. Spy*, March 14, 1771, and "The Scourge, I," in *ibid.*, May 9, 1771; "Humanity," *Boston Gaz.*, November 9, 1772. Hutchinson to Hillsborough, May 18, 1770, New England Papers, III, f. 80; Adams to Arthur Lee, Boston, November 3, 1772, and Adams to Sayre, November 23, 1770, in Cushing, *Writings of Samuel Adams*, II, 344, 69.

as 1774, Elbridge Gerry saw military training as a way of off-
setting colonists' fears of British regular troops, such that it
could "entirely unite us . . . and greatly add to the firmness of
our resolutions." For others, however, as Hutchinson noted already in 1770, the reason for arming was overt and hostile. "In
the present most critical season, the Military is part of the
armour of God," "Fervidus" told *Boston Gazette* readers on
May 18, 1772. "And we should all, as one man, be in utmost
readiness to resist, *even unto blood*, the cruel enemies of our
liberty" in what he was ready to call a "civil war."[45]

Not even independence was the universal bogey it had
been in 1765. If Britain did not restore America's rights, an
article in the *Essex Gazette* declared in early 1772, the colonies
would "soon put in practice their mediated plan, of the United
Provinces, after the example of the Dutch, and form an independent commonwealth." The plan was feasible, various
writers claimed, even advantageous. The Americans could
"offer a free trade to all nations in Europe," which would
"effectually secure the Americans from the invasion of foreign
enemies, for it will be the interest of the European powers to
prevent any one nation from acquiring more interest in
America than the rest." At the same time, America would
save an amount estimated from £2–6 million annually that was
currently spent on British duties, quit rents, or to satisfy the
extortionist tactics of the King's officers. The question of
America's independence, it was said, was only one of time:
"But by all the signs of the times, and appearances of things,
it is very near—tis not probable that it is of the distance of
fifteen years."[46] The event would, however, never occur on

45. Gerry to Boston Committee of Correspondence, April 4, 1774,
Elbridge Gerry Papers, Library of Congress, Washington, D.C.;
Hutchinson letter cited, n. 44. See also "A Military Countryman,"
Boston Gaz., January 27, 1772, and "Oliver Cromwell" in *ibid.*, Oc-
tober 19, 1772; also the Rev. William Gordon to Lord Dartmouth,
Jamaica Plain, Massachusetts, June 16, 1773: "A military spirit in-
creases, and the people are forming various companies of artillery."
Papers of William Legge, Earl of Dartmouth, D 1778/2/637; William
Salt Library, Stafford, England.

46. "Foresight," from *Essex Gazette*, in *Prov. Gaz.*, March 7, 1772.
See also "AN AMERICAN," *Boston Gaz.*, January 6, and *New London
Gaz.*, January 17, 1772; "Age and Experience," *Boston Gaz.*, January

the initiative of the colonists: it was contingent on a continuation of British oppression. Even Samuel Adams, who increasingly saw independence as a likely outcome of the British-American conflict, was consistent on this point. In 1765, he said Americans would never opt for independence "unless Great Britain shall exert her power to destroy their Libertys"; in 1774, he still foresaw "*the entire separation and independence of the colonies*" only if "the British administration and government do not return to the principles of moderation and equity."[47]

Revolutionary tendencies were most fully expressed before 1773 in local situations, particularly in Massachusetts after that colony's governor and judges accepted Crown salaries. Undeterred by a respect for the Crown or confidence in redress from England, some opponents were ready to proclaim their government dissolved: the governor's continued authority was denied; grand juries refused to sit under Crown-paid judges. Officials who accepted payment other than from the legislature, which was paymaster under the Massachusetts Charter of 1691, violated the constitution, writers claimed. The new salary system destroyed the constitution's balance, making Massachusetts government absolute, thus illegal and of no force. But the King was also immediately involved in the opposition to Governor Hutchinson: "A ruler independent on the people is a monster in government," "Mucius Scaevola" wrote in the *Massachusetts Spy*. "Such a one is Mr. Hutchinson; and such would George the third be, if he should be rendered Independent on the people of Great-Britain." The King's authority was for some tied to Hutchinson's, and the denial of one implied a denial of the other: the King could not free himself of his dependence on Parliament, "Scaevola" again wrote, so he had no legal right to free his colonial

---

11, and *N.Y. Jour.*, January 21, 1773 (and answer to this essay from "Age and Judgment," *N.Y. Jour.*, March 11, asking that discussion of independence be put aside "at this Time"); "An American" in *Boston Gaz.*, December 16, 1771, and "American Solon," in *ibid.*, December 23, 1771.

47. Adams to "G—— W——," Boston, November 13, 1765; to Dennis DeBerdt, December 16, 1766, and to Arthur Lee, Boston, April 4, 1774, in Cushing, *Writings of Samuel Adams*, I, 38, 113, and III, 100.

governors of that dependence. "And the moment that he or they attempt to render themselves independent on the people, that moment their authority ceases, they themselves break the compact with the people, and from that moment the people become alienated from their jurisdiction, and have a constitutional right to form their government anew." Rather than submit, it was better to "let the present system of government tumble into ruin, even though it should crush every tyrant to death."[48]

[I I I]

The scattered evidences of incipient revolution in England were misleading. Just as radical conclusions were pushed to extremes, the main body of the British opposition movement was in process of disintegration. Already in August 1770, reports arrived from England that the petition movement, which never had been united politically beyond the Middlesex election issue, had begun to abate. The fracas at the time of the lord mayor's commitment to the Tower of London was great; yet the next April, a London correspondent assured Philadelphians that the minority was declining daily: "Wilkes has lost his former popularity, and several others who bid fair to succeed him in the good opinion of the people have been 'bought off' . . . by the Ministry." After Parliament was prorogued and, because of that event, London's lord mayor and alderman were released, accounts reaching America agreed that everything was quiet and peaceful, with the ministry firmly established. In late 1771, the Supporters of the Bill of Rights split into two bitter factions, with the seceders forming a Constitutional Society; and a court-favored candidate, William Nash, was elected London's lord mayor. "There is no opposition now, nor any forming," Arthur Lee wrote his

48. *Mass. Spy*, November 14 and October 24, 1771 ("Mucius Scaevola"), October 3, 24, and November 22, 1771 ("Centinel"), and January 2, 1772, for "Rusticus": "We have prayed, we have entreated, supplicated, petitioned, addressed, to no purpose, and long suffered injuries with patience and submission," so now let us "SPURN the TYRANTS, PULL DOWN the TYRANNY they exercise."

brother, Richard Henry, in August 1772. Instead, there reigned in England "a calm, which seems to resign every thing to the will of a court, which is mediating and executing a systematic destruction of our liberties."[49]

In America, too, the radicals' support seemed to melt away. After the failure of the nonimportation movement in 1770, an apparent calm settled over political affairs that drove some colonial leaders, like James Warren of Plymouth, Massachusetts, to a near despondency, while in London Arthur Lee complained that the news from America had afflicted him with "such absolute despair, that I now give up all hope that our Country will escape Slavery." Luxury and corruption would bear down all freedom and liberty: the torrent was irresistible.[50]

Samuel Adams, however, recognized his countrymen's apparent placidity as a "sullen silence." Anyone who interpreted it as evidence that the colonists were reconciled to ministerial measures was wrong. Others agreed. Like Adams, John Dickinson in Pennsylvania, Richard Henry Lee in Virginia, and Ezra Stiles in Newport saw the "great Spirit of Liberty still going and operating with great force" in the "Body of the common people." Contention could never really end, the *South Carolina Gazette* asserted, until the Declaratory Act was repealed. Even the partial repeal of the Townshend duties could be seen as the product of bad British policy, like leaving splinters in a wound "which must prevent its healing, or in time occasion it to open afresh." One commentator explained the decline of agitation by the exhaustion of peaceful modes of seeking redress. "The reason why the people in the several provinces have not of late sent home petitions, remonstrances etc. and continued their publications in favour of liberty as frequent as heretofore," "Foresight" explained, "is they have

49. *N.Y. Jour.*, August 16, 1770 (London news, June 5), July 4, 1771 (London letter, April 22, via Philadelphia), and July 25, 1771 (London news, via Boston). *Prov. Gaz.*, July 21, 1771. Lee letter, August 17, 1772, in Lee, *Arthur Lee*, I, 207.

50. Warren to Samuel Adams, November 8, 1772, Samuel Adams Papers; Lee to Richard Henry Lee, September 10, 1770, Lee Family Papers, UVa, available in Paul P. Hoffman, ed., "Lee Family Papers, 1742–1795," University of Virginia microfilm (Charlottesville, 1966), Roll II.

already sufficiently informed the Parliament, and the people of Great-Britain, what their sentiments and intentions are, and are now waiting to see whether Great-Britain will restore their liberties."[51]

The cohesiveness of the American resistance movement in fact increased between 1768 and the early 1770's. Local politics, for example, became less of an obstacle to the opposition movement's growth once it became clear that the British government's American policy was rooted in more than temporary errors. In New York there had been two bitter "Sons of Liberty" factions in early 1769, one supporting the Delancey party, the other the Livingstonians. By July 1769, however, the process of uniting "to defend common rights" was under way, and Alexander McDougall, a Livingstonian, became by 1770 a leader of the Sons, along with former Delanceyites Isaac Sears and John Lamb.[52] In Philadelphia, too, Charles Thomson—a friend of the Anti-Proprietary leader Benjamin Franklin, who was perhaps for that reason only ambiguously involved with the predominantly Proprietary party Stamp Act opposition[53]—emerged as an active leader.

51. Adams to James Warren, March 25, 1771, *The Warren–Adams Letters, I* (Boston, 1917), 9; Dickinson to Arthur Lee, Philadelphia, September 31, 1771, in Lee, *Arthur Lee,* II, 304; Arthur Lee to Richard Henry Lee, September 23, 1772 (commenting upon R. H. Lee's optimism), UVa and "Lee Family Papers," Roll II; Stiles to Catharine Macaulay, November 13, 1772, Stiles Papers; *S.C. Gaz.,* May 7, 1772; Thomas Cushing, for the Massachusetts assembly, to Benjamin Franklin, June 29, 1771, in "Lee Family Papers," Roll II; and "Foresight," *Prov. Gaz.,* March 7, 1772.

Letters from the Philadelphia merchants' committee of 1769 were to the same effect. "We can have little expectation of a cordial union between both countries until there is an alteration in the Sentiments of Administration," it wrote Benjamin Franklin on April 18. The merchants had fought only for the repeal of the Townshend Act, but, they wrote London merchants on November 25, "the minds of the people" would not be satisfied until all recent revenue acts were repealed and things put "on the same footing they were before the late innovations." Sparks Mss., LXII, Vol. 7, pp. 188–9, 223, HUL.

52. Roger Champagne, "The Sons of Liberty and the Aristocracy in New York Politics," unpublished Ph.D. thesis, University of Wisconsin, 1960, chaps. 8, 9.

53. Thomson served on the Philadelphia committee that secured Stampman John Hughes's resignation in 1765, but his name never

Even the Philadelphia mechanics, whose loyalty to the Franklinites robbed the Stamp Act opposition of a popular base in that city, began by 1770 to abandon Joseph Galloway and other royalist Anti-Proprietary leaders. In short, as Isaac Sears put it, measures in support of the country's liberties were more important than men, or previous personal political loyalties; and the cause of Empire surmounted more petty local arguments.[54]

The network of private correspondences between colonists of radical sympathies also expanded during and immediately after the Wilkes agitation, and this, too, added cohesion to the colonial opposition effort. In part, this accomplishment was the work of Arthur Lee, the most prominent American in the London Wilkes movement, and a man who, with his brother William, largely took over Wilkes's American correspondence after Wilkes was released from prison and became absorbed in London affairs. Before leaving Virginia for London in 1768, Lee already planned to send "speedy and accurate information of the real designs of the British ministry . . . to leading men in the several colonies," so as to "enable them to harmonize in one system of opposition"; and he won John Dickinson to the idea. Once abroad, Arthur Lee not only wrote to Dickinson and his brothers, who became revolutionary leaders in Virginia, but established other correspondences, particularly with Samuel Adams and Joseph Warren. Moreover, he brought his colonial correspondents into direct contact with each other: through Arthur Lee's agency, Richard Henry Lee—the foremost radical leader in Virginia—began writing John Dickinson (1768) and Samuel Adams (1773). Other contacts were made independently. Joseph Reed visited Boston in 1769 and developed close friendships with some of the town's leaders. Reed, who also knew the Lees and other

---

appears in the correspondence of the Sons of Liberty and his surviving correspondence of the Stamp Act period indicates more a reluctant acquiescence than an enthusiastic support of the nonimportation effort of the period. See "The Thomson Papers, 1765–1816," NYHS *Colls. for 1878* (New York, 1879), 5–12.

54. Benjamin H. Newcomb, "Effects of the Stamp Act on Colonial Pennsylvania Politics," *W. M. Q.*, XXIII (1966), 272. Sears to printer, New York, May 5, in *N.Y. Jour.*, May 10, 1770.

English radicals through his wife's family in the City of London, moved to Philadelphia from Trenton in 1770 and became one of the town's revolutionary leaders. Another Philadelphia leader, Thomas Mifflin, developed New England contacts during a 1773 summer visit to Newport. Josiah Quincy, Jr.'s, trip from Boston to South Carolina in 1773 played an important part in consolidating this network. His journal records long conversations with leading colonists along the road home—often men like Cornelius Harnett, "the Samuel Adams of North Carolina"—and Quincy constantly tried to interest these contacts "with regard to a general and permanent Continental Literary Correspondence."[55]

This tenacity and unity of the American people was of particular importance, for in the wake of the Wilkes movement's collapse, the colonists, it seemed, had to assume the leadership in defending British freedom. From 1768 to 1770, they had waited, hoped, and trusted their English colleagues to carry the main responsibility of opposition; but such dependency was no longer feasible. Had Britons become "unfeeling to their condition," Samuel Adams asked Arthur Lee in 1771, or had "brute force at length become so formidable, that after having in vain petitioned those whose duty it is to redress their grievances, they are afraid to imitate the virtue of their ancestors in similar cases, and redress their grievances themselves?" The next year, he wrote Rhode Islander Henry Marchant of the "great concern" of the Friends of Liberty in Boston that the administration could carry an election in the City of London, "which has heretofore by her Independency and Incorruption been the great Security of the Freedom of the nation." Everything seemed to vindicate his observation of November 1770 that few Englishmen were worthy of America's confidence, that it was "the Business of America to take care of herself." John Dickinson drew the same conclu-

55. Lee, *Arthur Lee*, especially Lee's "Memoir," I, 244, and II, *passim*; James C. Ballagh, ed., *The Letters of Richard Henry Lee* (New York, 1911): I, *1762–1778*, 29, 82; William B. Reed, *Life and Correspondence of Joseph Reed* (Philadelphia, 1847), I, 40–1; Kenneth R. Rossman, *Thomas Mifflin and the Politics of the American Revolution* (Chapel Hill, 1952), 13; "Journal of Josiah Quincy, Junior, 1773," MHS *Procs.*, XLIX (1915–16), 424–81, especially 451, 457–8, 460.

sion from events in England. "As to our British friends," he
wrote in September 1771, "we ought to expect everything
from them but—assistance." And letters from London,
particularly from Wilkites like Arthur Lee or Stephen Sayre,
also agreed: the colonists must henceforth depend primarily
upon themselves for the defense of their liberties.[56]

But how should the radical leaders exercise this new responsibility? A true patriot, Adams wrote in 1771, would
"keep the attention of his fellow citizens awake to their
grievances," and not allow them to rest "till the causes of
their just complaints are removed." This patriotic task was
simplified in a virtuous country like America, where there was
an underlying "strong spirit of Liberty" surviving in the people
at large. In such a situation, the Boston Committee of Correspondence said, it required "only a sight of . . . daring In-
croachments, to produce a manly and effectual opposition to
them." As a result, top priority was given to publicizing
British actions; and that task was performed largely by the
new committees of correspondence. Those committees that
linked together the various provincial legislatures after the
suggestion of the Virginia burgesses in 1773 were designed
in part to communicate the "most early and authentic intelligence" of British innovations affecting the colonies. And net-
works of correspondence committees at local and county levels
were set up, according to Charles Thomson, so that "any
intelligence of importance" could be "quickly disseminated to
the whole body of the people." Once the people's eyes were
opened, the existence of a design against British liberties was
clear. "Our ship is in the hands of pilots who . . . are steering
directly under full sail to a rock," one 1772 writer said; "the
whole crew may see [this path] in full view if they *look the
right way*."[57]

56. Adams to Arthur Lee, Boston, July 31, 1771; to Marchant, January 7, 1772, and to Stephen Sayre, Boston, November 23, 1770, in
Cushing, *Writings of Samuel Adams*, II, 189, 306, 68; also supporting
judgment by "Solon," *Mass. Spy*, June 3, 1773. Dickinson to Arthur
Lee, September 21, 1771, in Lee, *Arthur Lee*, II, 304. Sayre to Adams,
London, September 18, 1770, and Lee to Adams, December 31, 1771,
in Samuel Adams Papers.

57. Samuel Adams as "Vindex," *Boston Gaz.*, January 21, 1771, and
Cushing, *Writings of Samuel Adams*, II, 149–50; Boston Committee

No immediate results were expected. The colonists had not yet been provoked enough, John Dickinson realized; but "thanks to the excellent spirit of administration," he had no doubt that the future would bring more severe measures, and that this future oppression would make the colonists far more actively attentive to their cause. As for the "calm friend of freedom," then, his task was to wait "till time shall ripen the period for asserting more successfully the Liberties of these countries," to be a man "on the watch to seize the happy opportunity, whenever it offers," ready to "call out new dangers." Always, then, the radicals' moves were geared to those of the British government, which was expected to condemn itself by its actions. "We cannot make Events," Samuel Adams later said. "Our Business is wisely to improve them."[58]

These expectations were amply fulfilled with the Tea Act of 1773, followed in 1774 by the "Intolerable Acts." The Boston Port Bill, the Administration of Justice Act, the Massachusetts Government Act, and the Quebec Act seemed to prove beyond all doubt the existence of a despotic plot: by punishing the Bostonians for their "patriotic efforts," by denying basic British rights to Britons in Massachusetts and Canada, annulling the Massachusetts Charter, and granting toleration to Canadian Roman Catholics, these acts flagrantly fulfilled those tendencies already discovered with more difficulty in British actions of the Wilkes period. The existence of "a regular, systematic plan" against American freedom became

---

of Correspondence to Nathan Sparhawk, Boston, March 31, 1773, "Minutes of the Committee of Correspondence," Book 3, p. 233, MHS (photostats of the originals in the NYPL). On strategy, see also "Fervidus," *Boston Gaz.*, March 16, 1772. Letter from Virginia, March 14, 1773, in *ibid.*, April 12, 1773. Thomson to David Ramsay, New York, November 4, 1786, "Thomson Papers," 218–19. The Pennsylvania committees were probably not organized before 1774, however. See Thomas Mifflin to Samuel Adams, May 21, 1774, Samuel Adams Papers, in which Mifflin anticipates the formation of committees of correspondence on the New England model "for the several Counties in the province which was never done on former Occasions."

58. Dickinson to Arthur Lee, Philadelphia, October 31, 1770, in Lee, *Arthur Lee*, II, 302–3; Dickinson to Samuel Adams, Fairhill, April 10, 1773, Samuel Adams Papers. Samuel Adams to Samuel Cooper, Philadelphia, April 30, 1776, in Cushing, *Writings of Samuel Adams*, III, 284.

"as clear as the sun in its meridian brightness."[59] And once this plan was so definitely proven, no colony could stand unaffected by the singling out of Massachusetts for punishment. At a time when British policy in Ireland or England was echoed in America and the West Indies, Massachusetts's fate was an immediate threat to all.

The emphasis on waiting and watching tied in well with two other lessons that Samuel Adams, who was rapidly becoming the architect of the final stages of the Revolution, learned from the agitation of the late 1760's and early 1770's. First, there was the instructive example offered by the Bill of Rights Society. Division among the London patriots had caused their important defeat in the London elections of 1771, Adams believed; and in general it was part of the ministry's "Machiavellian plan" to encourage divisions within its opposition. A continued consultation between patriots could help avoid disunity, but beyond this, patience was necessary, for "it requires time to bring honest Men to think and determine alike even in important matters." The conclusion was akin to a second lesson, drawn from the Regulators' defeat at the Alamance, one already "often inculcated in Massachusetts": "to let grievances be pretty generally felt before a few undertake to effect their redress." For final success, the revolutionary movement would have to be ready to compromise differences between the most radical and less ardent colonies: "great prudence, temper, and moderation" would have to be "mixed in our counsels, and made the governing principles of the contending parties," as George Washington later put it. Those colonies most advanced in their conclusions, most ready for war or independence, would have to hold back and wait, since "salvation from Slavery perpetual to us and our posterity" depended upon "Union and Harmony amongst ourselves (under God)."[60]

59. George Washington to Bryan Fairfax, Mount Vernon, July 4, 1774, in Fitzpatrick, *Washington Writings*, III, 228.

60. Adams to Henry Marchant, January 7, 1772, and to Samuel Cooper, Philadelphia, April 30, 1776, in Cushing, *Writings of Samuel Adams*, II, 306–7, III, 284. "Humanus," *Mass. Spy*, July 25, 1771. Washington to Joseph Reed, New York, April 15, 1776, Fitzpatrick, *Writings of Washington*, IV, 483. Baltimore to Norfolk and Ports-

The composite effect of the agitation of late 1769 and the early 1770's was apparent when open conflict with Britain resumed in 1773 and 1774. Through their own efforts and those of their fellow sons of liberty elsewhere, particularly in England, the colonial leaders gained the knowledge and experience that rendered their own later endeavors more mature, more politic, better adapted to the needs of their situation. At the same time, the nature of their agitation was transformed. Arms and independence were ready words in 1773 as they had not been when the conflict with Britain began in 1765 or recommenced in 1767. Once contentious but loyal subjects, by 1773 the American radical leadership was tentatively revolutionary.

---

mouth committees of correspondence, June 17, 1774, Purviance Papers. Philadelphians also deduced the need of unity from their observations of English opposition politics: see Philadelphia committee to John Collins of Rhode Island, December 15, 1769, Sparks Mss., LXII, Vol. 7, pp. 232-3.

CHAPTER EIGHT

THE MAKING OF AN
AMERICAN REVOLUTION,
1772–1776

MORE THAN THE LACK of an active following kept Americans like Samuel Adams from advocating the "last appeal" in the early 1770's. They were emotionally and intellectually unprepared for war and a potential withdrawal from the empire. Declarations of affection for Britain continued and hopes that independence could be averted were expressed on into late 1775, even by the man who finally wrote the Declaration of Independence.[1] The government had apparently violated the most elementary civil rights and acted upon a regularized plan for establishing despotic executive rule, which implied that American grievances would only multiply in coming years. Still, there was a possibility that the trend might be reversed. If nothing else, Joseph Warren suggested in 1773, chance might produce measures with "agreeable effects," it might unearth a way "to penetrate the Egyptian darkness . . . so palpable in the court atmosphere."[2]

Hopes generally centered, however, on more predictable developments. A change in ministry or a new Parliament could alter the tendency of events. Then, too, the King might

1. Thomas Jefferson to unnamed correspondent, Monticello, August 25, 1775, Papers of William Legge, Earl of Dartmouth, D 1778/2/ 1461, William Salt Library, Stafford, England.

2. To Arthur Lee, Boston, December 21, 1773, in Richard Henry Lee, *Life of Arthur Lee* (Boston, 1829), II, 262.

reverse his stand: somehow, the pleas of his aggrieved subjects might win his compassion and lead to basic reforms.
Finally, after all else failed, and arms became necessary, hope
remained that the British people would rise up like their
seventeenth-century ancestors to salvage their liberties. So
long as these possibilities remained, colonists could envisage a
solution to their problems like that won by other aggrieved
subjects in English history: a document might be negotiated
that would settle the questions of right at issue, altering or
further settling the distribution of power within the constitution, with government otherwise continuing much as it had
before the conflict arose. Significantly, colonial leaders discussed a hypothetical "American Bill of Rights," looking back
to the English Bill of Rights established in 1689. Only after
all these possibilities were ruled out did the colonists reject
their Mother Country and announce a revolution, not like
that of 1688 which had hitherto served as their model, but
an exclusively American Revolution, for national independence.

[I]

William Legge, Lord Dartmouth, replaced Lord Hillsborough
as secretary of state for the American colonies in August 1772,
and his appointment awoke renewed hope for reform. Dartmouth had served as president of the Board of Trade in the
Rockingham administration of 1765–6, which had repealed the
Stamp Act, and had given colonists a "general satisfaction" by
his performance in office. Moreover, Americans found him "in
point of moral virtue . . . unexceptionable," in contrast to the
rest of the King's ministers, and his virtue was buttressed by
strong religious sentiments—Arthur Lee in fact found the
new minister "religious *overmuch*, and even addicted to
methodism." For Lee, this religiosity indicated "a weak mind,
or hypocritical heart," but for most observers his appointment
was "considered as a favourable presage of a change of sentiments at Court." "From your unspotted character, from your
known attachment to the principles of religious and civil
liberty, and from your generous concern for the welfare of

your country," a widely reprinted English letter to Dartmouth claimed, "the public in general" expected that he would use his influence "to protect, to countenance, and support the just pretensions of all his Majesty's subjects to partake alike of his paternal care and affection."[3]

For the Americans, Dartmouth seemed to presage change, too, because he was willing to supplement biased official intelligence with direct private accounts from the colonies. As early as 1766, he expressed a readiness to receive first-hand reports on America from Stephen Sayre, who was then planning to visit several major colonial commercial towns. Six years later, Dartmouth again accepted an offer of intelligence from the Reverend William Gordon, a future historian of the Revolution who then lived near Boston and claimed to have frequent and unreserved conversations with the town's leaders. In 1773, the secretary took up a similar offer of a correspondence from the Philadelphia revolutionary leader Joseph Reed. Nor was the initiative for such exchanges always on the side of the colonists. Soon after taking office, Dartmouth wrote a private, personal letter to Thomas Cushing, speaker of the Massachusetts Assembly, assuring Cushing that he had "lost no Time" in laying the assembly's recent petitions before the King and expressing his strong desire that the differences between Britain and the colonies be resolved. For Cushing, the letter was enough to justify fully the Americans' confidence in the new secretary's wisdom and justice.[4]

3. *Prov. Gaz.*, October 17, 1772; Samuel Adams to Arthur Lee, Boston, November 3, 1772, in Lee, *Arthur Lee*, II, 193, and Lee's "Memoir," in *ibid.*, I, 256–7; "Probus" to Dartmouth, from the London *Political Register*, in *Pa. Jour.*, February 3, and *Mass. Spy*, January 21, 1773. See also the expressions of hope through Dartmouth in documents received by the Boston Committee of Correspondence and copied into their "Minutes," NYPL, and, in photostat, MHS: minutes of the Roxbury Town Meeting, December 14, 1772, pp. 24–8; Gloucester's instructions to its assembly representatives, 1772, p. 29; Acton town proceedings, January 18, 1773, p. 125, and those of Billerica, February 1, 1773, p. 193.

4. Sayre to Dartmouth, Philadelphia, December 13, 1766, and from New York, June 25, 1767, Dartmouth Papers, D 1778/2/258, 264. Gordon to Dartmouth, Jamaica Plain, Massachusetts, October 24, 1772, and June 16, 1773, in *ibid.*, D 1778/2/442, 637. Reed's initiative was conveyed by his father-in-law, Dennis DeBerdt. See DeBerdt to Dart-

These hopeful expectations were dispelled by Dartmouth's performance in office. From the outset of his service, suggestions were made for reforms that the new secretary had power to effect, but none of these was acted upon. In both London and colonial papers, "Probus" called on Dartmouth to dismiss the governor of Grenada; the secretary should, moreover, order the dissolution of Grenada's assembly with its new contingent of Roman Catholic members, then restore English government as it was first set up on the island after the Peace of 1763. And he should annul Lord Hillsborough's instructions for the military subjection of the Caribs on the Island of St. Vincent. Another writer demanded that Dartmouth dismiss from office and punish Massachusetts Governor Thomas Hutchinson and "the rest of the cabal" in the Bay Colony or it would be "manifest to the world" that Dartmouth was no independent force for good but "the puppet of the day, incapable to move unless some secret hand shall touch the MASTER WIRE."[5]

Dartmouth's orders setting up the *Gaspée* Commission were still more damaging to his reputation. The commission, according to the Boston Committee of Correspondence, was "so abhorrent from the principles of every free government, [that] our expectations from the change [in ministry] must be totally annihilated." Dartmouth's personal opposition to the provisions for bringing accused colonists to England for trial, which he thought illegal, was known. If he could not prevent such illiberal innovations, should he not, as "Junius Americanus" suggested, "atone for an incautious assumption of power, by an honourable resignation"? But bound by affection for his half-brother Lord North, and

---

mouth, August 14, 1773, in *ibid.*, D 1778/2/682, and Reed to DeBerdt, Philadelphia, January 4, 1772, in William B. Reed, *Life and Correspondence of Joseph Reed* (Philadelphia, 1847), I, 49. Dartmouth to Cushing, June 19, 1773, Dartmouth Papers, D 1778/2/641, and Cushing to Arthur Lee, Boston, September 20, 1773, in Lee, *Arthur Lee*, II, 238. Cushing's reply to Dartmouth, August 22, 1773, is also in the Dartmouth Papers, D 1778/2/692.

5. "Probus," *Pa. Jour.*, February 3, 1773, and *Mass. Spy*, January 21 and April 29, 1773; "An American," *Boston Gaz.*, October 4, and *Mass. Spy*, October 7, 1773.

fearful of embarrassing him by resigning so soon after taking office, Dartmouth remained in the government, giving his tacit backing even to measures he privately opposed.[6]

Evaluations of Dartmouth reflected these discouraging events. As early as November 1772, Samuel Adams trembled for the new secretary "lest he should make shipwreck of his virtue" in the other ministers' company. By the following April, Adams expressed doubt whether personal goodness was enough for a successful statesman. Letters from the Lees in London both shared and fed these doubts. Four months after Dartmouth took office, Arthur Lee wrote that he was "at least too moderate a character to attempt any thing grand or decisive." By the next June, Lee wrote Thomas Cushing that the secretary was "that kind of man who apparently meaning no ill, will never do any good." His comments to Samuel Adams were even harsher. "Though not so actively bad," Lee said, Dartmouth was "yet . . . as capable of adopting any unjust and arbitrary measure as my Lord Hillsborough"; and the "Rhode Island measure," in fact, proved him to be "a man after his majesty's own heart, arbitrary and hypocritical." By August 1774, the *Boston Gazette* was ready to print William Lee's conclusion that, "notwithstanding his fawning and deceitful expressions to the Americans," within the cabinet Dartmouth was "as determin'd and violent an enemy to [the colonists] as any in the country."[7]

The correspondence of Americans with Dartmouth reinforced this despair. It proved, in fact, more a record of irreconcilable differences than a means of reconciliation. Like

6. Boston Committee to Charlestown, January 1, 1771, in its "Minutes," 40–1. "Junius Americanus" [Arthur Lee], from London *Public Adviser*, in *Pa. Jour.*, October 6; *Prov. Gaz.*, October 2, *Boston Gaz.*, September 27, 1773. B. D. Barger, *Lord Dartmouth and the American Revolution* (Columbia, 1965), 77–8.

7. Samuel Adams to Arthur Lee, Boston, November 3, 1772, and April 9, 1773, in Lee, *Arthur Lee*, II, 193, 199; Arthur Lee to Samuel Adams, Middle Temple, December 24, 1772, and June 11, 1773, in *ibid.*, I, 224, 232, and see also 222, 226, 233–4. Arthur Lee to Thomas Cushing, June 10, 1773, PRO, CO 5/118, ff. 90–1. *Boston Gaz.*, August 22, 1774, and William Lee to Cushing, London, June 1, 1774, PRO, CO 5/118, ff. 26–7.

the Rockinghams of 1765–6, Dartmouth continued to assert the absolute supremacy of Parliament over all parts of the British Empire. He thought it perhaps politic that Parliament cease to exert its right "till some Occasion . . . in which the Expedience and Necessity of such Exercise should be obvious to every considerate Man in every Part of the Dominions of Great Britain," but he could never deny that authority, he wrote Thomas Cushing, for it was "inherent and inseparable from the supreme Authority of the State." It was then easy to conclude "that the liberties of America are not so much in danger from any thing that Parliament has done, or is likely to do here, as from the violence and misconduct of America itself." For Dartmouth, the "absurdity of the idea" that Britain intended to enslave the Americans was obvious, so, without further effort to dispel the colonists' fears, he advised that they "prudently acquiesce" in Parliament's laws. By doing so they would "perhaps obtain all they wish, and receive that indulgence and compliance with their desires which they never can extort by sullen opposition or undutiful resistance."[8]

The hopelessness of the proposal was manifest from the start. Soon after Dartmouth's letter to Cushing was privately circulated, the *Boston Gazette* printed an almost point-by-point refutation of the secretary's suggestions. And when Reed received a similar "confession of faith" from Dartmouth, he commented to a friend that it was "bad enough, God knows."[9] American fears of British designs could not be dispelled by offhanded assertions of their absurdity; and so long as their suspicions remained, submission was impossible. As Reed put it, capitulation to the claims of Parliament seemed "virtually and necessarily" to imply "a surrender both for myself and

8. Dartmouth to Cushing, June 19, 1773, Dartmouth Papers, D 1778/2/641; Dartmouth to Reed, July 11, 1774, in Reed, *Joseph Reed*, I, 72–4.

9. "A" to printers, *Boston Gaz.*, September 13 and 20, 1773. Hillsborough and Dartmouth both agreed on parliamentary supremacy, he pointed out, and differed only in their methods of establishing it: "when one fails of carrying the darling point by the terror of *fleets and armies*, another hopes to succeed in a more *gentle* way. A people may be coaxed or flattered into concessions, when they cannot be made to comply by force." Reed's comment in Reed, *Joseph Reed*, I, 74.

my children of the blessings of liberty." In short, though
both Dartmouth and the Americans hoped for a settlement,
it was unthinkable for Dartmouth that Parliament retreat,
while it was equally impossible for the Americans to back
down. The colonists viewed their opposition as more justified by English tradition than were Parliament's innovations.
There could no more be a "divine right of doing wrong" in
Parliament than in the King, Reed wrote, "and all the principles of the [Glorious] Revolution show that there are certain cases wherein resistance is justifiable to him." The
American proceedings that Reed reported to Dartmouth on
into 1775—the tea opposition, the gathering of support for
Boston after the Port Bill, the Continental Congress—were,
then, legitimate and honorable for Reed. For Dartmouth,
however, the narrative was no doubt as damaging as the
biased official information Reed sought to circumvent, for
it continued to document American resistance, which for
the colonial secretary was always unjustified, and the cause
of the whole unfortunate altercation.[10]

There remained a way out of the dilemma: Parliament
on its own might repeal its objectionable legislation and upset
the current government. There could be no hope, of course,
in the Parliament of 1768, which had repeatedly shown its
"subserviency" to the ministry; but the Septennial Act meant
that a new general election was necessary by 1775. In early
1773, John Wilkes saw the one remaining hope for British
freedom in "the Wisdom and Virtue of a future independent
Parliament" that would bring a "Vigour and Success to the
honest Efforts of all real Patriots for the Restoration of the
Constitution." Arthur Lee found English elections so corrupt
that he doubted whether an "independent, impeaching House
of Commons" could be procured; yet the prospect of a new
election played a central role in the patriots' strategy. In May

10. Reed to Dartmouth, July 25 and September 25, 1774, in *ibid.*, I,
72, 77. For Dartmouth's attitude toward the Tea Party, see his letter
to John Thornton, February 12, 1774, Dartmouth Papers, D 1778/2/
827 (the "late outrageous madness of the people of Boston" must be
abandoned and Americans must "return to a sense of the Duty . . .
all Subjects owe to the supreme Authority of The State" before
redress could come).

and again July 1774, William Lee recommended an immediate colonial nonimportation and nonexportation agreement, largely for its effect on the British electorate, while
in Virginia Richard Henry Lee saw the approaching election
as an effective restraint on the "Tory Ministers." "The wise
and good in Britain," he wrote, "are too well convinced of
the unmerited abuse we have received for 10 or 12 years
past not to produce consequences from a dispute with America,
fatal to the views of the Ministry at a general election." Even
the Continental Congress expressed warm confidence that
the British people would declare their sentiments for America
in the approaching election, for it still seemed inconceivable
in 1774 "that *they* the defenders of true religion, and the
asserters of the rights of mankind," would "take part against
their affectionate protestant brethren in the colonies, in favour
of *our open* and *their own* secret enemies."[11]

The timing and conduct of the election, however, was
under the government's control. "The thing I dread most,"
the Boston radical Thomas Young wrote in August 1774,
"is the sudden dissolution of the present Parliament and the
rechoice before the People are thoroughly possessed of the
whole information they need in these matters." His fears were
well placed, for on September 13 the King precipitously dissolved Parliament and issued writs for a new election. When
the news reached Arthur Lee—who so little expected the dissolution as to leave for a winter vacation in Italy—he rushed
back to London through snow and ice for the new crisis in
the empire's affairs.[12]

The Bill of Rights Society at least seemed ready. Two weeks

---

11. John Wilkes to Sir Fletcher Norton, speaker of the House of
Commons, in *Boston Gaz.*, June 14, 1773; Arthur Lee to Richard
Henry Lee, June 11, 1771, Lee Family Papers, UVa, available in
Paul P. Hoffman, ed., "Lee Family Papers, 1742–1795," University of
Virginia microfilm (Charlottesville, 1966), Roll II; William Lee to
Samuel Adams, May 14 and July 25, 1774, Samuel Adams Papers,
NYPL; Richard Henry Lee to Samuel Adams, April 24, 1774,
Chantilly, Virginia, in James C. Ballagh, ed., *The Letters of Richard
Henry Lee* (New York, 1911), I, 107. Congress's memorial to the
inhabitants of the British colonies, in *N.Y. Jour.*, November 3, 1774.

12. Young to Samuel Adams, Boston, August 21, 1774, in Samuel
Adams Papers; Lee's "Memoir," in Lee, *Arthur Lee*, I, 262–3.

earlier, it had recommended to British electors that all parliamentary candidates be required to endorse a series of reforms. The list included the redressing of Irish and American
grievances, and the impeachment of ministers responsible
for violating the rights of the Middlesex electors and for the
"military murders" at St. George's Fields. More fundamental
were demands for annual Parliaments and the exclusion of
all pensioners from the Commons, which together would have
undercut government control of the legislature. Middlesex
County led the way. On September 26, candidates John
Wilkes and John Glynn formally agreed to support the whole
slate of reforms. And it was hoped, the *New York Journal*
reported, "that the electors in every county, city, and town
in Great Britain, will insist upon the like engagements from
those they choose." Buoyed by such news, the radical press
at first retained some hopefulnes: it was the opinion of "the
most intelligent and best informed that the Ministry cannot
keep together much longer in its present Form," that "the
Cabinet has not been so completely embarrassed for these
twenty Years as at present," the *Providence Gazette* reported.
Wagering odds were 3 to 2 that the American acts would be
repealed by New Year's Day.[13]

Hope ended abruptly, however, once the new Parliament
convened. The King opened it in December 1774 with a
speech John Wilkes supposedly called a "BLOODY good one,"
an intended "American Death warrant." The monarch condemned the new nonimportation movement of the American
Congress; he spoke of a "most daring spirit of resistance and
disobedience to the law" in Massachusetts, and declared his
"firm and steadfast resolution to withstand every attempt to
weaken or impair the supreme authority of the Legislature

13. London news, August 27, in *Mass. Spy*, November 3, 1774;
N.Y. Jour., December 1, 1774; *Prov. Gaz.*, January 28, 1775. On
American interest in the election, see also Joseph Warren to Josiah
Quincy, Jr., Boston, November 21, 1774, in Richard Frothingham,
Life and Times of Joseph Warren (Boston, 1865), 395, and Josiah
Quincy Sr., to Josiah Quincy, Jr., Braintree, January 3, 1775, in
Josiah Quincy, *Memoir of the Life of Josiah Quincy, Junior . . .
1744–1775*, ed. Eliza S. Quincy (3rd edn., Boston, 1875), 184. Ian
Christie, "Wilkites and Election of 1774," *Guildhall Miscellany*, II,
No. 4 (London, October 1962), 155–64.

over all the dominions of the Crown." Both Lords and Commons merely repeated the King's words in their own addresses of thanks. Moreover, when Lord John Cavendish submitted an amendment to the address, asking that the Commons be given the government's American papers before it so fully endorse the King's indictment of the colonies, it was overwhelmingly defeated, 264 to 73. "Thus it appears that the continued and anxious Suspence of the Colonies is at an End," the *Providence Gazette* commented. Hopes of relief from the "Wisdom and Justice of this new Parliament" evaporated when the legislation decided to proceed "without the necessary Means of Information, in a Matter of such infinite Importance as the Preservation of America."[14] Not that information would have changed Parliament's opinion: after examining the American papers in February, the Parliament acceded to Lord North's suggestion and declared that a rebellion existed within Massachusetts and was encouraged by illegal combinations in several other colonies. Both houses, then asked the King to "take the most effectual measures to enforce *due* obedience to the laws and authority of the Supreme Legislature," assuring him that they would support him in that effort "at the hazard of their lives and properties." As one paper bitterly commented, Parliament acted "like a parcel of spanniels," whom the minister could make "jump backwards and forwards . . . over a stick, just as he pleases."[15]

Meanwhile, American attitudes toward the King also took a new turn. In 1772 it was widely assumed that the King acted largely under the influence of his advisors. This was not necessarily a redeeming factor, but it did allow some hope for change. After the failure of the English and American petitions of the late 1760's and early 1770's, it was clear, as Samuel Adams put it, that the aggrieved had reached the royal ear, but due to the "baneful Influence of corrupt and infamous Ministers and Servants of the Crown," they had not touched the royal heart. This implied that the King might

14. *Boston Gaz.*, February 6, and *Supplement* February 6; *Prov. Gaz.*, February 4, 1775.

15. Joint address of the Lords and Commons, February 7, in *Boston Gaz.*, April 10, 1775; *ibid.*, April 17, 1775.

yet be moved to pity and redress; or, as another writer noted in 1772, the "omnipotent Monarch . . . in Heaven" could always "turn crafty counsels into foolishness, and reprove Kings for his Peoples sake."[16]

The King's assent to the Intolerable Acts in 1774 undermined these hopes and moved his complicity in government actions onto a new level of seriousness. His assent to the Port Bill amounted to a formal leveling of war against Massachusetts, a writer in the *Essex Gazette* argued, and "if the King violates his sacred Faith to, and Compact with any one State of his Empire, he *discharges the same from their Allegiance to him, dismembers them from the Empire and reduces them to a State of Nature.*" In short, he "CEASES TO BE THEIR KING." His assent to the Quebec Act, which the King personally endorsed, was of even broader significance. "A prince who can give the royal assent to any bill which should establish popery, slavery and arbitrary power either in England or any of its dominions," an often-reprinted article claimed, "must be guilty of perjury; for it is, in express terms, *contrary to his coronation oath,*" in which he had promised to maintain "the *protestant reformed religion established by law*" in England and all her dominions. To establish Catholicism in Canada, as it was said the Quebec Act had done, went beyond anything either Charles I or James II had attempted. With striking frequency, newspapers referred to the "King's giving his royal assent to the obnoxious Quebec bill, and thereby breaking his coronation oath," the one formal tie that bound him to his people and them to him.[17]

Not everyone, of course, followed this line of reasoning. John Dickinson insisted in October 1774 that "every thing may yet be attributed to the misrepresentations and mistakes

16. Adams as "Valerius Poplicola" in *Boston Gaz.*, October 5, 1772, and Harry A. Cushing, ed., *The Writings of Samuel Adams* (New York, 1904–8), II, 334–5; "Joel," *Boston Gaz.*, May 25, 1772.

17. "Vox Vociferantis in Eremo," from *Essex Gazette*, in *Boston Gaz.*, August 15, 1774. "A Scotsman," from London *Public Advertiser*, in *Pa. Jour.*, November 23, 1774, and *Prov. Gaz.*, November 19, 1774. London news, July 2, in *Mass. Spy*, September 8, 1774; King quoted on Quebec Act in *Boston Gaz.*, August 22, 1774. *Prov. Gaz.*, August 27, 1774, and "Scipio" to the King, *Pa. Jour.*, October 5, 1774.

of ministers," that the present cause was that of "half a dozen . . . fools or knaves," not of Great Britain. Such men championed continued appeals to the King, most notably in the petitions of the Continental Congress. To others such petitions were hopeless from the start, and the failure of those of 1774 and 1775 vindicated their stance.[18] When allegiance to the King was still declared, it was often qualified in ways that made the pledge no longer binding: we and our posterity will be faithful subjects of the Brunswick kings, the town of Mansfield, Connecticut, said in October 1774, "as long as the Crown maintains inviolate the stipulated Rights of the People." Similarly in North Carolina, Granville County emphasized in August 1774 that the relationship of King and people was contractural such that a violation of the compact "would rescind the civil Institution binding both . . . together"; and a year later, Tryon County resolved to bear allegiance to the King only "so long as he secures to us those Rights and Liberties which the principles of our Constitution require." At least one *Boston Gazette* reader was ready by July 1775 to ink out thoroughly a formalistic reference to the King in an edict of his Provincial Congress.[19]

By 1775, moreover, writers frequently asserted what was only rarely claimed three years earlier: that the King was himself the center of the design for despotism. The trend was clear in 1774 when writers repeatedly noted that "a plan of despotism and arbitrary power, has incessantly been pursued during the present reign, thro' all the ministerial changes and manoeuvres," that "every Session of Parliament, and every Council Board at Whitehall since the year 1762, have produced some new exertions of arbitrary power against America." If this peculiar pattern could "explain all those intricate movements of government, which otherwise appear quite mysterious and unaccountable," did it not implicitly do so by indicting the one constant element in government, the one

18. Dickinson to Josiah Quincy, Jr., Fairhill, October 28, 1774, in Quincy, *Memoir*, 169. Pessimism on petitions: Chap. 7, *ns.* 38, 39.

19. Mansfield meeting in *New London Gaz.*, November 11, 1774; *N.C. Col. Recs.*, IX, 1034, and X, 163; *Boston Gaz.*, July 3, 1775, in Edward Green's collection, HUL.

man who remained through all other changes in personnel—George III?[20]

The conclusion was encouraged by some Letters from London. The King strongly supported the acts of 1774 to punish Massachusetts Bay and alter its government, wrote William Lee. "Lord North, Dartmouth, and some say, Lord Mansfield, have been against these measures; but the K[ing] with his usual obstinacy and tyr[annica]l disposition, is determined . . . to inslave you all." William's brother Arthur had leveled similar accusations since the King's rejection of the original London remonstrances, but his statements generally remained confined to private letters. Now public newspapers, particularly those in the North, concurred and elaborated the details of royal control. The King had made Lord North's proposal of hasty elections in 1774 so fully his own, it was charged, that it became "a piece of Hanoverian treachery, baseness and ingratitude, which . . . far exceeded all the artful villainy, and low cunning of the discarded Stuarts." Taking the country by surprise meant "that no opposition might be made to his creatures." There were 285 Members of the new Parliament "paid with the people's money to vote whatever Lord North proposes," another account from London claimed. And this venality lay under direct royal control. Eight agents who controlled the court party in Parliament received royal instructions in a tavern near the royal palace. The King was "his own secretary"; he arose every morning at 6 A.M. and "sends off his box with remarks on a bit of paper tied round each order." "The K[ing] overlooks their schemes and corrects them," the account said, "as well as gives orders how to proceed in the future." The infamous "Fish Bill" of Febraury 1775, which barred New Englanders from the North Atlantic fisheries and forbad them to trade

20. Extracts of letters from London in *Boston Gaz.*, May 23, 1774; "Sidney," *Pa. Jour.*, August 31, 1774. Also [John Dickinson] Letter II to the Inhabitants of the British Colonies in America, Philadelphia, in *Boston Gaz.*, June 27, 1774, and Paul L. Ford, ed., *The Writings of John Dickinson*: I, *Political Writings, 1764–1774*, in *Memoirs of the Historical Society of Pennsylvania*, XIV (Philadelphia, 1895), 473–4; Thomas Jefferson, *A Summary View* . . . (orig. pub., 1774), in Julian Boyd, ed., *The Papers of Thomas Jefferson*: I, *1760–1776* (Princeton, 1950), 125.

with anyone but Britain and the British West Indies, was thus attributed to "our *pious* Sovereign . . . from the best accounts . . . the grand promotor of these proceedings." The royal proclamation of August 23, 1775, which promised decisive military action against a rebellion "manifestly carried on for the purpose of establishing an independent empire," thus only augmented a disjunction of colonists from the Crown that was already well advanced. The King's words increased support for those who had attributed the outbreak of war in April 1775 to the Crown's offensive, and who interpreted that act as a crime that "totally dissolved our allegiance to the King of England as our King."[21]

[II]

These successive re-evaluations of the British government were of intense and basic significance to colonial leaders. They underlay decisions on what tactics to follow—as was clear, for example, in 1770 when Richard Henry Lee promised that the Virginia Assembly would pass "such Measures . . . as our intelligence from London shall render necessary," and in November 1774 when Joseph Warren noted that Massachusetts would avoid direct action and "bear the Inconvenience of living without government until we have some farther intelligence of what may be expected from England."[22] Hence the importance of accurate accounts from England not only of events, but evaluating the government,

21. William Lee to Richard Henry Lee, London, March 17, 1774, in Worthington C. Ford, ed., *Letters of William Lee* (Brooklyn, 1891), I, 83; "The Crisis II," *Mass. Spy*, May 24, 1775; extract of letter from London, February 24, *New London Gaz.*, April 28, 1775, and *Prov. Gaz.*, May 20, 1775. Extract of London letter, March 2, *N.Y. Jour.*, April 20, 1775; "Common Sense," *New London Gaz.*, April 12, 1776, and "Johannes in Eremo" [the Rev. John Cleaveland] to Gage, *Boston Gaz.*, July 17, 1775, and "Amicus Constitutionis," *New London Gaz.*, October 27, 1775. On King's speeches, Merrill Jensen, *The Founding of A Nation* (New York, 1968), 647, 649.

22. Richard Henry Lee to Arthur Lee, Chantilly, Virginia, April 5, 1770, UVa and "Lee Family Papers," Roll II; Warren to Josiah Quincy, Jr., Boston, November 21, 1774, in Frothingham, *Joseph Warren*, 395.

the public's feelings, the effect of American efforts, and prospects for the future. Such news could come from trusted friends in London: the colonial agents, William or Arthur Lee, Stephen Sayre, Benjamin Franklin. But as such correspondents increasingly feared interference with the mails, a free exchange of news and ideas could best be carried on in person.

For years, Americans in England on commercial or pleasure trips had taken time to meet and consult with resident Americans and American sympathizers; but by late 1774 and 1775, colonial delegates were sent to England in a systematic and politically purposeful way. Josiah Quincy, Jr.'s, closely planned trip to the South in 1773 fitted him well for such a mission. Equipped with an intimate knowledge of American sentiments gathered during his intercolonial travels and with plans for a personal correspondence extending from New England through the Southern colonies, Quincy sailed for London in September 1774. "Perhaps there never was an American," his father wrote him two months later, " . . . whose Abilities have raised the Expectations of their American Brethren more than yours." Carefully, Quincy measured the feelings of the British people; he consulted Lords Dartmouth and North; he discussed endlessly America's position with the Lees, Franklin, Joseph Priestly, Richard Price, Brand Hollis, and others who backed her cause.[23] On the basis of letters received from Quincy and Franklin in March 1775, Samuel Adams, Joseph Warren, and Benjamin Church urged increased defense preparations at the Massachusetts Provincial Congress, and the letters Quincy carried home with him that month were read openly in the Connecticut General Assembly, and their message carefully carried from there to Providence by two Rhode Island observers.[24]

23. Quincy to his wife, London, November 17, 1774, and January 11, 1775, in Quincy, *Memoir*, 197, 251. Quincy to his father, November 26, 1774, Josiah Quincy, Jr., Papers, f. 80, MHS. Also "Journal of Josiah Quincy, Jun., During His Voyage and Residence in England from September 28th, 1774, to March 3d, 1775," MHS *Procs.*, L (1916–17), 433–71.

24. "Intelligence" enclosed in Gage to Dartmouth, Boston, March 28, 1775, PRO, CO 5/92, ff. 126–7; unsigned letter to Capt. Wallace, Providence, May 4, 1775, PRO, CO 5/121, ff. 184–6.

Quincy was followed by other colonists: William Palfrey, who sailed December 1, 1774, made a brief visit to Charleston, and finally arrived in England in February; and Francis Dana, who sailed in April 1775 with more recent accounts of the Continental Congress than either Quincy or Palfrey had carried. From his radical activities as well as his mercantile business, Palfrey, like Quincy, had an impressive network of important correspondents throughout the colonies —with Benjamin Harrison and William Holt in Virginia, for example, Charles Thomson and Thomas Mifflin in Philadelphia, and Silas Downer in Providence.[25]

Interest in Britain differed, however, from what it had been at the height of the Wilkes movement. In no way were the colonists depending upon a catharsis in England, and the need for self-reliance tempered all their hopes of change there. Even while arguing in September 1773 that Lord Dartmouth could unite England and America "upon a fair, candid, and equitable footing," Thomas Cushing declared that he was "fully of opinion that it is to ourselves we ought to trust, and not to the persons who may be in power on [the other] side the water." John Holt's *New York Journal* said the same thing in February 1775 as reports came to America that Lord North's power was crumbling, and the friends of America increasing. Notwithstanding all these signs, the paper said, "not the least Relaxation on our Part should be admitted. The Preservation of our Rights and Liberties still depends on [our] Firmness, Union, Prudence, and Perseverance."[26]

By late 1774, American firmness clearly implied a readiness to use arms. Isolated pleas for military readiness appeared from the early 1770's; but the summonses took on a new immediacy, particularly in Massachusetts, after the tea parties and the Intolerable Acts. "We have hitherto employed

25. Frothingham, *Joseph Warren*, 448; Dr. Samuel Cooper to Benjamin Franklin, August 15, 1774 [April 1775?], BM King's Mss., 204; John G. Palfrey, "Life of William Palfrey," in Jared Sparks ed., *Library of American Biography*, 2nd Ser., VII (Boston, 1848), 342, 372–7, and Palfrey's correspondence in the Palfrey Family Papers, HUL.

26. Cushing to Arthur Lee, Boston, September 20, 1773, in Lee, *Arthur Lee*, II, 238; *N.Y. Jour.*, February 9, 1775.

lenient measures *more* than enough," "A PATAGONIAN" claimed
in the *Boston Gazette* for February 21, 1774; and by July,
John Adams was of the same mind. "What avails Prudence,
Wisdom, Policy, Fortitude, Integrity without Power, without
Legions?" he asked his friend James Warren.[27] After early
September, when a rumor that the British were cannonading
Boston caused a general mobilization in Massachusetts and
Connecticut,[28] more regularized procedures were established
for summoning military aid to Boston. Once the Continental
Congress recommended military training on September 28,
preparations throughout the colonies went forward systematically. Moreover, after the British placed an embargo on the
exportation of military stores to America, confrontations between royal officials and colonists over the control of domestic
ammunition supplies increased. In New Hampshire, for
example, a band of several hundred provincials seized Fort
William and Mary and carried away its cannons and gunpowder.[29] By December, Elbridge Gerry thought a civil war
was "almost unavoidable."[30]

The resort to force in 1774 and 1775 was more clearly
revolutionary than it had been at the time of the first tea
parties. In 1773, as during the resistances of 1765–6 and
1768–70, force was used to oppose a limited exertion of

27. "When Demosthenes . . . went Ambassador from Athens to the
other States of Greece to excite a Confederacy against Phillip," Adams
added, "he did not go to propose a Non-importation or Non-consump-
tion Agreement!" Adams to Warren, Braintree, July 17, 1774, in *The
Warren–Adams Letters*, I (Boston, 1917), 26.

28. Richard D. Brown, *Revolutionary Politics in Massachusetts;
The Boston Committee of Correspondence and the Towns, 1772–1774*
(Cambridge, 1970), 226–8; Richard Henry Lee to William Lee,
Philadelphia, September 20, 1774, in Ballagh, *Letters of Richard
Henry Lee*, I, 124. There is an excellent account in Franklin B. Dexter,
ed., *The Literary Diary of Ezra Stiles* (New York, 1901), I, especially
477–85.

29. The New Hampshire seizure occurred after Paul Revere brought
news of the arms embargo from Boston. See Gov. John Wentworth to
Gage, Portsmouth, December 14 and 16, 1774; Capt. Cochran, Commander of Castle William and Mary, to Wentworth, December 14,
1774, PRO, CO 5/92, ff. 48–52, and Wentworth to Dartmouth, December 20, 1774, PRO, CO 5/939.

30. Gerry to Samuel Adams, Boston, October 15, 1774, Samuel
Adams Papers.

British authority. By 1775, the validity of that authority as a whole was contested. Colonial writers denied vehemently that their war was a rebellion, for a rebellion opposed authority "founded . . . in the *constitution and laws of the government.*" By violating the constitution and the laws, the current rulers had forfeited their authority, so the Americans were only "taking up arms . . . against usurpation and tyranny," "against armed robbers, murders and usurpers."[31]

The contract between America and Britain might of course be renegotiated, with colonial rights more firmly established in an American Bill of Rights. It was clearly necessary, Elbridge Gerry noted, that some "constitutional check on the government at home be invented" to which Americans could recur whenever aggrieved in the future, and the terms of such a document were discussed by Samuel Adams and Arthur Lee in 1774. Even the young James Madison, who would one day compose such a document for the United States alone, was intrigued in 1774 by the possibility that a "Bill of Rights" might be adopted by Congress and confirmed by the King or Parliament, such that America's liberties would be "as firmly fixed, and defined as those of England were at the revolution."[32]

Yet without an overturning of the current British government, all of the peace plans actually offered in 1775 were, for the radical leaders, inadequate. Given the despotic intentions of the government, official peace initiatives were *prima facie* suspicious. "We know it has been the constant Practice of the King and his Junto ever since this Struggle began to endeavor to make us believe their Designs were pacifick, while they have been mediating the most destructive plans," Samuel Adams later wrote. Lord North's conciliatory proposal of 1775 was deemed by Congress "an insidious Manoeuvre calculated to divide us," and even Lord Chatham's

31. "A Church of England Man," *N.Y. Jour.*, November 10, 1774; "Johannes in Eremo" to Gage, *Boston Gaz.*, July 17, 1775.

32. Gerry to Samuel Adams, Marblehead, June 21, 1773, Elbridge Gerry Papers, Library of Congress, Washington, D.C.; Arthur Lee to Thomas Cushing, London, December 6, 1774, PRO, CO 5/118, ff. 92, 93; Madison to William Bradford, August 1, 1774, in William T. Hutchinson and William M. Rachel, eds., *The Papers of James Madison*, I (Chicago, 1962), 118.

scheme, which came nearest to satisfying the Americans' constitutional requirements, was considered dangerous while current officeholders kept their places. The House of Lords' ready rejection of the scheme as "too favourable to the Americans" was a blessing, "A.B" told *New York Journal* readers, since the otherwise seductive proposal left Parliament supreme judge of its powers under the agreement, and, given the character of Parliament, such an arrangement offered "very little security."[33]

The colonists were, however, not yet consciously molding an *American* war or an *American* revolution. They sought rather a British revolution, one that would reconstitute the British government with new rulers and a firmer establishment of basic rights and thereby save not only America, but Britain, too. The two causes seemed as closely interwoven in 1774 and 1775 as they had been at the height of the Wilkes agitation: "the Liberties of Great-Britain are so involved in those of America," a writer in the *Pennsylvania Journal* claimed, "that the instant the latter is enslaved, that instant absolute despotism is established in the former." And for Rhode Island's Samuel Ward, nothing was more evident "than . . . that the Liberty of America is the Life of Britain, and if Slavery takes place in this Country, Britain will fall a sacrifice to her own tyranny."[34]

The initiative for halting the "torrent of despotism" that threatened all British subjects equally had, however, left Wilkes's London for the New World, and the transfer, recognized by some colonists in 1770, was now commonly acknowledged abroad. "Our principal hopes of any effectual opposition is upon your part of the world, where corruption has not yet made so great a progress," a Dublin correspondent wrote to Philadelphia in March 1773. A year later, Arthur

33. Samuel Adams letter, April 16, 1776, *Warren–Adams Letters*, I, 224; Congress's "Declaration on Taking Up Arms," July 6, 1775, in Boyd, *Jefferson Papers*, I, 216; *N.Y. Jour.*, April 13, 1775. See also Joseph Warren to Arthur Lee, Cambridge, April 27, 1775 ("the colonies will sooner suffer depopulation than come into any measures with [the present ministry]"), and May 16, 1775, in Lee, *Arthur Lee*, II, 267, 270.

34. "Anglus Americanus," *Pa. Jour.*, June 29, 1774; Ward to Ezra Stiles, Boston, January 2, 1773, Ezra Stiles Papers, Beinecke Library, Yale University, New Haven, Connecticut.

Lee reported that the Friends of Liberty in England, too, were watching the Americans with anxiety, and considered their actions as decisive "either to establish or overturn the present plan of despotism." In short, as Britain declined "in virtue, liberty and political wisdom . . . the virtue and liberty of America" became "her brightest hope; if this fails, ruin stares her in the face." Soon it was said that not only Britain's future, but her current freedom was due only to the Americans: "All things . . . being ripe in England for the open introduction of arbitrary power," one widely reprinted article claimed, "nothing seems to have prevented it, but the struggles of the Americans to preserve their liberties"— hence the government's desperate determination to crush the colonists' opposition.[35] The responsibility was great, but so was the opportunity; for, as Samuel Purviance of Baltimore expressed it, the Americans could hope that their "Virtuous Struggles" would "embolden our Friends in England and Ireland to stand forth more boldly than hitherto, and convince a Despotic Administration of their Folly," and thus "secure the Liberties of the whole Brittish Empire."[36]

The colonists nonetheless continued to hope on into 1775 that America would not have to stand alone against the British government. Through most of 1774, prospects for English support seemed poor. "Universal Bribery and Corruption has Annihilated the little share of Liberty and Patriotism which Walpole left behind," an English correspondent wrote William Palfrey in March, "and I'm really at a Loss to judge which is the most venal and corrupt, the Minister or the House of Commons, the People or their Representatives." As the ministry sponsored the Intolerable Acts and thus unveiled

35. Irish letter in *N.Y. Jour.*, May 27, 1773; also Charles Lucas to Boston, in *Boston Gaz.*, March 18, 1771. Arthur Lee to Francis L. Lee, April 2, 1774, in Lee, *Arthur Lee*, I, 39–40. Statement from Boston *Evening Post* in *N.Y. Jour.*, April 17, 1774; extracts of London letters dated April 7 and 8, in *Prov. Gaz.*, May 23, *New London Gaz.*, May 20, and *Boston Gaz.*, May 23, 1774. In New York the letters were circulated in a separate handbill: see enclosure in Haldimand to Dartmouth, New York, May 15, 1774, PRO, CO 5/91, f. 47. London letter, October 9, 1773, in *N.Y. Jour.*, January 13, 1774, and Catharine Macaulay to Arthur Lee, [1773,] UVa and "Lee Family Papers," Roll II.

36. Samuel Purviance, Jr., to Samuel Adams, Baltimore, September 26, 1775, Samuel Adams Papers.

their designs "with a grossness, that one would think nothing but ignorance made drunk could overlook or mistake," the British population sat by supinely, and its silence seemed to indicate consent. "The People of this country are sunk in luxury," one correspondent concluded, "and wish only to get their hands into the purses of Americans to support them in it."[37]

But there were also reports in the fall of 1774 "that the people in England are rubbing up their eyes, and begin to awake." The government's haste "to secure every avenue to the Citadel of Despotism," Thomas Young explained, led the entire nation to take alarm. Thousands gathered at Parliament House when the King went there to give his assent to the Quebec Act, and the crowd "not only hissed, but it is said, pelted him from the House of Lords to the Palace, crying out *no Roman-catholic King: no Roman catholic religion! America forever!*" Marblehead's Elbridge Gerry congratulated the Boston Committee of Correspondence on "the Dawn of *Reason* appearing in the East," bringing hope that "we shall see . . . every corrupted Prostitute now in Government as effectually stigmatized by the People, as was wicked Cain under the peculiar Displeasure of his Maker." The City of London began to move again, too, and petitioned against the act, while in Falmouth—where a few days earlier America was so unpopular that a colonial captain had found the town disagreeable —news of the Quebec Act "so incensed the People that they declared for America, and imprecated every Anathema upon it, if it should submit to the late Acts of Parliament." Even the "highest Tories," it was said, suddenly began declaring "they will take up Arms if Attempts are made to enforce the Acts."[38]

News of the Americans' firmness also seemed to stimulate the shift in British opinion. Earlier, Joseph Warren said in November 1774, the ministry had "by bribes and falsehoods

37. George Peacock to Palfrey, London, March 4, 1774, Palfrey Papers, Part II, a, 151. Letter from Bristol [Henry Cruger?], July 20, in *Pa. Jour.*, October 5; *Mass. Spy*, October 20; *N.Y. Jour.*, October 20, 1774. Unsigned letter, *Pa. Jour.*, September 28, 1774.

38. Thomas Young to Samuel Adams, Boston, August 21, 1774, Samuel Adams Papers; Elbridge Gerry to Boston Committee of Correspondence, August 20, 1774, in *Boston Gaz.*, August 22, 1774.

deceived the nation" about America. Now, the eyes of the people were opening to "the coolness, temper, and firmness" of the Americans, to the unanimity of all the colonies in defense of their rights, and to their universal indignation at the injustices offered to Boston. "The tone of public conversation, which has been so violently against us, begins evidently to turn."[39] How important, then, were America's emissaries in England who carried the freshest and most accurate news of American developments, representatives who could themselves diffuse the spirit of the Americans. "I have lighted up the countenances of many," Josiah Quincy, Jr., wrote his wife on November 24, 1774; "I am speaking conviction every day to more. In short, I am infected with an enthusiasm which I know to be contagious."[40]

If the English people were to act upon their new convictions, however, it seemed by 1775 that they must do so by an insurrection. This had not been true the preceding fall when the Continental Congress addressed the British people, warning them that the government sought control over American lives and property so that it could "with the greater facility enslave you." The English people could then, it seemed, avert this fate through constitutional channels: "we hope," the address said, "that the magnanimity and justice of the British Nation will furnish a Parliament of such wisdom, independence and public spirit, as may save the violated rights of the whole empire."[41] This hope was dashed by the surprise election of 1774. The government's roughshod tactics made it clear, as Virginia's Richard Henry Lee put it, that only direct popular action could arrest its power, that the future would depend "on the firmness of [the colonists']

39. Joseph Warren to Middletown, Connecticut, Committee, from Boston, November 17, 1774, Frothingham, *Joseph Warren*, 391–2; also *N.Y. Jour.*, September 8, 1774, and London letter, January 2, in *Pa. Jour.*, *Postscript* March 9, 1775.

40. Quincy, *Memoir*, 210.

41. *Journals of the Continental Congress* (Washington, 1904–6): I, *1774*, 82, 90. Compare this with the "Address to the Inhabitants of Great Britain" adopted in July, 1775, in *ibid.*, II, 163–70, which mentions no legal channel to change. Action is nonetheless urged: "too late you may lament the loss of that freedom, which we exhort you, while still in your Power, to preserve."

own virtue, or on the general exertion of the people of England." The sudden election, Samuel Adams believed, could even indicate that Lord North was in serious trouble. "Had [the ministers] suffered the election to be put off till the spring," he suggested, "it might have cost some of them their heads."[42]

Gauging the chances for an English uprising became a primary concern of American representatives in England. Josiah Quincy, Jr., for example, was preoccupied with it from the first two weeks of his visit, which he spent, he told his wife, talking with all ranks of the people. He quickly confirmed reports that the people were rousing, and by November felt that any fair poll would find 20 to 1 in favor of the Americans. But the people did not act because their leaders were divided and because they were " 'cowed' by oppression. It is amazing," he reported, "it is incredible how much this is the case. Corruption, baseness, fraud, exorbitant oppression, never so abounded as in this island. . . . Englishmen—that boasted race of freedom—are sunk—are sunk in abject submission." For the most part, then, his conclusions were pessimistic; Americans should expect no aid from the British people, he advised in November, but depend upon themselves. He never absolutely ruled out the possibility of English support: "If the actions of this country are as correspondent with the sense, words, and declarations of its inhabitants as the words and doings of my American countrymen," he said, "I am sure this country will be convulsed." But the initial "If" indicated a continuing doubt, for Quincy grew "confirmed more and more every day" in his suspicion "that the commonality in this country are no more like the commonality in America than if they were two utterly distinct and unconnected people."[43]

Where Quincy doubted that the English people would act, others were unqualified in their promises of an English

42. Richard Henry Lee to Arthur Lee, [February 24, 1775,] Ballagh, *Letters of Richard Henry Lee*, I, 130; Richard Henry Lee to Samuel Adams, Virginia, February 4, 1775, Samuel Adams Papers; Samuel Adams to Arthur Lee, Cambridge, February 14, 1775, Lee, *Arthur Lee*, II, 223.

43. Quincy, as "Henry Ireton," to his wife, through whom he wrote to other Boston leaders, London, November 17 and 24, 1774, and January 12, 1775, in Quincy, *Memoir*, 195–7, 205–12, 258–9.

insurrection. "Hope nothing from the people here," a London letter of September 1774 advised, "—but if you persevere— we shall soon join you by the thousands." Later promises were even more explicit. "The Sword being once drawn against you," a London letter of December claimed, "will produce something very like a civil War in this Country in less than 12 months," while another message two months later offered a promise of even quicker relief. "If you hold out a few months, England will rise and do you justice, as well as relieve themselves [sic] from those accursed tyrants, who want to corrupt you and deprive you of both liberty and property." With the arrival of this advice came also the testimony of a Captain Callahan, who arrived at Marblehead from England in late April 1775, and related "that every Thing at London wears a strong Appearance of a speedy Rising against the present Administration."[44] One inhibition on English action, Quincy reported, was a pervasive doubt that the Americans were "*really in earnest.*" This was one factor leading him to conclude by December 1774 that his "*countrymen must seal their cause with their blood.*" "When you have shown that you are what Englishmen once were, whether successful or not, your foes will diminish, your friends amazingly increase," he promised—although, again, he was unclear whether or not an American war would spur an English one. For the colonists who read the letters he carried home with him in March 1775, however, there was no ambiguity. As the Rhode Islanders understood it, those letters said "that we must without delay prepare to fight it out, which will certainly effect a Revolution in England."[45]

If the objective was to inflame England, some still thought that measures of economic coercion—nonimportation, non-exportation, a refusal to pay British debts—might be more effective than American bloodshed. England remained lethargic because the English did not yet *feel* the privation of op-

44. *N.Y. Jour.*, October 27, 1774 (London letter, September 3, 1774), and February 9, 1775 (London letter, December 6). Extract of letters via New York in *New London Gaz.*, April 28 (also Callahan's report) and *Prov. Gaz.*, May 20, 1775.

45. Quincy to his wife, December 7 and 14, 1775, in Quincy, *Memoir*, 216–20, 224–7; letter to Capt. Wallace, Providence, May 4, 1775, reporting Rhode Island reception of Quincy's intelligence, PRO, CO 5/121, ff. 184–6.

pression, writers stressed. They basked in luxury, riches, and dissipation, with the Americans "ministering to their Pleasure by . . . plentiful Remittances." One writer in the *South Carolina Gazette* calculated that a strict nonimportation could reduce three million Englishmen who depended upon the export trade "to a starving Condition." "Thus, Hanibal-like," he suggested, "we can plant the war in our Oppressor's Country." "Stop all trade—be silent, be strong, be resolute," a letter from London recommended, "hold out only six months, and all will be well. England will rise on the occasion." So late as May 1, 1775, a royalist in Charleston reported that local leaders had been persuaded by information "from their friends in England that the Ministry dared not enforce the Acts of the Legislature, and that if they could only contrive to hang together a few months longer every extravagant demand their Congress had made would be complied with."[46] Josiah Quincy, Jr., in fact, gradually moved toward this view. In November 1774, he told his countrymen not to depend on commercial plans alone, and thereafter he announced bloodshed would be necessary for victory. But by January 1775 he, too, saw hope in economic measures. "If my countrymen, after deliberating, are convinced that they can keep the pure faith of economy . . . ," he wrote, "I will venture to assure them that they shall obtain a bloodless victory." Benjamin Franklin converted Quincy fully to this tactic in early March 1775. The manufacturers were already complaining about the loss of American trade, he said, and if nonimportation were adhered to for a year from the following September or to the next session of Parliament, "the day is won."[47]

46. London letter in *N.Y. Jour.*, Febraury 9, 1775; "Non Quis Sed Quid," Charleston, in *S.C. Gaz.*, July 4, 1774. The South Carolina writer was not yet talking of mobs overturning the British government, however, but hoped "that the Cry of Famine re-echoed from the thousands, rising in Mobs, will oblige the Parliament to adopt other Measures." London letter in *Prov. Gaz.*, June 11, 1774. Alexander Innes [to Dartmouth?], Charleston, May 1, 1775, PRO, CO 5/396, f. 137.

47. Quincy to his wife, November 24, 1774, and January 11, 1775, in Quincy, *Memoir*, 210, 252; Quincy, "Journal . . . 1774–1775," especially 468–9.

William Lee was also a fervent advocate of economic coercion. A twelve-months abstention from commerce, he advised his American correspondents, could force British merchants and manufacturers to "feel that your cause is their own and . . . consequently to fight your battles." If the Americans persevered, confirming and enlarging the Congress's plan, they could depend upon it, he wrote Richard Henry Lee in January 1775, "12 months must produce a Revolution here." But for him, economic coercion in no way precluded military action: in fact, he recommended that the colonists be prepared to resist force by force even as he urged the certain efficacy of commercial sanctions. Richard Henry Lee apparently shared this stance. He remained confident that economic sanctions would succeed, John Adams later claimed, as late as the dissolution of the first Continental Congress; yet in March 1775, he seconded Patrick Henry's proposal in the Virginia Provincial Congress that the colony be put in a state of defense.[48]

By March 1775, William Lee, along with his brother Arthur, Price, Priestly, and other American supporters in England—with the exception of Franklin—had decided that the issue would not be settled without fighting, and the sooner hostilities began the better. They questioned only whether New Englanders should initiate military action before reinforcements reached Gage, or continue to act defensively, waiting until a much stronger British army attacked them. It would be better if decisive action were taken with the approbation of the other colonies, William Lee wrote, but in all cases the decisive moment must not be lost.[49] There was, then, a basic

48. William Lee to Francis Lightfoot Lee, London, December 24, 1774, and to Richard Henry Lee, January 17, 1775, in Ford, *Letters of William Lee*, I, 103, 114. John Adams to William Wirt, January 23, 1818, in William Wirt Henry, *Patrick Henry, Life, Correspondence, and Speeches*, I (New York, 1891), 239–40, 259.

49. Quincy, "Journal, 1774–75," 468, where Quincy relates his telling Franklin the opinions of Price, Priestly, and the two Lees so as to suggest they were in essential agreement. The Lees' views are given in their letters of March 4 to Samuel Adams, carried to America by Quincy, in the Samuel Adams Papers. Price's agreement is apparent from William Lee's letter to Quincy, April 12, 1775, MHS *Procs.*, L, 494, where he says Price's opinion is still "that the Quarrel

cleavage within the ranks of Americans and American sympathizers in London by the spring of 1775: Quincy and Franklin remained convinced that economic coercion could win
victory without American bloodshed, while the Lees' coterie
believed that a quick resort to arms, defensive or presumptive,
was also necessary. As a result, Quincy carried no simple
message with him when he sailed for America in March.
Instead, he hoped to report the "sentiments" of America's
friends, "in what things they differed" as well as agreed, and
why, with the hope that even these divided counsels would be
of great service to his country.[50]

These intense discussions in London proved irrelevant for
the colonists. Already in 1774, Patrick Henry and John
Adams agreed that "We must *fight*, if we can't otherwise rid
ourselves of British taxation, all revenues, and the constitution
or form of government enacted for us by the British parliament." Nonconsumption and nonimportation agreements were
not a viable alternative to war. Although such plans could
"safely rest and be founded on the virtue of the majority,"
the need to enforce them on an unwilling minority implied
force and preparations to meet counterforce, "which will
directly produce war and bloodshed." Nor did it seem to
Elbridge Gerry that the administration would hesitate to "involve us in Blood rather than suffer their tyrannical plan to
be defeated by the mercantile Restrictions intended by the
Colonies." In short, even economic sanctions implied war.
The Franklin-Quincy proposal, that the colonies wait peacefully until their economic sanctions induced reactions in
England, was but another manifestation of man's natural inclination to "indulge in the illusions of hope" when there was,
Patrick Henry said in March 1775, "*no longer any room for
hope.*" The Americans' petitions and remonstrances had been
refused or answered with worse insults; the colonists had done
"everything that could be done, to avert the storm . . . now
coming on." War had become "inevitable," Henry declared,

---

can not be terminated without fighting, which the sooner it happens
the better." This was also apparently the opinion of Brand Hollis, who
by March 1775 looked forward to a new country, learning by British
mistakes, and erecting a model government for the world. See his
letter to Quincy, March 2, 1775, Josiah Quincy, Jr., Papers, f. 97.

50. Quincy, "Journal, 1774–75," 470.

"—and let it come! !"[51] A month later, when Quincy died at sea, the news of Lexington and Concord was already spreading through the continent.

[III]

After the outbreak of hostilities, the colonists waited for supporting action to develop abroad and encouraged it as best they could. In March 1775, Arthur Lee suggested that the Irish, who were still greatly attached to America, could aid the colonial cause. Lee advised the colonists either to plan nonimportation so as to favor the Irish or to send them an address explaining Congress's action, thereby directing Irish resentment toward the British. A strict adherence to the association would then produce, Lee promised, the "most intolerable distress and dangerous Insurrections" in Ireland as in England and force the British government to keep troops there that would otherwise be used against the United States. The Continental Congress complied and addressed the Irish people on July 28, 1775.[52] There were, in fact, encouraging signs of Irish sympathy. Dubliners instructed their parliamentary representatives to refuse any aid to Britain in its conquest of America, and went so far as to hold an extra-legal freeholders' meeting to consider the war. Like Dublin, the trading towns of Belfast and Cork petitioned the Crown to end the war with America. But more direct support never materialized; and in late 1775, the Irish Parliament condemned the colonists as rebels and granted the British 4000 Irish soldiers for use in America.[53]

---

51. John Adams to Hezekia Niles, Quincy, February 5, 1819, with "Broken Hints to be communicated to the Committee of Congress for the Massachusetts" (1774) in Hezekia Niles, *Principles and Acts of the Revolution in America* (New York, 1876), 107–8; Gerry to Samuel Adams, Boston, October 15, 1774, Samuel Adams Papers; reconstruction of Henry's speech of March 1775 in Henry, *Patrick Henry*, I, 262, 264.

52. Arthur Lee to Samuel Adams, London, March 4, 1775, Samuel Adams Papers; *Journals of the Continental Congress*, II, 212–18.

53. Robert B. McDowell, *Irish Public Opinion, 1750–1800* (London, 1944), 40–8; Maurice R. O'Connell, *Irish Politics and Social Conflict in the Age of the American Revolution* (Philadelphia, 1965), 23–35.

There were more promising signs of aid from England in 1775. Like Dublin, the City of London strongly supported the American cause. After petitioning against the Quebec Act alone, the Common Council protested the other Intolerable Acts, and, in February 1775, petitioned against the Fisheries Bill. The city publicly justified the Americans' resistance and declared that the government's efforts "to establish arbitrary Power over all *America*" affected Britons everywhere. After war broke out the Common Council asked George III to suspend hostilities, and continued to declare its sympathy for the Americans. Meanwhile, John Wilkes, London's lord mayor in 1775, strongly defended the colonists in Parliament.[54]

English assistance went beyond resolves and speeches. Subscriptions were opened to raise funds for the Americans. Wilkes, George Hayley, and several other "principal merchants and gentlemen" were said to have promised generous contributions in September 1774. One contributor from Gloucester offered his contribution for "the assistance of our worthy fellow subjects in America and against the corrupt traitors at home." In June 1775, colonial newspapers reported that London's Constitutional Society had ordered its treasurer to pay Franklin £100 for the relief of Boston.[55] Wilkes's secret help to the colonies was apparently still more important. First in 1775 at Mansion House, the residence of the lord mayor, then elsewhere in 1776, Wilkes dined together with Arthur Lee, who from November 1775 acted as confidential correspondent of the Continental Congress in London, and with the playwright Pierre Augustin Caron, known as Beaumarchais, who in 1776 became an agent through whom French aid was sent to the colonies. Well into 1776, Wilkes maintained a weekly correspondence with Beaumarchais, and served in the dangerous position of a middleman through whom funds collected

54. *Addresses, Remonstrances, and Petitions, Commencing the 24th of June, 1769, Presented to the King and Parliament, from the Court of Common Council and the Livery in Common Hall Assembled. . . .* (London [, 1778]), *passim*. O. A. Sherrard, *A Life of John Wilkes* (London, 1930), 273–7, and William P. Treloar, *Wilkes and the City* (London, 1917), 167–70.

55. *Prov. Gaz.*, November 5, 1774; *Boston Gaz.*, April 17, 1775; *Mass. Spy*, June 7, 1775.

from pro-American Englishmen were forwarded, via France, to the United States.[56]

This English support of America was recognized publicly by the King in his proclamation of August 1775. The American rebellion, he said, was "much promoted and encouraged by the traitorous correspondence, counsels and comfort of divers wicked and desperate persons within this realm." Although the proclamation is remembered most often because it declared the Americans to be rebels, it was aimed more immediately at suppressing this domestic support for the colonists. The king called on all his subjects at home and in his dominions "to use their utmost endeavours to withstand and suppress . . . rebellion, and to disclose . . . all treasons and traitorous conspiracies which they shall know to be against us, our crown and dignity," and for this purpose to give the secretary of state "due and full information of all persons who shall be found carrying on correspondence with, or in any manner or degree aiding or abetting" the Americans, that they might be brought to "condign punishment." When the proclamation was issued, Lord Mayor Wilkes allowed only the city's common crier to attend its reading.[57]

As the King's proclamation hinted, there were even fledgling signs of an insurrection in England, which was especially interesting to those ready to draw encouragement from the most radical fringe groups of English society. Throughout 1775 "The Crisis," a broadsheet published in England, stressed the unity of American and English grievances and went on to predict that if the sword were drawn in America, it would not long remain sheathed in England. Englishmen

56. See entries in Wilkes's Diary, BM Add. Mss., 30866, for September 6 and October 25, 1775; February 5, 10, and May 19, 1776. These, as well as other meetings with Americans, are not included in the Diary as printed in Treloar, *Wilkes and the City*, 259–89. Also Horace St. Paul (occasional substitute for the British ambassador to France) to Lord Weymouth, Paris, May 1, 1776, and Lord Stormont (British ambassador) to Weymouth, Paris, September 25, 1776, PRO, SP 78/299, ff. 68, 536; Stormont to Weymouth, Paris, November 20, 1776, PRO, SP 78/300, f. 249.

57. King's Proclamation of Rebellion, August 23, 1775, in Henry Steele Commager, *Documents of American History* (6th edn., New York, 1958), 96; Sherrard, *John Wilkes*, 277.

were not yet "so far degenerated as to TAMELY see a mercenary army of soldiers . . . BUTCHER their BRETHREN and FELLOW-SUBJECTS in America, because they are determined to defend their own rights and the British constitution." Once war broke out, "The Crisis" called upon Englishmen to follow the Americans' example and enter "an ASSOCIATION in defence of [their] common rights, and the rights of America." "Let us . . . punish the parricides," its author called, ". . . let us frustrate their present desperate and wicked attempt to destroy America, by joining with our injured fellow subjects, and bravely striking one honest and bold strike to destroy them . . . let us not leave the pursuit till we have their heads and their estates."[58]

One such association was formed near Leicester Fields in London. In August and September 1775, letters signed by its secretary, Thomas Joel, were sent into the country asking that other similar associations be established and that these maintain communication with London through committees of correspondence. The association's purpose, the letter said, was to avert ruinous consequences to English commerce and freedom from a loss of America; and more directly to support the constitution as established at the Glorious Revolution and the accession of the House of Hanover against "the designs of men, who seem determined to destroy all their excellent effects." The association also circulated a broadside, "Sidney's Exhortation," that called upon "EVERY GOOD MAN" to unite in the "COMMON CAUSE, and use his utmost Endeavours to wrest the POWER of GOVERNMENT out of Hands, that have exercised it WEAKLY and WICKEDLY." At least one American town seized upon these encouraging signs. In October 1775, the citizens of Middletown, Connecticut, pointed out to their assemblymen that "Committees of Association are forming throughout the kingdoms of Ireland and England," and that the associations were "the first step taken . . . which afterwards produced a glorious revolution."[59]

58. "The Crisis," III, V, and XXII, as reprinted in *Mass. Spy.*, May 31, June 14, and October 13, 1775; and in *Prov. Gaz.*, July 1 and 15, and October 7, 1775.
59. Some copies of Joel's letters were sent to Lord Dartmouth. Those originally sent to Litchfield and Blackburn, dated September

The reality of insurrection was another matter. The only such scheme in 1775 that left any traces was an extravagant, and perhaps completely spurious, plot to capture the King and return him to Hanover, which was charged to Stephen Sayre. According to depositions the government produced, Sayre sought to win over a young American officer, Francis Richardson, who was an adjutant at the Tower of London with important responsibilities for coordinating command. Sayre argued, according to Richardson's testimony, that both England and America would be ruined if there was no change in government, and Richardson could help avert that fate. The people were determined "to take the Government into their own hands," but no longer could they strike only at the ministers. "They must strike at the fountain head," Sayre explained—at the King himself. Richardson was to win the connivance of troops at the Tower through bribes, of which £1500 had already been distributed. On October 26, a week after their conspiratorial interview, George III would be seized as he went to the House of Lords and held in the Tower. Wilkes as lord mayor would summon a *posse* to prevent the Tower from being retaken; meanwhile, a new council would "annul the Authority of all Officers Civil and Military of which the aforesaid Stephen Sayre's party should disapprove," and the conspirators would ship the monarch off "to His German Dominions."[60]

The government's case against Sayre rapidly collapsed after it was brought into court on October 28, and later proceedings were dropped. From the start, Sayre denied Richardson's story. Although he had met with Richardson and told the adjutant that nothing could save England and America "but a total Change of Men and Measures," he had also expressed his belief, Sayre said, that "there was not spirit enough left

---

4 and 10, and "Sidney's Exhortation," are in the Dartmouth Papers, D 1778/2/1504, 1507, 1503. Middletown instructions in *New London Gaz.*, November 10, 1775.

60. Depositions sworn by Nicholas Nugent, October 23, 1775, and Francis Richardson, October 20, 1775, PRO, TS 11/542. See also T. B. Howell, ed., *A Complete Collection of State Trials and Proceedings for High Treason and Other Crimes and Misdemeanours from the Earliest Period to the Present Time*, XX (London, 1814), 1286–1315.

in this Country to bring such a Measure about." Later, Sayre was awarded £1000 damages in a suit for false arrest against William Henry, Earl of Rochford, who had issued the warrant against him. The ministers' belief that London radicals might plot to depose the King was not, however, completely implausible, for Sayre's associates were strong advocates of the right of revolution, and they did believe that George III was the source of all despotic measures. The alleged plot was also in keeping with Sayre's April 1775 statement to Samuel Adams that "high Convulsions" were necessary to save the Mother Country, and that if these were begun in America, they might "prove salutary even to us in England."[61]

For most observers, however, including Horace Walpole, the whole affair was a farce. The "nonsensical" character of the story, as well as the ministers' gravity in dealing with it (they apparently trebled the guards), "could not keep anybody from laughing." Were Sayre to be confined anywhere, Walpole suggested, it should be in Bedlam. Sayre's public reaction was surprisingly like Walpole's: when the charges against him were read, the *Boston Gazette* reported, Sayre and his counsel just laughed, and charged " 'that the whole was too ridiculous to be seriously attended to.' " Whether true or not, Sayre's comment, it would seem, admitted the bankruptcy of any American hopes of an English uprising.[62]

Already, in fact, the Americans were coming to see the futility of hopes for effective support from the British people. Their impression that widespread sympathy for them existed in England had grown disproportionately from reports out of London; now even there the weakness of radicalism was apparent. In December 1774 Joseph Reed, who had lived for years in London, and who had been a classmate of Sayre at Princeton, regretted that leadership of the well-disposed people of London and Middlesex had fallen exclusively into the hands of Wilkes, Sayre, and the Bill of Rights Society. "What a

61. Examination of Sayre before Earl of Rochford, October 23, 1775, PRO, TS 11/542; Sayre to Adams, April 4, 1775, Samuel Adams Papers.

62. Walpole to Sir Horace Mann, London, October 28, 1775, and to the Rev. William Mason, Strawberry Hill, October 25, 1775, in Paget Toynbee, ed., *The Letters of Horace Walpole. . .*, IX (Oxford, 1904), 277–8, and see also 271, 273. *Boston Gaz.*, February 19, 1776.

noble opposition to the present system of arbitrary power and corruption might have been formed by men of real virtue and wisdom," he wrote. Under current circumstances and leadership, he feared city patriotism would become "a standing jest throughout the kingdom." In September 1774, Samuel Adams still stressed the importance of coordinating American opposition with the efforts of their allies in Britain; but by November 1775, he had moved well beyond Reed's earlier pessimism. "I cannot conceive that there is any room to hope from the virtuous efforts of the people of Britain," he said flatly. "They seem to be generally unprincipled and fitted for the yoke of arbitrary power. The opposition of the few is feeble and languid—while the Tyrant is flushed with expectations from his fleets and armies." And Elbridge Gerry, who in 1773 had already concluded that colonial grievances arose "from the whole Gov[ernmen]t of G[reat] Britain," similarly expanded his indictment of the Mother Country. "NOT ONLY THE GOVERNMENT OF GREAT BRITAIN BUT THE COLLECTIVE BODY OF THE PEOPLE ARE CORRUPT AND TOTALLY DESTITUTE OF VIRTUE," he wrote in March 1776. "A.Z." expressed the same conviction in the *New London Gazette* for January 19, 1776. Oppression had so broken the spirit of the English people that the Americans could "expect but little aid from our friends in Great-Britain, how much soever they may be disposed to assist us." "It is not to be expected," he said, "they can support us in what they themselves have lost, and [are] utterly unable to regain." Even a New York Tory noticed a new turn in the thinking of "Ringleaders" because there had been "no Insurrections in England, on which they principally depended."[63]

The effect of British internal placidity was no less apparent among Virginians. In effect, the hopeful distinction that "Junius" had drawn in 1770 between King and corrupted Parliament on the one hand and the English people on the

63. Reed to Dennis DeBerdt, Philadelphia, December 24, 1774, in Reed, *Joseph Reed*, I, 89. Adams to Joseph Warren, Philadelphia, September 25, 1774, in Frothingham, *Joseph Warren*, 378; Adams to James Bowdoin, Philadelphia, November 16, 1775, in Cushing, *Writings of Samuel Adams*, III, 241. Gerry to unnamed correspondent, Philadelphia, March 26, 1776, Gerry Papers. Unsigned letter to Isaac Wilkens, New York, October 3, 1775, PRO, CO 5/134, f. 338.

other was finally effaced. In July 1775, George Washington noted that the news of Lexington and Concord "was far from making the Impression [in England] generally expected here." After Bunker Hill similarly led only to more severe reprisals against the colonists, Washington abandoned any hope of accommodation. By January 1776, he was ready to condemn not only the British government but "a nation which seems to be lost to every sense of virtue, and those feelings which distinguish a civilized people from the most barbarous savages." Jefferson, too, wrote in the summer of 1775 that the efforts of the British nation to aid the Americans had hitherto been "ineffectual"; but that the colonists could still "confide in the good offices" of their "fellow subjects beyond the Atlantic" in seeking to end British violence. "Of their friendly dispositions we do not yet cease to hope," he wrote, "aware, as they must be, that they have nothing more to expect from the same common enemy than the humble favor of being last devoured." The Continental Congress endorsed similar expressions of common cause in 1775 when it adopted a second address to the British people. "Soldiers who have sheathed their Swords in the Bowels of their *American* Brethren, will not draw them with more reluctance against you," it warned. A year later, however, any suggestion that the Americans "had friends in England worth keeping terms with" seemed to Jefferson "pusillanimous"; and the mid-1775 expressions of confidence gave way to an effusive indictment of the British people in Jefferson's draft of the American Declaration of Independence. They were, he charged, "unfeeling brethren," who had "given the last stab to agonizing affection" by re-electing the "disturbers of our harmony" and supporting their magistrates' military measures against the Americans.[64]

64. George Washington to Joseph Reed, Cambridge, January 31, 1776, and also February 10, 1776, and to Major General Philip Schuyler, July 28, 1775, in John C. Fitzpatrick, ed., *The Writings of George Washington* (Washington, 1931–44), IV, 297, 321, and III, 375; Virginia Resolutions of June 10, 1775 (of which Jefferson claimed authorship), Jefferson's draft of the Continental Congress's "Declaration on taking Up Arms," his notes on the Continental Congress's proceedings for July 2, 1776, and his draft of the Declaration of Independence, all in Boyd, *Jefferson Papers*, I, 173, 203, 314, 426–7. *Journals of the Continental Congress*, II, 163–70, especially 169–70.

Partisans in London came to the same conclusion in late 1775 and 1776. One correspondent wrote unctuously of dropping "a pious tear over the fallen virtue and majesty" of the English people. By August 1775, William Lee also believed that the "unaccountable supineness" that had seized the English friends of liberty meant "that a downfall of the British empire seems inevitable," and in 1776 even John Wilkes gave up his faith in the City of London. After failing in his bid for the office of chamberlain, Wilkes decided that London's liverymen were "no longer worthy the name of freemen," but had become "mean vassals, ignominiously courting, and bowing their necks to the ministerial yoke." "If we are saved," he said, "it will be almost solely by the courage and noble spirit of our American brethren, whom neither the luxuries of a court, nor the sordid lust of avarice in a rapacious and venal metropolis, have hitherto corrupted."[65]

[IV]

The failure of the English opposition meant, for one thing, that the Americans would have to fight alone. For this they were prepared: from 1774, while still hoping for support abroad, the colonial leaders increasingly prepared for battle as if they would have to fight unaided. For years, in fact, colonial newspapers had stressed the ability of the colonists alone to withstand Britain. Some articles sought primarily to build morale, asserting "that freedom will triumph in this country, over all its enemies," such that "the Americans will soon be objects of universal admiration and applause," kindling the spirit of liberty in other nations "until the most servile kindreds of the earth will be warmed into freedom." Freedom itself gave strength: it had supported the Corsicans until they gave in to the forces of corruption; it had sustained the Seven Provinces—whose area, it was claimed, was half that of Pennsylvania and whose population approximated that of Massa-

65. Unsigned letter, September 2, 1775, PRO, CO 5/40, ff. 17–20; William Lee to Ralph Izard, August 14, 1775, in Ford, *Letters of William Lee*, I, 168. Wilkes's comments, from the *Annual Register* for 1776, quoted in *ibid.*, 40–1.

chusetts—against the enormous power of Spain. "Three millions of people, armed in the holy cause of liberty, and in such a country as . . . we possess, are invincible by any force which our enemy can send against us," Patrick Henry claimed. There was, moreover, "a just God who presides over the destinies of nations; and who will raise up friends to fight our battles for us."[66]

Technical military advantages were also discussed. The size of their country gave the colonists an advantage over Britain which was, the newspapers claimed, not one-hundredth of America's size. If persecuted in the cities, the Americans could flee into the country and carry on the fight. Then, too, the Americans had weapons and were practiced in their use, unlike the average Englishmen, who had been disarmed by law. Certainly, thousands of "brave musqueteering Americans" were unmatched by the British army of 1775, described as "a number of mercenary, hacknied, tattered regiments, patched up by the most abandoned and debauched of mankind, the scum of the nation, the dregs of Irish and Scottish desperados."[67] Finally, the Americans felt strengthened by the conviction of their rightness and by the fact that they fought for their own liberties, and on a homeland that could not be created anew elsewhere. For Ezra Stiles these themes were inextricably bound. "Our fathers fled hither for Religion and Liberty," he wrote Catharine Macaulay on April 15, 1775. "If extirpated from hence, we have no new World to flee to. God has located us here, and by this . . . commands us to make a stand, and see the salvation of the Lord." Constantly, the colonists had prayed and fasted, asking the counsel of Heaven and committing their cause to God. "The Event is with the Lord of Hosts," Stiles said, "which we doubt not will be happy and Glorious. We are embarked in a glorious

66. Letter to the timid Americans, Providence, in *N.Y. Jour.*, June 17, 1773; *Mass. Spy*, February 9, 1775; Henry quoted in Henry, *Patrick Henry*, I, 265. Also "Age and Experience," *Boston Gaz.*, January 11, 1773 ("in a short time the Americans will be too strong for any nation in the world").

67. "An American," *Boston Gaz.*, November 25, 1771; extract of letter from England, June 22, *N.Y. Jour.*, September 8, 1774; "Cosmopolitan IV," *Mass. Spy*, November 17, 1775.

and animating Cause, and proceed . . . with undoubted Confidence of final success." The war "will indeed be expensive, extremely expensive," Jefferson wrote after the battle of Bunker Hill, yet "nobody now entertains a doubt but that we are able to cope with the whole force of Great Britain, if we are but willing to exert ourselves."[68]

The failure of English support meant, too, that the focus of the American effort changed. As Joseph Warren put it in April 1775, "*If America is an humble instrument of the salvation of Britain, it will give us the sincerest joy; but, if Britain must lose her liberty, she must lose it alone.*" Even the new concentration on saving only America had widespread implications. America could become a refuge for the oppressed of the world—perhaps the last refuge, for everywhere liberty seemed to be in flight. Not only had the forces of freedom been defeated in Corsica and England, but, it was said, were also being crushed in Sweden, where Gustavus III restored absolute government with a military *coup d'état* in August 1772; in Poland, due to Russian conquests; and in France, where the death of Louis XV in May 1774 had made way for the accession of Louis XVI, who was, Madison said, "a young ambitious monarch."[69] Concern was most marked, however, for those persecuted within the British Empire. "Should the sons of virtue in Britain and Ireland, after all their noble efforts in the cause of freedom, be borne down by the Torrent of despotism, and liberty be extinguish'd in British realms," "An American" promised in 1771, "America will open her arms wide to receive them, in her friendly bosom of peace and liberty they may spend their tranquil days, and breathe their last in the pure air of freedom." The theme was

68. Stiles letter in Stiles Papers; Jefferson to George Climer, July 5, 1775, in Boyd, *Jefferson Papers*, I, 186.

69. Warren to Arthur Lee, Boston, April 3, 1775, in Frothingham, *Joseph Warren*, 447; Madison to William Bradford, August 1, 1774, in Hutchinson and Rachel, *Madison Papers*, I, 118 and 23, n. 8. On the "last refuge" theme, see also "Anglus Americanus," *Boston Gaz.*, August 1, 1774; "Alarm V," *N.Y. Jour.*, November 18, 1773 ("If you suffer the iron rod of oppression to reach and scourge you here, remember you have no America to flee to for an asylum"); "J.R." in *Pa. Jour.*, June 22, 1774, and Arthur Lee to Samuel Adams, London, December 3, 1773, in Lee, *Arthur Lee*, I, 261.

endlessly repeated, not only by Americans but by the patrons of liberty abroad.[70]

Finally, the failure of English support raised for the last time the question of independence. The prospect was not new: the possibility had been discussed with seriousness since the early 1770's. For some, indeed, independence was a fact—already in 1772 one New Englander claimed Great Britain had "totally cancelled all obligations to continue [the Americans'] connection with her another day." By the same reasoning, Providence's Silas Downer found in the Intolerable Acts a great "deliverance." "The Time is come," he wrote William Palfrey in July 1774, ". . . that we are independent. By the passing of the late Acts in the British Parliament, every Tye is cut, and we set adrift." In September of 1774, Patrick Henry also told the Continental Congress that government was dissolved and "we are in a state of nature." The outbreak of war in 1775 led more people to the same conclusion.[71] For the ardent, then, the only problem remaining in mid-1775 was whether or not to recognize publicly a *de facto* state of independence. By 1776, advocacy of a Declaration of Independence had become the defining trait of American radicals.[72]

Several considerations had prevented the Americans from accepting independence, but gradually each of them was weakened or gave way. Political and military considerations provided significant deterrents to independence. Precipitous action might alienate moderate Americans, particularly those in the middle colonies; or it might provoke an English retaliation that the colonists could not withstand. But through 1775

---

70. *Boston Gaz.*, November 25, 1771. Also "The Preacher," *Mass. Spy*, March 24, 1774, and letter from the Bill of Rights Society to South Carolina, 1770, in *S.C. Gaz., Continuation* August 23, 1770: Society members hope "that when luxury, misrule and corruption, shall at length, in spite of all resistance, have destroyed this noble constitution here, our posterity . . . will find a welcome refuge in America."

71. "Humanity," *Boston Gaz.*, November 9, 1772; Downer to William Palfrey, Providence, July 12, 1774, Palfrey Papers, Part II, a, 60; John Adams's account of Henry's speech in Henry, *Patrick Henry*, I, 221. See also resolves of Mecklenburgh County Committee, May 31, 1775, in *N.C. Col. Recs.*, IX, 1282–5.

72. Bernard Mason, *The Road to Independence: The Revolutionary Movement in New York, 1773–1777* (Lexington, Ky., 1966), viii.

colonial unity increased. Since Parliament's acts of 1774, which made the American position so clearly correct, one Bostonian claimed, even old Tories were changing sides to "unite with the Majority of the People against Oppression." Lexington and Concord also had a great galvanizing effect: the "ever memorable 19th of April last," a writer recalled in 1776, "has so happily united the thirteen colonies" that few political tracts were needed or published thereafter compared to the "swarms" that preceded it.[73] Already in November 1774, Joseph Reed assured Josiah Quincy, Jr., that there was "no danger of the enemy being let in" through Philadelphia. "There is a band of staunch, chosen sons of liberty among some of our best families, who are backed by the body of the people in such a manner that no discontented spirit dares oppose the measures necessary for the public safety." For Reed, New York was the problem; but by February 1776, Eliphalet Dyer reported to Samuel Adams that even that weak point was "pretty well Secured" and that its military preparedness was "much owing to that Crazy Capt. Sears which Y[ork] Delegates would affect to Call him."[74]

The most important single restraint on any decision for independence, however, was the hope that somehow, whether by action of the ministry, Parliament, King, or the British people, an accommodation within the framework of the empire might yet be made between the colonists and Britain, with the "terms and limits of our union" ascertained and fixed "upon clear and solid ground." This hope lingered on into late 1775; but with the failure of the English people to rise in support of the Americans it was extinguished, and independence became imperative. It was at this time that Thomas Paine published *Common Sense*. The pamphlet was credited with converting many, particularly in the South, to independence; yet its emphasis upon immediate political, economic, and

73. The Rev. Samuel Stillman to Mrs. Patience Wright, Boston, April 13, 1774, Josiah Quincy, Jr., Papers, f. 74; "Probus," *Boston Gaz.*, March 11, 1776. The number of political tracts in radical newspapers did diminish after April 1775. Military reports took their place.

74. Reed to Quincy, November 6, 1774, in Quincy, *Memoir*, 173; Dyer to Adams, Lebanon, Connecticut, February 27, 1776, Samuel Adams Papers.

military expediency seemed aberrant in the context of American thought. Paine had arrived in the colonies only in 1774. For Americans who had lived through the whole of the controversy, independence emerged more directly from their decade-long fruitless search for redress within the empire. *Common Sense* was the work of an "original genius," said "An Independent Whig" in the *New York Journal*; but he objected to Paine's arguing for independence on the basis of expediency rather than "absolute necessity." "We must be either independent, or be reduced to the most abject state of slavery," he said; and responsibility lay not only in the malevolence of King, ministers, and Parliament, but now, too, in the "supineness of the [English] nation," which left the government to pursue schemes destructive to the public and thereby "obliged the colonies to go into a mode of self defence beyond what they ever intended." A writer in the *Pennsylvania Packet* used almost the same words. Because of the "usurpations of the British Parliament," the "insolence of the ministry," "the obstinacy and bloody mindedness of the king," and, finally, "the inhumanity of their brethren in Great Britain," the colonies concluded that independence was "the only means that could secure peace—liberty—and safety to America."[75]

The colonists' disillusionment with the British people, then, made it finally necessary for them "to dissolve the political bands" that bound them to Britain, to seize their independence. It was above all the penultimate paragraph of the Declaration of Independence, berating the British people for proving "deaf to the voice of justice and of consanguinity," that distinguished it from Congress's pronouncements of 1775. Jefferson's obsessive recollection that "we might have been a free and a great people together" if "a communication of grandeur and of freedom" were not "below their dignity," his pronouncement that the Americans could climb "the road to glory and

75. [Arthur Lee?] letter from England, September 2, 1775, PRO, CO 5/40, ff. 17–20; "Independent Whig," *N.Y. Jour.*, February 22, 1776; "Remarkable EVENTS in the year 1775," from *Pennsylvania Packet*, in *Boston Gaz.*, January 22, 1776. See also "Memorial," *New London Gaz.*, April 12, 1776: "the King and Ministry, Court and Nation, have been so far agreed to subject and inslave us . . . that we think it altogether inconvenient, absurd, improper, unjust and impossible, ever to be subject to that King, State, or Nation any more."

to happiness . . . apart from them," were omitted from the draft by Congress. Yet the essence remained: the British people would henceforth be considered no different from the "rest of mankind, enemies in war, in peace friends."[76]

In declaring their independence, the Americans, of course, for the first time formally attributed their repeated injuries to the "present King of Great Britain." It was he who had kept up standing armies without the legislatures' consent, who had imposed unconstitutional taxes, and deprived the colonists of trial by jury. The King was blamed, however, not because of any new discovery of his guilt—that had been first suspected and asserted after the failure of the London Remonstrances a half decade earlier. The reason lay rather in customary forms. By English revolutionary tradition, a people announced their acceptance of revolution by publicly attributing responsibility for unconstitutional acts to the King, who embodied the state's authority, rather than to his ministers. And although in fact a "long train of abuses and usurpations" in England and Ireland as well as America had convinced the colonists that there was a "design to reduce them under absolute despotism," only American grievances were cited. That was because, to the regret of the Americans, only they in the end proved ready and able to fight for their rights.

Independence became possible, finally, because of a corrosion of American affection for Britain, which was, John Dickinson said, the one basic and essential element in any lasting union of Britain with her colonies. During the mid-1760's, the most radical of colonists had taken great pride in their British affiliation, their membership in the freest government in the world. During the Stamp Act crisis, Dickinson feared only a future "dreadful revolution of sentiments" toward Britain; but by 1774, Joseph Reed told Lord Dartmouth that American fondness for Britain was already fading. In October 1775, an English observer in New York used stronger words: "the Minds of the People now begin to be sowered" against Britain, he said. Affection and a sense of kinship with Englishmen were not extinguished in 1775; but by then the Americans had learned, too, to speak of the Mother Country

76. Carl L. Becker, *The Declaration of Independence* (New York, 1948), 148–50, 182–4.

as "a vile imposter—an old abandoned prostitute—a robber, a murderer," a "*Jezebel.*" The English people were, it was once said, "remarkable throughout the world for a melancholy cast of mind," and even the Londoners, "enveloped in a foggy atmosphere, and breathing nothing but the grossness of a sea-coal air," came to be a people apart, inferior to the Spartan Americans.[77] It was this gradual change "in the minds and hearts of the people" that seemed revolutionary to contemporaries. Only because affection for Britain had been so deep did the change seem fundamental. Because the weaning of attachment was incomplete, and because, too, of the uncertainty in America's future, the decision for separation was not much happier for John Adams or even Arthur Lee than it was for John Dickinson, who in the end could not accede to the Declaration of Independence.[78]

77. Dickinson's *The Late Regulations Respecting the British Colonies.* . . . (Orig. pub., Philadelphia, 1765), in Ford, *Dickinson Writings*, I, 244; Reed to Dartmouth, Philadelphia, September 25, 1775, in Reed, *Joseph Reed*, I, 77; Peter Shires to the Rev. John Wesley, Montholly, New York, October 29, 1775, PRO, CO 5/134, f. 154. Letter to printer, New York, April 26, 1775, in *N.Y. Jour., Supplement* May 25, 1775; "Casca," *Pa. Jour.*, October 27, 1773.

78. Arthur Lee to Samuel Adams, June 23, [1773,] in Lee, *Arthur Lee*, I, 220 ("The first wish of my heart is that America may be free —the second is, that we may ever be united with this country"); also [Arthur Lee] letter of September 2, 1775, urging a postponement of independence until unavoidable because of his "rooted affection for the Stock from which we Sprung," PRO, CO 5/40, ff. 17–20. John Adams to James Warren, April 22, 1776, in which Adams wonders whether Americans would be happy under their new "free and popular governments," in S. E. Morison, *Sources and Documents Illustrating the American Revolution* (Oxford, 1929), 147.

CHAPTER NINE

REPUBLICANS, BY CHOICE

THE COLONISTS' CONSTITUTIONAL ARGUMENTS, their consistent respect for traditional procedures, even their efforts to contain violence have given later generations an impression that the American Revolution was hardly revolutionary at all. The colonists did not seek change; they set out to defend a constitutional system which had been established, they believed, with the Glorious Revolution of 1688. Here, however, they resembled many other revolutionaries of the seventeenth and eighteenth centuries, who also set out to restore an uncorrupted past.[1] Only when that goal proved unobtainable did contenders establish new regimes that differed profoundly from the past, transforming their own land and sometimes shifting a wider civilization as well.

The colonists sought a past that could not be rewon, if indeed it had ever existed. Hence, to protect liberty as they understood it, the Americans broke off from their Mother Country and undertook one of the earliest modern colonial wars for independence. The movement toward independence constituted the negative phase of the Revolution, a rejection of old and once-revered institutions and ties, which for contemporaries constituted a major upheaval in its own

1. Hannah Arendt, *On Revolution* (New York, 1965), 34–40, 153.

right. It, moreover, opened a second phase of more wide-spread influence: a revolution in constitutional forms. The achievement of profound political change in the state and federal constitutions of the 1770's and 1780's grew logically out of the popular agitation of the years before independence. The American leaders' concern with peace and good order, their technique of curtailing individual violence by organizing, in effect institutionalizing, mass force—which continued beyond the extra-legal institutions of the 1760's into the committees, conventions, and congresses of the mid-1770's—led naturally toward the re-establishment of regular government. The overall form of these new institutions had also been largely determined by July 1776. Disillusionment with the English constitution and with contemporary British rulers had proceeded simultaneously until it became clear that the new-founded American state should not be modeled after that of England. Instead, it would be what the colonists came to call "republican." This conversion to republicanism transformed "a petty rebellion within the Empire into a symbol for the liberation of all mankind"; it meant that Americans helped open what R. R. Palmer has called the "Age of the Democratic Revolution."[2]

[I]

As confidence in British justice increasingly soured in the 1770's, and as the righteousness of the Americans' cause seemed ever more clearly proven, the task of restraining popular violence became increasingly difficult. In the past, leaders had been able to divert mobs toward the "regular methods of proceeding"; but that tactic gradually became untenable. In January 1774, when a Boston crowd, apparently composed largely of sailors, seized John Malcom, a customs official

2. Cecelia M. Kenyon, "Republicanism and Radicalism in the American Revolution: An Old-Fashioned Interpretation," *W. M. Q.*, XIX (1962), 168; R. R. Palmer, *The Age of the Democratic Revolution,* I (Princeton, 1959). Miss Kenyon mistakenly thought the colonists' conversion to republicanism occurred "within a few months" in 1776 (p. 165).

long charged with "venality and corruption as well as . . . extortion in office," efforts were again made to secure Malcom's freedom with assurances that "the law would have its course with him." But the insurgents asked "what course had the law taken with Preston or his soldiers, with Capt. Wilson or Richardson?" Mob members claimed they had seen "so much partiality to the soldiers and customhouse officers by the present Judges, that while things remained as they were, they would, on all such occasions, take satisfaction their own way," and proceeded to tar and feather their victim.[3]

When justice could be imposed, as was claimed, only by the people, insurgents assumed an increased legitimacy and authority. Repeatedly, it was said that upheaval was only a product of oppression. As a result, those who supported or tried to enforce "tyrannic" British laws were the sources of disorder, and mobs became defenders of the peace. In October 1773, when Boston's Ebenezer Richardson appeared in Philadelphia, he was, the *Pennsylvania Journal* reported, pursued by "many well-wishers to peace and good order" who intended to tar and feather him.[4]

In effect, the restraint of established law was dissolved: when the people's "rights and properties cannot be secured by the laws of the land," it was maintained, opposition to unjust power could be measured "*only* by the perpetual and universally binding law of *self-defense*." Some writers seemed to declare an open season on men "combined to subvert our

3. Statement on Malcom's character in Gov. Josiah Martin to Lord Hillsborough, North Carolina, June 5, 1772, PRO, CO 5/303, f. 4; Frank W. C. Hersey, "Tar and Feathers: The Adventures of Captain John Malcom," CSM *Pubs.*, XXIV (*Trans.*, 1937–42), 429–73, especially 444–5. "Capt. [John] Wilson" of the British Fifty-ninth Regiment had urged Negro slaves in Boston to murder their masters. Hiller B. Zobel, *The Boston Massacre* (New York, 1970), 102. Malcom had been tarred and feathered the previous November in New Hampshire after he had unjustly seized the brig *Brothers*. He had also marched against the North Carolina Regulators, which contributed to his unpopularity in Boston. The immediate provocation of the January 1774 uprising was, however, Malcom's hitting Bostonian George Hewes with a large stick. See also *Boston Gaz.*, January 31, 1774, where the uprising is interpreted as one of the "effects of a government in which the people have no confidence."

4. *Pa. Jour.*, October 20, 1773.

civil government, to plunder and murder us," who by their acts forfeited any right to "protection in their persons or properties." As Locke said, they had "*put themselves in a state of war* with us . . . and being the aggressors, if they perish, the fault is their own." After the passage of the Intolerable Acts, which seemed to make British oppression manifest beyond the slightest doubt, any man holding office under those acts seemed to have "wittingly and willfully" broken "the sacred bond of his allegiance to the laws and constitution of his country, than which no act in the power of man to commit can be more attrociously criminal." By 1775, Loyalists were "the *Guy Fawk's* [sic] of the present Day . . . inexcusable in every point of View," whose crimes were "committed against the clearest Light," and who should be given "no Quarter" but made "to bow . . . and lick the Dust."[5]

The potential for widespread and undisciplined mob violence in these circumstances awoke a new emphasis upon internal restraint. "These tarrings and featherings," John Adams complained in 1774, "this breaking open Houses by rude and insolent Rabbles, in Resentment for private Wrongs or in pursuance of private Prejudices and Passions, must be discountenanced." Much as in 1765, ground rules were published, specifying when direct action was appropriate and how it should be exercised. Popular exertions were "right, justifiable, and commendable," it was stressed, only "in *some very extreme cases.*" The people should never punish misdemeanors that could be suppressed under the established laws, for that would be "a heinous insult upon the good laws of the land, and upon all those wise and worthy gentlemen that are in lawful authority." Even criminals who could not be prosecuted under current laws of the land should sometimes be overlooked because of their "insignificancy." And when the people resumed the judicial power that was originally theirs, they must act with all the safeguards and decorum that restrained civil magistrates. They "should ever be as judicious, deliberate, and cautious in making full enquiry whether the party

---

5. "Constitutional Catechism," *N.Y. Jour.*, December 9, 1773, and *Mass. Spy*, January 27, 1774; "Massachusettensis," and unsigned letter in *ibid.*, November 18, 1773, and August 11, 1774; "A Son of Liberty," *New London Gaz.*, September 29, 1775.

suspected be a real traitor, or criminal to a degree worthy of their notice, as any court of justice ought to do, and should give the accused as full and fair an opportunity to vindicate themselves if they are able." The people should appear in good order, and avoid property damage, "unless, perhaps, it may be requisite to force a door, or the like, in order to effect the good purposes designed." Punishment might indeed be carried out, but it should in no way be "of a sportive and ludicrous nature." "What should we think of our honorable courts if they should punish criminals by *tar and feathers* . . . ?"[6] In short, if regular judicial tribunals must be superseded, their procedures were not to be abandoned in revolutionary justice.

A body acting under such rules could hardly be thought of as a mob. As the formulator of these guidelines noted, "mob" implied "the most confused tumults," while the new procedures befitted more accurately the action of a "respectable confederated populace"—or, more concretely, the various committees and associations that proliferated in the colonies after the Tea Act reawoke colonial opposition. The tea resistance constituted, in fact, a model of justified forceful resistance upon traditional criteria. As in the Stamp Act crisis, resistance seemed mandatory because, as John Adams wrote, the tea duty represented "an attack upon a fundamental principle of the constitution," against which all efforts short of force had failed. Payment of the duty had to be prevented, yet volatile confrontations and the destruction of private property were to be avoided where possible. In Philadelphia and New York, local committees convinced the tea captains to return their ships to England without unloading. In Charleston, the imported East India Company tea was seized by customs officials after consignees refused to accept it and the tea ship had remained unladen in the harbor over the legal twenty-day waiting period; but local patriots rested confident that it would remain locked up and not be offered for sale, so no further action seemed necessary. Later in 1774, as tempers rose and

6. John to Abigail Adams, Falmouth, July 7, 1774, in L. Kinvin Wroth and Hiller B. Zobel, eds., *Legal Papers of John Adams* (New York, 1968), I, 140; letter to *Conn. Gaz.* reprinted in *New London Gaz.*, October 21, 1774.

"vigorous measures" were increasingly demanded, local committees nonetheless often ritualistically refused to lay hands on the tea themselves. At Charleston in November 1774, the proprietors and agents of some imported tea themselves emptied seven chests of the baneful leaf into the Cooper River in the presence of the Committee of Inspection and a large crowd. And at Annapolis, Maryland, in October 1775 the owners of imported tea "voluntarily" burned not only the tea, but the *Peggy Stewart* upon which it was shipped to the colonies.[7]

Only in Boston did all efforts to reship the tea fail; and only there did its impoundage by customs officials seem likely to lead to its distribution. Still the Bostonians "took every method that a people engaged in such a cause could take." They urged the consignees to order the tea's reshipment and unsuccessfully asked customs officials, then the governor, to issue the clearances needed for the ship's departure. Only when the waiting period was about to expire and the tea to be seized did the "Mohawks" set to work, and then with conspicuous self-discipline, making "very little noise," taking care to prevent property damage other than to the tea—a padlock accidently broken was supposedly replaced—and keeping plunder off-limits. One interloper who tried to hide some tea in his pockets was "stripped of his booty and his clothes together, and sent home naked," which seemed to Dr. Samuel Cooper "a remarkable instance of order and justice among savages." When they had completed their business, observers reported, the participants "silently departed" and the town remained "remarkably quiet"—"never more still and calm," John Adams insisted. After acting with such care the Tea Party actors could say, with John Scollay, that they had "acted constitutionally." For Adams, the night was even more glorious than that of August 14, 1765. "This is the grandest Event which has ever yet happened Since the Controversy

7. *Ibid.*; Adams, "Novanglus," in Charles F. Adams, ed., *The Works of John Adams* (Boston, 1850–6), IV, 88; Benjamin W. Labaree, *The Boston Tea Party* (New York, 1964), 152–9; John Drayton, *Memoirs of the American Revolution* (Charleston, 1821), I, 153–4; account from Annapolis, October 20, 1774, in Peter Force, ed., *American Archives*, 4th Ser. (Washington, 1937–46), I, 885–6.

with Britain opened!" he wrote. "The Sublimity of it, charms me!"[8]

In its leadership and in its guiding principles, the tea resistance was heir to the resistance movements of the 1760's. Philadelphia's old Son of Liberty William Bradford helped organize that town's proceedings, and John Dickinson endorsed resistance, although radical leadership there was passing to Charles Thomson, Joseph Reed, and Thomas Mifflin. Charleston's Christopher Gadsden, New York's Isaac Sears, John Lamb, and Alexander McDougall, Boston's Samuel Adams, Thomas Young, Joseph Warren, William Molineux, Josiah Quincy, Jr., and others of the old Sons of Liberty were all prominent in the Tea Act resistance. Once again, efforts were to involve the body of the people in opposition efforts. At Philadelphia, the tea resistance was concerted at large public meetings; Bostonians deliberated their actions not in regular town meetings, but in still broader "Meetings of the People of Boston and the neighbouring Towns," sometimes referred to significantly as "Body" meetings; and at New York, an "Association of the Sons of Liberty" was circulated through the population for signatures in November 1773 to obviate any criticisms of the resistance as representing only a vocal minority. The aim of "orderly resistance," with its demand that mass action be disciplined and extraneous violence be avoided, also remained intact. Thomas Young, for example, was one of the first to propose openly that the East India Company's tea be destroyed at Boston; but he also defended the consignee Francis Rotch before a crowd clamoring for "A mob! A mob!", and urged that Rotch's person and property be left unharmed. The Sons of Liberty's Association at New York also endorsed "the strongest terms of

8. "Destruction of the Tea, in the Harbor of Boston, December 16, 1773," MHS *Colls.*, 4th Ser., IV (Boston, 1858), especially John Scollay to Arthur Lee, Boston, December 23, p. 385; Dr. Samuel Cooper to Benjamin Franklin, Boston, December 17, p. 375, and testimony of Dr. Hugh Williamson, pp. 387–8. Adams to James Warren, Boston, December 17, 1773, in Elbridge H. Goss, *The Life of Colonel Paul Revere* (Boston, 1891), I, 134–5; Labaree, *Boston Tea Party*, 126–45; and Mercy Warren, *History of the Rise, Progress, and Termination of the American Revolution*, I (Boston, 1805), especially 102, 107.

opposition, without actual force," leaving the option of force open, as one commentator noted, for any future emergency that might "render the measure necessary."[9]

With the passage of the Intolerable Acts in 1774, the coercion of individuals seemed increasingly necessary for the community's interest: to prevent the Massachusetts Government Act from going into effect; to prevent artisans and merchants from supplying the British army at Boston; and, with the adoption of the Continental Association on September 5, to enforce adherence to the commercial and sumptuary restrictions enacted by the United States Congress. The very presence of persons loyal to Britain posed problems, particularly after the outbreak of war: "Why should persons who are preying upon the vitals of their Country be suffered to stalk at large, while we know they will do us every mischief in their power?" George Washington asked in November 1775. "Would it not be prudence to seize on those Tories who have been, are, and that we know will be active against us?" For others, "Tory" connoted not just those actively working against the Americans, but those who remained passive. Any persons who refused to sign the defense associations circulated in the spring and summer of 1775, and thereby to pledge their readiness to sacrifice "Lives and Fortunes to secure . . . Freedom and Safety," were easily singled out as "Persons inimical to the Liberty of the Colonies."[10]

Supporters of the Crown branded the result chaos. Oftentimes the King's courts were closed, and, as Lord Dunmore

9. Frederick D. Stone, "How the Landing of Tea was Opposed in Philadelphia by Colonel William Bradford and Others in 1773," *Pennsylvania Magazine of History and Biography*, XV (1891), 385–93; Labaree, *Boston Tea Party, passim*, especially 141 on Young; L. F. S. Upton, "Proceedings of Ye Body Respecting the Tea," *W. M. Q.*, XXII (1965), 287–300, especially 290 and *n.* 2; Roger Champagne, "The Sons of Liberty and the Aristocracy in New York Politics, 1765–1790," unpublished Ph.D. thesis, University of Wisconsin, 1960, 296–308; Force, *American Archives*, 4th Ser., I, 251–8.

10. Washington to Gov. [Jonathan] Trumbull of Connecticut, Cambridge, November 15, 1775, in *ibid.*, III, 1563; South Carolina Association, June 3, 1775, "Miscellaneous Papers of the General Committee, Secret Committee, and Provincial Congress, 1775," *South Carolina Genealogical and Historical Magazine*, VIII (1907), 141–2.

reported in December 1774, "There is not a justice of the
Peace in *Virginia* that acts, except as a Committee-man."
Massachusetts Loyalists complained that they had been "deprived of their liberty, abused in their persons, and suffered
such barbarous cruelties, insults, and indignities, besides the
loss of their property by the hands of lawless mobs and riots,
as would have been disgraceful even for savages to have committed." Without courts they had no hope of redress except,
of course, with the aid of the British army. And was the
Provincial Congress not responsible for such abuses? In
October 1774, it had demanded that all officials who had accepted or acted under authority from the Massachusetts Government Act publicly renounce their commissions within ten
days or "be considered as infamous betrayers of their country,"
as "Rebels against the State," whose names would be published repeatedly so that they would be sent "down to posterity
with the infamy they deserve." The Congress demanded further that those who renounce their offices not be molested for
past conduct; but in stigmatizing British partisans was it not,
as Lord Dunmore charged in Virginia, "inviting the vengeance
of an outrageous and lawless mob?" Although violence was
not directly incited, public wrath was only partially stayed.
But then were revolutionary institutions obliged to protect all
those entitled to protection under the old regime? The South
Carolina House of Assembly forthrightly denied this obligation. "In times like the present when a whole Continent is
engaged in one arduous struggle for their Civil Liberties," it
declared in August 1775, "if Individuals will wantonly step
forth and openly . . . condemn measures universally received
and approved, they must abide the consequences—It is not in
our power in such cases to prescribe Limits to Popular Fury."
Others agreed: the New York Provincial Congress, for example, simply declared certain delinquents to the cause "entirely put out of the protection of this Congress." In effect,
the state was being created anew, and those who chose to
abstain from the new arrangements were free to remain, suffering all the perils of a state of nature, or to leave. Even here,
however, the "outrages" of the people were purposeful: they
were aimed, for the most part, against public opponents of
the new American institutions and sought a more uniform

adherence to the new authority, so that the legal limbo of revolution might end.[11]

Disciplined collective coercion was preferred to that by vengeful individuals. When a mass of people assembled at Cape Cod in September 1774 to prevent the meeting of the county court at Barnstable and to ferret out British partisans, it began much as similar groups had done in the later months of the Stamp Act crisis. Rules of proceeding were adopted, outlawing the intemperate use of liquor, profane language, the invasion of property, or violence "otherwise than . . . shall be approved of and accounted necessary by our community for the accomplishing the errand we go upon." These rules were to be read daily "during our transitory state and temporary fellowship," as a "public testimony that we are neither friends to mobs or riots, or any other wickedness or abomination." The county conventions that sprang up in Massachusetts from July 1774 similarly sought "the discouragement of all licentiousness, and suppression of all mobs and riots," encouraging citizens "to observe the most strict obedience to all constitutional laws and authority." Occasionally, patriots proved impatient—Isaac Sears, for example, embarrassed his own Provincial Congress in November 1775 by marching into New York from Connecticut, disarming Loyalists along the way, then seizing the type of Loyalist printer James Rivington; and Patrick Henry spurned the arguments of Virginia's other revolutionary leaders in May 1774 when he marched to demand redress for the gunpowder Lord Dunmore had seized from the Williamsburg magazine. Yet not even Henry acted anarchically. "Strict orders were repeatedly given to the Volunteers to avoid all violence, injury, and insult towards the persons and property of every individual,"

11. Dunmore to Lord Dartmouth, Williamsburg, December 24, 1774, in Richard B. Harwell, ed., *The Committees of Safety of Westmoreland and Fincastle* (Richmond, 1956), 19; [Loyalists] to the Massachusetts Provincial Congress, Boston, February 23, 1775, and Massachusetts Provincial Congress Resolves of October 21, 1774, in Force, *American Archives*, 4th Ser., I, 1260, 839; South Carolina Commons House of Assembly to Governor William Campbell, August 18, 1775, in "Miscellaneous Papers," 193; New York Congress Resolves, December 21, 1775, in Force, *American Archives*, 4th Ser., IV, 435.

and Henry gave the King's receiver-general a receipt for the
£330 he took from the King's funds, promising to return all
funds in excess of that needed by the Virginia Convention
to replace the powder "unlawfully" seized by Lord Dunmore.
Like Sears, whose actions were sometimes praised outside
New York, Henry received the thanks and approval of his
own Hanover County Committee and of Orange County, where
the young James Madison was one of his admirers.[12]

The Continental Association of 1774 regularized procedures against dissidents. Under its terms, committees were
to be chosen in every county, city, and town throughout the
colonies by those able to vote for provincial assemblymen.
Complaints were to be made to these committees, and when a
majority of committeemen were satisfied of the accused's
guilt, the "truth of the case" was to be published in the local
newspaper. Provincial conventions and local committees were
allowed to enact further regulations for executing the association, and these bodies sometimes established detailed judicial procedures. In Connecticut, several counties agreed to
proceed against accused persons in an "open, candid and deliberate manner." Formal summonses would be given the
accused, who had then at least six days to prepare his defense; hearings would be open, and no convictions made "but
upon the fullest, clearest and most convincing proof." Revolution was no excuse for licentiousness: thus, one local New
York committee voted its disapproval of "all . . . unlawful
assemblies . . . unless judged necessary by the major part
of the Committee of the said Town or District." Persons

12. Agreement of the People from Plymouth and Bristol Counties,
at Rochester, Massachusetts, September 26, 1774, in Frederick Freeman, *The History of Cape Cod* (Boston, 1860), I, 430–2; Richard D.
Brown, *Revolutionary Politics in Massachusetts* (Cambridge, Mass.,
1970), 212–20. On Sears: *Boston Gaz.*, December 4, 1775, and Force,
American Archives, 4th Ser., III, 1626, 1707–8, and IV, 185–6, 393,
410, 422–3. Henry: *ibid.*, II, 540–1, and William T. Hutchinson and
William M. Rachel, *The Papers of James Madison*, I (Chicago, 1962),
144–7. Madison was proud of his colony's restlessness: see his letter to
William Bradford, [early March 1775,] 141: "How different is the
Spirit of Virginia from that of N[ew] York? A fellow was lately tarred
and feathered for treating one [of] our county committees with
disre[s]pect; in N. Y. they insult the whole colony and Continent
with impunity!"

accused of being Tories or enemies of their country were "to be complained of unto the Committee of the District or Town in which such person or persons may reside," whereupon the accused would be summoned, and the accuser invited to present "his evidence for trial." Nor were the decisions of local committees necessarily final. In March 1776, for example, the New Jersey Provincial Congress provided for appeals by nonassociators from their local township committee to the county committee, and finally to the Provincial Congress itself.[13]

"Trials" before committees were often aimed less at determining guilt than at giving committeemen an opportunity to "convert" the accused to the American cause: on March 6, 1775, the Cumberland County, New Jersey, Committee spent "much time . . . in vain" trying to convince one Silas Newcomb of his error in drinking East India tea despite the Continental Association before finally breaking off dealings with him and publishing his name as an enemy of American liberty. And boycotts were less often punishments than inducements to change. Thus, the committees of Waltham, Newton, Watertown, Weston, and Sudbury, Massachusetts, asked all persons to withhold commercial dealings with an unrepenting tea purchaser, Eleazer Bradshaw, "until there appears a reformation in said *Bradshaw*"; in October 1775, the Committee of Augusta County, Virginia, asked Virginians "to have no farther dealings, connection, or intercourse" with Alexander Miller, found guilty of calling the Americans rebels and impuning the motives of the Continental Congress, "until he, by his future behaviour, convinces his countrymen of his sincere repentance for his past folly"; and the Sussex County, New Jersey, Committee imposed a boycott upon George McMurtie, proved to have "spoke very contemptuously and disrespectfully of the Continental and Provincial Congresses," until he acknowledged his fault

13. Continental Association in Arthur M. Schlesinger, *The Colonial Merchants and the American Revolution* (New York, 1968), 611, and 487–8 on Connecticut procedures; New York Committee of Safety Minutes, September 14, 1775, including minutes of an August 3 meeting of the committee of Cambridge, Hoosack, and Bennington, in Force, *American Archives*, 4th Ser., III, 894, and IV, 1609.

in a Philadelphia or New York newspaper. Such testimonials
of repentence may not have evidenced any profound change
of heart; but in the early stages of the Revolution, at least,
convenience was considered a valid component of allegiance.[14]

The committee's primary dependence upon social and economic boycotts was not new. In some areas, indeed, the tactic seems to have scarcely abated during the so-called quiet
period after 1770: in 1773, Lord Dartmouth admitted to
Benjamin Franklin that the growth of the royalist party in
Massachusetts was inhibited less by violence than by social
isolation. Men of loyalist sympathies were "reviled and held
in Contempt, and People don't care to incur the Disesteem
and Displeasure of their Neighbours." Now the punishment
seemed particularly enlightened and appropriate for institutions that derived their "power, wisdom and justice, not from
scrolls of parchment signed by Kings but from the People,"
since infamy was "more dreadful to a freeman than the gallows, the rack, or the stake." With time, more imposing
sanctions were used: Loyalists might be fined, imprisoned,
have their property confiscated (although this was everywhere
fraught with controversy), or, better yet, be banished. One
student of loyalism has suggested that the committees' protracted proceedings were designed to encourage the Loyalists' going into exile, which advanced internal uniformity
of allegiance while reducing the occasions for violent reprisals.[15] The most significant exceptions to the rule of moderacy, which allowed dissidents to escape with their lives
and sometimes their property as well, lay with those accused
of inciting slave insurrections in the South. In 1775 a free
black, Thomas Jeremiah, was executed in South Carolina on

14. *Ibid.*, II, 34, and III, 937, 939–40, 951. See also Thomas Young
to Hugh Hughes, December 21, 1772: "We need not spill the blood
even of mistaken enemies if we can otherwise reduce them to reason,
and make them our friends." Miscellaneous Bound Documents, 1770–3,
MHS.

15. Franklin to Thomas Cushing, London, May 6, 1773, PRO, CO
5/118, f. 55; "Political Observations . . . ," from *Pennsylvania Packet*,
November 14, 1774, quoted in Schlesinger, *Colonial Merchants*, 432–3;
Chap. 1 of the manuscript for Prof. Mary Beth Norton's forthcoming
book, "The British-Americans: the Loyalist Exiles in England, 1774–
1789."

what the royal governor thought an unproven and improbable charge of fomenting a slave uprising, and similar accusations against James Simmons in Dorchester County, Maryland, caused him to be "adjudged nem. con. a Suit of Tarr and Feathers, which was immediately put into Execution," and banished from the province.[16]

Political considerations militated most strongly for restraint. On into April 1775, reconciliation with Britain seemed possible without the spilling of blood, if only the Continental Association could be enforced and incidents avoided that might detonate a military confrontation. Restraint seemed essential, too, to win the partisanship of moderates, and to gain time for the forging of American unity, upon which, everyone acknowledged, the success of their cause would depend.[17] Before Lexington and Concord, the responsibility for forbearance rested most heavily upon the people of Boston, who bore what Josiah Quincy, Jr., called a "treble pressure of public oppression" from the Intolerable Acts, and upon the inhabitants of the surrounding counties where incidents between American partisans and British officials or soldiers occurred regularly. "Nothing can ruin us but our Violence," Samuel Adams warned from Philadelphia in May 1774. He urged Joseph Warren "to implore every Friend in Boston by every thing dear and sacred to Men of Sense and Virtue to avoid Blood and Tumult." It was necessary to *"give the other Provinces opportunity to think and resolve,"* or Massachuetts would be left to perish alone, and the American cause with her. When it became established that the Continental Congress

16. Jeremiah: Gov. Lord William Campbell to Lord Dartmouth, Charleston, August 31, 1775, PRO, CO 5/396, ff. 225–9, and see also Henry to John Laurens, August 21, 1775, "The Papers of Henry Laurens in the Collections of the South Carolina Historical Society," microfilm by the South Carolina Department of Archives, Columbia, "Letterbook," Roll 5. Simmons: Gilmor Papers, Ms. 387.1, nos. 4, 5, MdHS.

17. See, for example, Charles Thomson to Samuel Adams and John Hancock, Philadelphia, December 19, 1773, in calendar of the Samuel Adams Papers, NYPL; Thomson to William Palfrey, May 10, 1774, Palfrey Family Papers, Pt. II, a, no. 189, HUL; John Dickinson to Thomas Cushing, Fairhill, December 11, 1774, PRO, CO 5/118, ff. 97–8.

would support Boston, still John Adams urged from Philadelphia that "blows may be spared, if possible, and all Ruptures with the Troops avoided."[18] Constantly, contemporary accounts indicate, the "warmest Patriots" fought to maintain the peace despite minor provocations and major incidents— during the "false alarm" of September 2, 1774, for example, when rumors that the British were cannonading Boston caused a general mobilization; or throughout the mass coercions of mandamus councillors who had been appointed to the New Provincial Council under the Massachusetts Government Act of 1774. "You are placed by Providence in the post of honor because it is the post of danger," Massachusetts people were told; "and, while struggling for the noblest objects,—the liberties of your country, the happiness of posterity, and the rights of human nature,—the eyes, not only of North America and the whole British Empire, but of all Europe, are upon you." How necessary, then, "that no disorderly behavior, nothing unbecoming our characters as Americans, as citizens, as Christians, be justly chargeable to us."[19]

18. Quincy to Dickinson, Boston, August 20, 1774, and to Samuel Adams, Boston, August 20, 1774, in Josiah Quincy, *Memoir of the Life of Josiah Quincy, Junior, of Massachusetts* (Boston, 1825), 170–4; Samuel Adams to Joseph Warren, Philadelphia, May 21, 1774, *The Warren–Adams Letters*, I (Boston, 1917), 26; John Adams to Richard Cranch, September 18, 1774, in the Josiah Quincy, Jr., Papers, f. 64, MHS.

19. On the role of the revolutionary leaders in keeping the peace, see letters from James Lovell, Boston, to Josiah Quincy, Jr., in London, Josiah Quincy, Jr., Papers, especially that of October 10–28, 1774, f. 66, and November 3, 1774, f. 69. Lovell indicated that the Boston leaders took over from the selectmen the task of maintaining order, and even conferred with General Thomas Gage "upon a Mode of keeping Peace and Quiet with eight Regiments and more scatter'd among us this Winter." On efforts to avoid a premature military confrontation in early September, 1774, see *Mass. Spy*, September 8, 1774, which tells how members of the Cambridge and Boston committees came quickly to Cambridge on hearing of the armed masses there, and how Thomas Young intervened to prevent a group of horsemen from pursuing Customs Commissioner Benjamin Hallowell into Boston. It is noteworthy that the "body" that secured the resignations of two mandamus councillors in Cambridge also unanimously passed a resolution signifying their "abhorrence of mobs, riots, and the de-

This continued concern for restraint and order within the revolutionary movement explains in part the breadth of its internal support. Modern studies indicate that at most 20 per cent, and perhaps much less, of the white population retained its loyalty to Britain.[20] The creed of ordered resistance, gradually transformed into ordered revolution, also accounts for attitudes toward the American military effort after April 19, 1775. The American army should act with dignity and restraint: one Connecticut company of soldiers adopted, for example, a carefully framed agreement "for preventing disorders, irregularities, and misunderstandings" in the course of its march to Cambridge and subsequent military service. Others developed more fully notions of enlightened war. Treat your prisoners with humanity, the Americans were advised, and make no hasty reprisals for the enemy's transgressions: "a generous reluctance in the exercise even of necessary severities will give a Solid reputation and dignity of character to your Arms and Actions that will well become the cause in which you are contending, and make you respectable in the eyes of Europe."[21]

But in Massachusetts, it seems, where hostility had been so long confined, old constraints were temporarily abandoned in the sudden release of wartime enthusiasm, until "the least hint from the most unprincipled fellow" became "quite sufficient to expose the fairest character to insult and abuse."

----

struction of private property." Even Lieutenant Governor Thomas Oliver reported that the crowd gathered on the morning of September 2 was "not a mad mob, but the freeholders of the county." As the day wore on he discovered that the mass became less manageable, and he witnessed the leaders' increasing difficulty in avoiding violence. See Force, *American Archives*, 4th Ser., I, 762–6, and Joseph Warren to Samuel Adams, September 4, 1774, in Richard Frothingham, *Life and Times of Joseph Warren* (Boston, 1865), 355–7, and 397 for Massachusetts Provincial Congress's Address to inhabitants, December 1774.

20. Paul Smith, "The American Loyalists: Notes on Their Organization and Numerical Strength," *W. M. Q.*, XXV (1968), 269; Wallace Brown, *The King's Friends: The Composition and Motives of the American Loyalist Claimants* (Providence, 1965), 250.

21. Agreement of Benedict Arnold's company at New Haven, April 24, 1775, *New London Gaz.*, June 16, 1775; [Arthur Lee?] to America, September 2, 1775, PRO, CO 5/40, f. 17–20.

For Joseph Warren, the need to repress such incidents, particularly at the hands of soldiers, indicated the necessity of transforming makeshift committees and congresses into established civil governments.[22] That step was finally ordered by the Continental Congress on May 10, 1776. It represented a logical conclusion to the long-term, gradual, but unforeseen shift of power from British to American institutions, and an eloquent testimonial of the revolutionaries' commitment to liberty and law.

[II]

By 1776 it had become clear not only that the Americans must found their own, independent governments, but also that those new governments would be distinctly different from that of Great Britain. America would be, in short, a republic. The very word inspired confusion, such that John Adams, perhaps the country's most learned student of politics, complained that he "never understood" what a republican government was and believed "no other man ever did or ever will." Compounded from the Latin *res publica*, "republic" meant "the *public good*, or the good of the whole," as Thomas Paine explained, "in contradistinction to the despotic form, which makes the good of the sovereign, or of one man, the only object of the government." Technically, then, even England's eighteenth-century constitution could have qualified as "republican"—had it worked in fact as it did in theory, restraining the power of King, nobles, and people, so that the public welfare triumphed over particular interests.[23]

But for Americans and Englishmen of the eighteenth century republicanism was also associated with the Common-

22. Warren to Samuel Adams, Cambridge, May 26, 1775, in Frothingham, *Joseph Warren*, 495–6.

23. Adams to Mercy Warren, Quincy, July 20, 1807, MHS *Colls.*, 5th Ser., IV (Boston, 1878), 353, and Bernard Bailyn, *The Ideological Origins of the American Revolution* (Cambridge, 1967), p. 282–3, *n*. 50. Paine quoted in Gordon Wood, *The Creation of the American Republic, 1776–1787* (Chapel Hill, 1969), 55–6.

wealth period of British history, when for a brief time England was ruled without King or lords; and indeed, "commonwealth" is the closest English equivalent to "republic." "Republic," then, had concrete institutional implications: it suggested a state in which all power flowed from the people, none from inherited title. In this sense, England was hardly republican, as Christopher Gadsden understood in 1763 when he insisted that the colonists were "no friends to republicanism," but loyal subjects of the King and the "most ardent lovers of that noble constitution of our mother country."[24] The Americans' later conversion to republicanism represented, then, more than a reaffirmation of traditional conceptions of the corporate free state, in which all private interests must be sacrificed for the common good. It meant that the people alone would allocate power. It meant that the United States would have neither legally established nobility nor King.

Revolution did not necessarily imply republicanism. England's Glorious Revolution of 1688 had turned out one monarch only to establish another. Nor did independence imply republicanism. As recently as 1766, when the Portsmouth, New Hampshire, Sons of Liberty mentioned independence (so as to express their "darkest Gloom and horror" at the prospect), that contingency implied for them "erecting an independent Monarchy here in America."[25] A decade later, however, revolution, independence, and republicanism were intimately interwoven causes, and indeed they had developed together. Disillusionment with monarchy was the major component of the new republicanism, and evidence of anti-monarchic sentiment began to emerge in the early 1770's, as attitudes toward George III began to change, until gradually all hereditary rule was rejected by the same arguments used against kingship. By the time Thomas Paine took up the cause of republicanism in *Common Sense*, there was little to be said on the subject that had not already been argued in the previous half decade. Both Englishmen and Americans

24. Wood, *Creation of the American Republic*, 56; Gadsden's "To the Gentlemen Electors of the Parish of St. Paul, Stono," February 5, 1763, in Richard Walsh, ed., *The Writings of Christopher Gadsden, 1746–1805* (Columbia, 1966), 48.

25. To Providence Sons of Liberty, April 10, 1766, Belknap Papers, 61.c.122, MHS.

participated in this reappraisal of British government. But since revolution developed only in the colonies, republican theories could be applied only in America.

Attitudes toward British institutions and the quality of British rule were logically and necessarily connected. Institutions were always judged by their performance; there was little place in radical eighteenth-century thought for any intrinsic reverential quality in government. As John Trenchard said in 1739, a government was "a mere Piece of Clockwork," with "Springs and Wheels" that had to be so arranged that the mechanism would "move to the publick Advantage." For a time, England's mixed constitution seemed to obviate the need for any further institutional experimentation. But when liberty appeared to be as vulnerable in British as in French or Spanish territory, this enthusiasm naturally disappeared. "My Ideas of the Eng[lish] Constitution have much diminished," Ezra Stiles wrote Catharine Macaulay in December 1773. As a model of mechanical expertise the value of the English constitution was gone: it seemed instead "to have become . . . a kind of fortuitous consolida[tion] of Powers now in Opposition to the true Interest of the people." So fundamental was the disorder that efforts to "patch up" or restore this "broken Constitution" seemed "almost as discouraging . . . as to essay the Recovery of an hydrop[si]cal Subject which with many Excellencies in it carries about it the seeds of inevitable Death." Even earlier praise was rescinded. Suddenly, it seemed that "England had been struggling under Diseases for ages. It has at Times and in some parts received a temporary Cure—but the Disorder is so radically seated as will at last baffle every political physician."[26]

England's failure meant that enlightened legislators had to return to the task of rearranging, even manufacturing anew the wheels and springs of government. Discussion of governmental forms first arose, in fact, with Corsica in mind. Pascal Paoli wanted to find the perfect constitution, and asked Jean-Jacques Rousseau to design one for him. Cath-

26. John Trenchard, *An History of Standing Armies in England* (London, 1739), 1; Stiles to Catharine Macaulay, December 6, 1773, Ezra Stiles Papers, Beinecke Library, Yale University, New Haven, Connecticut.

arine Macaulay interested herself in the problem and published
her own scheme, then added in a second edition (1769) a
letter of criticism from an unnamed American gentleman.[27]
But after Corsica's fall, the constitutionalists' efforts finally
centered on America, which because of England's degenera-
tion most urgently needed new institutions. America's government would have to be a "new phenomenon"; she would
have to "originate new Constitutions" should she fail, as
she must, to find successful remedies for the "Amend[men]t
and Melioration of old, injudiciously formed and decayed
Governments" like Britain's. Stiles hoped that the Americans
and the "Men of Genius and penetrat[in]g Observation" who
advised them would "take a large and comprehensive View
of the polities of the States and Countries around the Globe,"
and not only of Greece, Rome, and England. They should
avail themselves "of the Lights of Orientals and Asiatics, of
the World itself both in ancient and modern Ages."[28]

Inevitably, however, Americans would dwell most on the
familiar English constitution, seeking to retain its remaining
"excellencies" and eliminate its "hydropsical" elements. As
the colonies seemed "striding fast to independence" in April
1774, North Carolina's William Hooper predicted they would
soon adopt Britain's constitution, "purged of its impurities,
and from an experience of its defects guard against those
evils which have wasted its vigor and brought it to an un-
timely end." And in England a year later Brand Hollis, too,
hoped that the Americans, "knowing the errors of England,"
would avoid them, "fix their Liberties on a solid basis and
. . . show to the world a perfect form of Government where
Liberty and Justice shall act in Union."[29]

27. [François Pierre Guillaume] Guizot's *History of France . . . to
1848*, quoted in George P. Anderson, "Pascal Paoli, An Inspiration to
the Sons of Liberty," CSM *Pubs.*, XXVI (*Trans.*, 1924–6), 184;
Catharine Macaulay, *Loose Remarks on Certain Propositions to be
Found in Mr. Hobbes's Philosophical Rudiments of Government and
Society with a Short Sketch of a Democratical Form of Government in
a Letter to Signior Paoli . . . With Two Letters, one from an American
Gentleman . . .* (2nd edn., London, 1769).

28. Stiles to Mrs. Macaulay, December 6, 1773, Stiles Papers.

29. Hooper to James Iredell, April 26, 1774, *N.C. Col. Recs.*, IX,
985; Hollis to Josiah Quincy, Jr., March 2, 1775, Josiah Quincy, Jr.,

By then it was clear to many colonists that the major "error" of England's regime was its retention of monarchy, and of hereditary rule in general. The re-evaluation of monarchy began in earnest soon after George III spurned the London remonstrances and thereby became implicated in the "ministers'" plot. In September 1770, the Massachusetts Assembly heard a sermon on the ninth chapter of Nehemiah:

> Behold, we are Servants this day, and for the Land that thou gavest unto our fathers, to eat the fruit thereof, and the good thereof, behold we are Servants in it. And it yieldeth much increase unto the Kings *whom thou hast set over us because of our Sins*: also they have dominion over our bodies, and over our Cattle at their pleasure and we are in great distress.

The text, William Palfrey told John Wilkes, was "a Sermon in itself."[30] Thereafter, American writers continued to elaborate the argument that kings represented blights, not blessings. Two years before the outbreak of war, readers of the *Massachusetts Spy* were told by "A REPUBLICAN" that "Kings have been a curse to this and every other country where they have gained a footing"; of all men "Kings . . . are the least to be trusted." Unless "under such an *excellent* King as the   *present*," he suggested with sarcasm, "every man of sense and independency" would prefer a "well constructed REPUBLIC" to a monarchy. A speaker at the 1775 commencement in Princeton, New Jersey, made the same point by citing all the reigning monarchies—Sweden, Turkey, Russia, Prussia, France, Spain, and Portugal; even England, it seemed, had become "the land of slavery—the school of paricides and the nurse of tyrants." Indeed, the orator concluded, "the history of Kings and Emperors is little more

---

Papers, f. 97. Hooper, however, emphasized the extent of Britain's "dominion" rather than monarchy as the cause of her downfall.

30. Palfrey to Wilkes, Boston, October 23–30, 1770, CSM *Pubs.*, XXIV (*Trans.*, 1937–42), 421. Italics in the original.

than the history of royal villany. The supreme governor of the universe seems to have set up arbitrary Princes on purpose to shew us the concentrated depravity of the human heart."[31]

The combination of human nature and the "trappings of monarchy," in Milton's phrase, seemed peculiarly suited to produce tyranny. "Kings are but men . . . subject to all the passions of human nature," an article in a 1774 *New London Gazette* pointed out; thus they were "too prompt to grasp at arbitrary power, and to wish to make all things bend and submit to their will and pleasure." Their lofty situation fed this lust, as "Monitor" explained in the January 25, 1776, *New York Journal.* "Their being educated in a taste for luxury, magnificence and pleasure, and surrounded with a great tribe of favourites, flatterers, and sycophants, powerfully inclines them to rapaciousness."[32]

To some degree the same circumstances surrounded all hereditary officers, making them, for Arthur Lee among others, "an absurdity" for guaranteeing "that a vitious or immeritorious Son . . . enjoy that distinction and those privileges . . . given to the virtue and merit of his Father," which was "at once preposterous and pernicious." "The experience of all times and states has proved," he argued in 1775, that the nobility or patricians held ideas "dangerous to the Community," that they "always view the rights of the People with a malignant eye, and employ their power and influence to subvert them." And since kings were particularly pampered, "open to all the temptations the most formidable to frail humanity," it was "reasonable to expect that they would be oftener vicious than virtuous"—an outcome that "Monitor" claimed was "verified by the general experience of nations." So avid became their thirst for power, an earlier writer noted, that kings were "scarcely ever to be tamed; and

31. *Mass. Spy,* April 8, 1773; speech of September 27 in *New London Gaz.,* December 22, 1775, and see also Richard Parker to Richard Henry Lee, April 27, 1776, Lee Family Papers, UVa, available in Paul P. Hoffman, ed., "Lee Family Papers, 1742–1795," University of Virginia microfilm (Charlottesville, 1966), Roll II.

32. Article from the London *Public Ledger* in *New London Gaz.,* October 7, 1774.

the only sure method of preventing their doing mischief is, to muzzle them or draw their talons."[33]

Monarchy, in short, was a poor risk. "A good King is a miracle," a writer in the *Pennsylvania Packet* concluded in late 1774; and at the 1775 commencement in Princeton, it was said that only God could be entrusted with kingly power, for "it requires the wisdom, the goodness, and all the other attributes of a Deity to support it." Certainly, public advantages had been won from kings, even aside from the "vast increase of debt and taxes" that the "REPUBLICAN" of 1773 had called the only gift of monarchy. But these "signal benefits" were inadvertent, even "contrary to [the kings'] own intention": [34]

> To John's oppressions, and Henry the Third's weakness, we owe the two great charters. To Henry the Eighth we are indebted for our freedom from the power of the Court of Rome, and the Pope's supremacy. To James and Charles the First we are beholden for the petition of right; And lastly to James the Second's bigotry we must place the settlement of the revolution.

As of 1765, England's post-revolutionary kings, especially the Hanoverians, seemed to offer an exception to the dismal history of royalty; but ten years later it was said that William III could be "censured with as little ceremony as James the First, and his three immediate successors were all of them enemies of the people of England." Even the limited power granted the monarchs after 1688 had proved too much, and they, too, fitted the pattern of English dynastic pretensions as outlined by a writer in 1774. It was rare to find an instance where the Crown descended in a regular manner

33. Arthur Lee to Samuel Adams, December 10, 1775, Samuel Adams Papers; "Monitor," *N.Y. Jour.*, January 25, 1776; "A Republican," *Mass. Spy*, April 8, 1773.

34. Article from *Pennsylvania Packet* reprinted in *Prov. Gaz.*, December 17, 1774; Princeton oration in *New London Gaz.*, December 22, 1775; "A Republican," *Mass. Spy*, April 8, 1773; article from *St. James Chronicle* in *Boston Gaz.*, September 18, 1775.

for more than three generations, he claimed, probably because a dynasty that held the Crown over three successions
"increased their power to such a great degree as to be obnoxious to the people, and dangerous to their constitution,
rights, and liberties." No longer did it seem fitting to cite
the Glorious Revolution as the source of the Hanoverian
kings; instead, their common ancestry with the Stuarts was
stressed, and ultimately their descent from William the Con-
queror, who was, as an article of 1774 said, "a SON OF A
WHORE." "A French bastard landing with an armed banditti,
and establishing himself king of England against the consent
of the natives," Thomas Paine later observed, "is in plain
terms a very paltry rascally original." The nefarious tendency
of monarchy thus became universal through history; there
were no more exceptions.[35]

The whole discussion suggested what Paine made explicit: that it was "the republican and not the monarchical
part of the constitution of England which Englishmen glory
in, viz. the liberty of choosing an house of commons from
out of their own body." The constitution of England was
"sickly" only "because monarchy hath poisoned the republic,
the crown hath engrossed the commons."[36] For the Americans
who were suffering its effects, this illness was above all to
be avoided in the future. Joseph Warren wrote Samuel
Adams in May 1775 that he hoped never again to have to
enter a political war, and for that very end wished all the
"seeds of despotism" uprooted from American institutions. In
particular, he asked that "the only road to promotion may

35. *Boston Gaz.*, September 18, 1775; article from London *Public
Ledger* in *New London Gaz.*, October 7, 1774, and London *Chronicle*
in *Pa. Jour.*, April 13, 1774; Thomas Paine, *Common Sense and the
Crisis* (New York, n. d.), 24.
36. *Ibid.*, 26. See, too, the English radical tract "The Crisis," especially no. III, in *Prov. Gaz.*, July, 1775, which warned that "whenever the state is convulsed by civil commotions, and the constitution
totters to the centre, the throne of England must shake with it." Its
author looked forward to an upheaval in which "at ONE STROKE *all
the gaudy trappings of royalty may be laid in the dust,*" when "all
distinctions must cease; the common safety and the rights of mankind
will be the only objects in view; while the King and the peasant must
share one and the same fate, and perhaps fall undistinguished together."

be through the affection of the people." For the various states that set about "new modelling" their government the most pressing need, it seemed, was the freeing of their institutions from "that worst of plagues, the KING'S EVIL; which disorder," a writer in the *New London Gazette* prayed, " . . . will soon be [extir]pated from this otherwise happy land, and nevermore be suffered to infect it again."[37]

Beyond this republican conviction, constitutional ideas might differ. It was in opening up new areas of discussion that Paine made his main contribution: *Common Sense* prodded debate from the then-exhausted themes of Britain, her King, and institutions, toward a new controversy over the internal structure of republican government. In this debate, which was more concerned with "who should rule at home" than was the previous revolutionary struggle, the old colonial radicals apparently had little to say in common. The resistance movement was logically complete with independence. For some, in fact, its work was done once war became inevitable,[38] and by 1775 the sons of liberty began to go their separate ways. Many went into the army—Israel Putnam, for example, John Lamb, or William Palfrey, who sought a commission immediately after his return from England in the late spring of 1775. Others became absorbed in civilian offices, either in the Continental Congress or in their states; while some, like Paul Revere, lost their former importance and felt swept aside by the history they had helped create.[39] Even those who contributed their efforts to drafting the new constitutions diverged in outlook. The most marked contrast was perhaps between John Adams and Thomas Young, one of whom championed Massachusetts's

37. Warren to Adams, Cambridge, May 14, 1775, in Frothingham, *Joseph Warren*, 483; *New London Gaz.*, June 7, 1776.

38. See, for example, Thomas Young's letter of September 27 in *Mass. Spy*, October 6, 1774, explaining his recent departure from Boston: "I considered that I had faithfully done my part in possessing my countrymen with a sense of their natural and charter rights; and that my services in that way could be of little more importance to them, the time being now come when arms seem the proper arguments to hold up to our opponents."

39. Revere's complaints in a letter to John Lamb, Boston, April 5, 1777, in Goss, *Life of Paul Revere*, I, 280–1.

"conservative" state constitution, the other the "radical" constitution of Pennsylvania.

Problems remained to be solved. The meaning as well as forms of American republicanism had to be worked out more fully. The colonists' traditional emphasis upon communal rights had to be reconciled with an emergent concern for individual rights. And indeed, republicanism had yet to be durably established: on into the nineteenth century Americans were haunted by fears that their experiment would fail.[40] By the time the old radical coteries broke up, however, the outline of the new nation was clear. America would be independent of Britain; and her only king, as Paine put it, would be the law. No human monarchy would be installed, for kingship was incompatible with government by law, itself the basis of all political liberty. Americans became republicans not automatically and thoughtlessly, nor for lack of an alternative. They were republicans by conviction and by choice.

40. For the continuing story, see particularly Wood, *Creation of the American Republic*; Bailyn, *Ideological Origins of the American Revolution*, and Roger H. Brown, *The Republic in Peril: 1812* (New York, 1964).

APPENDIX

———————◦∞◦———————

THE SONS OF
LIBERTY OF
1765–1766

THE AMOUNT OF INFORMATION available on the Sons of
Liberty of 1765–6 varies substantially from colony to colony.
As a whole, and without intensive analysis, it makes clear
that the Sons of Liberty were respectable members of their
communities and included professional men, merchants, even
local officials—as Edmund and Helen Morgan have already
concluded.[1] Within that category there were, however, local
variations worth recounting in some detail. What follows, then,
is a summary of information now available on persons who
were members of the Sons of Liberty in the various towns
and provinces that became the United States.

The most complete single list of the American Sons of
Liberty is printed in Isaac Q. Leake's *Memoir of the Life
and Times of General John Lamb* (Albany, 1857), pages 3
and 4. Leake's catalogue is incomplete because it includes only
names that appeared in the correspondence of the New York
Sons of Liberty, to which he had access. On the other hand,
Leake includes men whose connection with the Sons of Liberty cannot be documented today since their names do not
appear in the surviving papers of John Lamb at the New-

1. *The Stamp Act Crisis: Prologue to Revolution* (New York,
1963), 231–40. The Morgans did not, however, confine their attention
to those whose involvement in the organized Sons of Liberty can be
documented, but instead studied the Stamp Act opposition more generally.

York Historical Society, which include the bulk of documents Leake cited or reprinted.

A detailed study of the Charleston, South Carolina, Sons of Liberty has been made by Richard Walsh for his *Charleston's Sons of Liberty: A Study of the Artisans* (Columbia, 1959). Walsh shows that the Charleston Sons of Liberty were drawn from the same mechanic population as were Christopher Gadsden's Artillery Company, the Fellowship Society, and the Charleston Fire Society, through which the Sons worked. Since Charleston was not formally included in the intercolonial correspondence network, the Charleston Sons of Liberty apparently had no correspondence committee. Several men associated with the Sons in Charleston can, however, be identified from lists of those who met with Gadsden, a merchant who served as an advisor to the group, at the local Liberty Tree in the fall of 1766. Two such lists are available. One, in Joseph Johnson's *Traditions and Reminiscences chiefly of the American Revolution in the South* (Charleston, 1851), page 28, was supposedly found among the papers of Judge William Johnson and had been written from memory about 1820 by George Flagg, the only surviving member of the group. The other, in R. W. Gibbes, *Documentary History of the American Revolution . . . 1764–1776* (New York, 1855), pages 10 and 11, is said to be from Gadsden's papers, and also to have been signed by Flagg. Of the men included, Johnson says, "All that are known were . . . reputably engaged in their maintenance—all in easy circumstances, none rich. At least half of them were master mechanics, the very bone and muscle of a thriving community." Walsh also testifies to their economic respectability.[2]

Like South Carolina, Virginia and North Carolina were not integrated into the Sons of Liberty correspondence union, although Norfolk, Virginia, might well have been had repeal been delayed. The Sons there resolved on March 31, 1766, that "a committee be appointed" to correspond with "the associated Sons and Friends of Liberty in the other British

2. Johnson, *Traditions*, 29; Walsh, *Charleston's Sons of Liberty*, 15–25, 29–33. The Gibbes and Johnson lists are almost identical except for spelling and, in some cases, the professions attributed to individuals. The Gibbes list includes professions, whereas Johnson

colonies in America." A letter from one Jer. Morgan to Governor Francis Fauquier, April 5, 1766, identified the committee chosen at that March 31 Norfolk meeting: the president, he says, was "Mr. Davis Parson of the Parish, Secretary Paul Loyel," and the other members included "Mr. Bush, Clerk of the County, Mr. Holt, Lawyer, Mr.

---

gives several brief biographies (28–34). The following list is from Gibbes, with Johnson's variations in parentheses.

1. Christopher Gadsden, merchant.
2. William Johnson, blacksmith. (He carried on "an intensive business" in partnership with Tunis Tebout; an active patriot on into the Revolutionary War.)
3. Joseph Veree, carpenter. (Later served in the first South Carolina Provincial Congress, 1775.)
4. John Fullerton, carpenter.
5. James Brown, carpenter. (A "retail merchant in Church street.")
6. Nath[anie]l Libby, ship carpenter. (Johnson spells his name "Lebby" and says he was a "boat-builder, a zealous patriot of great respectability.")
7. George Flagg, painter and glazier. (A native of Boston, and the closest friend of William Johnson.)
8. Tho[ma]s Coleman, upholsterer.
9. John Hall, coachmaker. (He was "engaged in mercantile pursuits"; all of his family were "firm patriots"; born in Bristol, England.)
10. W[illia]m Field, carver.
11. Robert Jones, sadler.
12. John Loughton, coachmaker. (Johnson lists a "John Lawton" who was a planter of English birth. He also lists a William Laughton as a partner with Uzziah Rogers and Benjamin Hawes in an "extensive business as coach and chair makers.")
13. "W." Rogers, wheelwright. (Johnson lists him as "UZ."—Uzziah —Rogers, and says he was a partner in a chair and coach-making establishment along with William Laughton and Benjamin Hawes.)
14. John Calvert, "Clerk in some office." (Johnson says he was "a very respectable man, a commission merchant and book-keeper.")
15. H[enry] Y. Bookless, wheelwright. (Stayed in Charleston during the British occupation and signed a complimentary address to Sir Henry Clinton.)
16. J. Barlow, sadler.
17. Tunis Teabout, blacksmith. (Johnson spells his name "Tebout"; a partner of William Johnson.)
18. Peter Munclean, clerk. (Johnson spells his name "Munclear.")
19. W[illia]m Trusler, butcher.
20. Robert Howard, carpenter. (Johnson says he was "a factor, a very respectable man.")

Anthony Lawson Do. ["ditto," i.e., lawyer], and Mr. Parker Merchant in Norfolk." The *Virginia Gazette* (Rind) of May 16, 1766, referred to those colonists who organized at Leedstown, Virginia, the previous February as "gentlemen"; and indeed, the 125 signatories to the Westmoreland County Association of February 27, 1766, who constituted for all practical purposes the local Sons of Liberty, included prominent members of Virginia's leading families grouped under the leadership of Richard Henry Lee.[3] The North Carolina uprising of February 1766 that formed an association much

---

21. Alexander Alexander, schoolmaster. (From Mecklenburg, N.C., and "educated in the whig principles of that distinguished district, at their academy in Charlotte.")

22. Ed[ward] Weyman, clerk of St. Philip's Church, and glass grinder. (Johnson says he was an upholsterer.)

23. Tho[ma]s Swarle, painter.

24. W[illia]m Laughton, tailor. (See above, no. 12.)

25. Daniel Cannon, carpenter. (Johnson says, though a "house-carpenter," Cannon was "the oldest and most influential mechanic in Charleston, and subsequently called Daddy Cannon. He owned all Cannonsborough.")

26. Benjamin Hawes, painter. (A partner in coach and chair business with William Laughton and Uzziah Rogers.)

3. Sons' Resolves in *Va. Gaz.* (Purdie and Dixon), April 4, 1766; Morgan letter in PRO, CO 5/1331, f. 78. The signers of the Westmoreland Association of February 27, 1766, are printed in Richard B. Harwell, ed., *The Committees of Safety of Westmoreland and Fincastle* (Richmond, 1956), 101–2: Richard Henry Lee, Will[iam] Robinson, Lewis Willis, Thos Lud[well] Lee, Samuel Washington, Charles Washington, William Sydnor, John Monroe, William Cocke, Will[ia]m Grayson, W[illia]m Brockenbrough, Moore Fauntleroy, Francis Lightfoot Lee, Thomas Jones, Rodham Kenner, Spencer Mottram Ball, Richard Mitchell, Joseph Murdock, Rich[ar]d Parker, Spence Monroe, John Watts, Rob[er]t Lovell, John Blagge, Charles Weeks, William Booth, Geo[rge] Turberville, Alvin Moxley, W[illia]m Flood, John Ballantine Jr., William Lee, Thomas Chilton, Richard Buckner, Will Chilton, Joseph Peirce, John Williams, Jno. Blackwell, Winder S. Kenner, W[illia]m Bronaugh, Will[iam] Peirce, John Berryman, Jno. Dickson, John Browne, Edward Sanford, Charles Chilton, Laur[ence] Washington, Sam[ue]ll Selden, Daniel McCarty, Jer. Rush, Edw[ar]d Ransdell, Townshend Dade, Laur[ence] Washington (*sic*), John Ashton, W[illia]m Brent, Francis Foushee, John Smith Jr., Will Balle, Thomas Barnes, Jos[eph] Blackwell, Reuben Meriwether, Edw[ard] Mountjoy, William J. Mountjoy, Thomas Mountjoy, John Mountjoy, Gilb[er]t Campbell, Jos[eph] Lane, Richard

like that in Westmoreland County, Virginia, similarly included persons of consequence, according to the royal governor: the "Mayor and Corporation of Wilmington and most all the gentlemen and planters of the counties of Brunswick, New-hanover, Duplin, and Bladen with some masters of vessels." Cornelius Harnett, an assemblyman and merchant who was perhaps the wealthiest local freeholder, apparently served as chairman.[4]

A handbill of the Maryland Sons of Liberty's proceedings of March 1, 1766, included a list of men who attended from Anne Arundel and Baltimore counties, and also some of the Sons of Liberty in Kent County. It named two lawyers who later signed the Declaration of Independence: William Paca (descendant of a wealthy planter; Philadelphia College, class of 1759; then student of law at the Middle Temple, London), and Samuel Chase (son of an Episcopal clergyman who studied law at Annapolis, and had been sent to the provincial assembly in 1763 at the age of twenty-two). Charles Carroll of Carrollton indicated that Baltimore gentlemen readily entered the Sons of Liberty's association in March 1766, but the subscribers at Annapolis were "men of little note." That town's gentlemen expected news of the Stamp Act's repeal to arrive imminently, and argued that "it was time to act desperately, when our affairs were desperate."[5] The New Jersey Sons were every bit as obscure

Lee, Daniel Tebbs, Fran[ci]s Thornton Jr., Peter Rust, John Lee Jr., Fran[ci]s Waring, John Upshaw, Meriwether Smith, Thomas Roane, James Edmondson, James Webb Jr., John Edmondson, James Banks, Smith Young, W. Roane, Rich[ard] Hodges, James Upshaw, James Booker, A. Montague, Richard Jeffries, John Suggitt, Jno. S. Woodcock, Robert Wormeley Carter, John Beale Jr., John Newton, Will[iam] [Bea]le Jr., Ch[arle]s Mortimer, John Edmondson Jr., Charles Beale, Peter Grant, Thomson Mason, Jona. Beckwith, James Sanford, John Belfield, F. W. Smith, John Augt. Washington, Thomas Belfield, Edgcomb Suggitt, Henry Francks, John Bland Jr., Ja[me]s Emerson, John Richards, Tho[ma]s Jett, Thomas Douglas, Max Robinson, John Orr, Thomas Logan, Jos[eph] Milliken, Ebenezor Fisher, Hancock Eustace.

4. *N.C. Col. Recs.*, VII, 174; R. D. W. Connor, *Cornelius Harnett; An Essay in North Carolina History* (Raleigh, 1909), 46–7.

5. Paca and Chase: B. J. Lossing, *Biographical Sketches of the Signers of the Declaration of American Independence* (New York, 1948), 146–50, 154–6, and Robert E. Casey, *The Declaration of In-*

as those in Annapolis. The names of several can be gleaned from their correspondence in the Lamb Papers. Leake lists these with the exception of Gershom Mott, who seems sometimes to have worked in close collaboration with the Sons in New York, and a Mr. Phillips, who signed a letter from Trenton on February 28, 1766.[6]

In Pennsylvania, only William Bradford, the printer of the *Pennsylvania Journal* and proprietor of Philadelphia's major coffeehouse, can be clearly identified as a Son of Liberty from the surviving correspondence in the Lamb Papers. An old but useful biography of Bradford indicates that the merchant and future revolutionary financier Robert Morris may also have been connected with the Sons. Leake included Isaac Howell with Bradford as members of the Philadelphia committee.[7]

The New York Sons of Liberty have been studied more than any other group—by Henry B. Dawson in *The Sons of Liberty in New York* (Poughkeepsie, 1859); Carl Becker in *The History of Political Parties in the Province of New York, 1760–1776* (Madison, 1909); Herbert Morais in "The Sons of Liberty in New York," in *The Era of the American Revolution*, edited by Richard B. Morris (New York, 1939), pages

---

dependence (New York, 1924), 62. The handbill of Maryland's proceedings of March 1, 1766, survives in the NYPL handbill collection, and the names are reproduced in Leake, *Life of John Lamb*, 3–4: Joseph Nicholson presented an address from Kent County signed by William Ringgold, William Stephenson, Thomas Ringgold Jr., and Joseph McHard, Gideon McCauley, Daniel Fox, Benj[amin] Binning, W[illia]m Bordley, Jarvis James, William Stukely, Joseph Nicholson Jr., James Porter, Thomas Ringgold, Ja[me]s Anderson, Tho[ma]s Smyth, W[illia]m Murray, Jos[eph] Nicholson, Geo[rge] Garnet, S. Boardley Jr., Peroy Frisby, Hen[ry] Vandike, and John Bolton. Anne Arundel County Committee: William Paca, Samuel Chase, Tho[ma]s B. Hands. Baltimore County Committee: John Hall, Robert Alexander, Corbin Lee, James Heath, John Moale, William Lux. Baltimore Town Committee: Thomas Chase, D. Chamier, Rob[er]t Adair, Patrick Allison, and W. Smith.

6. *Ibid.*, 4. The Committee of Upper Freehold: Daniel Hendrickson, Minister; Peter Imlay Jr., Joseph Holmes Jr., Peter Covenhoven Jr., and Elisha Lawrence Jr. Burlington: Richard Smith. New Brunswick: Henry Bickers.

7. *Ibid.*; John W. Wallace, *An Old Philadelphian, Colonial William Bradford, the Patriot Printer of 1776* (Philadelphia, 1884), 365–6.

269–89, and most recently by Roger Champagne in his un-published Wisconsin Ph.D. thesis of 1960, "The Sons of Liberty and the Aristocracy in New York Politics, 1765–1790." Morais gathered the names of people associated with the Sons and tried to discover their professions. He listed people connected with the Sons in various secondary accounts as well as documentary sources, and brought in men from Albany as well as New York City. He also seems to have included in his list men who became politically active only after the Stamp Act crisis. He was able to locate biographical material on eighteen out of a total of thirty-eight men. Eleven of the eighteen were merchants, four lawyers (here he included William Livingston and John Morin Scott, whose association with the Sons of Liberty of 1765–6 is doubtful), one a wealthy landlord and merchant, one a physician, and another a writer of popular ballads.

A more limited list, including only names that appeared on correspondence of the New York Sons and those of the men sent to New London to negotiate the military Sons of Liberty alliance in December 1765, contains ten names: Isaac Sears, John Lamb, Thomas Robinson, William Wiley, Gershom Mott, Joseph Allicocke, Hugh Hughes, Edward Laight, Flores Bancker, and Charles Nicoll. Hughes was a teacher; Sears, Lamb, Allicocke, Laight, Bancker, and Nicoll were merchants.[8]

The names of Albany's Sons of Liberty are perhaps the most accessible since ninety-four of them signed a "consti-tution" which, with ninety-two of the names, is printed in *The American Historian and Quarterly Genealogical Record* for April 1876.[9] A shorter list of the officers and committee

8. Biographies of several are available in John Austin Stevens, Jr., *Colonial New York. Sketches Biographical and Historical 1768–1784* (New York, 1867), 119, 160–1, 140–1, 153. On Laight, see also *N.Y. Gaz.*, May 7 and 28, 1767.

9. Edited by The Historical Society, Schenectady, New York, Vol. I, pp. 146–7: Tho[mas] Young, Peter Williams, Nanning Visscher, Abr. Ten Eyck, John Visscher, Jacob G. Lansingh, John Van Alen, John Ten Broeck, Henry J. Bogert, Nicholas Marselis, John De Garno, Henry B. Ten Eyck, Barent Ten Eyck, Comfort Sever, Jer. V. Rensselaer, Aril Lagrange, David Edgar, Matthew Watson, W[illia]m Bensone, Tho[mas] Stimtoy, Tho[mas] Lynott, David Smith, Har-

of the Albany Sons of Liberty chosen on March 3, 1766, was also printed. Beverly McAnear did not use these documents in his study of "The Albany Stamp Act Riots," but instead used Henry Van Schaack's list of those who were present at the earlier meetings of the Sons. There is, however, a considerable overlap in the lists as to individuals and even more so as to family names. McAnear's analysis of the membership indicated that the Sons were closely related to the legal government—either they themselves or other members of their families were in public office. Almost all were Dutch, indicating the Sons were led by "the older, conservative, property-holding, dominant social class in Albany." His list included only thirty-six people; of these, the ages of twenty could be identified. And of these, eighteen were twenty-one to thirty-five years of age, which led McAnear to conclude that the Sons in Albany were "a gathering of young men."[10]

The Connecticut Sons of Liberty were again, Oscar Zeichner concluded, men of standing. The names of those who were most active on the several Connecticut committees can be gathered, at least in part, from their correspondence in the Lamb Papers and from the names of persons appointed as a correspondence committee by the Sons' Hartford convention of March 25, 1766, which were published in the

---

manus Cuyler, Peter Hanson, Gysbert Fonda, Garret H. Roseboon, Peter Yates, Ph. Lansing, W. Marcius, Derik, Swart, Corneles V. Veghten, To. Young, John F. Pruyn, John Lansing, Richard Hilton, John Ransen, John T. Fisher, Abrah[a]m Eight, Jacob Evertsen, Barent Bogart, Peter Van Wie, William McIntosh, John Clint, Tho[mas] Lottridge, Jonathan Ruorrey, Abram Syle, Rob[er]t Henry, Jacob Cuyler, Cornelius Swits, B. Visscher, Bar. Roseboon, William Van Antwer, Abram Schuyler, Sanl Pruyn, Isaac Deforast, John Cluet Jr., William Van Corton, Henry Ten Eyck Jr., Gooje Van Schaick, Jacob Seigor, Barnardus halen Bake, John E. Bratte, Isaac Hogan, John T. Hansen, Clement Hallen Back, Willem Van Wie, John Scott, Jacob Roseboon, —————, Dan[ie]l Staly, Isaac Dean, Lucas Van Veghten, Cornl Wendell, Mynd. Roseboon, Dirk B. Van Schoonbovn, John Ganswoort, Barent Van Alen, Derik Roseboon, ——— Van ———, John Marselis, Jacob B. Bogart, Daniel Winne, William Thitto, Anthony S. Van Schaick, Gerrit Greverat, Peter W. Witbeck, Jacob Fralick, Joseph French, William Lottridge, Casparus Van Wie, John Gillman Jr., Jacob Hooghkirk, John Whiting, J. Roorback.

10. *W. M. Q.*, IV (1947), 486–98.

Connecticut Gazette (New Haven) on April 5, 1766. John Durkee of Norwich was perhaps the most prominent Connecticut Son of Liberty. He was the colony's corresponding secretary, the equivalent of John Lamb in New York. He had made his name in the Seven Years' War, rising to the rank of major. In peacetime, he operated a tavern at Norwich, and was well enough off to buy stock in the Susquehannah Company as early as 1761. He was in all likelihood the "commandant" of Connecticut's Stamp Act uprising of September 18, 1765. In 1769, he led a company of Susquehannah settlers into Pennsylvania territory, for which he was captured and jailed, and he went on to fight actively during the Revolutionary War.[11] Durkee's fellow townsman, Samuel Huntington, was also apparently connected with the Sons. He was from one of the colony's oldest families, although his father was a farmer of modest means. Huntington taught himself law and practiced in his native Windham, then, after 1760, in Norwich. He was elected to the general assembly in 1764, and to the council in 1765; he later became a signer of the Declaration of Independence, president of the Continental Congress, and governor of Connecticut. Windham's Hugh Ledlie, who operated a retail store, was on Connecticut's central correspondence committee.[12]

The redoubtable Israel Putnam of Pomfret was a leading Connecticut Son, who served on the correspondence committee appointed at the Hartford convention of March 1766. With Ledlie he also constituted the correspondence committee for Windham County. Putnam won renown in the Seven Years' War; in peacetime, he was a farmer and innkeeper, who held several local offices and often represented Pomfret in the general assembly. He supposedly organized the mass effort

11. Zeichner, *Connecticut's Years of Controversy* (Chapel Hill, 1949), 52; Amos A. Browning, "A Forgotten Son of Liberty," *Records and Papers of the New Haven County Historical Society* (New London), III (1912), Pt. 2, 257–9.

12. Huntington is mentioned in Sturges to New York Sons, March 25, 1766, Lamb Papers; and see Lossing, *Biographical Sketches*, 53–5. Ledlie: William D. Love, *The Colonial History of Hartford* (Hartford, 1914), 230, 316; he apparently later moved to Hartford. See John T. Farrell, ed., *The Superior Court Diary of William Samuel Johnson, 1772–1773*, in *American Legal Records*, IV (Washington, 1942), 160.

that won Ingersoll's resignation. Like Durkee, he was an explorer, and served on the field during the Revolutionary War.[13]

Besides Durkee, Ledlie, and Putnam, the Sons' convention at Hartford appointed five others to its correspondence committee: Jonathan Sturgis, Thaddeus Burr, Samuel Bradley, Jr., John Brooks, and Le Grand Cannon. Sturgis (or Sturges) was a graduate of Yale College, class of 1759, who was a lawyer in Fairfield when the Stamp Act agitation began. He later served in the general assembly, 1772–84, became a Fairfield judge of probate in 1775, and served as a Connecticut delegate to the Continental Congress 1785–7.[14] Burr, a Princeton graduate and landowner of moderate income, was born in 1735 into an old, politically prominent Fairfield family; he remained an active committeeman on into the Revolutionary War.[15] Little is known of Samuel Bradley, apparently also of Fairfield; John Brooks served on Stratford's committee for enforcing the Continental Association in 1774 and again, with Le Grand Cannon, on a Stratford committee to collect donations for Boston after the Port Bill was passed and, in December 1775, on the town's Committee of Observation. A local history identifies Cannon as "a merchant from New York City."[16]

Other persons have sometimes been associated with the Connecticut Sons. Isaac Leake lists a "Jo. Burrows," along with Durkee, Sturges, and Ledlie, as committeemen from that colony; and Zeichner says some of the most prominent persons in Connecticut, including ministers, merchants, and magistrates, supported the Sons. He lists Matthew Griswold and the Reverend Stephen Johnson of Lyme, Eliphalet Dyer

13. David Humphrey, *Essay on the Life of the Honorable Major-General Israel Putnam* (Boston, 1818), and William Farrand Livingston, *Israel Putnam: Pioneer, Ranger, and Major General* (New York, 1901).

14. Franklin B. Dexter, *Biographical Sketches of the Graduates of Yale College*, II (New York, 1886), 614–15.

15. Elizabeth H. Schenck, *The History of Fairfield, Fairfield County, Connecticut* (New York, 1905), II, *passim* on the Burr family; Jules David Prown, *John Singleton Copley* (Cambridge, Mass., 1966): I, *In America, 1738–1774*, 104.

16. Samuel Orcott, *A History of the Old Town of Stratford* (Fairfield, 1886), I, 372, 373, 382, 386, 426.

of Windham, and Jonathan Trumbull and William Williams of Lebanon among these. Trumbull (Harvard, 1927), an important but periodically bankrupt merchant, was said to head Lebanon's Sons of Liberty. He was later governor of Connecticut during the Revolutionary War.[17]

The Loyal Nine—a social club that served as the organized nucleus of Boston's Sons of Liberty—were conveniently identified by name and occupation in the diary of John Adams, who visited them in January 1766. Present were "John Avery Distiller or Merchant, . . . John Smith the Brazier, Thomas Crafts the Painter, [Benjamin] Edes the Printer, Stephen Cleverly the Brazier, [Thomas] Chase the Distiller, Joseph Field Master of a Vessell, Henry Bass [merchant]," and "George Trott Jeweller." It has been conjectured that Field's presence, like Adams's, was that of a guest, and that Henry Welles was the ninth member. When the historian William Gordon made up his list of those who prepared Boston's August 14 effigies, he gathered eight names, including Welles's, but excluding both Field and Trott. A letter from Thomas Crafts, Jr., to John Adams indicates strongly that Samuel Adams was also closely associated with the Nine, whether or not he was a formal member. It is unclear exactly how many Bostonians beyond these few were involved in any organized way with the Sons of Liberty, if indeed any were. In future years, however, the Sons of Liberty reassembled in numbers to celebrate the anniversary of the first Stamp Act uprising. A list of 355 Sons of Liberty (including 6 visitors), who assembled at Liberty Tree, Dorchester, on August 14, 1769, in the handwriting of the Sons' secretary at that date, William Palfrey, contains the names of all those connected with the Loyal Nine (including John and Samuel Adams) except Field and Welles.[18]

The names of several New Hampshire Sons of Liberty can be gathered from letters in the Belknap Papers at the Massa-

17. Leake, *John Lamb*, 4; Zeichner, *Connecticut's Years of Controversy*, 52; John Langdon Sibley and Clifford K. Shipton, *Biographical Sketches of Graduates of Harvard University* (Cambridge and Boston, Mass., 1873–), VIII, 276.

18. L. H. Butterfield, ed., *Diary and Autobiography of John Adams* (New York, 1964): I, *Diary 1755–1770*, 294; George P. Anderson, "A Note on Ebenezer Mackintosh," CSM *Pubs.*, XXVI (*Trans.*, 1924–

chusetts Historical Society: Samuel Griffeth, George Gains, Richard Champney, Joseph Bass, and Noah Parker. Champney was a merchant, Gains a cabinetmaker who became a Portsmouth selectman in 1776 and served on the 1777 Committee of Safety. The congregational minister and future president of Harvard, Samuel Langdon, drafted many of the Sons' letters; but perhaps the most interesting name associated with the New Hampshire Sons of Liberty is that of Colonel Theodore Atkinson. Atkinson did not sign documents but a draft of one of the Sons' letters is endorsed, probably by the eighteenth-century historian Jeremy Belknap, as being in "Col. Atkinson's handwriting." Moreover, an advertisement for a Sons' meeting of March 1766 is endorsed with a notation that "the Stampt Bonds that accompany . . . Mediterranean Passes were Deposited in the Hands of T. Atkinson Esq. to be at the disposall of the Sons of Liberty." Atkinson (Harvard, 1718), was the brother-in-law of Royal Governor Benning Wentworth; he was clerk of the council, province secretary, and colonel in charge of New Hampshire forces after Wentworth's accession to the chief magistracy. He apparently took little part in the subsequent revolutionary effort.[19]

Rhode Island's Sons of Liberty are among the groups of which most is known. In part this is due to the Providence Sons themselves, who obligingly identified their committee in a letter to New Hampshire of March 24, 1766, as "Paul Jew, James Angell, Silas Downer, Esqs. Mr. John Jenckes, Mr. John Brown Merchants, Mr. Jabez Bowen Junr. Physician, and Mr. William Goddard Printer." Of those identified simply as "Esquires," James Angell was currently Providence's town clerk; Downer (Harvard, 1747) was a scrivener, who performed tasks such as drawing up deeds and copying

6), 358–9; William Gordon, *The History of the Rise, Progress, and Establishment of the Independence of the United States of America* (London, 1788), I, 175; Crafts to Adams, Boston, February 15, 1766, in Charles F. Adams, ed., *The Works of John Adams* (Boston, 1850–6), II, 184; "An Alphabetical List of the Sons of Liberty who dined at Liberty Tree, Dorchester, Aug. 14, 1769," MHS *Procs., 1869–1870* (Boston, 1871), 140–2.

19. New Hampshire Sons to Edes and Gill, Portsmouth, February 6, 1766, and inscription on draft for the above, Belknap Papers, 61.c.111; Sibley and Shipton, *Harvard Graduates*, VI, 221–31.

legal papers. He drafted much of the Sons' correspondence. In a letter to the New York Sons, he said his property was "very small."[20]

The real wealth of information, however, is on Newport's Sons of Liberty, and comes mainly from Ezra Stiles's papers at Yale University, especially his "Stamp Act Notebook." Stiles gave the names of men on two Sons of Liberty committees: one to organize repeal celebrations in 1766, the other to organize celebrations of the first anniversary of repeal in 1767. He then identified the men, often giving provincial offices and family background as well as profession and religion. Moreover, the names of those on Newport's Sons of Liberty Correspondence Committee were included in a letter from Newport to the Providence Sons of April 4, 1766.[21] These three lists are much alike, and certainly agree on a core of ten committee members. The only name on the correspondence committee not included in either of Stiles's lists is that of Samuel Hall, printer of the *Newport Mercury*. The only person Stiles includes on both his lists who is not mentioned in the Sons' letter is Christopher Ellery, the merchant brother of William Ellery. Stiles says, moreover, that "Henry Marchant Esq. Atto[rney] at Law" was later added to the committee as a "genuine" Son of Liberty. Examination of the names on these various lists generally supports Stiles's contention that the committee "was as respectable as could have been chosen in Newport, and the most respectable Committee of the Sons of Lib[ert]y on this Continent," although the Sons of Liberty in Virginia and North Carolina, of whom Stiles knew little, rivaled the Newporters in social standing.

The Newport Sons' committee included Henry Ward and Metcalf Bowler, who had been Rhode Island representatives at the Stamp Act Congress in October 1765. Ward was secretary of the province, Bowler a deputy. Josias Lyndon, then age sixty-five according to Stiles, had for many years been clerk of the colony's general assembly and of the inferior court of common pleas for Newport County; he was

20. Providence to New Hampshire Sons in Belknap Papers, 61.c.120; Sibley and Shipton, *Harvard Graduates*, XII, 129–31; Downer to New York Sons, Providence, July 21, 1766, Peck Mss., III, 3, RIHS.

21. RIHS Mss., XII, f. 67.

"a Gent[leman] of an amiable and reputable Reputation, of Politeness and of a good Estate." William Ellery and his brother Christopher were sons of William Ellery, a wealthy Newport merchant who had served as judge, assistant, and deputy governor in Rhode Island, and possessed, according to Stiles, an estate of £20,000 sterling. William, Jr., like his father, was educated at Harvard (class of 1747) and then went into business as a merchant and, for a time, was naval officer in the colony. In 1770, he began practicing law. He was, Stiles wrote, "for Literature and sound Judgment equal to any Man in Town, and really [was] of the most Weight and Firmness of any of the Committee." He served in the Continental Congress, 1776–86, and signed the Declaration of Independence.[22]

John Channing, a man of fifty-three, was "a Gentleman of the greatest Politeness . . . of free and genteel Elocution," according to Stiles, "and a Merchant of the largest Business, transacting a Com[m]erce of Four Thousand Sterling a year." Of Thomas Freebody Stiles says little, except that he was called "Capt[ain]"; Robert Crook (or Crooke) was identified as "a Merchant of figure and of good Connexions." John Collins was a merchant, too; "Major" Jonathan Otis was identified only as a "very sensible worthy Man," religious, dedicated to the cause of liberty, and a remote relative of James Otis of Massachusetts. Charles Spooner, as noted earlier, was the only one on the committee "from among middling and lower life," and his membership was highly valued because he "united in himself the whole confidence of the plebians." In religious affiliation the group was diverse: Spooner, Lyndon, and Ward were Baptists; Crook, Bowler, and Freebody Episcopalians; Channing, Otis, Marchant, and the two Ellerys Congregationalists; and Collins a Quaker.

It is noteworthy that the occupations of the Sons of Liberty were generally urban in character. No simple farmers are

22. Besides Stiles, see Edward T. Channing, "Life of William Ellery," in Jared Sparks, ed., *Library of American Biography*, VI (Boston, 1836), 85–159.

listed—and, indeed, except for Virginia, hardly any whose livelihood came from the land. On the whole it seems that the need to organize the Stamp Act resistance was most acute within the towns where the stampmen usually lived, where commerce and government were centered, and the maintenance of order in the midst of resistance the most tenuous. Only later did the organized colonial opposition extend widely across the countryside. The Boston Sons of Liberty's interest in organizing other Massachusetts towns, for example, left little evidence of success, unlike the town's efforts to create a network of committees of correspondence after 1772.

There seems to have been a strong tendency for those most forthright against the Stamp Act to maintain that position against other instances of British "oppression" on into the Revolutionary War. Certainly, few became Loyalists: none of Boston's Loyal Nine became British partisans in the 1770's; none of the signers of the Westmoreland Association of 1766 appear on a list of Virginia claimants for compensation from Britain; and Joseph Johnson noted that of all those who met with Gadsden at Liberty Tree in 1766, only Henry Bookless later signed a complimentary address to Sir Henry Clinton, one index of Charleston's Loyalists.[23] Many Sons of Liberty remained active American leaders, as the biographies of Connecticut's Sons of Liberty suggests; and men like Samuel Adams, John Lamb, Isaac Sears, Richard Henry Lee, Cornelius Harnett, and Christopher Gadsden remained in the forefront of American opposition to Britain throughout the period.

On the other hand, some future Loyalists apparently found the Sons of Liberty congenial in the 1760's. Of 349 Massachusetts people who dined with the Sons of Liberty on the anniversary of the first Stamp Act uprising, at least 20 became Loyalists, and among them were some of the Bay Colony's most prominent British partisans—Thomas Brattle, John Erving, Samuel Quincy, Dr. John Jeffries. Indeed, a

23. James H. Stark, *The Loyalists of Massachusetts and the Other Side of the American Revolution* (Boston, 1910); list of Virginia claimants provided by Prof. Mary Beth Norton of Cornell University; Johnson, *Traditions*, 33.

handful of men who were active Sons of Liberty during
1765–6 themselves joined the Loyalists' ranks a decade later.[24]
On reflection, however, the participation of such men in the
early stages of the resistance movement is not bizarre. All
the Sons of Liberties considered themselves Loyalists in the
1760's. It was only later that loyalty to Britain and American
partisanship became incompatible.

24. Names on list cited *n.* 18 above compared with Stark, *Loyalists
of Massachusetts*. Prof. Norton has identified the following Sons of
Liberty of 1765–6 as Loyalists: Joseph Allicocke of New York,
Robert Alexander of Maryland, and the "Mr. Parker" of Norfolk, if
he was James Parker.

A LIST OF
UNPUBLISHED
MANUSCRIPT
SOURCES

[ENGLAND]

BRITISH MUSEUM, London. The Stowe Manuscripts, volumes 264 and 265, contain copies of reports on America compiled by the British government and the minutes of various governmental meetings of the Stamp Act period. Originals of most, but not all, of this material can also be found at the Public Record Office. The King's Manuscripts, volumes 201–4, include a series of letters between Benjamin Franklin, the Rev. Dr. Samuel Cooper, and Governor Thomas Pownall. Other useful material was found in volume 206 of the King's Manuscripts, which brings together the answers to circulars asking about the state of American manufacturing; in the Egerton Manuscripts, which include the Hutchinson family's papers; and in various Additional Manuscripts, including the correspondence of John Almon, the Newcastle, Hardwicke, and Liverpool series, and the correspondence of Josiah Martin (an army officer in the colonies who became North Carolina's governor 1771–6). The John Wilkes Papers—Additional Manuscripts 30865–96—were examined particularly for documents from Americans or pertaining to the colonies in any way, and some interesting unpublished material was found.

GUILDHALL LIBRARY, London. The John Wilkes Papers here are concerned almost exclusively with details of the government's proceedings against him, although the catalogues of his library were of interest. The Guildhall also has a very full collection of pamphlets on or by Wilkes. The Noble collection of newspaper clippings on prominent figures in the history of the City of London included some relevant items.

THE HOUSE OF LORDS RECORD OFFICE, London. This is the major parliamentary library and holds, among the Main Papers, perfect or nearly perfect collections of all documents presented to the Lords on disturbances in the colonies. These papers—listed fully in the *Journals of the House of Lords* for the dates on which they were presented to the House—represent, to a large extent, the cream of the American intelligence. Although the documents are copies of originals which can usually be found at the Public Record Office, the collection includes some items I found nowhere else.

THE PUBLIC RECORD OFFICE, London. Much unpublished material remains in the collections of the Public Record Office. Accounts of disturbances in the colonies and of changes in naval dispositions due to colonial events are available in the Admiralty I file, especially volumes 482–5, North American In-Letters (*i.e.*, to the Admiralty), 1759–77. The Privy Council Papers include many documents on events in the colonies presented to the Council. Those most relevant here are now classified as Privy Council I. See particularly volumes 51–6 (1765–74), with some addenda to these holdings in volume 60.

The Treasury Papers, kept in packets of loose documents, have not survived intact from the eighteenth century. Yet they contain important material not in the Colonial Office 5 file that American historians often use, such as letters from the stamp officials of 1765–6, and the reports of customs officials. The bulk of helpful material was in Treasury 1, particularly volumes between 437 and 522 (1765–76), although other scattered relevant documents were found in series beyond Treasury 1. The Treasury Solicitor Papers were consulted for material on certain state trials, especially that of Stephen Sayre in Treasury Solicitor 11, volume 542. The Chatham Papers, Public Record Office 30/8, had some helpful items, especially in volume 97, and sections of the

State Papers were studied for information on Wilkes's relationship with Beaumarchais.

The largest body of pertinent material, however, remains in the Colonial Office Papers, particularly the fifth series (CO 5). Historians have traditionally relied on Charles M. Andrews's *Guide to the Materials for American History to 1783, in the Public Record Office of Great Britain*, 2 volumes (Washington, 1912–14), but I found that a greater sense of the structure of this particular file could be gained from the Public Record Office's *Lists and Indexes*, Number XXXVI. *Colonial Office Records, Preserved in the Public Record Office* (London, 1911). Particularly helpful material was found in CO 5, volumes 40, intercepted letters, 1770–82; 83–93, military dispatches, 1763–76; 118, containing the letters of Benjamin Franklin, John Dickinson, William and Arthur Lee, and others, taken from Thomas Cushing's house at Boston in 1775, and commented upon by the Rhode Island Loyalist Thomas Moffatt; 119–21, Admiralty Papers submitted to the Secretary of State, 1771–August 1775; 133, with documents on the tea crisis; 134–5, miscellaneous documents, 1771–6, particularly helpful for 1775; 145, 146, and 154, Secretary of State's correspondence with the Treasury and Custom House, 1771–5; 159 and 160, Secretary of State's correspondence with the Attorney and Solicitor General, which concerns legal issues raised during the Anglo-American conflict; 219, extracts of letters from General Thomas Gage to the Secretary of State, 1765–7 (continued in volumes 233–5); 241–2, copies of dispatches from the Secretary of State to the governors; and 246, private letters of the Secretaries of State. Volumes from the high 200's to the end of the CO 5 file (volume 1450) are arranged by colony. These were used except where the material included has been published, as was particularly the case for North Carolina, New Jersey, and New York.

SHEFFIELD CENTRAL CITY LIBRARY, Sheffield. The Wentworth–Woodhouse Papers include the papers of the second Marquis of Rockingham. These contain some revealing letters from colonists, and more material throwing light on English politics.

WILLIAM SALT LIBRARY, Stafford. The Dartmouth Papers here form the most useful collection, with the exception of the Public Record Office, in England for a study of the years before American independence. It includes several letters by Sons of Liberty not found elsewhere, as well as other very informative materials.

[UNITED STATES]

HARVARD UNIVERSITY, HOUGHTON LIBRARY, Cambridge, Massachusetts. Houghton's large Sparks collection includes much relevant material on the American Revolution. See particularly the letterbooks of Governor Francis Bernard (Sparks Manuscripts IV, of which volumes 4 and 5 were used most intensively), Papers Relating to New England (Sparks Manuscripts X, volumes 2–4, which present a graphic picture of the nonimportation movement of 1768–70 in Boston), and the Letters of Philadelphia Merchants of 1769, among the Charles Thomson Papers (Sparks Manuscripts LXII, volume 7). Bernard's correspondence at the Public Record Office, which includes enclosures not in the letterbooks, was sometimes preferred to the Houghton collection. The Palfrey Family Papers were of central importance to this book because they include, in Part II, the correspondence of William Palfrey, secretary of the Boston Sons of Liberty and correspondent of John Wilkes. Houghton also houses the Arthur Lee Papers, but I used instead either published versions of Lee's letters or the microfilm edited by Paul P. Hoffman of the "Lee Family Papers, 1742–1795," issued by the University of Virginia, Charlottesville, in 1966.

THE LIBRARY OF CONGRESS, Washington, D.C. The Elbridge Gerry Papers were the most important collection for this study. Little new was found in the Charles Thomson Papers.

MARYLAND HISTORICAL SOCIETY, Baltimore. Informative unpublished material particularly on the period 1774–6 was found in the Purviance (MS. 1394) and Gilmor (MS. 387.1) Papers, which include documents collected by the Baltimore Committee of Correspondence. The society also has a useful set of transcripts of Samuel Chase letters compiled from other repositories on the east coast.

MASSACHUSETTS ARCHIVES, State House, Boston. Volumes XXV–VII of the Massachusetts Archives's collections contain the papers of Lieutenant Governor, then Governor, Thomas Hutchinson. A typescript is available at the Massachusetts Historical Society.

MASSACHUSETTS HISTORICAL SOCIETY, Boston. Letters from Boston sent to Quincy when he was in London constitute a particularly informative part of the Josiah Quincy, Jr., Papers. The Belknap Papers include the New Hampshire Sons of Liberty's correspondence from the Stamp Act period. See particularly the documents numbered 61. c. 100–50. The five volumes of Miscellaneous Bound Documents for 1765–76 also contain important items, such as three very full letters from Thomas Young to the New York Son of Liberty Hugh Hughes. Many of the other important collections at the Massachusetts Historical Society have been published. Attention should be drawn, however, to the minutes and correspondence of the Boston Committee of Correspondence, 1772–4, which constitute part of the George Bancroft Collection at the New York Public Library. These are available in photostat at the Massachusetts Historical Society.

NEW-YORK HISTORICAL SOCIETY, New York. The papers of John Lamb and of Alexander McDougall were essential for this book. Many of Lamb's papers were published by Isaac N. Leake. The McDougall Papers are particularly rich for the 1770's, and his correspondence with Josiah Quincy, Jr., Samuel Adams, and William Cooper in 1774 and 1775 is very useful.

NEW YORK PUBLIC LIBRARY, New York. The Samuel Adams Papers include many letters written to Adams by such men as John Dickinson, Charles Thomson, and Christopher Gadsden. Adams's own letters have been published. Occasional references have been made here to the "Calendar" to the papers, which includes brief summaries of letters now missing in the manuscript itself. Some items in the Chalmers collection were also consulted. The Bancroft manuscripts include the minutes and correspondence of the Boston Committee of Correspondence: see above, under Massachusetts Historical Society.

THE PENNSYLVANIA HISTORICAL SOCIETY, Philadelphia. Several William Bradford letters, and some documents referring to the Sons of Liberty, are among the Society's collections, but these did not prove particularly informative for this study.

THE RHODE ISLAND HISTORICAL SOCIETY, Providence. The correspondence of the Providence Sons of Liberty from the Stamp Act period is in the Rhode Island Historical Society Manuscripts, volume XII (for 1750–75). See also the Peck Manuscript, III, which has other relevant documents, including a long and revealing letter by Silas Downer, and the Samuel Ward Papers. Ward's letters from May 1775 to March 1776 have been printed. Henry Marchant's "Journal of Voyage from Newport in the Colony of Rhode Island to London . . . began July 8th 1771" is also available at the Rhode Island Historical Society on microfilm.

UNIVERSITY OF VIRGINIA LIBRARY, Charlottesville. The Lee Family Papers have been microfilmed along with other Lee papers at Harvard and the American Philosophical Society. See above, under Harvard University.

YALE UNIVERSITY, BEINECKE LIBRARY, New Haven, Connecticut. The Ezra Stiles Papers contain sermons, letters, and various other personal writings, including his "Stamp Act Notebook." Stiles considered political activism outside the proper sphere of a minister, but he knew Newport's radicals and had many contacts in Connecticut and other colonies as well as correspondents in England. He was an acute observer of people and events, and recorded much of what he saw and heard.

INDEX

A NOTE ABOUT THE AUTHOR

PAULINE MAIER was born in St. Paul, Minnesota, in 1938. She received her A.B. from Radcliffe College in 1960 and her Ph.D. from Harvard University in 1968. She has taught at the University of Massachusetts, Boston, since 1968 and is currently an assistant professor there. Her article "Popular Uprisings and Civil Authority in Eighteenth-Century America," upon which Chapter 1 of this book is based, was awarded the prize for the best article in *The William and Mary Quarterly* during 1970.

A Note on the Type

This book was set in Monticello, a Linotype revival of the original Roman No. 1 cut by Archibald Binny and cast in 1796 by The Philadelphia type foundry Binny & Ronaldson. The face was named Monticello in honor of its use in the monumental fifty-volume *Papers of Thomas Jefferson*, published by Princeton University Press. Monticello is a transitional type design, embodying certain features of Bulmer and Baskerville, but it is a distinguished face in its own right.